Designing Qualitative Research

FIFTH EDITION

Catherine Marshall
University of North Carolina at Chapel Hill

Gretchen B. Rossman
University of Massachusetts, Amherst

Los Angeles | London | New Delhi
Singapore | Washington DC

For information:

SAGE Publications, Inc.
2455 Teller Road
Thousand Oaks, California 91320
E-mail: order@sagepub.com

SAGE Publications Ltd.
1 Oliver's Yard
55 City Road
London EC1Y 1SP
United Kingdom

SAGE Publications India Pvt. Ltd.
B 1/I 1 Mohan Cooperative Industrial Area
Mathura Road, New Delhi 110 044
India

SAGE Publications Asia-Pacific Pte. Ltd.
33 Pekin Street #02-01
Far East Square
Singapore 048763

Printed in the United States of America

Library of Congress Cataloging-in-Publication Data

Marshall, Catherine, 1946-
Designing qualitative research/Catherine Marshall, Gretchen B. Rossman.—5th ed.
p. cm.
Includes bibliographical references and index.
ISBN 978-1-4129-7044-0 (pbk.)
1. Social sciences—Research—Methodology. I. Rossman, Gretchen B. II. Title.

H62.M277 2011
300.72—dc22 2009045113

Printed on acid-free paper

10 11 12 13 14 10 9 8 7 6 5 4 3 2 1

Acquisitions Editor: Vicki Knight
Associate Editor: Lauren Habib
Editorial Assistant: Ashley Dodd
Production Editor: Sarah K. Quesenberry/Astrid Virding
Copy Editor: QuADS Prepress (P) Ltd.
Proofreader: Ellen Brink
Indexer: Kathleen Paparchontis
Typesetter: C&M Digitals (P) Ltd.
Cover Designer: Candice Harman
Marketing Manager: Stephanie Adams

Designing Qualitative Research

FIFTH EDITION

This new edition is dedicated to all our many students—those we have worked with in the past, those we are working with now, and those we will work with in the future, either directly and face-to-face or through this new edition.

Our students, and the many other students of qualitative research, carry on the qualitative traditions with style and grace and also forge new pathways that build bridges across traditions and take up multidisciplinary, hybrid forms of qualitative inquiry. Collectively, our quantitative report of past students adds up to close to 75 doctoral dissertations, over 25 master's theses, and over 800 class or workshop participants. Our qualitative report of past students fits into three themes: the puzzled and questing, the true believers, and the "Well, I hate statistics so I might as well try this" categories.

We look forward to the work of our future students, and readers, no matter what their stance toward qualitative inquiry. We hope this new edition challenges preconceptions and moves forward this variegated field we work in.

Catherine Marshall and Gretchen Rossman

CONTENTS

LIST OF TABLES

LIST OF FIGURES

LIST OF VIGNETTES

PREFACE TO FIFTH EDITION

Since the first edition of *Designing Qualitative Research*, the context for systematic inquiry has undergone seismic shifts. As we prepared for this newest edition, we went "all out." This fifth edition can stand alone: We have added extensive material on philosophy, history, and genres of qualitative inquiry, including discussions on cultural studies, queer theory, and critical race theory. There is more attention to the ways in which research can be attuned to policy and practice—ranging from problem identification all the way to the format for the presentation of findings. We have a new chapter dedicated entirely to trustworthiness and ethics (Chapter 3), and discussions of ethical issues are interwoven throughout the text. Thus, throughout the book there is substantial new material on trustworthiness, validity, and general ethical considerations. In addition, we have greatly expanded our guidance for data analysis at the proposal stage and for managing analysis in preparing the writing of final reports.

Specifically, all chapters have been substantially revised in terms of tone and reader-friendliness and have been updated in terms of references, although some of the grandfathers and grandmothers are still there. What is also new to this edition is that all chapters end with a list of Key Concepts.

Where appropriate in terms of data collecting, we have indicated key considerations for the observer who is visually impaired or has other physical limitations throughout the chapters. And we have added a new section (in Chapter 6) on interviewing across differences in social identities.

Now, with a warmer climate for qualitative inquiry on many university campuses, we have placed less emphasis on defending and more emphasis on asserting the appropriateness of qualitative inquiry. We believe that the momentum supporting the "goodness" of qualitative inquiry for many kinds of cultural questions moves us past conservative trends stipulating that appropriate—and acceptable—inquiry can take only one form: the randomized, controlled experiment. Such stipulations are written into policy governing research and evaluation of federally funded programs. So this edition reflects these turns of events. We honor the university, as *the* institution that continues the struggles against political waves and protects alternative inquiry. Universities are still reasonably gentle places to find support for qualitative research.

As we now write, we find that qualitative research methodology has matured. This fifth edition addresses the advances and challenges presented by provocative developments and new applications. The book originally met the need for advice on designing qualitative research, given the complexity, the flexibility, and the controversies of its many genres. That need persists: Doctoral students, research managers, policy analysts, and researchers anticipating multimethod team research will continue to find clear and direct guidance in this edition. Qualitative designs are currently used in research in the fields of health behavior, education, urban planning, public relations and communications, sociology, international studies, psychology, management, social work, health policy, nursing, and more. Our focus tends to be on research in applied fields such as many of these. While we acknowledge the many developments that have come from autoethnography, performance ethnography, and cultural studies, as examples, our primary audience continues to be those working in fields that demand practical answers to complex questions.

Originally, *Designing Qualitative Research* was written because qualitative reports were intriguing but mystical. Earthy, evocative ethnographies seemed to just appear by magic. Researchers and students had no guidance for learning from such work. A few researchers provided chapters or appendixes describing their procedures. Texts extolled the philosophical stances and the cultural premises of qualitative research. We originally wrote this book to fill the void, to provide specific advice on design. Then, and now in this fifth edition, we benefit from the research experience of those who first systematically documented their designs and processes and also from the probing questions of our doctoral students. Thus, we provide readers connections to the classics of ethnography and other qualitative genres as well as present the issues and design dilemmas of researchers with new questions for the new century. Furthermore, this edition extends and deepens the discussion in the previous edition about strategies for incorporating into qualitative methodology the challenges posed by postmodernists, feminists, critical race theorists, and those who demand that research be directly useful to the researched.

This fifth edition continues to provide vignettes to illustrate the methodological challenges posed by the intellectual, ethical, political, and technological advances affecting qualitative research design. Vignettes include, for example, researchers' challenges in designing research with refugee and immigrant populations, and new sections address issues of translating into English and dealing with institutional review boards. Other vignettes of interest include discussions of researchers' explicitly political stances toward promoting democracy while conducting evaluations of community development and critical theorists' puzzling over reporting research without colonizing those who allowed them into their lives. Because qualitative design is not linear, different pedagogical strategies are required; the vignettes, we hope, assist readers in transferring suggestions about design to applications in their own research.

We have between us a collective total of 55 years of teaching qualitative methodology to graduate students! At 10 to 20 per class each year for each of us, just think how many qualitative researchers we've helped produce! Nothing keeps us attuned to qualitative research dilemmas more than the challenges our students present in classes and dissertations. We wish to thank the many hundreds who have continuously pressed for innovative approaches and posed research questions fresh from real-life problems; many have graciously allowed us to use their questions in vignettes. Finally, we, and our readers, benefit from the contributions of reviewers in scholarly journals and in anonymous reviews as well as from critical suggestions from our own students. We thank Aaron Kuntz and Melanie Schoffner for agreeing that their "dialogues between learners," originally appearing in the fourth edition, be used in this one. While they are no longer students, they continue to be learners, just as we are. We appreciate the specific editorial and writing contributions of Paul St. John Frisoli in creating and balancing the substantial revisions, and we thank Mavis Jarnigan for her calm, steadfast management of complex rewrites for this new edition. We also thank Vicki Knight at Sage Publications for her ongoing guidance and wisdom in producing this edition, and we thank the following reviewers who contributed important insights, which we have incorporated: Jennifer Esposito, Georgia State University; Peter Hessling, North Carolina State University; Lesley Rex, University of Michigan; Sandra Scharlemann, Concordia University. We hope our efforts will continue to provide a practical guide, assisting researchers as they craft sound, thoughtful, and sensitive proposals for qualitative inquiry that is robust and ethical.

ABOUT THE AUTHORS

Catherine Marshall is a professor in the Department of Educational Leadership at the University of North Carolina at Chapel Hill. After completing her PhD at the University of California, Santa Barbara, and a postdoctoral fellowship at the University of California, Los Angeles (UCLA), she served on the faculty of the University of Pennsylvania and at Vanderbilt University before taking her current position at North Carolina. The ongoing goal of her teaching and research has been to use an interdisciplinary approach to analyze the cultures of schools, state policy cultures, gender issues, and social justice issues. She has published extensively on the politics of education, qualitative methodology, women's access to careers, and socialization, language, and values in educational administration. Her honors include the Campbell Award for Lifetime Intellectual Contributions to the Field, given by the Politics of Education Association (2009); the University Council for Educational Administration's Campbell Award for Lifetime Achievement and Contributions to Educational Administration (2008); the American Educational Research Association's (AERA) Willystine Goodsell Award for her scholarship, activism, and community building on behalf of women and education (2004); and a Ford Foundation grant for Social Justice Leadership (2002). In the American Educational Association, she was elected to head the Politics and Policy Division, and she also created an AERA Special Interest Group called Leadership for Social Justice.

Marshall is the author or editor of numerous other books. These include *Activist Educators: Breaking Past Limits*; *Culture and Education Policy in the American States*; *The Assistant Principal: Leadership Choices and Challenges*; *The New Politics of Gender and Race* (editor); and *Feminist Critical Policy Analysis* (Vols. 1 and 2). Early in her scholarly career, while conducting qualitative research on policy and teaching literally hundreds of doctoral students how to adopt and adapt the qualitative approach into workable proposals, she recognized a need and began to develop this book.

Gretchen B. Rossman is a professor of international education at the Center for International Education at the University of Massachusetts, Amherst. She received her PhD in education from the University of Pennsylvania with a specialization in higher education administration. She has served as a visiting professor at Harvard University's Graduate School of Education. Prior to coming to the University of Massachusetts, she was Senior Research Associate at Research for Better Schools in Philadelphia. With an international reputation as a qualitative methodologist, she has expertise in qualitative research design and methods, mixed-methods monitoring and evaluation, and inquiry in education. Over the past 25 years, she has coauthored nine books, two of which are editions of major qualitative research texts (*Learning in the Field*, third edition [in preparation], with Sharon F. Rallis, and the present fifth edition of *Designing Qualitative Research*, with Catherine Marshall—both widely used guides for qualitative inquiry). She is also currently writing a book to be titled *Introduction to Inquiry* (with Sharon Rallis). She has also authored or coauthored over 40 articles, book chapters, and technical reports focused on methodological issues in qualitative research synthesis, mixed-methods evaluation, and ethical research practice, as well as the analysis and evaluation of educational reform efforts both in the United States and internationally.

Professor Rossman has served as principal investigator (PI) or co-PI on several large United States Agency for International Development–funded projects (in the Southern Sudan, Malawi, and India); as co-PI on a World Bank–funded multigrade schooling project (Senegal and Gambia); as lead trainer for a Save the Children–funded participatory monitoring and evaluation of professional training (Azerbaijan); and as external evaluator on several domestic projects, including a Department of Education–funded reform initiative, a National Science Foundation–funded middle-grades science initiative, and a number of projects implementing more inclusive practices for students with disabilities. She regularly presents papers at the annual meetings of the American Evaluation Association, the American Educational Research Association (AERA), and the Comparative & International Education Society (CIES). She recently completed a two-year term serving as program chair for the qualitative research section of AERA's Division on Methodology.

1 Introduction

There are limits to what the rationalizing knowledge epitomized by statistics can do. No matter how precise, quantification cannot inspire action, especially in a society whose bonds are forged by sympathy, not mere calculation.

—Mary Poovey (1995, p. 84)

Qualitative research methodologies have become increasingly important modes of inquiry for the social sciences and applied fields, such as education, regional planning, health sciences, social work, community development, and management. Long dominated by research methods borrowed from the experimental sciences, the social sciences now present a sometimes confusing array of alternative genres. From anthropology came ethnomethodology, ethnoscience, and the more familiar ethnography. Sociology has yielded symbolic interactionism and the Chicago School. Phenomenology derives directly from strands of Western philosophy, and interdisciplinary work has spawned sociolinguistics, discourse analysis, life histories, and narrative analysis. Psychology has contributed to clinical methodology.

The critical traditions, including postmodern, poststructuralist, and postcolonial perspectives, contribute to critical discourse analysis, a variety of feminist research approaches, critical race theory and analysis, queer theory and analysis, cultural studies, critical ethnography, and autoethnography. An emerging and intriguing mode of representation is performance ethnography, and the explosion of computer-based technologies has spawned Internet ethnography and multimodal forms of inquiry. Action research and participatory research, often explicitly ideological and emancipatory, intend to critique and radically change fundamental social structures and processes and to reconceptualize the entire research enterprise. Many of these genres, derived from traditional and interdisciplinary scholarship, are now frequently used in policy studies and professional fields. Over a decade ago, and still true today, Denzin and Lincoln (1994) noted, "The extent to which the 'qualitative revolution' is taking over the social sciences and related professional fields is nothing short of amazing" (p. ix).

Each of these disciplinary traditions rests on somewhat different assumptions about what constitutes proper inquiry within the qualitative, or interpretive, paradigm. Throughout this text, we refer to *qualitative research* and *qualitative methodology* as if they were one agreed-on approach. If this were the case, it might be reassuring to the novice researcher, but unfortunately it is not. As Denzin and Lincoln (2005) wrote, "Qualitative research is a field of inquiry in its own right. It crosscuts disciplines, fields, and subject matters. A complex, interconnected family of terms, concepts, and assumptions surround [*sic*] the term *qualitative research*" (p. 2).

Qualitative research genres exist in great variety, and many excellent texts serve as guides to their assumptions and approaches. Many qualitative researchers, despite their various methodological stances, tend to espouse some common values and enact a family of procedures for the conduct of a study. They are intrigued by the complexity of social interactions expressed in daily life and by the meanings that the participants themselves attribute to these interactions. They are also exquisitely aware that they work in and through interpretations—their own and others'—layered in complex hermeneutic circles. These interests take qualitative researchers into natural settings, rather than laboratories, and foster pragmatism in using multiple methods—"a wide range of interconnected interpretive practices" (Denzin & Lincoln, 2005, p. 4)—for exploring a topic. Thus, qualitative research is pragmatic, interpretive, and grounded in the lived experiences of people. Rossman and Rallis (2003) offer five general hallmarks of qualitative research and four typical stances of researchers who practice it.

Qualitative research typically

- is enacted in naturalistic settings,
- draws on multiple methods that respect the humanity of the participants in the study,
- focuses on context,
- is emergent and evolving, and
- is fundamentally interpretive.

Qualitative researchers, they maintain, tend to

- view social worlds as holistic and complex,
- engage in systematic reflection on the conduct of the research,
- remain sensitive to their own biographies/social identities and how these shape the study (i.e., they are reflexive), and
- rely on complex reasoning that moves dialectically between deduction and induction (see Table 1.1).

Table 1.1 Characteristics of Qualitative Research and Researchers

Qualitative research
• Takes place in the natural world • Uses multiple methods that are interactive and humanistic • Focuses on context • Is emergent rather than tightly prefigured • Is fundamentally interpretive
The qualitative researcher
• Views social phenomena holistically • Systematically reflects on who she is in the inquiry • Is sensitive to his personal biography and how it shapes the study • Uses complex reasoning that is multifaceted and iterative

SOURCE: Adapted from Rossman and Rallis (2003, pp. 8, 10). Used with permission.

Qualitative research, then, is a broad approach to the study of social phenomena. Its various genres are naturalistic, interpretive, and increasingly critical, and they typically draw on multiple methods of inquiry. This book is intended to be a guide for researchers who have chosen some genre of qualitative methods in their effort to understand—and perhaps change—a complex social phenomenon and who seek to develop solid proposals for **ethical research practice** as they plan their inquiry.

* * * * *

The insightful case study, the rich description of ethnography, the narratives of complex personal journeys all are the products of systematic inquiry. In their beginnings, however, they were modest research proposals. Two decades ago, qualitative researchers had to search hard to find useful guidelines for writing thorough, convincing research proposals. Since then, many useful texts have been published (we cite several at the end of this chapter); these texts provide guidance in learning how to craft a solid research proposal. They help to fill the gap created, for example, by policy analyses that offer findings and recommendations with few details on how the research led to them and by published reports of qualitative research that lack sufficient detail to provide strong examples of how they were designed. All too often, beginning qualitative researchers have difficulty learning how to design a useful and generative study from such reports. Other reports are written as if the process unfolded smoothly, with none of the messiness inherent in any research. These versions are difficult to learn from. This book provides specific guidance for writing strong and convincing proposals for ethical research grounded in the assumptions and practice of qualitative methodology.

Although qualitative research has an accepted place in formal research arenas—the "amazing takeover" described above—dissertation committees and reviewers for funding agencies still need to see proposals that are well developed, sound, rigorous, and ethical. This book, organized as a guide through the process of writing a qualitative research proposal, shows how to write a proposal that may well convince reviewers by defining explicit steps to follow, principles to adhere to, and rationales for the strengths of qualitative research.

Sociologists, clinical psychologists, community health workers, criminologists, anthropologists, political scientists, regional planners, and others from a range of the social sciences and applied fields will find this guide useful. Although many of the examples come from education (because of our own backgrounds), the principles, challenges, and opportunities are transferable across disciplines and into other applied fields.

This book does not replace the numerous texts, readers, and journal articles that are important for learning about various qualitative genres and the nuances of their preferred methods. It is meant to complement those resources that explicate the philosophical bases, historical development, principles and methods of practice, and findings of qualitative studies. Its purpose is to give practical, useful guidance for writing proposals that fit within the qualitative paradigm and that are successful.

We should mention here, as a cautionary note, that many of the examples presented here—indeed, the entire structure and organization of the book—suggest that the processes of proposal development are linear and transparent. As we note throughout the text, this is not the case. The vignettes are written in well-polished prose, often because they are the final versions of sections in successful proposals. The structure of the book may suggest that one proceeds from Point A to Point B in a seamless and quite logical manner. Such are the challenges of presenting an iterative, recursive process in formal academic writing. The looping back and forth, the frustrations—such things are masked. We trust that the reader will keep this in mind.

CONSIDERATIONS

When considering writing a proposal for a research study that will use qualitative methods, the researcher will find it valuable to weigh three interrelated concerns; we refer to these as the "**do-ability**," the "**should-do-ability**," and the "**want-to-do-ability**."

"Do-Ability": Considerations of Feasibility

One set of considerations captures the feasibility, the "do-ability," of the study. Judgments about resources (time, money), access to the site or population of interest or both, and the researcher's knowledge and skills come into play here. Proposals seeking external funding and those for dissertation research must include a discussion of resources. Strategies to gain access to a site or to identify participants for the study should also be discussed. Throughout the proposal, the researcher should demonstrate her competence to conduct a thorough, ethical, qualitative research study. In citing the methodological literature and discussing pilot studies or previous research, the researcher demonstrates her experience in conducting qualitative research and familiarity with the ongoing discourse on methodology, thereby situating her own work within the evolving context of research.

Thus, this set of questions focuses on considerations of feasibility. Are there sufficient resources to support the conduct of the study? Are access and willing participation likely in the setting? Is the study focused enough so it can be completed? Does the researcher provide evidence of methodological competence?

"Should-Do-Ability": Considerations of Potential Significance and Ethics

Another set of considerations in building a solid proposal is to argue that the study has the potential to contribute to theorizing and research—the ongoing discourse in a social science discipline or an applied field; to policy issues and policy making; and/or to issues of practice. The researcher should argue that the study will likely contribute to scholarship, policy, and/or practice and address the familiar question "So what?" He should respond cogently and knowledgeably when asked why the study should be conducted. Thus, this set of considerations centers on the following questions: Should the study be conducted? How will it contribute to scholarship? Policy deliberations? Practice?

However, another crucial facet of these "should" considerations is the critically important area of ethics and ethical practice: What ethical concerns or issues may arise? What resources can the researcher draw on to respond sensitively to these issues? Because ethical concerns are so important in any inquiry involving human beings, we return to this topic in Chapter 3 and highlight it throughout the book.

"Want-to-Do-Ability": Considerations of Sustained and Sustaining Interest

This set of questions captures the researcher's engagement with the topic. Far removed from the days of assertions of the dispassionate scientist, the qualitative researcher (and all researchers, we claim) cares deeply about the topic that she inquires about. Qualitative research, however, is neither naively subjectivist nor biased (all too common criticisms). Rather, qualitative methodologies acknowledge that *all* research in the social science disciplines and applied fields may well be subjective (in the sense of a subjective caring) and shift the discourse to a discussion of epistemology and to strategies for ensuring trustworthy and credible studies (which we discuss more fully in Chapter 3). Thus, this third set of considerations captures the importance of commitment and compelling interest to sustain the study from design to implementation to analysis to writing up the final report.

The proposal, then, is an argument that makes the case and convinces reviewers that the study can be done and should be done and that there is sufficient energy and interest to sustain it.

THE CHALLENGES

Research proposals consist of two major sections: (1) the **conceptual framework** and (2) the design and research methods. Roughly corresponding to the *what*—the substantive focus of the inquiry—and the *how*—the means for conducting it—these two sections describe in detail the specific topic or issue to be explored and the methods proposed for exploration. In a sound, well-developed, well-argued proposal, the sections are integrally related: They share common epistemological assumptions; research questions and methods chosen to explore the topic are congruent and relate to one another organically.

To achieve this goal, researchers who would conduct qualitative research face several challenges, for example, in

- developing a conceptual framework for the study that is thorough, concise, elegant, and generative;
- planning a design that is systematic and manageable, yet flexible; and
- integrating these into a coherent argument that convinces the proposal readers (a funding agency or a dissertation committee) to approve the study.

They should also

- demonstrate their *competence* to conduct the study (introduced above in the "do-ability" considerations),
- depict how they will be mindful about issues of *ethical practice* (introduced above in the "should-do-ability" considerations), and
- provide details of strategies to ensure that the study is *trustworthy.*

Each of these topics is taken up throughout the book (see the Overview at the end of this chapter), providing guidance at the proposal development stage to help meet these challenges. In the rest of this chapter, we provide an overview of the need to develop a coherent conceptual framework and a solid design. We then turn to the necessity for the researcher to demonstrate competence to conduct the study.

Conceptual Framework

The first major section of the proposal—the conceptual framework—demands a solid rationale. In examining a specific setting or set of individuals, the writer should show how she is studying a case in a larger phenomenon. By linking the specific research questions to larger theoretical constructs or to important policy issues, the writer shows that the particulars of this study serve to illuminate larger issues and therefore hold potential significance for that field. The doctoral student in economics, for example, who demonstrates that his qualitative case studies of five families' financial decision making are relevant for understanding larger forces in the marketplace, has met this condition. The case studies are significant because they illuminate in detail larger economic forces while focusing on individuals.

A **research design** also can stipulate phenomenological, in-depth interviewing as the sole method of data collection. For example, by linking that approach to socialization theory, one can begin to build a case for the proposal, a case that grounds it in important theoretical and empirical literatures. We develop the logic undergirding the conceptual framework in Chapter 4.

Design and Methods

The second major section of a proposal, also requiring a sound rationale, is devoted to the design of the study and the selection of specific methods. This section demonstrates that the study is feasible. The writer should show that the design and methods are the result of a series of decisions he has made based on knowledge gained from the methodological literature and previous work. Those decisions should not derive just from the methodological literature, however. Their justification should also flow logically from the research questions and from the conceptual framework.

Because qualitative research proposals are at times unfamiliar to reviewers, the logic supporting the choice of the proposed methods must be sound. Ensuring a clear, logical rationale in support of qualitative methods entails attention to six topics:

1. The *assumptions* of qualitative approaches in general and for the specific genre or hybrid approach of the study
2. The **trustworthiness** of the overall design
3. Consideration of the *ethical issues* that may arise
4. The *choice of the overall design*, with an accompanying rationale for selecting a site, a sample, the participants, or any combination of these

5. The rationale behind the selection of *specific data collection methods* and how these will help inform the research questions
6. A realistic projection of the *resource needs* to implement the study as planned

To anticipate the Overview of the book at the end of this chapter, the first topic is discussed in Chapter 2, trustworthiness and ethics are elaborated in Chapter 3, Chapter 4 takes up the important task of building a conceptual framework, and Chapter 5 discusses design considerations—the *how* of the study. Chapters 6 and 7 discuss a variety of methods for gathering data. Chapter 8 presents ways to describe the researcher's intended approach to data analysis. Chapter 9 offers examples of projecting resource needs, and Chapter 10 focuses on the writing of the final report. In addition to these considerations, however, is the crucial need to argue that the researcher is competent to conduct the study (discussed in the next section).

Researcher Competence

Another challenge facing the writer is to explicitly and implicitly demonstrate competence. The exact standard of competence applied for evaluating the proposal depends on the purpose and scope of the research. Standards applied to a dissertation proposal will likely differ from those used to evaluate a multiyear-funded project written by established researchers. Paradoxically, even though dissertation research is intended to provide an opportunity for learning the craft, all portions of the dissertation proposal will be subjected to careful scrutiny. Writers will be expected to show their capability by thorough attention to every facet of the conceptual framework and the research design. Established researchers, on the other hand, may not receive such careful scrutiny because their record of previous work engenders trust and the logic of good faith preserves standards for research. Although this may seem unfair, it nevertheless is the reality of proposal evaluation.

To demonstrate competence, then, proposal writers should refer to their previous work and discuss the strengths and weaknesses of the pilot study as well as their coursework and other relevant education. The high quality of the proposal's organization and its conceptual framework must be discussed, along with the relevant literature and design. All this entails building a well-supported argument that convinces reviewers of the study's importance and soundness.

DEVELOPING AN ARGUMENT

Central to this book is the premise that developing a proposal is a process of building an *argument* that supports the proposal. Like the logic of formal debate or the reasoning in a position paper, a research proposal is intended to convince the reader that the research holds potential significance and relevance, that the design of the study is sound, and that the researcher is capable of conducting the study successfully. The proposal writer must, therefore, build a logical argument for the endeavor, amass evidence in support of each point, and show the entire enterprise to be conceptually integrated. As Maxwell (2005) notes, "A proposal is an argument *for* your study. It needs to explain the logic behind the proposed research, rather than simply describe or summarize the study and to do so in a way that nonspecialists will understand" (p. 119).

To illuminate this process of building an argument to support qualitative research, we offer two fictitious vignettes. The first describes a doctoral student of sociology convincing her dissertation committee that qualitative methods are best suited for exploratory research on the culture of a hospital. She intends to uncover patterns in the work lives of participants that will lead to important improvements in the treatment of patients. Vignette 2 shows researchers building a rationale based on the strengths of qualitative methods for policy analysis. The researchers had to convince legislators that qualitative methods would yield useful, vivid analyses that could inform the policy-making process. Following the vignettes, we develop the implications for building an argument in support of qualitative proposals and then provide an overview of the rest of the book.

VIGNETTE 1 Justifying Fieldwork to Explore Organizational Culture

As O'Brien reviewed the notes she had written to help with the proposal defense, she realized that her strongest argument rested on two aspects of the proposed study's significance: its exploratory purpose and its commitment to improving patient treatment in large urban hospitals. She realized that the latter aspect might be construed as biased, but if she kept the rationale grounded in the need to better understand complex interactions, tacit processes, and often hidden beliefs and values, she could demonstrate the study's clear potential to improve practice.

Her committee was composed of two quantitatively trained sociologists and a medical anthropologist. She knew she had the support of the anthropologist, whose advice had been crucial during the several proposal drafts she had written. The sociologists, however, were more likely to be critical of the design.

O'Brien decided to begin her presentation with an explication of the four purposes of research (exploration, explanation, description, and prediction) to link the purpose of her proposed study to general principles regarding the conduct of inquiry. She could then proceed quite logically to a discussion of the ways in which exploratory research serves to identify important variables for subsequent explanatory or predictive research. This logic could allay the concerns of the two quantitatively oriented sociologists, who would search the proposal for testable hypotheses, instrumentation and operationalization of variables, and tests of reliability.

The second major justification of the study would develop from its significance for practice. O'Brien recalled how she had reviewed empirical studies indicating that organizational conditions had a significant effect on

(Continued)

VIGNETTE 1 **(Continued)**

wellness and hospital-leaving rates. What had not been identified in those studies were the specific interactions between hospital staff and patients, the widely shared beliefs about patients among the staff, and the organizational norms governing patient treatment. Her research, she would argue, would help identify those tacit, often hidden, aspects of organizational life. This, in turn, could be useful both for policy regarding health care and for practice in health care facilities.

That O'Brien would be engaging in exploratory research where the relevant variables had not been identified and uncovering the tacit aspects of organizational life strongly suggested qualitative methods. Fieldwork would be most appropriate for discovering the relevant variables and building a thorough, rich, detailed description of hospital culture. By linking her proposed research to concepts familiar to the quantitative sociologists, O'Brien hoped to draw the sociologists into the logic supporting her proposal and to convince them of its sound design.

A researcher's first task, even before formulating the proposal, is quite often to convince critics that the research has the potential to be useful (for theoretical development in the field, in currents of empirical research, in policy issues, and/or in concerns of practice). O'Brien faced this challenge and developed a rationale supporting her choice of qualitative research methods. In many cases, and especially in policy research, one can appeal to policymakers' frustration with previous research. The researcher should build an argument that may well convince them that qualitative research will lead to strong, detailed conclusions and recommendations. The next vignette shows how two policy analysts convinced their superiors that they could answer pressing questions with qualitative methods.

VIGNETTE 2 **Convincing Policymakers of the Utility of Qualitative Methods**

Why, six months after state legislators had allocated \$10 million to provide temporary shelters, were homeless families still sleeping in cars? Keppel and Wilson, researchers in the legislative analyst's office, knew that the question demanded qualitative research methodology. Convincing their skeptical superiors, however, would be a real challenge. They scoured their texts on research methods, selected convincing phrases and examples, and prepared a memo to demonstrate the viability of qualitative research and to build the capacity of the legislative analyst's office in that direction. They argued that, too often, the office's research and evaluations missed the mark. The memo began with a quote about how an approximate answer to the right question is better than an exact answer to the wrong question. The winning points, though, in their presentation to their superiors came from two major sources. They first pointed out the numerous implementation questions concerning homelessness that needed to be explored in the real-world setting. Second, they pointed out that certain subtleties of the policy implementation process had to be explored to fully understand what was happening.

They spoke of needing to discover the right questions to ask so that the systematic collection of data would follow. Thus, Keppel and Wilson convinced their superiors that their findings would help define the important questions, describe patterns of implementation, and identify the challenges and barriers that could lead to more effective policy outcomes.

In Vignette 2, we see researchers convincing others that a qualitative study was needed. This underscores the notion that researchers proposing qualitative inquiry do best by emphasizing the promise of quality, depth, and richness in the findings. They may, however, encounter puzzlement and resistance from those accustomed to surveys and quasi-experimental research and may need to translate between qualitative and quantitative paradigms. Researchers who are convinced that a qualitative approach is best for the research question or problem at hand should make a case that "thick description" (Geertz, 1973, p. 5) and systematic and detailed analysis will yield valuable explanations of processes.

OVERVIEW OF THE BOOK

This chapter has introduced the key issues and challenges in developing a solid and convincing proposal for qualitative research. Chapter 2 provides brief discussions of several qualitative research genres, with mention of intriguing new developments from the critical perspectives. This helps the qualitative researcher situate his proposal within one of these genres or within some wonderfully hybrid mix.

Because of their increasing importance to the research enterprise, social life, and human well-being, research ethics are the central consideration of this book. We discuss ethics more fully in Chapter 3 and revisit ethical considerations throughout the other chapters. Also in Chapter 3, we discuss concerns of ensuring trustworthy, credible qualitative research studies and considerations at the proposal stage.

In Chapter 4, we turn to the complex task of building a conceptual framework around the study. This process entails moving beyond the initial puzzle or intriguing paradox by embedding it in appropriate traditions of research—"currents of thought" (Schram, 2006, p. 63)—linking the specific case to larger theoretical domains. This framing argument also should demonstrate the "problem" that the proposed study will explore, which then links the study to its hoped-for significance for larger social policy issues, concerns of practice, and people's everyday lives, or to some combination of these. Thus, the study's general focus and research questions, the literature, and the significance of the work are interrelated. We call this the substantive focus of the study—the *what*.

Chapter 5 presents a detailed discussion of the *how* of the study. Having focused on a research topic with a set of questions or a domain to explore, the proposal should describe how systematic inquiry will yield data that will provide answers to the questions. The writer should discuss the logic and assumptions of the overall design and the methods, linking these directly to the focus of the study and justifying the choice of qualitative methods.

Chapter 6 describes the primary methods of data collection typically used in qualitative inquiry: in-depth interviewing, observation, participant-observation, and analyzing artifacts and material cultures including documents. Chapter 7 offers somewhat more specialized methods that may supplement the primary ones or that could be used in and of themselves as the primary method for a particular study. These two chapters are not intended to replace the many exemplary texts that deal in great detail with specific methods; rather, we present a brief discussion of various alternatives and discuss the ways they can be generative as well as challenges in their implementation. Chapter 8 describes ways to discuss in a preliminary manner how the complicated tasks of managing, recording, and analyzing qualitative data will be accomplished during implementation of the study. This discussion is necessarily brief because the writer cannot specify the exact categories and themes for analysis at the proposal stage, but he can still describe the strategy he will use and link this to the conceptual framework of the study.

Chapter 9 describes the complex, dialectical process of projecting the resources necessary for the study. Time, personnel, and financial resources should be considered. Finally, Chapter 10 revisits the image introduced here of the proposal as an argument, focusing on strategies for writing up or presenting the research with the notion of audience as central. We also return to the key considerations of trustworthiness discussed in Chapter 2 and offer strategies for evaluating the soundness and competence of a qualitative proposal, with special attention to building a logical rationale and answering challenges from critics.

Throughout the book, we use vignettes to illustrate our points. Most of these are drawn from our own work and that of other social scientists; some have been written by our graduate students, and they are given full credit for this; and a few are fictitious with no references to published work. The principles depicted in the vignettes apply to research grounded in several disciplines as well as in the applied fields; they challenge you, the reader, to apply them to your own design.

Two themes run through this book. The first is that *design flexibility* is a crucial feature of qualitative inquiry, even though demands for specificity in design and method seem to preclude such flexibility. We urge the researcher to think of the proposal as an initial plan: one that is thorough, sound, well thought out, and based on current knowledge. The proposal reveals the researcher's sensitivity to the setting, the issues to be explored, and the ethical dilemmas sure to be encountered, but it also reminds the reader that considerations as yet unforeseen (Milner, 2007) may well dictate changes in this initial plan. Therefore, the language used in discussing the design and methods is sure, positive, and active, while reserving for the researcher the right to modify what is currently proposed.

The second theme, which we have already introduced, is that the *proposal is an argument.* Because its primary purpose is to convince the reader that the research shows promise of being substantive and will likely contribute to the field, that it is well conceived, and that the researcher is capable of carrying it through, the proposal should rely on reasoning and evidence sufficient to convince the reader: The logic undergirding it should be carefully argued. All this will demonstrate a thorough knowledge of both the topic to be explored and the methods to be used. At times, we give guidance and use terminology that should assist in translating qualitative design assumptions for more quantitatively oriented audiences. In describing the proposal as an argument, we often mention the reader of the proposal to remind you, the reader of this book, that a sense of audience is critically important in crafting a solid research proposal.

Finally, toward the end of several chapters, you will find a dialogue between two graduate students that we hope will provide a model of the kind of dialogues you will have with others learning about qualitative proposals. The dialogue participants, Melanie and Aaron, were our graduate students during the preparation of the fourth edition of this book. Melanie is now Assistant Professor of English Education at Purdue University, and Aaron is Assistant Professor of Qualitative Research at the University of Alabama, Tuscaloosa. We also provide citations for further reading and include a list of key terms at the end of each chapter.

Dialogue Between Learners

Hi Aaron,

So, if we're to work together during the book revision, I suppose we should introduce ourselves! I'm Melanie, Catherine Marshall's research assistant and a doctoral candidate in UNC-CH's education program. I'm in the dissertation phase right now—just finished my data collection—and I'm working on my analysis now. Not surprisingly, I chose to do a qualitative study. Because I'm focused on teacher education, reflection, and technology, for my study I chose to follow a group of student teachers who agreed to maintain Weblogs during their year of graduate study. I am looking at the "results" of their Weblogs for reflectivity, ownership, attitude toward technology, so on and so forth. A qualitative approach really supports my desire to include the students' voices in the study, while providing a framework that encourages multiple answers and flexible methods—and I know I'm lucky that there is support for these factors in my program.

What about you? What are your research interests? Are you focusing on qualitative approaches? What helped you make the decision one way or the other? Do you have support for that decision?

Looking forward to working with you,

Melanie

(Continued)

(Continued)

Melanie,

Great to hear from you. Like you, I'm also in the dissertation phase, only just barely. I'm working on narrowing down my proposal and thinking through the many choices that reveal themselves to someone beginning a qualitative research project. I'm interested in merging two interests of mine in my dissertation: the philosophical assumptions we make when we structure universities along disciplinary lines and faculty activism. Though they both might seem rather disparate, I'm hoping to bring them together by examining the effect (if any) of the disciplines on how faculty define and render activism in their daily work. I have support for looking at this qualitatively, though I think mainly because I've made it known from the day I started here that I don't have much love for quantitative work; my values simply don't match up with the overarching assumptions that make quantitative work possible.

I'm looking forward to e-mailing a bit more.

Take care,

Aaron

FURTHER READING

Introductions to Qualitative Research

Bogdan, R. C., & Biklen, S. K. (2006). *Qualitative research for education: An introduction to theory and methods* (5th ed.). Boston: Allyn & Bacon.

Corbin, J., & Strauss, A. (2008). *Basics of qualitative research: Techniques and procedures for developing grounded theory* (3rd ed.). Thousand Oaks, CA: Sage.

Eisner, E. W. (1991). *The enlightened eye: Qualitative inquiry and the enhancement of educational practice.* New York: Macmillan.

Ellingson, L. L. (2009). *Engaging crystallization in qualitative research: An introduction.* Thousand Oaks, CA: Sage.

Flick, U. (2009). *An introduction to qualitative research* (4th ed.). London: Sage.

Glesne, C. (2005). *Becoming qualitative researchers: An introduction* (3rd ed.). New York: Longman.

Hesse-Biber, S. N., & Leavy, P. (2006). *The practice of qualitative research.* Thousand Oaks, CA: Sage.

Janesick, V. J. (2004). *"Stretching" exercises for qualitative researchers* (2nd ed.). Thousand Oaks, CA: Sage.

Patton, M. Q. (2002). *Qualitative research and evaluation methods* (3rd ed.). Thousand Oaks, CA: Sage.

Pope, C., & Mays, N. (2006). *Qualitative research in health care.* Oxford, UK: Blackwell.

Rossman, G. B., & Rallis, S. F. (2003). *Learning in the field: An introduction to qualitative research* (2nd ed.). Thousand Oaks, CA: Sage.

Silverman, D. (Ed.). (2004). *Qualitative research: Theory, method, and practice* (2nd ed.). London: Sage.

Silverman, D., & Marvasti, A. (2008). *Doing qualitative research: A comprehensive guide* (2nd ed.). Thousand Oaks, CA: Sage.

Willis, J. W. (2007). *Foundations of qualitative research: Interpretive and critical approaches.* Thousand Oaks, CA: Sage.

On Qualitative Research Design and Proposal Writing

Biklen, S. K., & Casella, R. (2007). *A practical guide to the qualitative dissertation.* New York: Teachers College Press.

Creswell, J. W. (2007). *Qualitative inquiry and research design: Choosing among five approaches* (2nd ed.). Thousand Oaks, CA: Sage.

Creswell, J. W. (2009). *Research design: Qualitative, quantitative, and mixed methods approaches* (3rd ed.). Thousand Oaks, CA: Sage.

Herr, K., & Anderson, G. L. (2005). *The action research dissertation: A guide for students and faculty.* Thousand Oaks, CA: Sage.

Maxwell, J. A. (2005). *Qualitative research design: An interactive approach* (2nd ed.). Thousand Oaks, CA: Sage.

Merriam, S. B. (2009). *Qualitative research: A guide to design and implementation.* San Francisco: Jossey-Bass.

Piatanida, M., & Garman, N. B. (1999). *The qualitative dissertation: A guide for students and faculty.* Thousand Oaks, CA: Corwin Press.

Schram, T. H. (2006). *Conceptualizing and proposing qualitative research* (2nd ed.). Upper Saddle River, NJ: Pearson Prentice Hall.

KEY CONCEPTS

Conceptual framework

"Do-ability"

Ethical research practice

Research design

Researcher competence

"Should-do-ability"

Trustworthiness

"Want-to-do-ability"

2

Qualitative Research Genres

Qualitative methodologists attempt to organize the various genres or approaches into categories or strands; this can be useful for the proposal writer, who can situate his study within one of these strands. We refer to these as *methodological currents of thought*, employing Schram's (2006) quite useful phrase to describe theoretical and empirical strands that inform a conceptual framework. Historically, this categorizing was relatively straightforward; with the amazing proliferation of genres, however, the task has become more challenging. This chapter provides a brief summary of historical ways of organizing qualitative research genres, followed by discussions of genres that offer alternatives, at times with a focus on a specific population and often from a critical stance with emancipatory goals. Our purpose here is to help the proposal writer situate his study to provide a more nuanced argument for his specific approach.

Historically, qualitative methodologists developed typologies to organize the field. Focusing specifically on education, Jacob (1987, 1988) described six qualitative traditions: human ethology, ecological psychology, holistic **ethnography**, cognitive anthropology, ethnography of communication, and symbolic interactionism (see Table 2.1). Atkinson, Delamont, and Hammersley (1988) critiqued Jacob's typology and offered seven somewhat differing ones: symbolic interactionism, anthropology, sociolinguistics, ethnomethodology, democratic evaluation, neo-Marxist ethnography, and feminism. Creswell (1998) discussed biography, **phenomenology**, grounded theory, ethnography, and case study as the major strategies. And Patton (2002) provided a much longer list of theoretical orientations in qualitative inquiry; his list included, in part, ethnography, **autoethnography**, phenomenology, symbolic interaction, ecological psychology, systems theory, chaos theory, and grounded theory. Somewhat more recently, Denzin and Lincoln (2005) recognized case studies; ethnography, participant observation, and **performance**

ethnography; phenomenology and ethnomethodology; grounded theory; life history and *testimonio*; historical method; action and applied research; and clinical research.

Building on the discussion provided in Gall, Borg, and Gall (1996), analysis of these lists, especially those with similar entries, shows a focus in three major genres: (1) *society and culture*, as seen in ethnography, **action research**, case studies, and often grounded theory; (2) *individual lived experience*, as exemplified by **phenomenological**

Table 2.1 Historical Typologies of Qualitative Research

Jacob (1987, 1988)	Atkinson, Delamont, and Hammersley (1988)	Creswell (1998)	Patton (2000) (partial)	Denzin and Lincoln (2005)
Overlapping genres				
Holistic ethnography Cognitive anthropology	Anthropology Neo-Marxist ethnography	Ethnography	Ethnography Autoethnography	Ethnography Performance ethnography
Ethnography of communication	Sociolinguistics		Narrative inquiry	Life history and *testimonio*
Symbolic interactionism	Symbolic interactionism Ethnomethodology	Phenomenology	Phenomenology Ethnomethodology	Phenomenology Ethnomethodology
		Grounded theory	Grounded theory	Grounded theory
		Case study		Case studies
Genres specific to author/s				
Ecological psychology	Democratic evaluation	Biography	Ecological psychology	Historical method
Human ethology	Feminism		Heuristic inquiry	Action research
			Social construction and constructivism	Clinical research

approaches, some feminist inquiry, life histories, and *testimonio*; and (3) *language and communication*—whether spoken or expressed in text—as in sociolinguistic approaches, including **narrative analysis** and discourse and conversation analysis. We offer a short description of these major genres below and then turn to other genres that offer critical opportunities for qualitative inquiry.

MAJOR GENRES

A Focus on Society and Culture: Ethnographic Approaches

Ethnography is the hallmark of qualitative inquiry and, as Patton notes (2002), "the earliest distinct tradition" (p. 81). Derived from anthropology and qualitative sociology, ethnographies study human groups, seeking to understand how they collectively form and maintain a culture. Thus, *culture* is a central concept for ethnographies. Focusing on an analysis of actions and interactions within the group, culture "describes the way things are and prescribes the ways people should act" (Rossman & Rallis, 2003, p. 95).

Ethnographers—those who inscribe (graph) the culture (ethnos)—typically study groups, communities, organizations, or perhaps social movements through long-term immersion in the setting and by using a variety of data collection methods. Through the approach of participant observation (discussed in Chapter 6), ethnographers describe and analyze patterns of interactions, roles, ceremonies and rituals, and artifacts of that cultural group.

Classical ethnography has been enriched by variations on its central principles and practices. **Internet ethnography** and **critical ethnography** are discussed briefly below as newer developments; others within this genre include autoethnography (see Jones, 2005) and **public ethnography** (see Tedlock, 2005), as well as the new form of representation, performance ethnography (see Alexander, 2005). These variations offer flexible new approaches, but all derive from the foundational principles of classical ethnography.

A Focus on Individual Lived Experience: Phenomenological Approaches

Phenomenological approaches seek to explore, describe, and analyze the meaning of individual lived experience: "how they perceive it, describe it, feel about it, judge it, remember it, make sense of it, and talk about it with others" (Patton, 2002, p. 104). Derived from the German philosophy of phenomenology, this family of approaches typically involves several long, in-depth interviews with individuals who have experienced the phenomenon of interest. Analysis proceeds from the central assumption that there is an *essence* to an experience that is shared with others who have also had that experience. The experiences of those participating in the study—those who have had a similar experience—are analyzed as unique expressions and then compared to identify the essence.

One excellent example of phenomenological approaches is Mosselson's (2006) study of the essence of the experience of being an adolescent female immigrant, where identity conflicts and issues are explored through a series of in-depth interviews. The phenomena of interest are typically framed as processual—being, becoming, understanding, and knowing. Recent developments call for more evocative and poetic forms of representation of phenomenological studies (see Todres & Galvin, 2008).

A Focus on Talk and Text: Sociolinguistic Approaches

Related to ethnographic approaches in their interest to understand the meanings that participants derive from and construct in social interactions and settings, sociolinguistic approaches focus on communicative behavior: talk and text. Researchers within this genre tend to record naturally occurring talk for analysis. The ubiquity of "talk" makes it quite generative for analysis. As Peräkylä (2005) notes,

> Face-to-face social interaction (or other live interaction mediated by phones and other technological media) is the most immediate and the most frequently experienced social reality. The heart of our social and personal being lies in the immediate contact with other humans. (p. 874)

Analyzing talk, then, is a central focus for **discourse analysis**, **critical discourse analysis**, conversation analysis (see Peräkylä, 2005), microethnography, and other variations within this genre. The focus for inquiry may be how particular speech events are accomplished, how identity is established and reproduced, or how social identity characteristics shape communicative behaviors.

In the past two decades, a critical turn has taken place in the social sciences, humanities, and applied fields. Some qualitative researchers have espoused postmodern, postpositivist, and postcolonial theoretical perspectives that critique traditional social science (see Ashcroft, Griffiths, & Tiffin, 2000; Connor, 1989; Denzin & Lincoln, 2005; Rosenau, 1992). These scholars challenge the historical assumption of neutrality in inquiry and assert that *all* research is interpretive and fundamentally political, spoken "from within a distinct interpretive community that configures, in its special way, the multicultural, gendered components of the research act" (Denzin & Lincoln, 2005, p. 21). They argue further that research involves issues of power and that traditionally conducted social science research has silenced many marginalized and oppressed groups in society by making them the passive objects of inquiry. Qualitative research is deemed especially guilty because of its historical complicity with colonialism (Bishop, 2005).

Those espousing these critical perspectives have developed research strategies that are openly ideological and have empowering and democratizing goals. We list some of these critical approaches as well as emerging ones in Table 2.2.

Table 2.2 Critical and Emerging Genres

Scholarly Traditions	Qualitative Research Genres
Critical theory	Critical ethnography Autoethnography
Queer theory	Queer analysis
Critical race theory	Critical race analysis
Feminist theories	Feminist research methods
Interdisciplinary studies	Cultural studies Multimodal studies
The Internet	Internet ethnography

We argue that either traditional or more critical and postmodern assumptions can undergird each genre. Traditional qualitative research assumes that (a) knowledge is not objective Truth but is produced intersubjectively; (b) the researcher learns from participants to understand the meaning of their lives but should maintain a certain stance of neutrality; and (c) society is reasonably structured and is orderly.[1] Critical theory, critical race theory, feminist theories, **queer theory**, **cultural studies**, and postmodern and postcolonial perspectives also assume that knowledge is subjective but view society as essentially conflictual and oppressive. These positions critique traditional modes of knowledge production (i.e., research) that have evolved in settings structured to legitimize elite social scientists and to exclude other forms of knowing. Critical race theorists and feminists, particularly, point to the exclusion of knowledges and truths from traditional knowledge production (Harding, 1987; Ladson-Billings, 2000; Ladson-Billings & Donnor, 2005; LeCompte, 1993; Matsuda, Delgado, Lawrence, & Crenshaw, 1993). By means of such challenges, it becomes clear that the assumptions behind research questions must be interrogated, deconstructed, and sometimes dismantled and reframed (Marshall, 1997a; Scheurich, 1997). Such inquiry could contribute to radical change or emancipation from oppressive social structures, either through a sustained critique or through direct advocacy and action taken by the researcher, often in collaboration with participants in the study. All these critiques share four assumptions:

> (a) Research fundamentally involves issues of *power*; (b) the research report is not transparent, but rather it is *authored* by a raced, gendered, classed, and politically oriented individual; (c) race, class, and gender [among other social identities] are crucial for understanding experience; and (d) historically, *traditional research has silenced* members of oppressed and marginalized groups. (Rossman & Rallis, 2003, p. 93)

These newer perspectives on qualitative research contain three injunctions: As researchers, we should

1. examine how we represent the participants—the Other (Levinas, 1979)—in our work;
2. scrutinize the "complex interplay of our own personal biography, power and status, interactions with participants, and [the] written word" (Rossman & Rallis, 2003, p. 93); and
3. be vigilant about the dynamics of ethics and politics in our work.

One implication of these concerns is that qualitative researchers pay close attention to their participants' reactions and to the *voice* they use in their work as a representation of the relationship between themselves and their participants.[2] Another is that the traditional criteria for judging the adequacy or trustworthiness of a work have become essentially contested. As a result, the novice researcher might be left floundering for guidance as to what *will* constitute thoughtful and ethical research. We discuss these issues in Chapter 3.

As noted above, those frustrated with traditional qualitative research may find greater flexibility of expression in narrative analysis, action and **participatory action research**, cultural studies, Internet ethnography, critical ethnography, feminist approaches, **critical race theory and analysis**, or queer theory and analysis, to mention a few of the more critical genres under the qualitative inquiry umbrella. Each embraces the changing of existing social structures and processes as a primary purpose and, when framed by explicitly critical orientations, and has openly political agendas and often emancipatory goals. We briefly discuss each below.

CRITICAL GENRES

Narrative Analysis

An interdisciplinary approach with many guises, narrative analysis seeks to describe the meaning of experience for those who frequently are socially marginalized or oppressed, as they construct stories (narratives) about their lives. Life histories, biographies and autobiographies, oral histories, and personal narratives are all forms of narrative analysis.

Each specific approach assumes that storytelling is integral to understanding lives and that all people construct narratives as a process in constructing and reconstructing identity (Sfard & Prusak, 2005). Some approaches focus on the sociolinguistic techniques a narrator uses, others on life events and a narrator's meaning making. When framed by feminist or critical theory, narrative analysis also can have an emancipatory purpose (Chase, 2005), as when stories are produced and politicized as counternarratives to prevailing oppressive "grand narratives" (we discuss this below under critical race theory and queer theory). Critical discourse analysis makes explicit a theoretical focus on issues of power, access to linguistic resources, and the ways these resources are distributed unevenly across both dominant and marginalized populations (see Rogers, 2004).

Action Research and Participatory Action Research

Action research challenges the claim of neutrality and objectivity by traditional social science and seeks full, collaborative inquiry by all participants, often to engage in sustained change in organizations, communities, or institutions (Stringer, 2007). It seeks to decentralize traditional research by staying committed to local contexts rather than to the quest for Truth and to the liberation of research from its excessive reliance on the "restrictive conventional rules of the research game" (Guba, 1978, as quoted in Stringer, 1996, p. x). When ideally executed, action research blurs the distinctions between researcher and participants, creating a democratic inquiry process. It is often practiced in organizational contexts and in education, where professionals collaboratively question their practice, make changes, and assess the effects of those changes (Kemmis & McTaggart, 2005; McNiff & Whitehead, 2003; Sagor, 2005). Also active in social work, business management, and community development (Hollingsworth, 1997), researchers who engage in action research do so to improve their practice.

More visible in international work, participatory action research draws on the precept of emancipation, as articulated by Freire (1970), that sustainable empowerment and development must begin with the concerns of the marginalized (Park, Brydon-Miller, Hall, & Jackson, 1993). In addition to an explicit commitment to action, the hallmark of participatory action research is full collaboration between researcher and participants in posing the questions to be pursued and in gathering data to respond to them. It entails a cycle of research, reflection, and action. Examples include research by Maguire (2000) on battered women, by Phaik-Lah (1997) in Malaysia on World Bank projects, and by Titchen and Bennie (1993) on training for nursing.

Cultural Studies

By Paul St. John Frisoli

The domain of cultural studies encompasses a broad range of perspectives and interpretations of "culture." Major themes throughout the discipline include acknowledging what we know, the relationship of that knowledge to who we are—our identities—and examining the relationship between the "knower" and the one who is "giving" the knowledge. Gray (2003) explains that "one of the key characteristics of cultural studies is that of understanding culture as constitutive of and constituted by 'the lived,' that is the material, social, and symbolic practices of everyday life" (p. 1). Within this domain, scholars underline the importance of deconstructing the intersection of language, text, power, and knowledge to gain a better understanding of how we craft representations of our life worlds (Gray, 2003, 2004; Ryen, 2003; Saukko, 2008). These scholars argue that language and text, when associated with power, help shape how we see, differentiate, and interpret the world around us to find our place within it (Prior, 2004). Research is embedded within the meaning-making process, which can contribute to and endorse discursive representations that in turn objectify a research participant's lived experiences. Research is part of the process of "forming the social mosaic" creating different social realities (Saukko, 2008, p. 471). Cultural studies examines these liminal spaces to "interrogate issues of domination and power" (hooks, 2004, p. 156) in order to surface different linguistic and textual interpretations and representations. This process relates to *feminist theory* and *critical race theory*, which break down "essentialist notions of difference" (hooks, 2008, p. 457) to offer opportunities for creating multiple discourses from voices that are frequently left out of the academy.

In qualitative research, cultural studies offer a lens to acknowledge a researcher's place and position of power, while recognizing how the researcher's past can shape the ways in which she represents the world of another (Gray, 2003; Ryen, 2003; Saukko, 2008). This process requires researchers to uncover their "fractured fragmented identities" (Gannon, 2006, p. 474) and recognize how hegemonic messages influence their identities and therefore their interpretations of reality (Saukko, 2003). Expressions of Barthes's (1972) notion of the body as fragmented, dispersed, continuous, and changing are materialized through a variety of approaches of cultural studies based in ethnography, which include montage, poetry, and performance (discussed below). These become different and legitimate forms of ethnography that depict the multisided and complex nature of a researcher's methodology and interpretive process. Autoethnography, a type of ethnography where the researcher is central to the inquiry process, is another generative means to demonstrate the "liminal, dynamic, and contingent" (Gannon, 2006, p. 480) selves/bodies that construct knowledge within cultural spaces.

Internet/Virtual Ethnography

By Paul St. John Frisoli

Emerging from the basic principles of ethnography, Internet ethnography, also known as **virtual ethnography**, is considered a method and methodology for conducting qualitative research. The Internet is loosely defined as a medium for communication, a venue to connect across physical borders, and a socially constructed space (Markham,

2004, p. 119). Therefore, this medium is seen as both a tool and a site for qualitative research, developed from the observation that social life in contemporary society communicates, interacts, and lives more online; for ethnographers to better understand the "social world," they must adjust their research methods to reflect these changes (Garcia, Standlee, Bechkoff, & Cui, 2009; Markham, 2004).

When the Internet is conceptualized as a tool, researchers may conduct and distribute e-mail or Web-based surveys, interview participants either synchronously in chat rooms or asynchronously via e-mails, create discussion boards and group blogs, or suggest online journaling for participants. This method challenges the assumed rapport-building ethnographic approaches of "being there, being part of an everyday life of a community or culture" (Flick, 2006, p. 265). Critics argue that with Internet ethnography, there are "removed social context cues such as gender, age, race, social status, facial expression and intonation resulting in a disinhibiting effect upon group participants" (Williams, 2007, p. 7). However, others argue that though these methods may prevent the researcher and participants from interacting face-to-face, they allow for more reflective, participant-driven textual responses, especially when rigorous and systematic qualitative research principles are enacted (Flick, 2006; Garcia et al., 2009; Mann & Stewart, 2002, 2004; Williams, 2007). One advantage of using the Internet for qualitative studies is that it allows researchers to conduct interviews in remote areas of the world while sitting in their offices, have day-to-day synchronous and asynchronous communication, and speak with individuals who may not be able to participate in face-to-face interviews because of physical barriers or protection issues (Mann & Stewart, 2002). We provide more details on the Internet and computer applications as tools for research in Chapter 7.

When the Internet is conceptualized as a site for research, the focus shifts to understanding and analyzing the medium as a central feature of contemporary social life and, therefore, as noted above, ripe for study. Particularly relevant is the work of Markham (2004), who takes a cultural studies approach to legitimate use of the Internet as both a tool and a "discursive milieu that facilitates the researcher's ability to witness and analyze the structure of talk, the negotiation of meaning and identity, the development of relationships and communities, and the construction of social structures as these occur discursively" (p. 97). As a result, Internet ethnography also identifies the World Wide Web as socially constructed virtual worlds (Hine, 2000) that can be researched to understand how people give meaning to their spaces. Virtual communities are graphical online environments in which people construct and represent their identities in the form of characters, also known as avatars. The avatars, representing research participants, are subject to participant observation to better understand the social construction of these virtual domains. Participating in these worlds may well ensure more anonymity, where participants may be more likely to disclose information because they may not be inhibited by a face-to-face social hierarchy with the researcher (Garcia et al., 2009). The virtual can offer a sense of safety where individuals feel freer to reconfigure their identities in order to express themselves and relate to those who are like them (Markham, 2004).

However, this world is an uncertain one, where maneuvering within it has yet to produce context-specific, agreed-on research ethics such as privacy, identity authenticity, and informed consent. We discuss ethical issues associated with the Internet in Chapter 7. Researchers and participants alike are able to create their own identities that may differ from who they say they really are. Researchers can "lurk" online to begin identifying study participants without such individuals knowing (Mann & Stewart, 2004). It is also unclear if a researcher has the right to extract text from individuals' blogs, discussion boards, and other publicly accessible information without permission. The Internet, as a new tool and site, is dynamic and fluid; its generativity for the development of qualitative research is just emerging.

Critical Ethnography

Critical ethnography is grounded in theories assuming that society is structured by class and status as well as by race, ethnicity, gender, and sexual orientation to maintain the oppression of marginalized groups. As defined by Madison, "Critical ethnography begins with an ethical responsibility to address processes of unfairness or injustice within a particular *lived* domain" (2005, p. 5). Historically, critical ethnography developed from the commitment to radical education in several works sharply critical of accepted teaching practice (hooks, 1994; Keddie, 1971; Sharp & Green, 1975; Weis, 1990; Weis & Fine, 2000; Young, 1971). Later work of this type has focused on the constraints on adopting radical teaching practices (Atkinson et al., 1988). Critical ethnography can also go beyond the classroom to ask questions about the historical forces shaping societal patterns as well as the fundamental issues and dilemmas of policy, power, and dominance in institutions, including their role in reproducing and reinforcing inequities such as those based on gender and race (Anderson, 1989; Anderson & Herr, 1993; Kelly & Gaskell, 1996; Marshall, 1991, 1997a).

We should note here the recent development of *postcritical ethnography*, which moves beyond critical ethnography to explicitly incorporate postmodern perspectives. This discourse community develops critical social narratives that are ethnographies in the traditional sense but in which the involved social scientist explicitly takes a political stand (Everhart, 2005). Postcritical ethnographers use narrative, performance, poetry, autoethnography, and ethnographic fiction as their forms of representation. Their goal is to take a stand (like participatory action researchers) and have greater impact than that allowed by a 20-page article in an academic journal or a book read by 40 people (Noblit, Flores, & Murillo, 2005). An example closely linked to the more familiar autobiography is the genre of autoethnography, mentioned above, which has evolved over the past two decades. Using the self as both subject and object, its inquiry proceeds through "multiple layers of consciousness, connecting the personal to the cultural" (Ellis & Bochner, 2000, p. 739). The self is deployed as an exemplar through which social processes and identities are constructed and contested, changed and resisted.

Another of postcritical ethnography's forms of representation that has entered the lexicon of qualitative scholars is the notion of performance. Performance ethnography has become a critical mode of representing ethnographic materials, "the staged reenactment of ethnographically derived notes" (Alexander, 2005, p. 411). Embodying cultural knowledge through performance not only depicts cultural practice but might also lead to social change, as actors and audience reconceptualize their social circumstances. This genre finds representation in popular theater (Boal, 1997, 2002), arts-based studies (Barone & Eisner, 2006), music (Said, 2007), and other media. It also evokes the notion of "cultural performance": the methods and resources available to members of a community or social identity group to construct and reconstruct (perform) those identities. (See Denzin, 2005, for an example.)

Feminist Theories and Methodologies

Feminist theories can be used to frame research across issues and disciplines. These theories place gender relations at the center of any inquiry and usually have critical and emancipatory aims, with a focus on women. Importantly, feminist perspectives increasingly incorporate the recognition of multiple intersectionalities of identity. Thus, gender, sexuality, race, religion, country of origin, language, age or generation, health and physical abilities, class, social networks, and so on, all combine in fluid ways (Friend, 1993; Herr, 2004; Young & Skrla, 2003). Gender is not the sole, essential, and fixed category identifying a person.

Feminist work ranges from examination of videotapes of mothers and young children showing the power of language in conveying gendered expectations for boys and girls (Gelman, Taylor, & Nguyen, 2004), gender differences in schools (Clarricoates, 1987), and the development of adolescent girls (Griffin, 1985; Lees, 1986) to the challenges made by Indonesian women to male dominance in shaman rituals as well as in school superintendent positions (Scott, 2003; Tsing, 1990) and studies of the effect of poverty and food insecurity on the relationships between boys and girls in South Africa (Bhana, 2005). Feminist perspectives "uncover cultural and institutional sources and forces of oppression.... They name and value women's subjective experience" (Marshall, 1997a, p. 12). By combining feminist and critical perspectives, scholars dismantle traditional policy analysis that has failed to incorporate women (Marshall, 1997a) and create research agendas that turn critical thought into emancipating action (Lather, 1991).

Different feminisms frame different research goals (Collins, 1990; Marshall, 1997a; Tong, 1989). For example, socialist and women's-ways feminisms focus on women in leadership positions to expand leadership theory. Power-and-politics feminisms identify patriarchy as a key structure for understanding experience. Such theory can frame examinations of the state-imposed oppression of women in welfare, medical, and other systems the state regulates. It can identify how the institutional practices

> were developed in a way, and continue to function in a way that specifically benefits one group of people. [In the United States] that group is Euro-American, middle- to upper-class, and usually male . . . [and the ways] the standard operating procedures tend to hurt those people who do not fit the above profile. (Laible, 2003, p 185)

Such theories help frame research identifying "the political choices and power-driven ideologies and embedded forces that categorize, oppress, and exclude" (Marshall, 1997a, p. 13).

Feminist theories now move far beyond the demand that the voices and the lives of women and girls be included in studies. This "add women and stir" response is inadequate. Feminist researchers have expanded qualitative inquiry especially by focusing on the power imbalances between the researcher and the researched, by expanding collaborative research, and by asserting that reflexivity is a strategy for embracing subjectivity, replacing pretences of objectivity (Marshall & Young, 2006; Olesen, 2000). Recent work focuses on indigenous worldviews, drawing on postcolonial theory and perspectives (see Cannella & Manuelito, 2008).

Critical Race Theory

Critical race theory emerged from a strand of critical theorizing applied to the U.S. legal system called critical legal studies. With links to critical theory generally, the feminist critique of the principles and practice of law, and postcolonial theory, critical race theorists take up issues of racism, racial oppression, and racial discrimination as their central focus for analysis. Those within this genre argue that legal decisions—both historical ones and those belonging to the present day—reflect the intersection of racism, sexism, and classism and that legal principles are not applied uniformly, with race as the central differentiating quality. They further argue that race is socially constructed and argue against practices that promote or express racial discrimination.

Derrick Bell, the sometimes controversial legal scholar, is credited with initiating and sustaining the advocacy and ideology inherent in critical race theory with his persistent critique of the liberalism of the U.S. civil rights movement. (Bell's legal papers, speeches, and academic publications are archived at the New York University Archives at http://dlib.nyu.edu/findingaids/html/archives/bell.html.) In the mid-1990s, the field of education began to take up the core arguments and analytic focus of critical race theory. Notable in this field is Ladson-Billings (1997, 2000, 2001, 2005; Ladson-Billings & Tate, 2006), whose work centered on issues of race in teaching practice and educational research. Her early work highlighted the pedagogical practices of teachers who had great success teaching African American students. More recently, Dixson (2005; Dixson, Chapman, & Hill, 2005; Dixson & Rousseau, 2005, 2007) have applied the qualitative methodology of portraiture (see Lightfoot, 1985; Lightfoot & Davis, 1997) to analyses of issues of race and racism, focusing specifically on "jazz methodology" (Dixson, 2005).

Other methodologies associated with critical race theory include storytelling (narrative analysis) and the production of counterstories to balance the hegemonic, often white, representations of the experiences of African Americans and other racially oppressed groups, primarily in the United States. Thus, critical race theory's methodological emphasis on storytelling and its political commitment to counterhegemonic representations have links with postcolonialism's emphasis on *testimonio*—giving witness to social injustices—and the production of counternarratives.

Critical race theory and analysis takes up an explicitly political agenda, with its focus on racial discrimination, white supremacy, and advocacy for redressing past injustices. In its avowedly political stance, critical race theory has much in common with certain strands of feminism (especially the more critical strands) and with queer theory and analysis, to which we now turn.

Queer Theory and Analysis

By Paul St. John Frisoli

Stemming from lesbian feminism, poststructuralism, and the civil rights and gay and lesbian political movements of the 1960s, queer theory attempts to deconstruct social categories and binary identities to demonstrate the fluidity and transparency of otherwise demarcated boundaries within the social world. Queer theorists argue that identity is not unitary but multiple, therefore allowing for an unstable acceptance of the different lived experiences of people (Jagose, 1996; Seidman, 1996; Stein & Plummer, 1996). Judith Butler (1999) is considered to be the unofficial "founder" of queer theory, with her pivotal work, *Gender Trouble*, which argues that gender and sexuality are performative, meaning that individuals subconsciously act out these normalized socially constructed identity categories that serve specific purposes in society. Therefore, naturally and definitively assumed standards such as heterosexuality are deconstructed to demonstrate that every aspect of a person's identity is based on norms, rules, and cultural models (Jagose, 1996). Defining these concepts as queer is to acknowledge the possibilities, the fluidities, and the processes and not fix them into a concrete discipline. Therefore, queer theory does not solely highlight sexuality but recognizes "that identities are always multiple or at best composites with literally an infinite number of ways which 'identity-components' (e.g., sexual orientation, race, class, nationality, gender, age, able-ness) can intersect or combine" (Seidman, 1996, p.11). However, critics highlight the point that the political origins of queer theory and at times the continued politicization of a "gay identity" and equal rights in the "sexual minority movement" fix and essentialize a universal identity category based on sexual orientation (Walters, 2004). Postcolonial queer theory scholars highlight the importance of recognizing the role of colonialism, postcolonialism, and globalization in imposing cultural imperialistic ideas of sexuality that fail to take non-Western cultures and histories into account (Altman, 2001).

Queer theory has played a pivotal role in qualitative studies to unravel supposedly scientific data that reified, objectified, and pathologized "homosexuals" and other socially marginalized groups as deviant to society (Rhyne, 2000). Of equal importance, the deconstructing nature and acceptance of the fluidity concept have currently made a variety of contributions to qualitative inquiry that include favoring multiple methods that foster researcher and participant understanding and collaboration and researcher reflexivity and self-awareness during multiple stages of the research project to recognize the lens through which the researcher interprets someone else's life world (Kong, Mahoney, & Plummer, 2002). Queer theory also allows postcolonial scholars to present new types of non-Western queer identities that offer insights that debunk narrow understandings of sexuality.

* * * * *

The preceding discussion is intended to provide ways of categorizing a variety of qualitative research genres and approaches as well as to briefly describe some of the emerging strands that derive from the critical, feminist, and postmodern critiques of traditional social science inquiry. As we note, systematic inquiry in each genre occurs in a natural setting rather than an artificially constrained one, such as a laboratory. The approaches, however, vary depending on theory and ideology, the focus of interest (individual, group or organization, or a communicative interaction, such as a text or a Web site), the degree of interaction between researcher and participants in gathering data, and the participants' role in the research. The discussion was intended to provide some sense of the array of approaches under the qualitative research umbrella. This text, however, cannot do justice to the detailed and nuanced variety of qualitative methods; we refer you to additional sources at the end of this chapter. Some of these sources are classic—the "grandmothers and grandfathers" in the field; others reflect emergent perspectives. Our purpose in this book is to describe the generic process of designing qualitative research that immerses researchers in the everyday life of a setting chosen for study. These researchers value and seek to discover participants' perspectives on their worlds and view inquiry as an interactive process between the researcher and the participants. The process is descriptive, analytic, and interpretive, and it uses people's words, observable behavior, and various texts as the primary data. Whether or not some single methodological refinement is qualitative could be debated in another arena. We hope to give practical guidance to those embarking on an exciting, sometimes frustrating, and ultimately rewarding journey into qualitative inquiry.

In the next chapter, we turn to the important considerations of trustworthiness and ethics. At the proposal stage, how might the researcher argue that her study will address the canons of trustworthiness? And which ones? She should also demonstrate a deep sensitivity to the ethical issues that may arise during the conduct of the study. These are taken up in the next chapter.

FURTHER READING

Major Genres

On Ethnography

Atkinson, P. A., & Delamont, S. (Eds.). (2008). *Representing ethnography: Reading, writing and rhetoric in qualitative research.* London: Sage.

Atkinson, P. A., Delamont, S., Coffey, A., Lofland, J., & Lofland, L. (Eds.). (2007). *Handbook of ethnography.* London: Sage.

Crang, M., & Cook, I. (2007). *Doing ethnographies.* Thousand Oaks, CA: Sage.

Fetterman, D. (2009). *Doing ethnography: Step-by-step* (3rd ed.). Thousand Oaks, CA: Sage.

Gobo, G. (2008). *Doing ethnography.* London: Sage.

Pink, S. (2009). *Doing sensory ethnography.* London: Sage.

Tedlock, B. (2005). The observation of participation and the emergence of public ethnography. In N. K. Denzin & Y. S. Lincoln (Eds.), *The SAGE handbook of qualitative research* (3rd ed., pp. 467–481). Thousand Oaks, CA: Sage.

Ybema, S., Yanow, D., Wels, H., & Kamsteeg, F. (2009). *Organizational ethnography: Studying the complexity of everyday life.* London: Sage.

On Phenomenology

Beverly, J. (2000). Testimonio, subalternity, and narrative authority. In N. K. Denzin & Y. S. Lincoln (Eds.), *Handbook of qualitative research* (2nd ed., pp. 555–565). Thousand Oaks, CA: Sage.

Caelli, K. (2000). The changing face of phenomenological research: Traditional and American phenomenology in nursing. *Qualitative Health Research, 10*(3), 366–377.

Center for Advanced Research in Phenomenology. (2005). *What is phenomenology?* Retrieved May 9, 2009, from www.phenomenologycenter.org/phenom.htm

Cohen, M. Z., Kahn, D. L., & Steeves, R. H. (2000). *Hermeneutic phenomenological research: A practical guide for nurse researchers.* Thousand Oaks, CA: Sage.

Groenewald, T. (2004). A phenomenological research design illustrated. *International Journal of Qualitative Methods, 3*(1), Article 4. Retrieved May 9, 2009, from www.ualberta.ca/~iiqm/backissues/3_1/html/groenewald.html

Kvale, S., & Brinkmann, S. (2009). *Interviews: Learning the craft of qualitative research interviewing* (2nd ed.). Thousand Oaks, CA: Sage.

Moustakas, C. (1994). *Phenomenological research methods.* Thousand Oaks, CA: Sage.

Van Manen, J. (Ed.). (1995). *Researching lived experience: Human science for an action sensitive pedagogy.* Albany: State University of New York Press.

Wronka, J. (2008). *Human rights and social justice: Social action and service for the helping and health professions.* Thousand Oaks, CA: Sage.

On Socio-Communications Studies

Roth, W.-M. (2001). Gestures: Their role in teaching and learning. *Review of Educational Research, 71*(3), 2–14.

Schiffrin, D., Tannen, D., & Hamilton, H. (Eds.). (2001). *Handbook of discourse analysis.* Oxford, UK: Blackwell.

Specialized Genres

On Narrative Analysis and Critical Discourse Analysis

Chase, S. E. (2005). Narrative inquiry: Multiple lenses, approaches, voices. In N. K. Denzin & Y. S. Lincoln (Eds.), *The SAGE handbook of qualitative research* (3rd ed., pp. 651–679). Thousand Oaks, CA: Sage.

Cheek, J. (2004). At the margins? Discourse analysis and qualitative research. *Qualitative Health Research, 14*(8), 1140–1150.

Clandinin, D. J., & Connelly, F. M. (2000). *Narrative inquiry: Experience and story in qualitative research.* San Francisco: Jossey-Bass.

Czarniawska, B. (2004). *Narratives in social science research.* Thousand Oaks, CA: Sage.

Daiute, C., & Lightfoot, C. (2004). *Narrative analysis: Studying the development of individuals in society.* Thousand Oaks, CA: Sage.

Josselson, R. (Ed.). (1996). *Ethics and process in the narrative study of lives.* Thousand Oaks, CA: Sage.

Josselson, R., & Lieblich, A. (Eds.). (1993). *The narrative study of lives.* Newbury Park, CA: Sage.

Peräkylä, A. (2005). Analyzing talk and text. In N. K. Denzin & Y. S. Lincoln (Eds.), *The SAGE handbook of qualitative research* (3rd ed., pp. 869–886). Thousand Oaks, CA: Sage.

Riessman, C. K. (2007). *Narrative analysis: Methods for the human sciences.* Thousand Oaks, CA: Sage.

Rogers, R. (Ed.). (2004). *An introduction to critical discourse analysis in education.* Mahwah, NJ: Lawrence Erlbaum.

Ten Have, P. (2007). *Doing conversation analysis* (2nd ed.). Thousand Oaks, CA: Sage.

On Action Research

Greenwood, D. J., & Levin, M. (2007). *Introduction to action research: Social research for social change* (2nd ed.). Thousand Oaks, CA: Sage.

Kincheloe, J. L. (1991). *Teachers as researchers: Qualitative inquiry as a path to empowerment.* London: Falmer.

McNiff, J., & Whitehead, J. (2003). *Action research: Principles and practice.* London: Routledge.

McNiff, J., & Whitehead, J. (2009). *Doing and writing action research.* London: Sage.

Noffke, S. E., & Somekh, B. (Eds.). (2009). *The SAGE handbook of educational action research.* London: Sage.

Reason, P. W., & Bradbury, H. (2006). *Handbook of action research* (concise paperback ed.). Thousand Oaks, CA: Sage.

Sagor, R. (2005). *Action research handbook: A four-step process for educators and school teams.* Thousand Oaks, CA: Corwin.

Stringer, E. T. (2007). *Action research: A handbook for practitioners* (3rd ed.). Thousand Oaks, CA: Sage.

Stringer, E. T., Christenson, L. M., & Baldwin, S. C. (2009). *Integrating teaching, learning, and action research: Enhancing instruction in the K-12 classroom.* Thousand Oaks, CA: Sage.

On Participatory Action Research

Brock, K., & McGee, R. (2002). *Knowing poverty: Critical reflections on participatory research and policy.* Sterling, VA: Earthscan.

Cooke, B., & Kothari, U. (Eds.). (2001). *Participation: The new tyranny?* London: Zed Books.

Hart, R. A. (1997). *Children's participation: The theory and practice of involving young citizens in community development and environmental care.* London: Earthscan.

Hickey, S., & Mohan, G. (Eds.). (2004). *Participation: From tyranny to transformation?* London: Zed Books.

Kemmis, S., & McTaggart, R. (2005). Participatory action research: Communicative action and the public sphere. In N. K. Denzin & Y. S. Lincoln (Eds.), *The SAGE handbook of qualitative research* (3rd ed., pp. 559–603). Thousand Oaks, CA: Sage.

Maguire, P. (2000). *Doing participatory research: A feminist approach.* Amherst, MA: Center for International Education.

McIntyre, A. (2008). *Participatory action research.* Thousand Oaks, CA: Sage.

McNiff, J., & Whitehead, J. (2009). *Doing and writing action research.* London: Sage.

McTaggart, R. (Ed.). (1997). *Participatory action research: International contexts and consequences.* Albany: State University of New York Press.

Park, P., Brydon-Miller, M., Hall, B., & Jackson, T. (Eds.). (1993). *Voices of change: Participatory research in the United States and Canada.* Toronto, Ontario, Canada: Ontario Institute for Studies in Education Press.

Van der Riet, M. (2008). Participatory research and the philosophy of social science: Beyond the moral imperative. *Qualitative Inquiry, 14*(4), 546–565.

Whyte, W. F. (Ed.). (1991). *Participatory action research.* Newbury Park, CA: Sage.

On Critical and Postcritical Ethnography

Carspecken, P. F. (1996). *Critical ethnography in educational research: A theoretical and practical guide.* New York: Routledge & Kegan Paul.

Crang, M., & Cook, I. (2007). *Doing ethnographies.* Thousand Oaks, CA: Sage.

Cruz, M. R. (2008). What if I just cite Graciela? Working toward decolonizing knowledge through a critical ethnography. *Qualitative Inquiry, 14*(4), 651–658.

Gitlin, A. (Ed.). (1994). *Power and method: Political activism and educational research.* New York: Routledge.

Madison, D. S. (2005a). *Critical ethnography: Method, ethics, and performance.* Thousand Oaks, CA: Sage.

Madison, D. S. (2005b). Critical ethnography as street performance: Reflections of home, race, murder, and justice. In N. K. Denzin & Y. S. Lincoln (Eds.), *The SAGE handbook of qualitative research* (3rd ed., pp. 537–546). Thousand Oaks, CA: Sage.

Marcus, G., & Fischer, M. (1986). *Anthropology as cultural critique: An experimental moment in the human sciences.* Chicago: University of Chicago Press.

Morrow, R. A., with Brown, D. D. (1994). *Critical theory and methodology.* Thousand Oaks, CA: Sage.

Noblit, G. W., Flores, S. Y., & Murillo, E. G., Jr. (Eds.). (2005). *Postcritical ethnography: Reinscribing critique.* Cresskill, NJ: Hampton Press.

Weis, L. (1990). *Working class without work: High school students in a de-industrializing economy.* New York: Routledge.

Weis, L., & Fine, M. (Eds.). (2000). *Construction sites: Excavating race, class, and gender among urban youth.* New York: Teachers College Press.

On Performance Ethnography and Arts-Based Qualitative Inquiry

Alexander, B. K. (2005). Performance ethnography: The reenacting and inciting of culture. In N. K. Denzin & Y. S. Lincoln (Eds.), *The SAGE handbook of qualitative research* (3rd ed., pp. 411–441). Thousand Oaks, CA: Sage.

Bagley, C. (2008). Educational ethnography as performance art: Towards a sensuous feeling and knowing. *Qualitative Research, 8*(1), 53–72.

Barone, T., & Eisner, E. (2006). Arts-based educational research. In J. L. Green, G. Camilli, & P. B. Elmore (Eds.), *Handbook of complementary methods in education* (3rd ed., pp. 95–108). New York: Routledge.

Boal, A. (1997). *Theater of the oppressed.* London: Pluto Press.

Boal, A. (2002). *Games for actors and non-actors* (2nd ed.). London: Routledge.

Denzin, N. (2003). *Performance ethnography: Critical pedagogy and the politics of culture.* Thousand Oaks, CA: Sage.

Furman, R., Langer, C. L., Davis, C. S., Gallardo, H. P., & Kulkarni, S. (2007). Expressive research and reflective poetry as qualitative inquiry: A study of adolescent identity. *Qualitative Research, 7*(3), 301–315.

Madison, D. S., & Hamera, J. (Eds.). (2005). *Handbook of performance studies.* Thousand Oaks, CA: Sage.

Miller-Day, M. (2008). Performance matters. *Qualitative Inquiry, 14*(8), 1458–1470.

Said, E. W. (2007). *Music at the limits: Three decades of essays and articles on music.* New York: Columbia University Press.

On Internet/Virtual Ethnography

Dicks, B., Mason, B., & Atkinson, P. (2005). *Qualitative research and hypermedia.* London: Sage.

Dicks, B., Soyinka, B., & Coffey, A. (2006). Multimodal ethnography. *Qualitative Research, 6*(1), 77–96.

Gajjala, R. (2004). *Cyber selves: Feminist ethnographies of South Asian women.* New York: AltaMira Press.

Garcia, A. C., Standlee, A. I., Bechkoff, J., & Cui, Y. (2009). Ethnographic approaches to the Internet and computer-mediated communication. *Journal of Contemporary Ethnography, 38*(1), 52–84.

Hine, C. (2000). *Virtual ethnography.* London: Sage.

Mann, C., & Stewart, F. (2002). Internet interviewing. In J. Gubrium & J. A. Holstein (Eds.), *Handbook of interview research: Context and method* (pp. 603–627). Thousand Oaks, CA: Sage.

Mann, C., & Stewart, F. (2004). Introducing online methods. In S. N. Hesse-Biber & P. Leavy (Eds.), *Approaches to qualitative research: A reader on theory and practice* (pp. 367–401). New York: Oxford University Press.

Markham, A. N. (2004). Internet communication as a tool for qualitative research. In D. Silverman (Ed.), *Qualitative research: Theory, method, and practice* (2nd ed., pp. 95–124). London: Sage.

Olesen, V. (2009). Do whatever you can: Temporality and critical, interpretive methods in an age of despair. *Cultural Studies: Critical Methodologies, 9*(1), 52–55.

Williams, M. (2007). Avatar watching: Participant observation in graphical online environments. *Qualitative Researcher, 7*(1), 5–24.

On Feminist Research

Brown, L. M. (2005). In the bad or good of girlhood: Social class, schooling, and white femininities. In L. Weis & M. Fine (Eds.), *Beyond silenced voices: Class, race, and gender in United States schools* (2nd ed., pp. 147–161). Albany: State University of New York Press.

Butler, J. (1999). *Gender trouble: Feminism and the subversion of identity.* New York: Routledge.

Calas, M., & Smircich, L. (1996). From "the woman's" point of view: Feminist approach to organization studies. In S. R. Clegg, C. Hardy, & W. R. Nord (Eds.), *Handbook of organization studies* (pp. 218–257). London: Sage.

Cannella, G. S., & Manuelito, K. D. (2008). Feminisms from unthought locations: Indigenous worldviews, marginalized feminisms, and revisioning an anticolonial social science. In N. K. Denzin, Y. S. Lincoln, & L. T. Smith (Eds.), *Handbook of critical and indigenous methodologies* (pp. 45–59). Thousand Oaks, CA: Sage.

Dillard, C. B. (2003). The substance of things hoped for, the evidence of things not seen: Examining an endarkened feminist epistemology in educational research and leadership. In M. D. Young & L. Skrla (Eds.), *Reconsidering feminist research in educational leadership* (pp. 131–159). Albany: State University of New York Press.

Harding, S. (Ed.). (1987). *Feminism and methodology.* Bloomington: Indiana University Press.

Herr, R. S. (2004). A third world feminist defense of multiculturalism. *Social Theory & Practice, 30*(1), 73–103.

Hesse-Biber, S. N., & Leavy, P. (2007). *Feminist research practice: A primer.* Thousand Oaks, CA: Sage.

Hill Collins, P. (1991). *Black feminist thought.* New York: Routledge.

Kleinman, S. (2007). *Feminist fieldwork analysis.* Thousand Oaks, CA: Sage.

Laible, J. (2003). A loving epistemology: What I hold critical in my life, faith, and profession. In M. D. Young & L. Skrla (Eds.), *Reconsidering feminist research in educational leadership* (pp. 179–192). Albany: State University of New York Press.

Lather, P. (1991). *Getting smart: Feminist research and pedagogy with/in the postmodern.* New York: Routledge & Kegan Paul.

Lather, P. (2007). *Getting lost: Feminist efforts towards a double(d) science.* Albany: State University of New York Press.

Marshall, C. (Ed.). (1997). *Feminist critical policy analysis: A perspective from primary and secondary schooling.* London: Falmer.

Marshall, C., & Young, M. (2006). Gender and methodology. In C. Skelton, B. Francis, & L. Smulyan, *Handbook of gender and education.* Thousand Oaks, CA: Sage.

Nielson, J. (Ed.). (1990). *Feminist research methods: Exemplary readings in the social sciences.* Boulder, CO: Westview.

Olesen, V. (2000). Feminisms and qualitative research into the new millennium. In N. K. Denzin & Y. S. Lincoln (Eds.), *Handbook of qualitative research* (2nd ed., pp. 215–255). Thousand Oaks, CA: Sage.

Olesen, V. (2005). Early millennial feminist qualitative research: Challenges and contours. In N. K. Denzin & Y. S. Lincoln (Eds.), *The SAGE handbook of qualitative research* (3rd ed., pp. 235–277). Thousand Oaks, CA: Sage.

Reinharz, S. (1992). *Feminist methods in social research.* New York: Oxford University Press.

Scott, J. W. (1986). Gender: A useful category of historical analysis. *The American Historical Review, 91*(5), 1053–1075.

Young, M. D., & Skrla, L. (2003). Research on women and administration: A response to Julie Laible's loving epistemology. In M. D. Young & L. Skrla (Eds.), *Reconsidering feminist research in educational leadership* (pp. 201–210). Albany: State University of New York Press.

On Cultural Studies

Barker, C. (2003). *Cultural studies: Theory and practice* (2nd ed.). Thousand Oaks, CA: Sage.

Barthes, R. (1972). *Mythologies.* London: Cape.

Gannon, S. (2006). The (im)possibilities of writing the self-writing: French poststructural theory and autoethnography. *Cultural studies: Critical methodologies, 6*(4), 474–495.

Gray, A. (2003). *Research practices for cultural studies: Ethnographic methods and lived cultures.* London: Sage.

Hall, S. (Ed.). (1997). *Representation: Cultural representations and signifying practices.* London: Sage.

hooks, b. (2004). Culture to culture: Ethnography and cultural studies as critical intervention. In S. N. Hesse-Biber & P. Leavy (Eds.), *Approaches to qualitative research: A reader on theory and practice* (pp. 149–158). New York: Oxford University Press.

Miller, G., & Fox, K. J. (2004). Building bridges: The possibility of analytic dialogue between ethnography, conversation analysis, and Foucault. In D. Silverman (Ed.), *Qualitative research: Theory, method, and practice* (2nd ed., pp. 35–55). London: Sage.

Prior, L. (2004). Following Foucault's footsteps: Text and context in qualitative research. In S. N. Hesse-Biber & P. Leavy (Eds.), *Approaches to qualitative research: A reader on theory and practice* (pp. 317–333). New York: Oxford University Press.

Ryen, A. (2002). Cross-cultural interviewing. In J. Gubrium & J. A. Holstein (Eds.), *Handbook of interview research: Context and method* (pp. 335–354). Thousand Oaks, CA: Sage.

Saukko, P. (2003). *Doing research in cultural studies: An introduction to classical and new methodological approaches.* London: Sage.

Saukko, P. (2008). Methodologies for cultural studies: An integrative approach. In N. K. Denzin & Y. S. Lincoln (Eds.), *The landscapes of qualitative research* (3rd ed., pp. 457–475). Thousand Oaks, CA: Sage.

Surber, J. P. (1998). *Culture and critique: An introduction to the critical discourse of Cultural Studies.* Boulder, CO: Westview Press.

On Critical Race Theory

Bernal, D. D. (2002). Critical race theory, Latino critical theory, and critical raced-gendered epistemologies: Recognizing students of color as holders and creators of knowledge. *Qualitative Inquiry, 8*(1), 105–126.

DeCuir, J. T., & Dixson, A. D. (2004). "So when it comes out, they aren't that surprised that it is there": Using critical race theory as a tool of analysis of race and racism in education. *Educational Researcher, 33,* 26–31.

Dixson, A. D., & Rousseau, C. K. (2005). And we are still not saved: Critical race theory in education ten years later. *Race, Ethnicity, & Education, 8*(1), 7–27.

Dixson, A. D., & Rousseau, C. K. (2007). *Critical race theory in education: All God's children got a song.* New York: Routledge.

Ladson-Billings, G. J. (1997). *The dreamkeepers: Successful teachers of African-American children.* San Francisco: Jossey-Bass.

Ladson-Billings, G. J. (2001). *Crossing over to Canaan: The journey of new teachers in diverse classrooms.* San Francisco: Jossey-Bass.

Ladson-Billings, G. J. (2005). *Beyond the big house: African American educators on teacher education.* New York: Teachers College Press.

Ladson-Billings, G. J., & Donnor, J. (2005). The moral activist role of critical race theory scholarship. In N. K. Denzin & Y. S. Lincoln (Eds.), *The SAGE handbook of qualitative research* (3rd ed., pp. 279–301). Thousand Oaks, CA: Sage.

Yosso, T. J. (2005). Whose culture has capital? A critical race theory discussion of community cultural wealth. *Race, Ethnicity, & Education, 8*(1), 69–91.

On Queer Theory

Butler, J. (1999). *Gender trouble: Feminism and the subversion of identity.* New York: Routledge.

Halperin, D. M. (1990). *One hundred years of homosexuality and other essays on Greek love.* New York: Routledge.

Hawley, J. C. (2001a). *Postcolonial and queer theories: Intersections and essays.* Westport, CT: Greenwood Press.

Hawley, J. C. (2001b). *Postcolonial, queer: Theoretical intersections.* Albany: State University of New York Press.

Jagose, A. (1996). *Queer theory: An introduction.* New York: New York University Press.

Rhyne, R. (2000). Foucault, Michel (1926–1984). In G. E. Haggerty (Ed.), *Gay histories and cultures: An encyclopedia* (Vol. 2, pp. 337–338). New York: Garland.

Seidman, S. (1996). *Queer theory/sociology.* Cambridge, MA: Blackwell.

Stein, A., & Plummer, K. (1996). "I can't even think straight": "Queer" theory and the missing sexual revolution in sociology. In S. Seidman (Ed.), *Queer theory/sociology* (pp. 129–144). Cambridge, MA: Blackwell.

Sullivan, N. (2003). *A critical introduction to queer theory.* New York: New York University Press.

Queer Theory and Qualitative Research:

Allen, L. (2006). Trying not to think "straight": Conducting focus groups with lesbian and gay youth. *International Journal of Qualitative Studies in Education, 19,* 163–176.

Donelson, R., & Rogers, T. (2004). Negotiating a research protocol for studying school-based gay and lesbian issues. *Theory Into Practice, 43*(2), 128–135.

Grossman, A. H., & D'Augelli, A. R. D. (2006). Transgendered youth: Invisible and vulnerable. *Journal of Homosexuality, 51,* 111–128.

Kong, T. S., Mahoney, D., & Plummer, K. (2002). Queering the interview. In J. F. Gubrium & J. A. Holstein (Eds.), *Handbook of interview research: Context and method* (pp. 239–258). Thousand Oaks, CA: Sage.

Mayo, C. (2007). Queering foundations: Queer and lesbian, gay, bisexual, and transgender educational research. *Review of Research in Education, 31,* 78–94.

McCready, L. T. (2004). Understanding the marginalization of gay and gender non-conforming Black male students. *Theory Into Practice, 43,* 136–143.

KEY CONCEPTS

Action research

Autoethnography

Critical discourse analysis

Critical ethnography

Critical race theory and analysis

Cultural studies

Discourse analysis

Ethnography

Feminist theories and methodologies

Internet ethnography

Narrative analysis

Participatory action research

Performance ethnography

Phenomenological approaches

Phenomenology

Public ethnography

Queer theory

NOTES

1. Burrell and Morgan (1979) provide one useful way for understanding research paradigms and the assumptions they embrace; Rossman and Rallis (2003) rely on their conceptualization to help situate various qualitative research genres. The discussion here draws on the work of Rossman and Rallis.

2. We address this more fully in Chapters 3 and 7, but here we note that participants may disagree with the researcher's report and that passive constructions ("The research was conducted") suggest anonymity and distance whereas active ones ("We conducted the research") claim agency.

3

Trustworthiness and Ethics

As we have indicated in Chapters 1 and 2, when developing a proposal for qualitative research, the writer needs to address certain key issues and considerations to demonstrate that the study, as designed, is well thought out, responds to criteria or canons for good research practice (depending on the genre), and is likely to be implemented with an ethical mindfulness. This chapter takes up these important issues, building on the previous discussions and forecasting further, sometimes more specific, recommendations to come in subsequent chapters.

Historically, concerns with the **trustworthiness** or goodness of qualitative research drew from the natural and experimental sciences for direction. Thus, **reliability**, **validity**, **objectivity**, and **generalizability**—borrowed from more quantitative approaches—were the criteria against which the soundness of a qualitative study was judged. This period of time has been characterized as one of "physics envy" (Rossman, Rallis, & Kuntz, in press), where reliability, validity, and generalizability were "the holy trinity . . . , worshipped with respect by all true believers in science" (Kvale, 1996, p. 229). With the postmodern turn/s, however, these canonical standards have been challenged, as has the very notion of putting forth criteria itself (Schwandt, 1996). A range of ways to conceptualize soundness (often referred to as "validity," using the historic term) has emerged. We discuss several approaches to trustworthiness and then build the argument that trustworthiness considerations cannot be separated from ethical concerns.

TRUSTWORTHINESS

A critical moment in the development of qualitative methodologies occurred when Lincoln and Guba published *Naturalistic Inquiry* in 1985. This text addressed central questions that determine the trust we have in research: Do we believe in the claims that a research report puts forward? On what grounds do we judge these as credible? What evidence is put forward to support the claims? How do we evaluate it? Are the claims potentially useful for the problematic we are concerned with? These questions capture concerns with validity, reliability, objectivity, and generalizability while broadening and deepening them.

Lincoln and Guba (1985) put forward alternative constructs to capture these concerns: **credibility**, **dependability**, confirmability, and **transferability**. Moreover, they offered a set of procedures to help ensure that these standards of trustworthiness would be met. For validity/credibility, they urged qualitative researchers to be in the setting for a long period of time (**prolonged engagement**); share data and interpretations with participants (**member checks**); triangulate by gathering data from multiple sources, through multiple methods, and using multiple theoretical lenses; and discuss their emergent findings with critical friends to ensure that analyses are grounded in the data (**peer debriefing**). They also firmly critiqued the positivist assertion that objectivity is possible and argued for alternative logics to better capture the usefulness of qualitative studies.

Their work was generative. Subsequent writing on the canons of trustworthiness often invokes their work and uses both their terminology and their procedural recommendations. For example, in 2000, Creswell and Miller list the following procedures to help ensure the rigor and usefulness of a qualitative study:

- **Triangulation**
- **Searching for disconfirming evidence**
- Engaging in reflexivity
- Member checking
- Prolonged engagement in the field
- Collaboration
- Developing an **audit trail**
- Peer debriefing

Most of these were articulated by Lincoln and Guba (1985). Another example can be found in Maxwell (1996, pp. 92–98), where he develops a checklist of validity tests:

- Searching for alternative explanations
- Searching for discrepant evidence and negative cases
- Triangulation
- Soliciting feedback from those familiar with the setting and from strangers
- Member checks
- Rich data
- Quasi statistics to assess the amount of evidence
- Comparison

We could offer other examples. As Kvale noted (1996, p. 231), Lincoln and Guba's (1985) work "reclaimed ordinary language terms," making these ideas more accessible. And many others have invoked their work, either as a starting point for a critique or to deepen the ideas they developed. There are few major texts about qualitative inquiry that do not cite this seminal work (see, e.g., Bodgan & Biklen, 2007; Creswell, 1998, 2002; Flick, 2009; Kvale, 1996; Kvale & Brinkmann, 2009; Marshall & Rossman, 2006; Patton, 2002; Wolcott, 2001; Yin, 2003) And despite the postmodern turn/s that challenge the notion of validity, the argument is still persuasive that "determining reliability and validity remains the qualitative researcher's goal" and that "claim[ing] that reliability and validity have no place in qualitative inquiry is to place the entire paradigm under suspicion" (Morse & Richards, 2002, p. 168). What is now contested is how these key terms are to be defined, by whom, for which research project, and for what audience.

The older terms—*reliability*, *validity*, *objectivity*, and *generalizability*—and Lincoln and Guba's (1985) modernization of them—*credibility*, *dependability*, *confirmability*, and *transferability*—tend to focus on design-stage considerations. Decisions at the design stage forecast what the researcher intends to do during implementation of the study, thereby demonstrating how the study design will likely ensure that the data and their interpretations will be strong and credible. However, the postmodern turn in the humanities and social sciences has encouraged a radical questioning of the "regulatory demand" implied by considerations of validity. As Corbin and Strauss (2007) lament,

> The notion of judging the quality of research seemed so clear before postmodernist and constructionist thinking pointed out the fallacies of some of our ways. Now I wonder, if findings are constructions and truth a "mirage," aren't evaluative criteria also constructions and therefore subject to debate? (p. 297)

Thus, the debate on validity rages on, offering a confusing array of choices for the proposal writer. Cho and Trent (2006) offer a useful way for organizing the various writings on validity. They put forward the notions of "**transactional validity**" and "**transformational validity**" to capture the essential arguments in the foundationalist/antifoundationalist debate.

Transactional or Transformational Validity?

Cho and Trent (2006) argue that historic approaches to ensuring validity (including the work of Lincoln & Guba, 1985) can be described as transactional, involving participants in the research project to validate themes, interpretations, and/or findings. They write,

> This approach assumes that qualitative research can be more credible as long as certain techniques, methods, and/or strategies are employed during the conduct of the inquiry. In other words, techniques are seen as a medium to insure an accurate reflection of reality (or at least, participants' constructions of reality). (p. 322)

Thus, stipulating that one will engage in member checks (the central procedure, they argue), which invite participants to confirm one's findings, and the extent to which one will design and implement a study using triangulation as a strategy will help ensure validity. Through member checks, the participants can correct the researcher's (perhaps not quite accurate) representations of their worlds. Through triangulation (using data sources, methods, theories, or researchers), the validity of specific knowledge claims is argued to be more robust. In both procedures, the goal is a more accurate, objective, and neutral representation of the topic under inquiry.

Given the complexity of the diverse genres and subgenres that coexist under the qualitative-inquiry umbrella, Cho and Trent (2006) provide some refreshing simplicity. Drawing on the work of Donmoyer (2001), they offer a table that summarizes the main purposes of a qualitative genre; the fundamental questions; validity as a process; and the major criteria for validity within those broad purposes. Table 3.1 suggests a key point that we have made thus far: Criteria vary, as do the major qualitative genres.

The "transactional" family of approaches has been critiqued for its emphasis on **convergence** and **corroboration** and for its assumption that procedures can help ensure a more accurate rendering of the topic. Cho and Trent (2006) argue that another family of validity approaches has emerged from this critique—what they refer to as "transformational validity." Writers within this category take quite seriously the notion (central to qualitative inquiry) that multiple perspectives, including those of the researcher-writer, exist; they thus grapple with ways to ensure that those voices are represented transparently and that the full dynamics of the research process are examined and critiqued. For some of these approaches, the processes and end results of the inquiry are the most important (e.g., empowerment, civic action, and greater efficacy); researcher reflexivity becomes central (discussed more fully in Chapter 8). They write that within this family of approaches,

> the question of validity in itself is convergent with the way the researcher self-reflects, both explicitly and implicitly, upon the multiple dimensions in which the inquiry is conducted. In this respect, validity is not so much something that can be achieved solely by way of certain techniques. (p. 324)

Within this family are the "transgressive approaches" to validity articulated by Lather (1993, 2001) and Koro-Lundberg (2008), among others. These scholars seek to interrogate the term *validity* and encourage methodologies that express the dynamics and complexities of individuals interacting within a particular sociohistorical site. Perhaps best known within this family is Lather's conception of **catalytic validity**—"the manner in which the process of research re-orients participants to their reality to stimulate *transformative* [italics added] possibilities" (Rossman et al., in press). Also, quite generative is the conceptualization by Kirkhart (1995) of *multicultural validity*, which carries an explicit **social justice** agenda.

Table 3.1 Use of Validity in Five Overarching Purposes Undergirding Contemporary Qualitative Research

Purpose	Fundamental Questions	Validity as a Process	Major Validity Criteria
"Truth" seeking	What is the correct answer?	Progressive induction	Member check as technical Causality-based triangulation
Thick description	How do the people under study interpret phenomena?	Holistic Prolong engagement	Triangulated, descriptive data Accurate knowledge of daily life Member check as recursive
Developmental	How does an organization change over time?	Categorical/back and forth	Rich archives reflecting history Triangulated, member check as ongoing
Personal essay	What is the researcher's personal interpretation?	Reflexive/aesthetic	Self-assessment of experience Public appeal of personal opinion of a situation
Praxis/social	How can we learn and change educators, organizations, or both?	Inquiry with participants	Member check as reflexive Critical reflexivity of self Redefinition of the status quo

SOURCE: Cho & Trent (2006, p. 326), adapted from Donmoyer (2001, pp. 175–189). Reprinted with permission.

Of note for the validity debate is the recent introduction of the concept of **crystallization** as an alternative to triangulation. First brought into the research methodology discourse by Richardson (1997), the concept has provided a flexible way of thinking about validity. The triangle is critiqued as a rigid structure with only three fixed points, while crystals are "prisms that reflect externalities *and* refract within themselves" (p. 92). Crystals thus offer multiple perspectives, colors, and refractions. Conceptualizing validity through the metaphor of the crystal calls on a methodology that demands self-critique or self-reflexivity. Ellingson (2009) develops the methodology of crystallization, offering a figure that depicts qualitative inquiry genres along a continuum. She articulates various positions along this continuum for thinking about crystallization (see Figure 3.1).

In sum, recent discourse on validity in qualitative inquiry offers the proposal writer alternatives for developing arguments to convince the reader that her study is well conceptualized and will be conducted rigorously and ethically. These arguments, with appropriate and convincing rationales, should be grounded in the appropriate literature.

* * * * *

While the debate rages about what should constitute criteria for assessing the trustworthiness of qualitative inquiry, who makes those determinations, and the attendant discussion of what constitutes "evidence," many qualitative researchers, especially those writing proposals for the first time, find a firm grounding in the ideas and procedures first articulated by Lincoln and Guba (1985). We would caution beginners, however, to bring their constructs up to date and to incorporate current thinking about the nuances of writing to convince a reviewer that the proposed study will be conducted rigorously and that the resulting assertions ("findings") will rest on solid methodological practice.

BRINGING ETHICS INTO TRUSTWORTHINESS

Although they are useful, we have observed that notably absent from many of the methodological discussions about validity are explicit discussions of the principles and practice of ethical research as central to the trustworthiness of any study. Some transformational approaches suggest a focus on the ethical with their commitment to social justice and to the disruption of hegemonic structures, but an explicit focus on the ethical is frequently absent. When moral principles are discussed, moreover, the paramount considerations of **respect for persons**, **beneficence**, and justice are often reduced to the procedural matters of gaining **informed consent**, as noted above. We believe the researcher must think beyond being careful with procedural matters and documentation for the protection of human subjects. At the proposal stage, the potential trustworthiness and goodness of a study should be judged not only by how competently it is designed (according to the norms and standards of a discipline) but also by how ethically engaged the researcher is likely to be during the study's conduct.

For criteria for trustworthiness and for ethics, we argue that reasoning must move beyond the procedural to focus on matters of relationships—with participants, with stakeholders, with peers, and with the larger community of discourse. Writing about their research in the allied health field, Davies and Dodd (2002) argue that

Figure 3.1 Qualitative Continuum

	Qualitative Continuum		
	Art/Impressionist	**Middle-Grounded Approaches**	**Science/Realist**
Goals	To unravel accepted truths To construct personal truths To explore the specific To generate art	To construct situated knowledges To explore the typical To generate description and understanding To trouble the taken-for-granted To generate pragmatic implications for practitioners	To discover objective truth To generalize to larger population To explain reality "out there" To generate scientific knowledge To predict and control behavior
Questions	How do we/can we cope with life? What other ways can we imagine? What is unique about my or another's experience?	How do participants understand their world? How do the participants and author co-construct a world? What are the pragmatic implications of research?	What does it mean from the researcher's point of view? What is the relationship among factors? What behaviors can be predicted?
Methods	Autoethnography Interactive interviewing Participant observation Performance Sociological introspection Visual arts	Semistructured interviewing Focus groups Participant observation/ethnography Thematic, metaphoric, and narrative analysis Grounded theory Case studies Participatory action research Historical/archival research	Coding textual data Random sampling Frequencies of behaviors Measurement Surveys Structured interviews

(Continued)

Figure 3.1 (Continued)

	Qualitative Continuum		
	Art/Impressionist	**Middle-Grounded Approaches**	**Science/Realist**
Writing	Use of first-person voice Literary techniques Stories Poetry/poetic transcription Multivocal, multigenre texts Layered accounts Experiential forms Personal reflections Open to multiple interpretations	Use of first-person voice Incorporation of brief narratives in research reports Use "snippets" of participants' words Usually a single interpretation, with implied partiality and positionality Some consideration of researcher's standpoint(s)	Use of passive voice "View from nowhere"(Haraway, 1988) Claim single authoritative interpretation Meaning summarized in tables and charts Objectivity and minimization of bias highlighted
Researcher	Researcher as the main focus or as much the focus of research as other participants	Participants are main focus, but researcher's positionality is key to forming findings	Researcher is presented as irrelevant to results
Vocabularies	Artistic/interpretive: inductive, personal, ambiguity, change, adventure, improvisation, process, concrete details, evocative experience, creativity, aesthetics	Social Constructionist/Positivist: inductive, emergent, intersubjectivity, process, themes, categories, thick description, co-creation of meaning, social construction of meaning, standpoint, ideology (e.g., feminism, postmodernism, Marxism)	Positivist: deductive, tested, axioms, measurement, variables, manipulation of conditions, control, predication, generalizability, validity, reliability, theory driven
Criteria	Do stories ring true, resonate, engage, move? Are they coherent, plausible, interesting, aesthetically pleasing?	Flexible criteria Clarity and openness of processes Clear reasoning and use of support Evidence of researcher's reflexivity	Authoritative rules Specific criteria for data, similar to quantitative Proscribed methodological processes

SOURCE: Ellingson (2009, pp. 8–9). Reprinted by permission of Sage Publications.

> ethics are an essential part of rigorous research. Ethics are more than a set of principles or abstract rules that sit as an overarching entity guiding our research . . . . Ethics exist in our actions and in our ways of doing and practicing our research; we perceive ethics to be always in progress, never to be taken for granted, flexible, and responsive to change. (p. 281)

They further urge that "ethics is not treated as a separate part of our research—a form that is filled in for the ethics committee and forgotten" (p. 281). Thus, at the proposal stage, addressing the large questions posed at the beginning of this section as well as engaging explicitly with the ethics of everyday practice will go far to convince proposal readers that the study is likely to be designed and conducted in trustworthy ways.

ETHICS: FOCUSING ON PEOPLE

Developing a sound proposal entails building an argument that is cogent and persuasive and that demonstrates that the researcher has an exquisite sensitivity to both the procedural and the everyday **ethical issues** (Guillemin & Gillam, 2004) inherent in research with human beings—what might be called *big E* and *little E* issues. For any inquiry project, ethical research practice is grounded in the moral principles of *respect for persons*, *beneficence*, and *justice*. *Respect for persons* captures the notion that we do not use the people who participate in our studies as a means to an end (often our own) and that we do respect their privacy, their anonymity, and their right to participate—or not—which is freely consented to. *Beneficence* addresses the central dictum, *primum non nocere* (first, do no harm)—first developed in medical fields. This means that the researcher does whatever he reasonably can to ensure that participants are not harmed by participating in the study. Finally, *justice* refers to distributive justice—that is, considerations of who benefits and who does not from the study, with special attention to the redress of past societal injustices.

In universities and other institutions that receive federal funding, questions about how the researcher relates to participants—ethical matters—come under the jurisdiction of **institutional review boards** (IRBs), which are charged with ensuring the protection of human subjects in all research conducted under the auspices of that institution. Such boards serve important defining and policing roles in judging what is considered **ethical practice** with human subjects, frequently requiring researchers to pass the appropriate **Collaborative Institutional Training Initiative** (CITI) modules. We discuss nuances of informed consent forms and working with institutional review boards more fully—and more pragmatically—in Chapter 5.

Of the three moral principles, respect for persons usually receives the most attention in institutional policies and procedures. Through the informed consent form, the researcher assures review boards that participants are fully informed about the purpose of the study, that their participation is voluntary, that they understand the extent of their commitment to the study, that their identities will be protected, and that there are minimal risks associated with participating. (We provide an example in Chapter 5.) However, developing informed consent forms—as one must do for research conducted under the aegis of any institution receiving federal funding—is just the minimum requirement. While necessary for research proposals, this procedural matter is just the beginning of demonstrating that the writer is likely to conduct the study with deep sensitivity to the ethics of everyday research practice (Rossman & Rallis, in press) and the often unforeseen issues (Milner, 2007) that may arise. While procedures matter—one must, after all, include an informed consent form with the research proposal—how we relate to the persons who participate in a study and the ethical issues that may arise should also be addressed in the proposal. Above all, at the proposal stage, qualitative researchers must demonstrate that they understand ethical practice as complex processes, not mere events. Ethical practice is ongoing; obtaining a signature on an informed consent form is merely one observable indicator of the researcher's sensitivity (see Bhattacharya, 2007, for an excellent discussion of the complexities of informed consent).

As we have witnessed over the years, this has had important consequences: Graduate students with whom we work speak in coded language about IRB approval, appearing to believe that such approval certifies their research as "ethical." At times, engaging with the thorny issues associated with ongoing ethical practice appears tedious, unproductive, and unnecessary. Cultural differences in interpretation of standard forms, such as informed consent, are sidelined; discussions about the ethical representation of what participants have shared are lost; and epistemological questions about the knowledge claims made in written texts gloss over the crucial relational foundation that generated those claims (Gunzenhauser & Gerstl-Pepin, 2006).

We suggest that the writer attend to the deeper relational matters by explicitly addressing issues that may arise in her proposed research. Specifically, we encourage our students to view the standard forms as only a starting point. We encourage them to provide a critique of the apparent lack of intercultural awareness embedded in such forms and their attendant explanations. These forms and guidelines typically provide little direction on how to mediate between the demands of a U.S.-based (and Eurocentric) university and the sensibilities of quite different cultural groups. For example, informed consent presumes that an individual can freely give his or her assent to participate in a research study. However, this assumption does not travel well across national boundaries, especially into more collectivist cultures. What does this notion of individual rights mean in a nation-state where the concept of the individual is blurred and the group is paramount and where one's obligations extend well beyond the self? And what happens to the assumption that an individual is free to participate or withdraw from a study at any time without prejudice when one is a civil servant, obligated by ties to the government to participate? Furthermore, how is the requirement that a participant sign the informed consent form viewed in cultures where literacy is not prevalent or, more ominously, where giving one's consent by signing a document or making one's mark on it puts one at risk in an authoritarian regime? Finally, how can the researcher give even reasonable assurances of protection from harm without fully understanding the consequences of village women participating in a study in a deeply patriarchal society? Vignette 3, written by Aaron Kuntz, who appears as one of the dialogue partners at the end of some chapters, illustrates the challenges of forecasting the deeply personal aspects of ethical qualitative inquiry practice.

VIGNETTE 3 Challenges in Anticipating Ethical Issues

By Aaron Kuntz

I didn't truly appreciate the subtle ethical implications of my methodological decisions until I had already completed my data collection. I was engaged in a study on faculty activism and thought I had covered all my ethical bases in both my dissertation proposal and IRB document preparation. After all, I had successfully defended my proposal with little methodological fanfare—the bulk of the questions from my committee were on the content of my research, not as much on the ethics of how I proposed to collect, analyze, and represent my data. Furthermore, my application sailed through the IRB process without even one recommendation for improvement. I took my proposal through the proper procedures and set about conducting my study, secure in the thought that my dissertation had been verified as both valid and ethical.

The practical implications of conducting an ethical study came into the foreground when a study participant stopped midsentence to ask, "This is all anonymous right? You won't connect this to my name or anything like that?" I assured the participant that everyone in the study would be given pseudonyms and all identifying markers would be stripped from written documents—after all, that's what was in my IRB application. The same question concerning anonymity came up with two additional participants, and I offered similar assurances. It wasn't until later in my research process that I realized that such basic methodological decisions held layered ethical tensions.

After collecting my data, I set about my analysis and began to think about the findings. This is when the subtlety of ethics hit me—how was I to adequately depict the stories of my participants' lives without breaching the pledge of anonymity? How could I represent participants as dynamic, complex humans and, at the same time, remove any and all identifications that might depict who they were? In short, how was I to represent participants fully and, at the same time, incompletely? In a discussion with my dissertation chair, I was advised to simply separate quotations from identities. That is, I should understand my transcripts as textual data removed from the actual narrative of participants' lives. Yet this position stood in direct opposition to my belief in giving participants a "voice" in my study. I maintained an ethical position that separating participant utterances from the participants themselves was wrong and continued a long history of misrepresenting and silencing participants within research studies. I wanted to honor those who participated in my study by allowing their distinctly individual voices to emerge and not be lost amidst a collective jumble of thematized quotations.

(Continued)

VIGNETTE 3 (Continued)

Over time, I realized that ethical decision making was not adequately resolved or even anticipated by a series of institutional procedures (e.g., IRB or a dissertation proposal defense) but instead involved a process of on-the-ground experiences in need of reflexive reasoning. Instead of merely writing about the content of my research, I began a series of analytic memos detailing the ethical quandaries I experienced throughout the day-to-day practices of my research. Here, I noted the tension between maintaining anonymity and representing participants as more than simply the "subjects" of my study. I also noted inconsistencies between my espousal of postmodern interpretations of identity as fragmented and incomplete and a romanticized vision of representing the "whole selves" of those who participated in my study. In a way, these analytic memos gave me the opportunity to step outside a study that consumed my life at that particular time—to make strange the familiar—and this process of defamiliarizing my research process brought otherwise unacknowledged ethical tensions to the fore and required newly reasoned research practices.

I regret that these ethically laden analytic memos never made it into the finished product of my dissertation; they had an effect but were never named or directly referenced. Mainly, my regret lies in the fact that those who read my study will never encounter the process of my reasoning—they only have access to the end product. I suppose at the time I didn't feel as though there was a space for me to include the ethical process inherent in my research, that the formality of the dissertation left no room for discussions of my ethics-in-practice. Now, I wonder about the ethical implications of not including such a process for my readership—of not including them in such ethically laden decisions.

* * * * *

Vignette 3 represents coming face-to-face with the "**ethically important moments**" (Guillemin & Gillam, 2004; Rossman & Rallis, in press) that might arise in the everyday conduct of a study—ones that the writer should discuss in the proposal. We suggest that these issues can be discussed in a section of the research design specifically devoted to "ethical considerations" and augmented in the discussion of the researcher's "personal biography," "social identities," or "positionality," where the potential thorny interactions of power, status, social identity, and cultural difference should be explored. Chapter 5 will address more details for writing this section of the research design.

Viewing the moral principles that guide research practice as *relational*, rather than merely as some procedural hoops that one must jump through, centers the inquiry on people, which is where, we argue, it should be. Explicitly valuing participants and recognizing the potential interpersonal impact of the inquiry helps demonstrate that the researcher will be deeply ethical. Their stances and decisions, then, will likely be grounded in what Kirkhart (1995) has termed *interpersonal validity*—that is, "the trustworthiness of understandings emanating from personal interactions" (p. 4). "This dimension of validity concerns itself with the skills and sensitivities of the researcher in how one uses oneself as a knower, as an inquirer" (Reason & Rowan, 1981, in Kirkhart, 1995, p. 4). This concept of interpersonal validity inextricably intertwines ethics with trustworthiness.

* * * * *

The preceding discussion is intended to sensitize the proposal writer to the important considerations of trustworthiness, or validity, and ethics in developing a convincing proposal. The specific emphases that the writer puts forward will depend, to some extent, on the genre of qualitative inquiry in which his study is situated. Thus, a proposal drawing on autoethnographic methods will need to demonstrate a deep familiarity with theorizing and pragmatic examples of that genre, specifically as those writings address validity and ethical issues.

However, the details of ensuring (or trying to ensure) that a study will be seen as trustworthy and ethical depend on the conceptual framework in which the writer situates her study within traditions of theorizing and research, discusses potential significance, and poses research questions. These, in turn, may well depend on the design of the study and the specific methods of data collection chosen. At this moment, it will be useful to remind the reader of the complexity of developing a proposal where recycling and revisiting ideas and decisions is just part of the game. A full understanding of the stances and strategies for ensuring trustworthiness and the potential ethical issues that might arise will only emerge after the writer of the proposal has made some initial decisions about the conceptual framework, the study's design, and generative data collection methods. We turn to these next in Chapters 4 (conceptualizing the study), 5 (design), 6 (primary data collection methods), and 7 (secondary and specialized methods). While this need to consider all elements at the same time is frustrating, it mirrors the complex processes of writing in general. So bear with it!

FURTHER READING

Adams, T. E. (2008). A review of narrative ethics. *Qualitative Inquiry, 14*(2), 175–194.

Beach, D. (2003). A problem of validity in educational research. *Qualitative Inquiry, 9*(6), 859–873.

Bhattacharya, K. (2007). Consenting to the consent form: What are the fixed and fluid understandings between the researcher and the researched? *Qualitative Inquiry, 13*(8), 1095–1115.

Cho, J., & Trent, A. (2006). Validity in qualitative research revisited. *Qualitative Research, 6*(3), 319–340.

Cho, J., & Trent, A. (2009). Validity criteria for performance-related qualitative work: Toward a reflexive, evaluative, and co-constructive framework for performance in/as qualitative inquiry. *Qualitative Inquiry, 15*(6), 1013–1041.

Davies, D., & Dodd, J. (2002). Qualitative research and the question of rigor. *Qualitative Health Research, 12*(2), 279–289.

Ellingson, L. L. (2009). *Engaging crystallization in qualitative research: An introduction.* Thousand Oaks, CA: Sage.

Flick, U. (2009). *An introduction to qualitative research* (4th ed.). Thousand Oaks, CA: Sage.

Guillemin, M., & Gillam, L. (2004). Ethics, reflexivity, and "ethically important moments" in research. *Qualitative Inquiry, 10*(2), 261–280.

Hostetler, K. (2005). What is "good" education research? *Educational Researcher, 34*(6), 16–21.

Kirkhart, K. E. (1995). Seeking multicultural validity: A postcard from the road. *Evaluation Practice, 16*(1), 1–12.

Kvale, S. (1995). The social construction of validity. *Qualitative Inquiry, 1*(1), 19–40.

Lather, P. (1993). Fertile obsession: Validity after poststructuralism. *Sociological Quarterly, 34*(4), 673–693.

Lather, P. (2001). Validity as an incitement to discourse: Qualitative research and the crisis of legitimation. In V. Richardson (Ed.), *Handbook of research on teaching* (4th ed., pp. 241–250). Washington, DC: American Educational Research Association.

Maxwell, J. A. (2004). Causal explanation, qualitative research, and scientific inquiry in education. *Educational Researcher, 33*(2), 3–11.

Milner, H. R. (2007). Race, culture, and researcher positionality: Working through dangers seen, unseen, and unforeseen. *Educational researcher, 36*(7), 388–400.

Rallis, S. F., & Rossman, G. B. (in press). Reflexive research practitioners. *International Journal of Qualitative Studies in Education, 23*(3).

Rossman, G. B., & Rallis, S. F. (in press). Everyday ethics: Reflections on practice. *International Journal of Qualitative Studies in Education, 23*(3).

Sikes, P., & Goodson, I. (2003). Living research: Thoughts on educational research as moral practice. In P. Sikes, J. Nixon, & W. Carr (Eds.), *The moral foundations of educational research: Knowledge, inquiry and values* (pp. 32–51). Berkshire, UK: Open University Press.

Wolcott, H. F. (2002). *Sneaky kid and its aftermath: Ethics and intimacy in fieldwork.* Walnut Creek, CA: AltaMira.

KEY CONCEPTS

Audit trail

Beneficence

Catalytic validity

Collaborative Institutional Training Initiative

Convergence

Corroboration

Credibility

Crystallization

Dependability

Ethical issues

Ethical practice

Ethically important moments

Generalizability

Informed consent

Institutional review boards

Member checks

Objectivity

Peer debriefing

Prolonged engagement

Reliability

Respect for persons

Searching for disconfirming evidence

Social justice

Subjectivity

Transactional validity

Transferability

Transformational validity

Triangulation

Trustworthiness

Validity

The What of the Study

Building the Conceptual Framework

What is research? What is a research proposal? How do the two relate to each other? The social scientist may view research as a process of trying to gain a better understanding of the complexities of human experience—by asking basic questions. With somewhat different purposes, other researchers ask applied and practical questions aimed at contributing possible solutions to pressing challenges (as, perhaps, in nursing or educational research). In some genres of research, the aim is to identify productive ways to take action based on the research findings. Through systematic and sometimes collaborative strategies, the researcher gathers information about actions and interactions, reflects on their meaning, arrives at and evaluates conclusions, and eventually puts forward an interpretation, most frequently in written form.

Quite unlike its pristine and logical presentation in journal articles—"the reconstructed logic of science" (Kaplan, 1964, p. 67)—research is often confusing, messy, intensely frustrating, and fundamentally nonlinear. In critiquing the way journal articles display research as a supremely sequential and objective endeavor, Bargar and Duncan (1982) describe how "through such highly standardized reporting practices, scientists inadvertently hide from view the real inner drama of their work, with its intuitive base, its halting time-line, and its extensive recycling of concepts and perspectives" (p. 2). This drama is delightful but also daunting.

The researcher begins by attending to interesting, mysterious, curious, or anomalous phenomena that he observes, discovers, or stumbles across. Like detective work or the most ethical traditions in investigative reporting, research seeks to explain, describe, explore, and/or critique the phenomenon chosen for study. Emancipatory genres, such as those represented by some critical, feminist, or postmodern work, also make explicit their intent to act toward the change of oppressive circumstances. The commitment of these emancipatory genres to social justice is increasingly present in all genres of qualitative inquiry. Thus, the research proposal is *a plan for engaging in systematic inquiry* to bring about a better understanding of the phenomenon and/or to change **problematic** social circumstances. As discussed in Chapters 1 and 2, the finished proposal should demonstrate that (a) the research is worth doing, (b) the researcher is competent to conduct the study, and (c) the study is carefully planned and can be executed successfully.

A proposal for the conduct of any research represents *decisions* the researcher has made—that a theoretical framework, design, and methodology will generate data appropriate and adequate for responding to the research questions and will conform to ethical standards. These decisions emerge through intuition, complex reasoning, and the weighing of a number of possible research questions, possible **conceptual frameworks**, and alternative designs and strategies for gathering data. Throughout, the researcher considers the "should-do-ability," "do-ability," and "want-to-do-ability" of the proposed project (discussed in Chapter 1). This is the complex, dialectical process of designing a qualitative study. This chapter discusses how, in qualitative design, you are choosing, from among possible research questions, frameworks, approaches, sites, and data collection methods, the one most suited to your research project. Building the research proposal demands that the researcher consider all the elements of the proposal *at the same time.* As noted in Chapter 1, this recursive process is complex and intellectually challenging because the researcher needs to consider multiple elements—multiple decisions and choices—of the proposal simultaneously.

But how to begin? This is often the most challenging aspect of developing a solid proposal. A quick answer is "Start where you are." Long ago, Anselm Strauss (1969) said, "The naming of an object provides directive for action" (p. 22). He pointed to how powerfully mobilizing it is to give one's project a name—to be able to put it into a short simple sentence.

Our experience suggests that research interests may have their origins in deeply personal interests, professional commitments and concerns, intriguing theoretical frameworks, methodological predilections, and/or recurring social problems. Whatever their source, these interests must be transformed into a logical proposal that articulates key elements and demonstrates competence. We offer one model for those elements, recognizing that much thought and drafting have preceded this formal, public writing.

SECTIONS OF THE PROPOSAL

Proposals for qualitative research vary in format but typically include the following three sections: (1) *the introduction*, which includes an overview of the proposal, a discussion of the topic or focus of the inquiry and the general research questions, the study's purpose and potential significance, and its limitations; (2) *a discussion of related literature* or "currents of thought" (Schram, 2006, p. 63), which situates the study in the ongoing discourse about the topic and develops the specific intellectual traditions to which the study is linked; and (c) *the research design and methods*, which detail the overall design, the site or population of interest, the specific methods for gathering data, a preliminary discussion of strategies for analyzing the data and for ensuring the trustworthiness of the study, a biography of the researcher, and ethical and political issues that may arise in the conduct of the study. In all research, these sections are interrelated—each one building on the others. They are listed in Table 4.1. In qualitative inquiry, the proposal should reserve some flexibility in research questions and design because these are likely to change. The qualitative research proposal is, actually, the researcher's very best reasoning about how he justifies his questions and how he can proceed to find answers. The next section provides some strategies for building a clear conceptual framework while retaining the flexibility to allow the unanticipated to emerge.

BUILDING THE CONCEPTUAL FRAMEWORK: TOPIC, PURPOSE, AND SIGNIFICANCE

The proposal should present a convincing argument, showing how the proposed research will likely be meaningful and will contribute to improving the human condition. In the outline provided in Table 4.1, the introductory section presents an overview of this argument because it (a) describes the substantive focus of the research—the topic—and its purpose; (b) frames it in larger theoretical, policy, social, or practical domains and thereby develop, its significance; (c) poses initial research questions; (d) forecasts the literature to be reviewed; and (e) discusses the limitations of the study. The proposal writer should organize the information so that a reader can clearly ascertain the essence of the research study. This section, along with the review and critique of related literature, forms the conceptual framework of the study and informs the reader of the study's substantive focus and purpose. We share the good advice of Schram (2006), who suggests that, on the way to developing the theoretical framework, the researcher should be able to say, "Here's how I am positioning my problem within an established arena of ideas, and here's why it matters" (p. 62). The conceptual framework doesn't come out of the sky, or even from one theorist's book. Rather, it is developed by the researcher herself, and the task, says Schram, is in " uncovering what is relevant and what is problematic among the ideas circulating around your problem, making new connections, and then formulating an argument that positions you to address that problem" (p. 63). The design section (discussed in Chapter 5) then describes how the study will be conducted and showcases the writer's ability to conduct the study.

Although our outline has separate sections, the researcher's narrative of the first two sections—the Introduction and the Review and Critique of the Literature—is derived from his thorough familiarity with the literature on relevant theory, empirical studies, reviews of previous research, and informed essays by experts. His careful review

Table 4.1 Sections of a Qualitative Research Proposal

Introduction
Overview Topic and purpose Significance for knowledge, for practical and policy problems, and/or for action. Framework and general research questions Limitations
Literature review and critique of related research
Theoretical traditions and currents of thought for framing the question Review and critique of related empirical research Essays and opinions of experts and insiders
Design and methodology
Overall approach and rationale Site or population selection and sampling strategies Access, role, reciprocity, trust, rapport Personal biography Ethical and political considerations Data collection methods Data analysis procedures Procedures to address trustworthiness and credibility
Appendixes (may include entry letters, data collection and management details, sampling strategies, timelines, budgets, notes from pilot studies)
References

of the related literature accomplishes three main purposes. First, it provides evidence that the study has potential **significance for practice and policy** and is likely to contribute to the ongoing discourse about the topic (often referred to as contributing to "knowledge"). Second, it identifies the important intellectual traditions that guide the study—the "currents of thought" that frame the study. Third, it identifies gaps in what is known—by critiquing previous research, by extending existing theory, or by pointing to practices and policies that are not working. These elements constitute the building blocks for a conceptual framework and help refine important and viable research questions. Before writing this section, the researcher probably has an intuitive sense that his questions are important or that he has pragmatic reasons for zeroing in on these questions. After writing the Introduction and the Literature Review, he will be quite convincing in his argument and assertion that the research has larger meaning.

Because of the interrelatedness of the sections and because writing is developmental and recursive—a "method of inquiry" itself (Richardson, 2000, p. 923)—the writer may find it necessary to rewrite the research questions or problem statement after reviewing the literature or to refocus on the significance of the research after its design is developed. Bargar and Duncan's (1982) description of "extensive recycling of concepts and perspectives" (p. 2) captures this dialectical process. Our advice is that the writer be sensitive to the need for change and flexibility: Be prepared to rewrite sentences numerous times, not rush to closure too soon, and learn to love the word processor's functions. Sound ideas for research may come in a moment of inspiration, but the hard work is in developing, refining, and polishing the idea—that is, the pursuance of the intellectual traditions that surround the idea—and in the methods used for exploring it.

The Overview Section

The first section of the proposal provides an overview of the study for the reader. It introduces the topic or problem and the purpose of the study, the general research questions it will address, and how it is designed. This section should be written crisply, engage the reader's interest, and foreshadow the sections that follow. First, the topic or problem that the study will address is introduced, linking this to practice, policy, social issues, and/or theory, thereby forecasting the study's significance. Next, the broad areas of theory and research to be discussed in the literature review are outlined. Then, the design of the study is sketched, focusing on the principal techniques for data collection and the unique features of the design. The short Overview provides a transition to a more detailed discussion of the topic, the study's significance, and the research questions.

The Section Introducing the Topic

The curiosity that inspires qualitative research often comes initially from observations of the real world, emerging from the interplay of direct experience with emerging theory, of political commitment with practice, as well as from growing scholarly interests, as noted above. At other times, a topic derives from a review and critique of the empirical research and traditions of theory. Beginning researchers should examine journals specifically committed to publishing extensive reviews of literature (e.g., *Review of Educational Research*, the *Annual Review of Sociology*, the *American Review of Public Administration*, and the *Annual Review of Public Health*), peruse policy-oriented publications to learn about current or emerging issues and challenges in their fields, and talk with experts about crucial issues. They might also reflect on the intersection of their personal, professional, and political interests. Those with little experience with literature reviews can greatly benefit from the "road map" format in Bloomberg and Volpe's (2008) *Completing*

Your Qualitative Dissertation. It breaks down into meaningful and more manageable pieces the steps and stages of undertaking research—the ways of using different theorists, ways to be selective and to integrate critiques, and ways to move from the review of literature to a conceptual framework.

Inquiry cycles between theory, practice, research questions, and personal experience. A research project may begin at any point in this complex process. Considering possible research questions, potential sites, and individuals or groups to invite to participate in the research may lead to a focus for the study. Imagining potential sites or groups of people to work with may reshape the focus of the study. Thinking about sites or people for the study also encourages the researcher to think about her positionality and possible strategies for gathering data. The researcher may know of a site where intriguing issues of practice capture her imagination. Developing the research project proceeds dialectically, as possible focuses of the research, questions, sites, and strategies for gathering data are considered.

Crabtree and Miller (1992) offer useful conceptualizations of the *cycle of inquiry.* They argue that a metaphor for the process of much qualitative research is embedded in "Shiva's circle of constructivist inquiry," Shiva being the Hindu god of dance and death (see Figure 4.1). The researcher enters a cycle of interpretation with exquisite sensitivity to context, seeking no ultimate truths. He must be faithful to the dance but also stands apart from it, discovering and interpreting the "symbolic communication and meaning . . . that helps us maintain cultural life" (p. 10). The researcher looks critically at experience and the larger social forces that shape it. Often, he searches for expressions of domination, oppression, and power in daily life. Then his goal is to unmask this "false consciousness" and create "a more empowered and emancipated consciousness by reducing the illusions" of experience (pp. 10–11). He may be inspired to embed empowerment goals, such as critical indigenous consciousness, in his research goals, like Lee (2006) in her study of University of New Mexico's summer leadership program. Thinking about this site and the issues and people in it fosters analysis about which research questions are likely to be significant for practice. These questions then shape decisions about gathering data. Whatever the qualitative genre or research goal, the cycle of inquiry entails question posing, design, data collection and discovery, analysis, and interpretation. It entails the use of theory throughout, but especially for question posing and for guiding interpretation and explanation.

The *problematic* of an everyday world issue for institutional ethnography is the realization of the project of inquiry, according to Smith (2005), that begins "in the actualities of peoples' lives with a focus of investigation that comes from how they participate and are hooked up into institutional practices" (p. 107). Especially in applied fields, such as management, nursing, community development, education, and clinical psychology, a strong autobiographical element often drives the study. For example, one student of international development education studied the dilemmas in refugee and immigrant groups in the United States because of her own professional work with similar groups in community development (Jones, 2004). Another student studied Indonesian farmers' views on land use because of her political commitment to indigenous peoples (Campbell-Nelson, 1997). And yet another student explored the

Figure 4.1 Shiva's Circle of Constructivist Inquiry

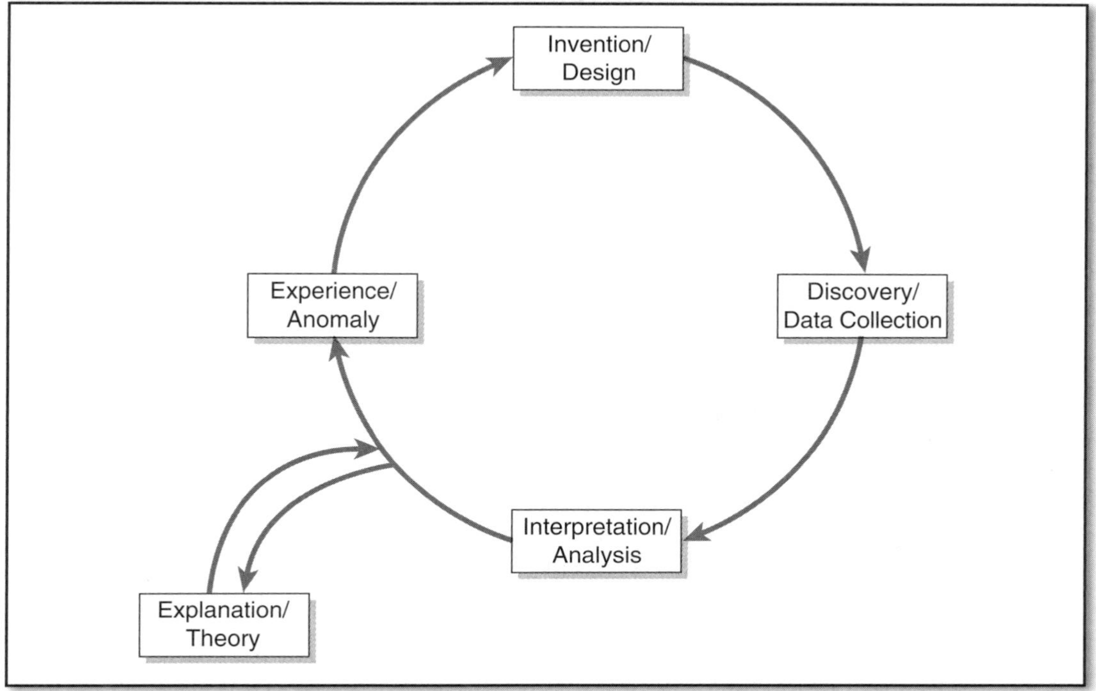

SOURCE: Crabtree and Miller (1992, p. 10). Reprinted with permission.

deep experiences of coping among HIV/AIDS orphans and other vulnerable children in her native village in Kenya (Ochiel, 2009). A final example is the student of social psychology, deeply committed to the protection of the environment, who studied environmental attitudes from the perspective of adult development theory (Greenwald, 1992).

One's personal biography is often a source, an inspiration, and an initial way of framing a research question. In qualitative research genres, the influences of biography are often stated explicitly (although such statements more often are placed later, under "Research Design"—see Chapter 5). The following quote illustrates such a statement:

> I strongly believe that for Black, Latina/o, Asian American, and Native American youth to succeed in this nation, we must have strong Black, Latina/o, Asian American, and Native American teachers. I also know, however, that many of us have been socialized through racially biased educational systems and carry skewed perceptions of ourselves, our communities, and other non-White racial or ethnic groups. (Kohli, 2009, p. 3)

He continues with descriptions of sources for these beliefs, both personal and research based. By developing and including such personal biography statements, qualitative researchers show potential readers that they are addressing aspects of themselves that have led to their research focus and interest. Later, we will show how this is useful for the research design (in Chapter 5), data analysis (in Chapter 9) and presentation of findings (in Chapter 10) sections.

In Vignette 4, we see a researcher, Paul Frisoli, beginning the challenge of taking a practical and policy question about West African youth and then combining this with his search for a focus that will give him personal significance. From his **"Eureka" moment**, he is energized to search the literature and identify manageable data collection strategies.

* * * *

VIGNETTE 4 Intertwining My Research, My Self, and Real-World Significance

I've been living and working throughout West Africa for the past seven years. It's been a fantastic experience, but at times I feel like I'm leading two separate lives. At home, I'm a gay man ready to jump into a same-sex marriage while also working on zeroing in on a dissertation research topic. In West Africa, I'm the practitioner who does not disclose his sexuality or divulge information about his life back home. Compounding this sense of contradictory identities is the realization that my research topic isn't clicking. I've been interested in issues about youth in West Africa for my dissertation research but have been unsure how to proceed.

My "Eureka" moment was the recognition of how to fuse my research topic with my own homo/heteroidentities! This came at a time when issues of sexuality seemed to be popping up more frequently all over the world: Iceland designated the first ever openly homosexual Prime Minister. California rescinded same-sex marriage benefits. A major American motion picture depicting the life of Harvey Milk, the first openly gay American politician in the 1970s, was screened in major theaters throughout the country.

Homosexuality in African countries has also been in the news: Senegalese men staged a same-sex marriage to promote awareness that homosexual people do exist in West Africa. The Gambian president reported the need to cut off the head of any gay person in his country. Once again in Senegal, eight HIV/AIDS awareness public health workers who provided help and assistance to men-who-have-sex-with-men were arrested and imprisoned for eight years for violation of sodomy laws and enacting criminal activities. In summary, young men of differing sexualities are being persecuted in West Africa, while gay people are being chosen as heads of state. I realized that, in this divided world in which we live, my multiple identities may not be so odd after all. I want to know about other people who may be experiencing similar disjointed sexual lifestyles. More specifically, I would want to ask the following question to West African men: What is it like to live a life that does not fit into a clean heteronormative lifestyle? This is my "want-to-do-ability"— a study to understand the lived experiences of young West African men who do not entirely conform to hegemonic concepts of gender and sexuality. My partner, Brad, told me that this project is also about me trying to discover something about myself, which is an assertion that I also believe to be true and valid for the want-to-do-ability of such a project.

Why is this important to anyone but me? How would I go about doing such a study? Doing research in the contexts where people are being imprisoned and threatened did not seem like a safe space for my participants or myself. An Internet search with key words such as "gay" and "Africa" yielded a number of young African men's blogs. Many of the blogs talked about identity issues in relation to their family, social, and professional lives. I immediately recognized the power of using the Internet to express oneself in a way that is safe, anonymous, and informative. These young men seem to have become Internet activists, using the Internet as a space for sharing their experiences, stories, and thoughts about their sexual identities. Not all of them claim to be "gay," but they talk about their own discovery processes. These public blogs have also allowed not so gay-friendly Africans to respond, introducing voices that concur with hegemonic political and social discourses found throughout scholarly texts and the media.

Now this is territory uncharted in previous research! I imagine that the value of this study will be to describe and analyze the presence of counterhegemonic sexualities in order to give voice to a population of people whose emotional, educational, and health needs may be different from those of other men. I'm now thinking that this study should be done, is potentially do-able, and that I certainly want it to be done.

* * * * *

For Paul, and for all researchers, the challenge is to demonstrate that this personal interest—increasingly referred to as the researcher's *positionality*—will not preordain the findings or bias the study. Sensitivity to the methodological literature on the self and on one's social identities in conducting inquiry, interpreting data, and constructing the final narrative helps accomplish this. Knowledge of the epistemological debate about what constitutes knowledge and knowledge claims, especially the critique of power and dominance in traditional research, is also valuable (see Chapter 2 on critical ethnography, feminist research, participatory action research, and postmodern perspectives).

When direct experience stimulates the initial curiosity, the researcher needs to link that curiosity to general research questions. The mouth of the conceptual **funnel**, if you will, contains the general, or "grand tour," questions the study will explore; the specific focus for the proposed study is funneled from these questions.

Figure 4.2 illustrates the funnel as a metaphor (as illustrated in Benbow's 1994 study about the development of commitment to social action). The mouth of the funnel represents the general conceptual focus—for example, the general issue of social activism and its role in ameliorating oppressive circumstances. The researcher then narrows the focus as in a funnel. Social activism becomes more researchable when the focus is on individuals who have demonstrated intense commitment to social causes or, possibly, on social movements such as group phenomena. A research question (or set of questions) can then funnel down to a more manageable and narrower focus on how life experiences help shape commitment to social activism. Researchers with very general and vague questions can benefit from putting their thoughts through the exercise represented by the funnel.

Figure 4.2 The Conceptual Funnel

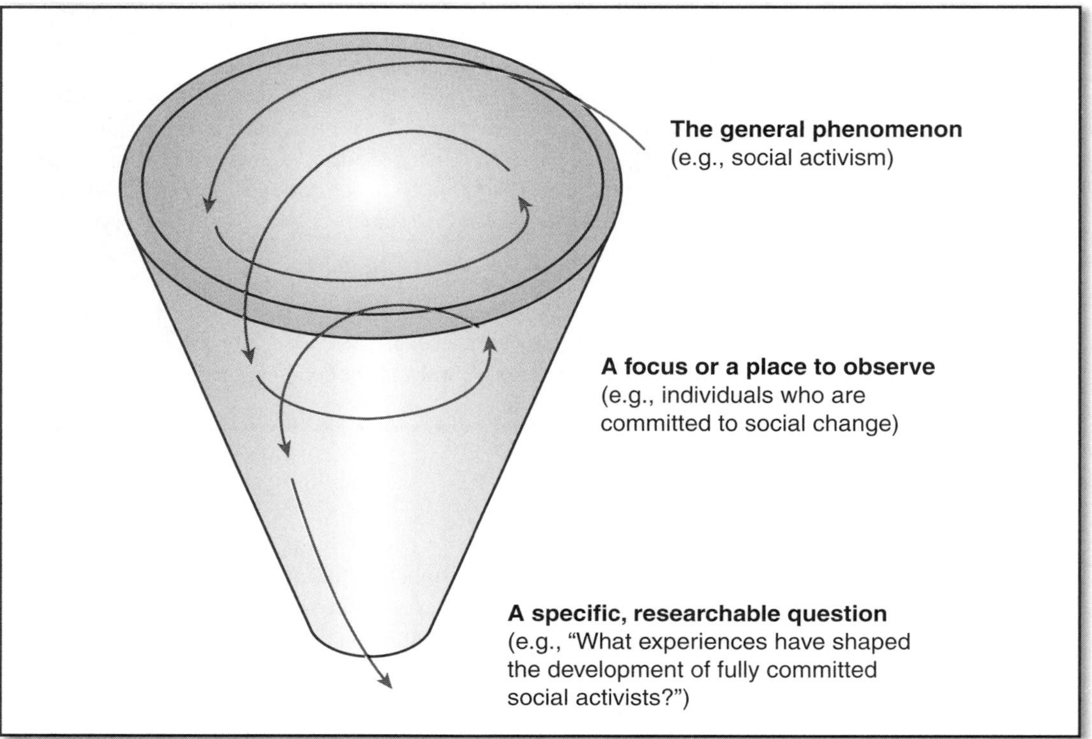

Formal theories have traditionally been used to develop research questions and are useful as funnels or lenses for viewing the topic of interest. However, there is another meaning to "theories," that is, the **personal theories**—theories in use or tacit theories (Argyris & Schön, 1974)—that people develop about events as ways to reduce ambiguity and explain paradox. If research inspiration derives from personal or tacit theory, however, the researcher should move beyond these and be guided by systematic considerations, such as existing theory and empirical research. Tacit theory (one's personal understanding) together with formal theory (from the literature) helps bring a question, a curious phenomenon, a silenced or marginalized population, or a problematic issue into focus and raises it to a more generalized perspective. The potential research moves from a troubling or intriguing real-world observation (e.g., a teacher reflecting, "These kids won't volunteer in class no matter how much it's rewarded"), to personal theory (e.g., the teacher saying, "I think they care more about what other kids think than they do about their grades"), to formal theory (e.g., the teacher considering doing research and using developmental theories of motivation to frame her thinking), to concepts and models from the literature (e.g., the teacher-researcher identifying previous research on students' behavior in the classroom mediated by the informal expectations of the student subculture). These coalesce to frame research, providing a focus for this hypothetical teacher-researcher's study in the form of a research question such as "What are the expectations of the student subculture concerning class participation?" Schram (2006) says that theory is a way of asking, pulling from

> a constellation of ideas and issues brought into focus by your inquiry . . . [and] provides something of a legitimizing and a narrowing influence upon the wide-ranging trajectories of hunches, tentative musings, and other forms of entry-level theorizing in which you have engaged. (p. 61)

To recapitulate, this complex process of conceptualizing, framing, and focusing a study typically begins with a personally defined question or identified problem. Personal observations are then transformed into systematic inquiry by reviewing the work of other scholars and practitioners on the topic, thereby building a theoretical rationale and conceptual framework to guide the study. Research questions can then be refined, and the design of the study can be more tightly focused; decisions about where to go, what to look for, and how to move to real-world observations become more specific. As the researcher moves back and forth through these various stages, the guidelines given in Figure 4.3 can help him visualize the process of moving from personal observations, to conceptual framework, to a specific focus, and finally to useful and/or creative questions connected to the literature and to real-life observations. They then help him visualize the research design: Where can one do this study? With whom? How can I actually gather data? How shall I plan for data analysis and reporting?

Framing the Research Process

However, the process is not nearly as linear as Figure 4.3 portrays. When, for example, the researcher is planning for the last "bubble" in the figure (categories, themes, patterns for findings), he will be asking himself what themes might be there and how the literature can help here.

And when he is at the very last stage, "Reports and publications," he will harken back to the very first stage, recalling his original causal observations and concerns or desires for change as he decides on the reporting formats and calculates what audiences to address and to whom he will be reporting.

Figure 4.3 and these questions are intended to be suggestive of others to pose when going through this difficult process of conceptualizing and designing. However, this process applies generically, whether the research is set in an urban neighborhood; with a legislative body; in a rural village in West Timor, Indonesia; or with newly arrived immigrant groups. Also, the process applies generically, whether the research question is about health, human sentiments, leadership, economies, community building, rituals, or any other topic.

Figure 4.3 Framing the Research Process

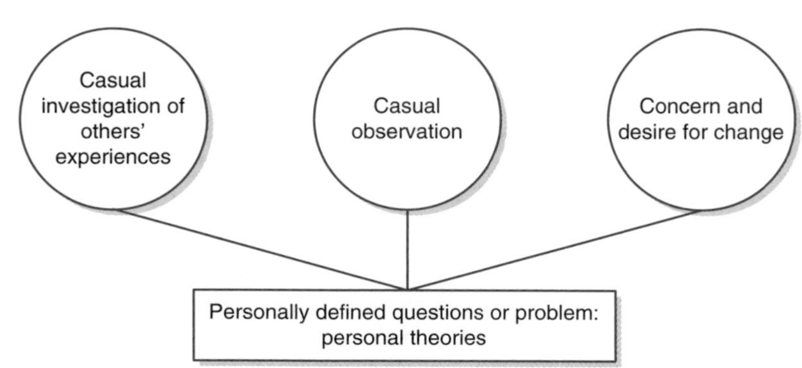

Personal Theories, Hunches, Curiosities

How do I move from casual observations to systematic inquiry? What previous research, existing theoretical frames, expressions of concern, and calls for change from people affected by the problem should focus my research?

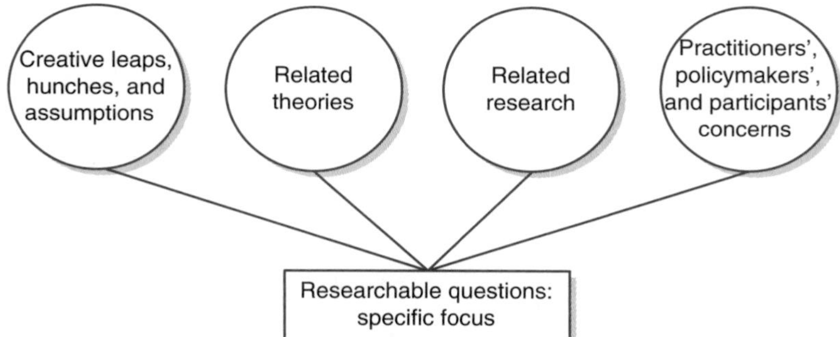

Literatures Frame Questions and Design

Guiding Questions and Focus

Now that the literature review has revealed an array of settings, populations, and methodological traditions used in previous research on similar questions, what is my focus? What will be the most creative and useful questions? What do I assume or guess I will see? What settings and populations can I observe and gather data from to explore these questions? What will I look at? How do I connect the concepts in the literature to behaviors and interactions in natural settings? How can I gain access? Record data? Decide whether to move to other settings or data collection strategies?

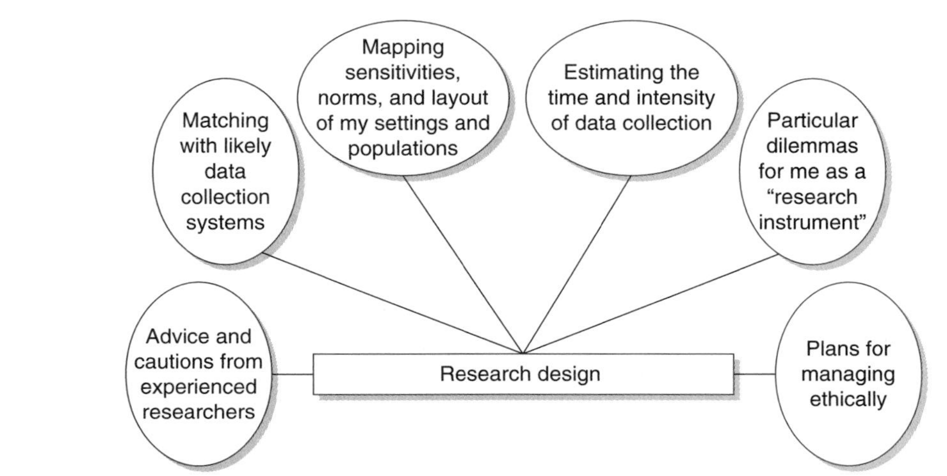

Research Design, Data Collection, and Management

As I gather data, what strategies will I use to organize my data? How will I move towards identifying patterns, and work systematically to ensure that I am working towards identifying useful and significant themes and trustworthy reports?

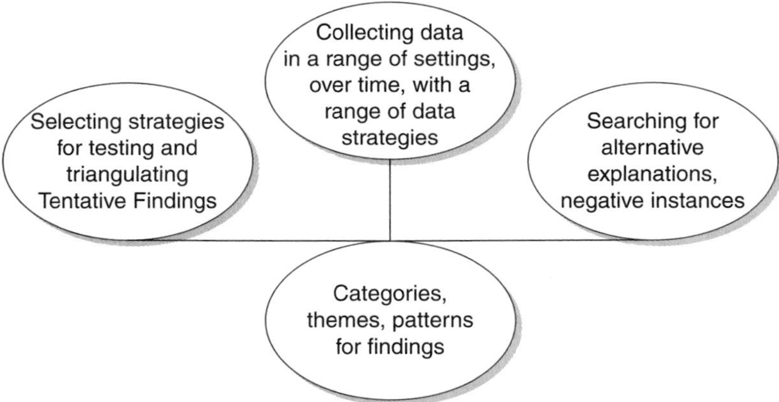

Reporting Findings, Conclusions

What modes of reporting are ethical, useful for my career, useful for helping people? How inventive should I be? What traditions in qualitative reporting make the most sense for my purposes? How do I demonstrate to readers the trustworthiness, the transferability and the utility of my findings as well as the limitations of my research and the new research challenges it has uncovered? Should I provide specific recommendations for change? Who is my audience?

Reports and Publications

This early work of conceptualizing is the most difficult and intellectually rigorous in the entire process of proposal writing. It is messy and dialectical, as alternative frames (scholarly traditions) are examined for their power to illuminate and sharpen the research focus. As noted earlier, exploring possible designs and strategies for gathering data also enters into this initial process. The researcher must let go of some topics and captivating questions as he fine-tunes and focuses the study to ensure its do-ability. Although this entails loss, it bounds the study and protects the researcher from impractical ventures. As Paul realized in Vignette 4, simply jumping into interviewing and observation in West Africa would put people in jeopardy and plainly would not work.

Intuition in this phase of the research process cannot be underestimated. Studies of eminent scientists reveal the central role of creative insight—intuition—in their thought processes (Briggs, 2000; Hoffman, 1972; Libby, 1922; Mooney, 1951). By allowing ideas to incubate and maintaining a healthy respect for the mind's capacity to reorganize and reconstruct, the researcher finds that richer research questions evolve. This observation is not intended to devalue the analytic process but instead to give the creative act its proper due. Bargar and Duncan (1982) note that research is a process

> that religiously uses logical analysis as a critical tool in the *refinement* of ideas, but which often begins at a very different place, where imagery, metaphor and analogy, intuitive hunches, kinesthetic feeling states, and even dreams and dream-like states are prepotent. (p. 3)

Initial insights and recycled concepts begin the process of bounding and framing the research by defining the larger theoretical, policy, or social problem or issue of practice that the study will address. This complex thinking also begins to establish the study's parameters (what it is and what it is not) and to develop the conceptual framework that will ground it in ongoing research traditions.

The Section Describing the Purpose of the Study

The researcher should also describe her intent in conducting the research—its purpose. Generally embedded in a discussion of the topic (often only a sentence or two but important nonetheless), a statement of the purpose of the study tells the reader what the research is likely to accomplish. Historically, qualitative methodologists have described three major purposes for research: *to explore*, *explain*, or *describe* a phenomenon. Synonyms for these terms could include *understand*, *develop*, or *discover*. Many qualitative studies are descriptive and exploratory: They build rich descriptions of complex circumstances that are unexplored in the literature. Others are explicitly explanatory: They show relationships (frequently as perceived by the participants in the study) between events and the meaning of the relationships. These traditional discussions of purpose, however, are silent about critique, action, advocacy, empowerment, or emancipation—the purposes often found in studies grounded in critical, feminist, or postmodern assumptions. The researcher can assert *taking action* as part of the intention of the proposed study, as in action research. He can assert *empowerment* (the goal of participatory action research) as a goal. But he can only, at best, discuss how the inquiry *may* create opportunities for empowerment (see Table 4.2).

The discussion of the topic and purpose also articulates the *unit of analysis*—the level of inquiry on which the study will focus. Qualitative studies typically focus on individuals, dyads, groups, processes, or organizations. Discussing the level of inquiry helps focus subsequent decisions about data gathering.

Table 4.2 Matching Research Questions and Purpose

Purpose of the Study	General Research Questions
Exploratory	
To investigate little-understood phenomena To identify or discover important categories of meaning To generate hypotheses for further research	What is happening in this social program? What are the salient themes, patterns, or categories of meaning for the participants? How are these patterns linked with one another?
Explanatory	
To explain the patterns related to the phenomenon in question To identify plausible relationships shaping the phenomenon	What events, beliefs, attitudes, or policies shape this phenomenon? How do these forces interact to result in the phenomenon?
Descriptive	
To document and describe the phenomenon of interest	What are the salient actions, events, beliefs, attitudes, and social structures and processes occurring in this phenomenon?
Emancipatory	
To create opportunities and the will to engage in social action	How do participants problematize their circumstances and take positive social action?

The Section Describing the Significance and Potential Contributions of the Study

Convincing the reader that the study is likely to be significant and should be conducted entails building an argument that links the research to important theoretical perspectives, policy issues, concerns of practice, or social issues that affect people's everyday lives. Think of it as an opportunity to discuss ways in which the study is likely to contribute to policy, practice, or theory or to measures for taking social action. Who might be interested in the results? With what groups might they be shared? Scholars? Policymakers? Practitioners? Members of similar groups? Individuals or groups usually silenced or marginalized? The challenge here is to situate the study as addressing an important problem; defining the problem shapes the study's significance.

A clinical psychologist might identify a theoretical gap in the literature about isolation and define the topic for an ethnography of long-distance truck drivers. Such a study may be relatively unconcerned with policy or practice; its contributions to theory, however, are preordained. A feminist sociologist could frame a study of discriminatory thinking among business executives for policy and practice by addressing the problem of persistent sexism in the workplace. A study of the impact of welfare reform on the lives of adult learners in basic-education courses could focus either on policy issues or on how this recurring social problem plays out in the lives of the learners. In that event, theory is less significant. The researcher develops the significance of the study by defining the problem. Some researchers are inspired and add a dimension of action to the study's significance for policy and practice. When overly narrow views of policy and practice miss a range of meanings and needs, qualitative researchers want to provide a holistic presentation and use their research as a tool for action (Lee, 2006; Wronka, 2008).

Funding opportunities often focus on a question. A welfare-to-work grants program calling for a multisite evaluation of programs for the so-called hard to employ might provide funding and an already interested audience. It also has direct significance for policy. These are rare opportunities for the researcher. Be wary of research opportunities focused on policy for their potential to seduce the researcher into agendas serving primarily the powerful elite (Anderson, 1989; Marshall, 1997a; Scheurich, 1997). Recall the discussion of explicitly ideological research in Chapter 1. For further discussion of these issues, see Smith (1988).

A study may well be able to contribute understanding and opportunities for action in all four domains, but it is unlikely to contribute equally to all four; the statement of the topic should thus emphasize one of them. For example, a study on the integration of children with disabilities into regular classrooms could be significant for both policy and practice. Framing this as a policy study requires that the topic be situated in national and state policy debates on special education. Framing it as most significant for practice would require the researcher to focus on structures supporting inclusive classrooms. Both frames are legitimate and defensible; the researcher's challenge is to argue for the study's potential contributions to the domains in which he is most interested. This, in turn, has implications for the literature review and the design of the study.

Significance for Knowledge

The discussion of the study's significance for theory is often an intellectual odyssey, which the researcher can pursue more fully in the review of related literature. At this point in the proposal, the researcher should outline the project's potential contribution to knowledge by describing how it fits into theoretical traditions in the social sciences or applied fields in ways that will be new, insightful, or creative. The significance statement should show how the study will contribute to research traditions or foundational literatures in new ways.

Often, the proposal identifies gaps in the literature to which the study will contribute. If the research is in an area for which theory is well developed, the study may be a significant test or expansion of the theory. The researcher may use concepts developed by previous researchers and formulate questions similar to those used in previous research. Data collection, however, may be in a different setting, with a different group, and certainly at a different time. Thus, the results of the research will constitute an extension of theory that will expand the generalizations or more finely tune the theoretical propositions. The contribution of such research is the expansion of previous theory. When researchers conceptualize the focus of the study and generate the research questions, they may draw on a body of theory and related research that is different from previous research. Significance of this sort, however, generally derives from an extensive and creative review of related literature. Having developed that section of the proposal, the writer then incorporates references to and summaries of it in the significance section. This type of significance is treated fully in the next section, on the review of related literature. Generally, by answering the question "How is this research important?" the researcher can demonstrate the creative aspects of the work.

The development of theory takes place by incremental advances and small contributions to knowledge through well-conceptualized and well-conducted research. Most researchers use theory to guide their own work, to locate their studies in larger scholarly traditions, or to map the topography of the specific concepts that they will explore in detail. In addition, some very creative research can emerge when a researcher breaks theoretical boundaries and reconceptualizes a problem or relocates the problem area. For example, Bronfenbrenner (1980) reconceptualized children's learning processes by applying the concept of *ecology* to child development theory. Weick's (1976) metaphor of schools as loosely coupled systems profoundly altered theoretical conceptualizations of educational organizations. Often, researchers follow a theoretical pragmatism, being "shamelessly eclectic" in the creative application of concepts from one discipline to another (Rossman & Wilson, 1994).

Significance for Practical and Policy Problems

The significance of a study for policy can be developed by discussing formal policy development in that area and presenting data that show how often the problem occurs and how costly it can be. For example, to demonstrate the significance of a study of the careers of women faculty, the researcher could present statistics documenting persistently lower salaries for women than men at comparable ranks; this is the problem that the study will address. The study's potential contributions to university compensation policies could then be spelled out. Based on that, contributions to the university degree program policy could then be articulated. In another example, the researcher could describe recent changes in welfare law and discuss how this reform was developed with little regard for those most affected, which is the problem the study will address. Potential contributions of the study to further reform of welfare law could then be described. In developing the topic and how the study might contribute to policy in that area, the researcher would demonstrate that the general topic is one of significant proportions that should be studied systematically.

A study's importance can also be argued through summaries of the writings of policymakers and informed experts who identify the topic as important and call for research pursuing the general questions. Statistical presentations of the incidence and persistence of the problem, as well as calls for research by experts, demonstrate that the study addresses an important topic, one of concern to policymakers in that area. In applied fields such as education, health policy, management, regional planning, and clinical psychology, for example, demonstrating a study's significance to policy—whether international, national, state, regional, or institutional—may be especially important.

Situating a study as significant for practice follows the same logic as developing significance for policy. The argument here should rely on a discussion of the concerns or problems articulated in the literature. This will involve citing experts, referencing prior research, and summarizing incidence data. Recall the preceding discussion of a study about the inclusion of children with disabilities. The researcher who wants this study to focus on issues of practice would discuss the literature detailing the concerns of teachers about meeting the needs of children with disabilities in their classroom. The study's potential contributions, then, would be improvement in teachers' classroom practice. Shadduck-Hernandez's (1997) proposal for her dissertation research about immigrant and refugee college students' sense of ethnic identity summarized the incidence data on enrollment and the paucity of culturally relevant experiences for them in the college curriculum. This set up her assertions of the study's potential contributions to pedagogical practice in university classrooms.

Significance for Action

Finally, a study may be significant for its detailed description of life circumstances that express particular social issues. Such a study may not influence policy, contribute to scholarly literature, or improve practice; it may instead illuminate the lived experiences of interest by providing rich description and foster taking action. Action research and participatory action research genres stipulate taking action as central to their work. In these cases, researchers should argue that the proposed inquiry and its attendant action will likely be valuable to those who participate, as well as to others committed to the issue. The challenge here is to identify how and in what ways.

Maguire's (2000) study with battered women was a participatory action research project. Her study's primary contributions were not intended for scholarly traditions, policy, or practice per se; rather, they were meant for the women involved in the work and for others committed to alleviating the abuse of women. The work was important because it focused on a major social issue. In contrast, Browne's (1987) study of battered women who kill their assailants made a different and significant contribution. It provided a critique of the legal system, which does little to protect women under threat; it then led to increased activism for women in these circumstances. Lather and Smithies's (1997) study collaborating with HIV-positive women invited the reader to enter into the women's lives so as to create new connections and the possibilities for action.

Through a discussion of relevant scholarship and the concerns of practice, the significance section articulates the topic to be studied and argues that further investigation of this problem has the potential to contribute to scholarship, policy, practice, or a better understanding of recurring social issues. This section defines who is likely to have an interest in the topic and therefore how and in what ways the study may contribute.

Of course, researchers preparing proposals for funding should adjust their statements about significance to the needs and priorities of the funding agencies. The foundation that takes pride in funding action projects or interventions will want to see statements about how the proposed research will directly help people or change a problematic situation. On the other hand, when seeking funds from an agency whose goals include expanding knowledge and theory (e.g., the National Science Foundation), to demonstrate the significance of the research, the researcher should emphasize the undeveloped or unsolved theoretical puzzles to be addressed.

The Section on the Conceptual Framework and Research Questions

Qualitative approaches to inquiry are uniquely suited to uncovering the unexpected and exploring new avenues. This demands flexibility in the proposal so that data gathering can respond to increasingly refined research questions. Herein lies a dilemma, however. The proposal should be sufficiently clear, both in research questions and design, so that the reader can evaluate its do-ability; on the other hand, the proposal should reserve the flexibility that is the hallmark of qualitative methods. This suggests that the research questions should be general enough to permit exploration but focused enough to delimit the study—not an easy task.

Focusing the study and posing general research questions are best addressed in a developmental manner, relying on discussions of related literature to help frame and refine the specific topic. Often, the primary research goal is to discover those very questions that are most probing and insightful. Most likely, the relevant concepts will be developed during the research process, but the research proposal must suggest themes based on one's knowledge of the literature.

Initial questions should be linked to the problem and its significance and should forecast the literature to be reviewed. Questions may be theoretical ones, which can be studied in a number of different sites or with different samples. They may focus on a population or class of individuals; these too can be studied in various places. Finally, the questions may be site specific because of the uniqueness of a specific program or organization. The study of refugee and immigrant college experiences (Shadduck-Hernandez, 1997; 2005) could have been conducted in any setting that had newcomer students; the theoretical interest driving the research was not linked to a particular organization. A study of an exemplary sex education program, however, can be conducted only at that site because the problem identified is one of practice. Thus, the questions posed are shaped by the identified problem and, in turn, constrain the design of the study.

Examples of *theoretical questions* include the following:

- How does play affect reading readiness? Through what cognitive and affective process? Do children who take certain roles—for example, leadership roles—learn faster? If so, what makes the difference?
- How does the sponsor-protégé socialization process function in professional careers? Does it work differently for women? For minorities? What processes are operating?
- What are the assumptions of medical staff and laypeople about how "positive thinking" affects coping with cancer?

Questions focused on *particular populations* could include the following:

- How do neurosurgeons cope with the reality that they hold people's lives in their hands? That many of their patients die?
- What happens to women who enter elite MBA programs? What are their career paths?
- What is the life of the long-distance truck driver like?
- How do school superintendents manage relations with school board members? What influence processes do they use?
- What happens to change-agent teachers during their careers? Do organizational socialization processes change or eliminate them? Do they burn out early in their careers?
- What are the life and career experiences of women PhDs who come from very poor families of origin?

Finally, *site-specific* and *policy-focused* research questions might take the following form:

- Why is the sex education program working well in this school but not in the others? What is special about the people, the plan, the support, and the context?
- How do the school-parent community relations of an elite private school differ from those in the neighboring public school? How are the differences connected with differences in educational philosophies and outcomes?
- What are the ways in which lobbying groups influence pollution control policy in the Massachusetts legislature?

- Why is there a discrepancy in the perceptions of the efficacy of affirmative action policy between university officials and groups of students of color at the University of North Carolina? What explains the discrepancy?

These are typical examples of initial questions developed in the proposal. They serve as boundaries around the study without unduly constraining it. The questions focus on interactions and processes in sociocultural systems and in organizations and thus link to important research literature and theory, but they are also grounded in everyday realities. The goal of this section of the proposal is to explicate the questions, thereby further focusing the study, and to forecast the literature to be discussed in the next section. Vignette 5 shows early development of an introductory statement for a pilot-study proposal.

* * * *

VIGNETTE 5 An Initial Statement

A doctoral student from China, Fan Yihong (2000), became deeply concerned about the fundamental purposes of education, especially as enacted in universities. Her experiences in universities in China and the United States led her to see that much of the organizational practice—procedures, norms, disciplinary boundaries—on both continents was deadening human spirit and creativity. She immersed herself in organizational theory, science and technology, and the development of the "new sciences" and complex systems theory in relation to Eastern philosophy. During this journey, she came on the emerging theories of the holographic universe and the holotropic mind (Capra, 1975, 1982, 1996; Senge, 1990; Wilber, 1996) that stress the wholeness of people, events, nature, and the world, and the innate capacity of the mind to comprehend reality in a holistic manner. Based on these interests, she posed four overarching research questions that would allow her to integrate the various complex intellectual traditions that framed her study:

1. What serves as triggers and preconditions for individuals to change their worldviews?
2. What processes have they undertaken to enable them to transform their changed ways of knowing to their changed ways of doing and then to their changed ways of being, finally becoming transformed human beings?
3. What characterizes these change processes?
4. How does individual awakening, recognizing the need for change, help bring about collective and organizational transformational change?

The potential significance of the study was described in terms of its contributions to understanding how personal and organizational transformation is possible, through rich descriptions of people and organizations that were radically different from traditional ones. Thus, the study would potentially contribute theory and practice, building a thoughtful and detailed analysis of the processes of transformation.

* * * * *

Fan Yihong (2000) has introduced the topic—the persistent problem of confining versus liberating educational environments, posed the preliminary general research questions, and forecast the study's potential significance. While this approach is not at all typical, it represented congruence with her theoretical framework and personal epistemology and cosmology. Following are two examples of other introductory paragraphs. Each states the topic, discusses the purpose, stipulates the unit of analysis, and forecasts the study's significance:

> Children with physical handicaps have unique perceptions about their "bodiedness." Grounded in phenomenological inquiry, this study will explore and describe the deep inner meaning of bodiedness for five children. The study will result in rich description through stories of these children's relationships with sports. The central concept of bodiedness will be explicated through the children's words. Those working with children with physical handicaps, as well as policymakers framing programs that affect them, will find the study of interest.
>
> The Neighborhood Arts Center in Orange, Massachusetts, is an award-winning program that serves all members of its community. The purpose of this study is to explain the success of this program in bringing arts to members of this low-income community. The study will use an ethnographic design, seeking detailed explanations of the program's success. The study will help decision makers and funders design similar programs that involve groups historically underrepresented in the arts. (Adapted from Rossman & Rallis, 2003)

Delineating the Limitations of the Study

All proposed research projects have limitations; none is perfectly designed. As Patton (2002) notes, "There are no perfect research designs. There are always trade-offs" (p. 223). A discussion of the study's limitations demonstrates that the researcher understands this reality—that he will make no overweening claims about generalizability or conclusiveness about what he has learned.

Limitations derive from the conceptual framework and the study's design. A discussion of these limitations early on in the proposal reminds the reader of what the study is and is not—its boundaries—and how its results can and cannot contribute to understanding. Framing the study in specific research and scholarly traditions places limits on the research. A study of land use in Indonesia, for example, could be situated in development economics; reminding the reader that the study is framed this way helps allay criticism. The overall design, however, indicates how broadly applicable the study may be. Although no qualitative studies are generalizable in the probabilistic sense, their findings may be transferable. A discussion of these considerations reminds the reader that the study is bounded and situated in a specific context. The reader, then, can make decisions about its usefulness for other settings. As important, though, is that statements about limitations, while acknowledging limits to generalizability, should reemphasize the qualitative study's very different purposes and strengths. As we discussed in earlier chapters, one chooses a qualitative approach to understand phenomena from the participants' perspectives and to explore and discover, in depth and in context, what may have been missed when studies were done with predetermined assumptions. So qualitative researchers must assert that traditional "gold standards" such as generalizabity, replicability, control groups, and the like are not the right criteria to aim for. We will return to this point in Chapter 9. Still, in conceptualizing and in framing the design, the sites, the sampling, and the management of data, we do aim to maximize the value of our research by anticipating questions and challenges. When, for example, we want to explore and discover the range of responses of men diagnosed with prostate cancer, we would face questions such as the following: What is lost by limiting the study to easily accessible and articulate middle-class males? Or to males in Austin, Texas? Or to patients but not spouses and doctors? For another example, when our purpose is to uncover the crucial elements in "successful" programs for pregnant and parenting teens, we would face the following questions: Must my sample include programs with comparable budgets to maximize comparability? But if I study many programs, how can I get the in-depth participant observation and interviewing I need, with my limited budget? Have I focused too narrowly by accepting others' definitions of "successful"? These are difficult questions, which will be revisited in Chapter 6 and later chapters. Early on, we may have only best guesses and hopes about what can be done. Later, these guesses and hopes will be refined in the research design, then again in planning the time and budget for the study, and probably again in the field.

Write the Introduction in draft or even outline. As one proceeds through the Literature Review, many of the details of the Introduction become evident. You will redo the Introduction, ultimately, when all other parts of the proposal are complete. Then and only then can one actually write an Introduction. Keep it short and engaging. In the end, it should be the "warm-up" to situate the reader for the full proposal. The time-constrained (or lazy) reader should be able to know, generally, what is being proposed, just by reading the Introduction.

LITERATURE REVIEW AND CRITIQUE OF RELATED RESEARCH

A thoughtful and insightful discussion of related literature builds a logical framework for the research and locates it within a tradition of inquiry and a context of related studies. The literature review serves four broad functions. First, it demonstrates the underlying assumptions behind the general research questions. If possible, it should display the research paradigm that undergirds the study and describe the assumptions and values the researcher brings to the research enterprise. Second, it demonstrates that the researcher is knowledgeable about related research and the scholarly traditions that surround and support the study. Third, it shows that the researcher has identified some gaps in previous research and that the proposed study will fill a demonstrated need. Finally, the review refines and redefines the research questions by embedding them in larger traditions of inquiry. We describe the literature review as a *conversation* between the researcher and the related literature.

Theoretical Traditions for Framing the Questions

As the researcher conceptualizes the research problem, he locates it in a tradition of theory and related research. Initially, this may be an intuitive locating, chosen because of the underlying assumptions, such as how the researcher sees the world and how he sees the research questions fitting in. As the researcher explores the literature, however, he should identify and state those assumptions in a framework of theory. This could be child development theory, organizational theory, adult socialization theory, critical race theory, or whatever theory is appropriate. This section of the literature review provides the framework for the research and identifies the area of knowledge the study is intended to expand.

Related Research, Reviewed and Critiqued

The next portion of the review of literature should, quite literally, review and critique previous research and scholarly writing that relates to the general research question. This critical review should lead to a more precise problem statement or refined questions because it demonstrates a specific area that has not yet been adequately explored or shows that a different design would be more appropriate. If a major aspect of the significance of the study arises from a reconceptualization of the topic, it should be developed fully here. Cooper (1988) provides a discussion of the focus, goal, perspective, coverage, organization, and audience for a literature review.

Essays and Opinions of Experts

In this section of the literature review, the researcher presents the practitioner's, and even the journalist's and policymaker's, words. It is an opportunity to show that, in addition to academic scholars and authors of journal articles, people outside the academy have spoken about the need to find answers, to explore reasons why, and to find new ways to look at a problem. Government reports, lobbyists' assertions, newspaper articles, and even person-on-the-street accounts can be included. The reader understands that the sources for this section may be less credible to scholarly readers than peer-reviewed sources. However, these sources often have the credibility that comes from direct personal experience and an insider's knowledge about a situation. Thus, quotes from state legislators and from the machinist union trade paper's editorials on the health problems of unemployed machinists can be cited to enhance or deepen insights regarding unemployment that were reviewed earlier from the scholarly research viewpoint.

Summarizing the Literature Review in a Conceptual Framework

Researchers develop an argument, throughout the literature review, by identifying the literatures that are useful and demonstrating how some literatures are dated, limited, or leave some questions unanswered. The argument buttresses the conceptual framework to be used and the questions to be asked. Figure 4.4 was derived from a literature review of organization theory, leadership theory, literature on the realities of school administrators' careers, and also government and professional associations' laments over administrator burnout and shortage (Marshall, 2008). The framework was created to buttress the proposal's argument—in this case the argument that research is needed to discover what organizational experiences support and entice healthy, engaged, and creative school administrators.

Model for Envisioning a Multi-Researcher, Multi-Focal Study

The framework was used to graphically display the argument that had been developed in the literature review. It also was used to identify ways in which seven related questions could be studies constructed to coordinate with each other, to point to possible sites and foci, and to clarify their significance for policymakers wringing their hands over administrator shortages and burnout. Finally, it shows the potential of the large project to take policymakers' worries and expand them, to show how the relevant policy issues should include the health, creativity, and engagement of administrators.

Some researchers find it useful to draw a **pictorial model** that identifies domains and relationships (as in concept mapping). Such pictures are not meant to predict one's findings but rather to present the researchers' current, proposal-stage thoughts about how things work. Figure 4.5 is one example of a simple conceptual model that can help a researcher envision her study's questions about the factors that affect patients' access to treatment.

Figure 4.4 Model for Envisioning a Multi-Researcher, Multi-Focal Study

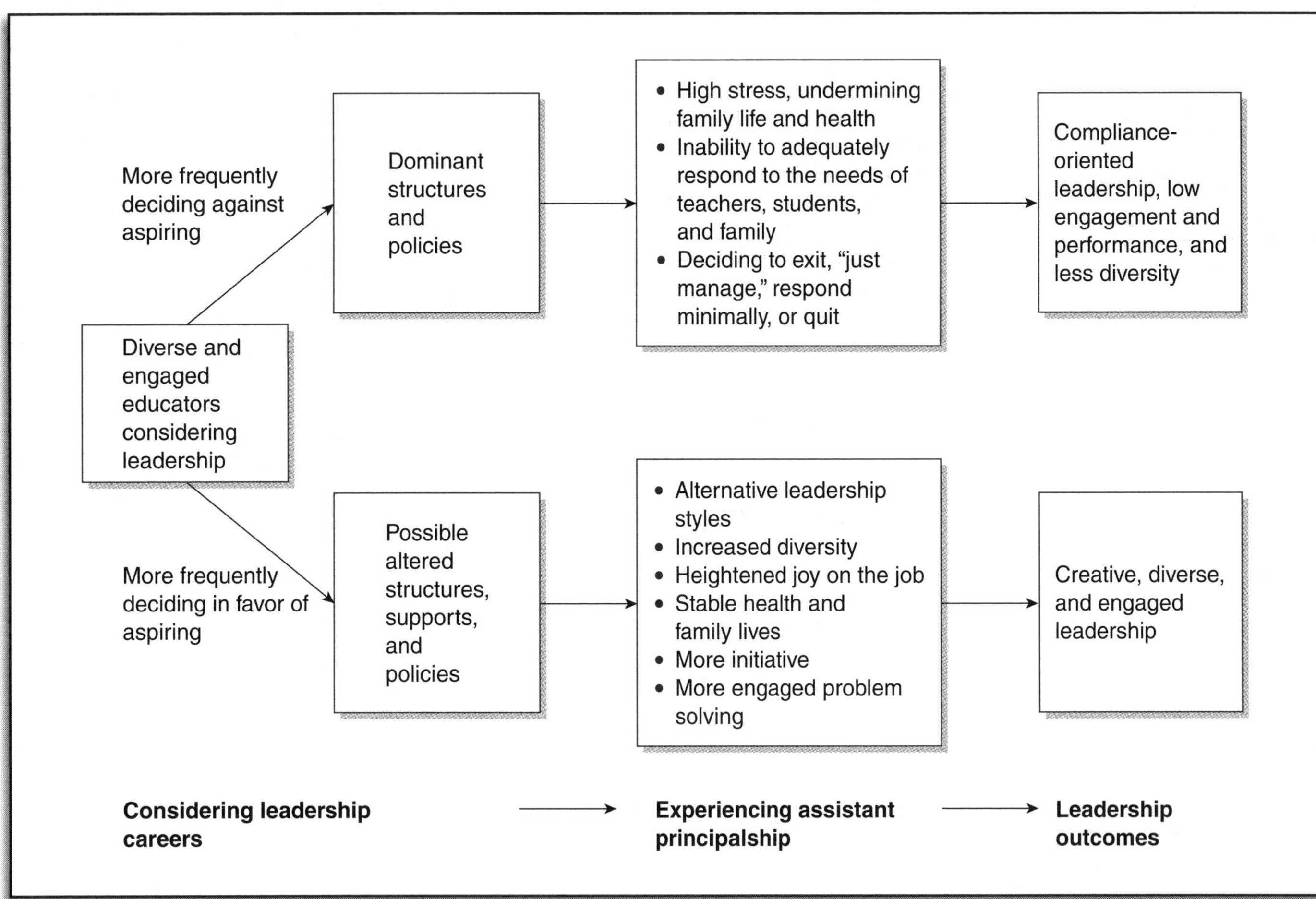

Figure 4.5 Example of a Simple Conceptual Model

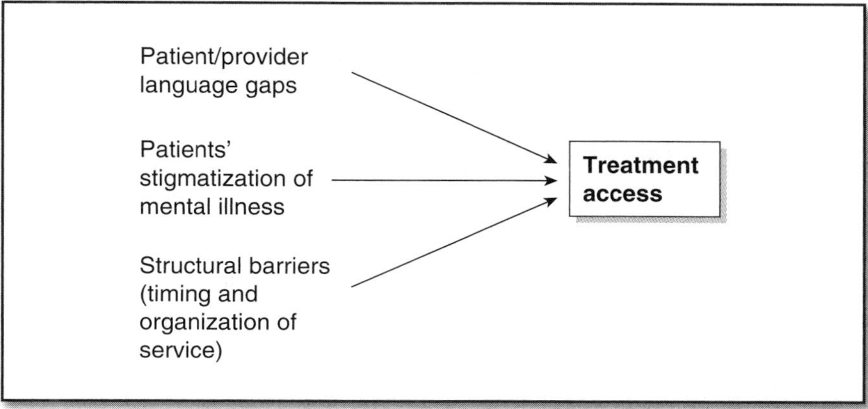

SOURCE: Schensul (2008, p. 519). Reprinted with permission.

Example of a Simple Conceptual Model

An extended example of integrating and dovetailing the significance of the review sections is provided in Vignette 6. Look for the ways in which the literature review led Marshall (1979, 1981, 1985b) to find new possibilities for pursuing the research questions.

* * * *

VIGNETTE 6 Building Significance Through the Literature

When Marshall (1979) was researching the general problem of women's unequal representation in school administration careers, she first reviewed the work of previous researchers. Many researchers before her had conducted surveys to identify the attributes, positions, and percentages of women in school administration. A few researchers had identified patterns of discrimination.

In a significant departure from this tradition, Marshall reconceptualized the problem. She looked at it as a problem in the area of adult socialization and looked to career socialization theory and found useful concepts such as role strain, sponsorship, aspiration formation, and more. From a review of this body of theory and related empirical research on the school administrative career, including recruitment, training, and selection processes, and on women in jobs and careers, Marshall framed a new question. She asked, "What is the career socialization process for women in school administration? What is the process through which women make career decisions, acquire training and supports, overcome obstacles, and move up in the hierarchy?"

(Continued)

VIGNETTE 6 (Continued)

This reconceptualization came from asking the significance question: Who cares about this research? The question encouraged a review of previous research that demonstrated how other research had already answered many questions. It showed that women were as competent as men in school administration. But a critical review of this literature argued that this previous research had asked different questions. Marshall could assert that her study would be significant because it would focus on describing a process about which previous research had only an inkling. The new research would add to theory by exploring career socialization of women in a profession generally dominated by men. It would also identify the relevant social, psychological, and organizational variables that are part of women's career socialization. This established the significance of the research by showing how it would add to knowledge.

The literature review also established the significance of the research for practice and policy, with an overview of the issues of affirmative action and equity concerns. Thus, the research question, literature review, and research design were all tied in with the significance question. Responding to this question demanded a demonstration that this was an area of knowledge and practice that needed exploration. To ensure exploration, qualitative methods were the most appropriate for the conduct of the study.

* * * * *

As Vignette 6 shows, the literature review can identify established knowledge and, more important, develop significance and new questions and often turn old questions around. This "initiating function" (Rossman & Wilson, 1994) of the literature review can be quite creative. It helps to try "out if-then propositions" and "thought experiments" (Schram, 2006, p. 67), where the researcher playfully generates possible linkages and relationships that can be made between theory and what might be discovered in data collection. For example, in a thought experiment in the research described above in Vignette 6, Marshall (1979) posed a guiding hypothesis that if women anticipate the role strain to be incurred by the piling on of mothering roles, administrative tasks, as well as doubts that women can be "tough" leaders, they will repress any aspirations to school leadership positions. Thus, such a thought experiment yields guiding hypotheses and some clues about how to ask questions and how to be sensitized to themes in her data, and she has more confidence that she can move from the dryness of literature review to the liveliness of real people and real lives in her data collection.

The review, moreover, provides intellectual glue for the entire proposal by demonstrating the sections' conceptual relatedness. The researcher cannot write about the study's significance without knowledge of the literature. He cannot describe the design without a discussion of the general research topic. A proposal is divided into sections because of tradition and convention, not because of a magical formula. To organize complex topics and to address the three critical questions posed at the beginning, however, the structure we provided in Table 4.1 is recommended. Vignette 7 illustrates how the conceptualization of a study can be creative and exciting, as the researcher forges links among historically disparate literatures.

VIGNETTE 7 Creative Review of the Literature

When research questions explore new territory, a single line of previous literature and/or theory may be inadequate for constructing frameworks that usefully guide the study. A case in point is that of Shadduck-Hernandez (1997; 2005), a graduate student in international development education, who searched the literature for a way to frame her study of a community service learning initiative serving refugee and immigrant youth and undergraduate students at a major research university.

Shadduck-Hernandez's forays into the literature on community service learning and the relationships between institutions of higher education and the communities they serve identified a substantial gap. Previous studies described the demographics about participants in community service learning projects, noting that typical projects involved white, middle-class undergraduate students working with communities of color. However, few critiqued the hegemonic practice embodied in such projects or called into question the continuing Eurocentric values in university and community relations. It became clear that previous research had failed to conceptualize the problem in terms of a sustained critique of the university, from the perspectives of those often marginalized from mainstream university discourse—refugee and immigrant students of color.

Having established that the study was situated in scholarly writing and research on community service learning and university-community relations, Shadduck-Hernandez still felt incomplete. This literature helped establish the context for her study but did not provide theoretical concepts or propositions that would help illuminate students' experience. She turned to the literature on critical pedagogy to more fully frame the principles of the project. She also discussed situated learning theory with its key notions of context, peer relations, and communities of practice to provide analytic insights into the learning milieu of the project. Finally, she relied on the anthropological concept of funds of knowledge—"the strategic and cultural resources that racially and ethnically diverse and low-income students and communities possess" (pp. 115–116). Her discussion of these literatures was tested against their usefulness in understanding community service learning among similar and familiar ethnic groups and for developing a gentle but quite pointed critique of the university.

* * * * *

Vignette 7 shows a creative blending of several strands of literature for framing the research. The integration of literatures helped shape a research focus that was theoretically interesting yet could help inform policy and practice in universities. Broad reading and knowledge of the history of institutions of higher education relative to their local communities—richly augmented by more **theoretical literature** on critical pedagogy, situated learning, and funds of knowledge—created a variegated and highly creative synthesis. Rather than narrowly constructing the study to focus on only one topic, the researcher searched widely for illuminating constructs from other disciplines. This work, although at times tedious, confusing, and ambiguous, enhances the research to follow and demonstrates that the researcher has engaged in significant intellectual work already.

The literature review serves many purposes for the research. It supports the importance of the study's focus and may serve to validate the eventual findings in a narrowly descriptive study. It also guides the development of explanations during data collection and analysis in studies that seek to explain, evaluate, and suggest linkages between events. In grounded-theory development, the literature review provides theoretical constructs, categories, and their properties that can be used to organize the data and discover new connections between theory and phenomenon.

The sections of the proposal discussed thus far—introduction, discussion of the topic and purpose, significance, general research questions, and literature review—stand together as the conceptual body of the proposal. Here, the major (and minor) ideas for the proposal are developed, their intellectual roots are displayed and critiqued, and the writings and studies of other researchers are presented and critiqued. All this is intended to tell the reader (1) what the research is about (its subject), (2) who ought to care about it (its significance), and (3) what others have described and concluded about the subject (its intellectual roots). All three purposes are interwoven into these sections of the proposal.

The final major section—research design and methods—must flow conceptually and logically from all that has gone before; these are discussed in Chapters 5 to 7. In the design and methods section, the researcher makes a case, based on the conceptual portion of the proposal, for the particular sample, methods, data analysis techniques, and reporting format chosen for the study. Thus, the section on design and methods should build a rationale for the study's design and data collection methods. Here, the researcher should develop a case for using qualitative methods. These topics are also discussed in Chapters 5 to 7.

Although there are parallels, proposals for qualitative research differ—sometimes substantially—from proposals for quantitative research. In the development of a qualitative proposal, the researcher first orients the proposal reader to the general topic to be explored. This will not involve a statement of specific research questions, propositions to be tested, or hypotheses to be examined. It can include a general discussion of the puzzle, the unexplored issue, or the group to be studied. Discussion becomes more focused through the literature review because, in exploratory studies, it is hard to predict which literature will be the most relevant; the focus of the study may best be served by an intersection of literatures.

In some cases, the literature review yields cogent and useful definitions, constructs, concepts, and even data collection strategies. These may fruitfully result in a set of preliminary **guiding hypotheses.** Using the term *guiding hypotheses* may assist readers accustomed to more traditional proposals. It is essential, however, that the researcher explain that guiding hypotheses are tools used to generate questions and search for patterns; they may be discarded when the researcher gets into the field and finds other exciting patterns of phenomena. This approach retains the flexibility needed to permit the precise focus of the research to evolve. By avoiding precise hypotheses, the researcher retains her right to explore and *generate* questions. The guiding hypotheses illustrate for the reader some possible directions the researcher may follow, but the researcher is still free to discover and pursue other patterns.

We do not intend to suggest that proposal development proceeds in a linear fashion, as we have noted earlier. Specifically, in Chapter 1, we argued that conceptualizing a study and developing a design that is clear, flexible, and manageable is dialectic, messy, and just plain hard work. As the researcher plays with concepts and theoretical frames for the study, he often entertains alternative designs, assessing them for their power to address the emerging questions. Considering an ethnography, a case study, or an in-depth interview study as the overall design will, in turn, reshape the research questions. So the process continues as the conceptual framework and specific design features become more and more elegantly related. The challenge is to build the logical connections between the topic, the questions, and the design and methods.

Dialogue Between Learners

Melanie,

In reading through the first few chapters, I'm struck with the trials of striving to give a sense of order to the messiness of qualitative research. We try to imagine that there is some type of logical order to our work, only to find that different aspects of our research designs bump into and merge with one another. I think about this often when we talk about conceptual framework in our classes. As a student, I feel that I'm often looking for the "right" theoretical lens with which to make sense of my qualitative work. It is, of course, a hopeless quest. There doesn't ever seem to be a perfect fit to our own research contexts. Yet in classes, we try one on and see how it fits, and then we try on another and see how the fit may be different. And then, of course, we begin our own work on dissertations and suddenly we're meant to, in some way, construct our own. Perhaps we piece a few theoretical perspectives together, finding links and overlaps that others might not have intuited. And it's all so very messy and, at times, disconcerting. I'm just beginning work on my dissertation and am (obviously) struggling a bit with this desire (hope?) for clarity.

Sorry to ramble so. Hope all is well,

Aaron

(Continued)

(Continued)

Aaron,

I completely agree with you about the messiness of qualitative research. I'm in the dissertation phase now, too, you know, and the theoretical piece is killing me! In theory (no pun intended), I understand what we mean by conceptual framework, but I have such a hard time articulating that in my own work. How do I pull from disparate works to create a logical whole? At what point does the framework stand on its own? How do I successfully craft a framework when the pieces are still coming together as I dig into the analysis?

One thing I've slowly realized about qualitative research—and I hope this is a legitimate understanding!—is that the process is not only nonlinear but hopelessly intertwined, almost like we're struggling to unravel a Gordian knot of our own making. Sometimes the interest in my research subject is the only thing that keeps me picking away at my confusion! Like you said, it's messy and it's complex, and it's frustrating—perhaps that's part of the appeal?

I'm afraid I'm rambling now as I'm quite tired and rather hungry. So time for a late dinner and bed!

Melanie

Note: These paragraphs are adapted from Rossman and Rallis (2003).

FURTHER READING

Barbour, R. (2008). *Introducing qualitative research: A student's guide to the craft of doing qualitative research.* Thousand Oaks, CA: Sage.

Bloomberg, L., & Volpe, M. (2008). *Completing your qualitative dissertation.* Thousand Oaks, CA: Sage.

Cheek, J. (2000). An untold story? Doing funded qualitative research. In N. K. Denzin & Y. S. Lincoln (Eds.), *Handbook of qualitative research* (2nd ed., pp. 401–420). Thousand Oaks, CA: Sage.

Cheek, J. (2008). Funding. In L. M. Given (Ed.), *The SAGE encyclopedia of qualitative research methods* (pp. 360–364). Thousand Oaks, CA: Sage.

Coley, S. M., & Scheinberg, C. A. (2000). *Proposal writing* (2nd ed.). Thousand Oaks, CA: Sage.

Creswell, J. W. (1998). *Qualitative inquiry and research design: Choosing among five traditions.* Thousand Oaks, CA: Sage.

Creswell, J. W. (2003). *Research design: Qualitative, quantitative, and mixed methods approaches* (2nd ed.). Thousand Oaks, CA: Sage.

Glesne, C. (2006). *Becoming qualitative researchers: An introduction* (3rd ed.). Boston: Pearson.

Janesick, V. J. (1994). The dance of qualitative research design. In N. K. Denzin & Y. S. Lincoln (Eds.), *Handbook of qualitative research* (pp. 209–219). Thousand Oaks, CA: Sage.

Kohli, R. (2008, April). *Breaking the cycle of racism in the classroom: Critical race reflections from future teachers of color.* Paper presented at the meeting of AERA, San Diego, CA.

Lee, T. S. (2006). "I came here to learn how to be a leader": An intersection of critical pedagogy and indigenous education. *InterActions: UCLA Journal of Education and Information Studies, 2*(1), 1–24.

Locke, L. F., Spirduso, W. W., & Silverman, S. J. (2000). *Proposals that work: A guide for planning dissertations and grant proposals* (4th ed.). Thousand Oaks, CA: Sage.

Madison, D. S. (2005). *Critical ethnography: Method, ethics, and performance.* Thousand Oaks, CA: Sage.

Marshall, C. (2008). *Making the impossible job possible.* Unpublished grant proposal, University of North Carolina at Chapel Hill.

Maxwell, J. A. (2005). *Qualitative research design: An interactive approach* (2nd ed.). Thousand Oaks, CA: Sage.

Piantanida, M., & Garman, N. B. (1999). *The qualitative dissertation: A guide for students and faculty.* Thousand Oaks, CA: Corwin Press.

Schram, T. H. (2006). *Conceptualizing and proposing qualitative research.* Upper Saddle River, NJ: Pearson.

Silverman, D. (2005). *Doing qualitative research* (2nd ed.). Thousand Oaks, CA: Sage.

Smith, D. E. (2005). *Institutional ethnography: A sociology for people.* Lanham, MD: AltaMira Press.

Strauss, A., & Corbin, J. (1990). *Basics of qualitative research.* Newbury Park, CA: Sage.

Strauss, A. L. (1969). *Mirrors and masks.* Mill Valley, CA: Sociology Press.

Weis, L., & Fine, M. (2000). *Speed bumps: A student-friendly guide to qualitative research.* New York: Teachers College Press.

Wronka, J. (2008). *Human rights and social justice: Social action and service for the helping and health professions.* Thousand Oaks, CA: Sage.

Ybema, S., Yanow, D., Wels̀, H., & Kamsteeg, F. (2009). *Organizational ethnography: Studying the complexity of everyday life.* London: Sage.

KEY CONCEPTS

Conceptual framework

"Eureka" moment

Focusing

Funnel

Guiding hypotheses

Personal biography

Personal theories

Pictorial model

Problematic

Related research

Significance for knowledge

Significance for practice and policy

Theoretical literature

5

The How of the Study

Building the Research Design

In the research proposal, one section is devoted to a description of the design and methods. This serves three purposes:

1. It presents a plan for the conduct of the study.
2. It demonstrates that the researcher is capable of conducting the study.
3. It asserts the need for, and offers strategies to preserve, the flexibility of design that is a hallmark of qualitative methods. The latter purpose is often the most challenging.

Eight major topics are addressed in the research design section of the proposal: (1) the qualitative genre, overall strategy, and **rationale**; (2) **site selection**, population selection, and **sampling**; (3) the researcher's **entry**, **role**, and **ethics**; (4) data collection methods; (5) data management; (6) data analysis strategy; (7) trustworthiness; and (8) a management plan or time line. Woven into these is the challenge of presenting a clear, do-able plan—with concrete, specific details—while maintaining flexibility in its implementation. After discussing this challenge, we address the first three topics. Later, Chapters 6 and 7 describe data collection methods, followed by a discussion of strategies for managing, analyzing, and interpreting qualitative data in Chapter 8. Considerations for managing the entire research process (using a management plan, budget, and time line) and organizing data collection and management are presented in Chapter 9. All along, we are building up to Chapter 10, in which we provide advice on modes of presenting and writing up qualitative research.

MEETING THE CHALLENGE

How do researchers maintain the needed flexibility of design so that the research can "unfold, cascade, roll, and emerge" (Lincoln & Guba, 1985, p. 210) and still present a plan that is logical, concise, and thorough, meeting the criterion of do-ability? The research design section should demonstrate to the reader that the overall plan is sound and that the researcher is competent to undertake the research, capable of employing the chosen methods, and sufficiently self-aware and interested to sustain the effort necessary for the successful completion of the study. This design and the researcher's defense of it must stand up to questioning. After all, the design must convince reviewers that the researcher is able to handle a complex and personal process, often making decisions in the field during the unfolding, cascading, rolling, and emerging.

The researcher should demonstrate to the reader that he reserves the right to modify the original design as the research evolves: Building flexibility into the design is crucial. The researcher does so by (a) demonstrating the appropriateness of and the logic of using qualitative methods for the particular research question and (b) devising a proposal that includes many of the elements of traditional proposals. At the same time, he reserves the right to change the implementation plan during data collection. As mentioned earlier, this section of the proposal should discuss the rationale for and logic of the particular qualitative genre in which the study is grounded, the overall strategy, and the specific design elements. At times, however, the researcher may need to justify qualitative research, in general, before situating the proposed study in a genre. We address the reality of this issue first and then focus on specific genres and approaches.

JUSTIFYING QUALITATIVE RESEARCH

In recent years, the value and prestige of qualitative inquiry have risen in some fields. Still, given the historical domination of social science research by traditional, quantitative models and the current conservative climate of the federal government, the researcher may well have to develop a justification for qualitative methods in general. Before describing the specific genre and approach, she should show how and why the research questions will be best addressed in a natural setting, using exploratory approaches. To accomplish this, the strengths of qualitative methodology should be emphasized by elaborating the value of such studies for the following types of research (Lincoln & Guba, 1985; Marshall, 1985a, 1987):

- Research that seeks cultural description and ethnography
- Research that elicits multiple constructed realities, studied holistically
- Research that elicits tacit knowledge and subjective understandings and interpretations
- Research that delves in depth into complexities and processes
- Research on little known phenomena or innovative systems
- Research that seeks to explore where and why policy and local knowledge and practice are at odds
- Research on informal and unstructured linkages and processes in organizations
- Research on real, as opposed to stated, organizational goals
- Research that cannot be done experimentally for practical or ethical reasons
- Research exploring novel, ignored, or often marginalized populations
- Research for which relevant variables have yet to be identified

Further support is found in the many excellent introductory texts on qualitative methods that describe the characteristics and strengths of qualitative methods (see Chapter 1, Further Reading). Drawing on these sources, the researcher proposing a study in a particular setting (e.g., a hospital ward or social service agency) could argue that human actions are significantly influenced by the setting in which they occur and that one should therefore study that behavior in those real-life natural situations. The social and physical setting—schedules, space, pay, and rewards—and internalized notions of norms, traditions, roles, and values are crucial aspects of an environment. Thus, for qualitative studies, context matters. The researcher can argue that the study must be conducted in the setting where all this complexity operates over time and where data on the multiple versions of reality can be collected. For a study focusing on individuals' lived experience, the researcher can also argue that human actions cannot be understood unless the meaning that humans assign to them is understood. Because thoughts, feelings, beliefs, values, and assumptions are involved, the researcher needs to understand the deeper perspectives that can be captured through face-to-face interaction and observation in the natural setting.

Critiquing and demonstrating the limitations of quantitative, positivist approaches can be an excellent strategy for justifying the use of qualitative methodology. The researcher might argue that the objective scientist, by coding the social world according to preordained operational variables, destroys valuable data by imposing a limited worldview on the subjects (a consideration for all studies, qualitative or otherwise, we would argue). The researcher might further critique experimental models by noting that policymakers and practitioners are sometimes unable to derive meaning and useful findings from experimental research and that the research techniques themselves have affected the findings. The lab, the questionnaire, and so on have become artifacts. Subjects are suspicious and wary. Sometimes they are aware of what the researchers want and try to please them. And the researcher could describe the ways in which stories—complex narratives of personal experience—are masked by quantitative methods or, worse, displaced by them.

In short, the strengths of qualitative studies should be demonstrated for research that is exploratory or descriptive and that stresses the importance of context, setting, and participants' frames of reference. A well-reasoned and convincing explanation for qualitative methods should include a concise but strong rationale that is firmly grounded in the conceptual framework and that justifies the specific data collection methods. The rationale should show how the selection of methods flows from the research questions. Two examples illustrate this. For Glazier's (2004) ethnographic study on the ability of the collaborative work of Arab and Jewish teachers in Israel to influence understanding of the Other, the compelling argument was that triangulation of qualitative data allows for multiple perspectives. Mishna (2004) also made a strong argument that a study using interviews with children and parents about bullying needs a qualitative methodology to capture context, personal interpretation, and experience. As Mishna pointed out,

> Qualitative data . . . privileges individuals' lived experience . . . Increasing our understanding of the views of children and adults is key to developing effective interventions. . . . We know surprisingly little about the dynamics of school bullying relationships. . . . It is vital to have children's perspectives when trying to identify the processes involved in problematic peer relations. (p. 235)

Notice how this researcher first presented what was already known, then what was still needed, and then why this topic needed a qualitative approach.

THE QUALITATIVE GENRE AND OVERALL APPROACH

Although acceptance of qualitative inquiry is currently widespread, at times it is necessary to provide a rationale for the particular genre in which a study is situated. Recall the discussion in Chapter 2 in which we argued that the many nuanced traditions of qualitative research can be categorized into those focusing on (a) *individual lived experience,* (b) *society and culture,* and (c) *language and communication.* The most compelling argument emphasizes the unique strengths of the genre for research that is exploratory or descriptive, that accepts the value of context and setting, and that searches for a deeper understanding of the participants' lived experiences of the phenomenon under study. One assumption common to all genres is that people express meaning about some aspect of their lives. This follows Thomas's (1949) classic proposition that in the study of human experience, it is essential to know how people define their situations: "If men [*sic*] define situations as real, they are real in their consequences" (p. 301). When a proposal presents the logical and compelling connections—the epistemological integrity—between the genre, the overall strategy, the research questions, the design, and the methods, this is quite convincing.

Overall Strategies

Qualitative research embraces a rich diversity of overall design, as discussed in Chapter 2. We can, generally, identify three distinct strategies, as displayed in Table 5.1.

Qualitative Genre and Overall Strategy

A study focusing on individual lived experiences typically relies on an **in-depth interview strategy**. Although this is often supplemented with other data (e.g., journal writing by the participants), the primary strategy is to capture the deep meaning of experience in the participants' own words.

Studies focusing on society and culture in a group, a program, or an organization typically espouse some form of **case study** as a strategy. This entails immersion in the setting and rests on both the researcher's and the participants' worldviews.

Research focusing on language and communication typically involves **microanalysis, discourse analysis**, or **textual analysis**, through which speech events, including text, and subtle interactions are recorded (often on videotape) and then analyzed. Directly linked to the qualitative genre and research questions, each strategy stipulates the focus of the inquiry (individual, group, interactions) and the overall approach to collecting data.

These three broad strategies are distinct from each other in the **complexity of design** and the **closeness of interaction** between researcher and participants. In-depth interview

Table 5.1 Qualitative Genre and Overall Strategy

Genre	Main Strategy	Focus of Inquiry
Individual lived experience	In-depth interviews	Individuals
Society and culture	Case study	Groups or organizations
Language and communication	Microanalysis or text analysis	Speech events and interactions

strategies are elegant in design, relying on a seemingly simple method for gathering data. Microanalyses frequently encompass more of the complexities of context than in-depth interview strategies, relying on some form of observation often complemented by interviews. Case study, the most complex strategy, may entail multiple methods—interviews, observations, historical and document analysis, and even surveys. Following the same logic, interview strategies require close, personal interactions between researcher and participants, often over long periods of time. Case studies may be less intimate than those involving participant observation (discussed in Chapter 5), which fosters close relationships. With their focus on observation, microanalyses tend to lie somewhere in the middle of this continuum. These continua are presented in Figure 5.1.

The strategy is a kind of road map, a proposed plan for undertaking a systematic exploration of the phenomenon of interest; the research methods are the specific tools for conducting that exploration. In-depth interview strategies stipulate a primary data collection method—interviewing. In case studies and microanalyses, the combination of methods proposed for collecting data may be quite complex. A study of the impact of welfare reform, for example, could be a case study of agencies in several cities and could rely on an array of methods, ranging from in-depth interviewing to document analysis of employment records over time. A study of student engagement in math lessons could employ the strategy of microanalysis of classroom interactions, perhaps including direct observation (through videotape) supplemented by interviews of teachers and students and by analysis of student work. The strategy frames the study by placing boundaries around it, identifying the analytic focus. The researcher, by choosing a strategy, is making many major decisions, using his judgment of the best approach to focus in on the questions posed in the conceptual portion of his proposal.

In developing the strategy, the researcher needs to consider its **informational adequacy** and **efficiency** (Zelditch, 1962) and an array of ethical considerations. To discern

Figure 5.1 Complexity of Design and Interaction

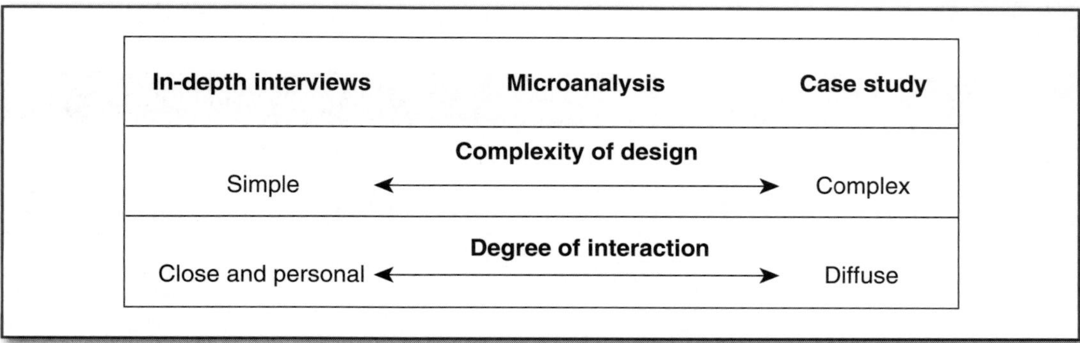

the adequacy of the strategy, ask whether this research design can be carried out without harming people or significantly disrupting the setting. Ask whether it is likely to foster responses to the research questions thoroughly and thoughtfully. Will this strategy elicit the information one seeks? (See questions of the study's do-ability in Chapter 1.) Does this plan allow adequate data to be collected, given the constraints of time, financial resources, **access**, and cost to participants and researcher? To these, we would add ethical considerations. Will the proposed strategy violate the participants' privacy or unduly disrupt their everyday worlds? Are they putting themselves in danger or at **risk** by participating in the study? Will the study violate their human rights in some way? (We address these ethical issues more fully later in this chapter.) The range of possible qualitative strategies is small. Which is chosen depends on the research questions, on the genre, on ethics, and on the time frame possible for the study.

In addition to developing a strong, supported rationale for the genre and strategy, this section of the proposal should assert and preserve the right to modify aspects of the design as the research proceeds. Early investigations of a phenomenon can also demonstrate the benefits of maintaining some flexibility. Illustrating this is Geer's (1969) description of **first days in the field**. She describes the qualitative researcher's immersion in the setting, beginning with some analytic concepts that were identified in previous research, guided by the theoretical framework and related research questions. These help the researcher determine what situations to observe, whom to interview, and what to ask. The researcher should establish the need and the right to determine the precise focus of the research after these first days in the field when new insights begin to clarify patterns and focus the relevant themes. Asserting this need for flexibility may result, however, in frequent check-ins with a dissertation committee chair. Major changes may require a new review by an **institutional review board** (or internal review board; IRB) committee.

Piloting

Pilot studies can be useful, not only for trying out strategies but also to buttress the argument and rationale for a genre and strategy. When the researcher proclaims that he is capable of conducting the proposed research and provides a description and assessment of a qualitative pilot study with intriguing preliminary data, doubters are often persuaded. As Sampson (2004) notes,

> While pilots can be used to refine research instruments such as questionnaires and interview schedules, they have greater use still in ethnographic approaches to data collection in foreshadowing research problems and questions, in highlighting gaps and wastage in data collection, and in considering broader and highly significant issues such as research validity, ethics, representation, and researcher health and safety. (p. 383)

Pilot interviews help in understanding oneself as a researcher. Piloting also helps the researcher find ways to eliminate barriers such as resistance to tape recorders and mistrust of the researcher's agenda, as Smith (1999) describes in his research on the fears of social workers. Even without a pilot study, the researcher can demonstrate her ability to manage qualitative research by describing initial observations or interviews. These experiences usually reveal fascinating questions and intriguing patterns. Piloting will yield a description of initial observations useful to demonstrate not only one's ability to manage this research but also the strengths of the genre for generating enticing research questions. Thus, describing a pilot study or initial observations strengthens a proposal.

Demonstrating the Traditions

One purpose of the research design section is to demonstrate that the researcher is capable of conducting qualitative research. Thus, the design section should quote materials from courses in qualitative methodology or from independent reading to demonstrate, through other researchers' publications, the qualitative research tradition that the proposed design is following. The quotations and citations are not used merely to impress readers with the number of the citations but to provide solid evidence that the researcher has entered into the critical conversation about methodology. This demonstrates knowledge of the historical and ongoing methodological discourse about qualitative inquiry and of the specific genre in which the study is situated. An increasing number of researchers have provided descriptions of the rationale for an evolving research design; both classical and newer works are referenced at the end of this chapter. Those that provide appendixes on methodology are particularly useful.

Once the overall approach and supporting rationale have been presented, the proposal outlines the setting or population of interest and plans for more specific sampling of people, places, and events. This outline provides the reader with a sense of the scope of the proposed inquiry and of whether the intensity, amount, and richness of the data will encourage full responses to the research questions. The researcher may devise a chart showing questions to explore, potential rich settings, and specific data collection strategies to display the logic of the design.

Researcher Identity, Voice, and Biases

Research designs should include reflection on one's **identity** and one's sense of **voice** and perspectives, assumptions, and sensitivities. These are key elements in a proposal's discussion of the choice of the research questions, as mentioned in Chapter 4. Recall that, in Chapter 4, we spoke of the passion and excitement and insight that can stimulate a research project that come from one's identity, experience, and values (also known as **biases**). But they should be articulated as elements of the researcher role, access, ethics, entry (addressed later in this chapter), and also data management, analysis, and reporting (to be addressed in Chapters 8–10). When they are out in the open, they are more manageable and the reader of the final report can assess how those elements of identity affected the study. The schema presented in Figure 5.2 usefully portrays the range of questions to consider, both for proposals and for final reports. This figure can serve as a guide for a proposal section where researchers "come clean" with assumptions, any prior observations or associations that might influence the research, and any personal connections and histories that could be useful or, conversely, could be seen as harmful bias.

Once the research begins, this section of the research design can serve as the first entry in the researcher's **field notes** devoted to **self-reflections**. These notes will be reflections on what worked (or not) in gaining access, entry, maintaining access, ethics, and gathering data. They will assist in the maintenance of the research instrument. They will include things as simple as "Next time, make sure to bring a bottle of water and a clean shirt" or "The anger and mistrust I felt while conducting that interview should give me caution as I assess the quality of the interview data, but they might also give me insight when I analyze the data that seemed to hit at others' repressed anger toward this person who has power over them." Thus **emotions**, passions, and biases are turned into research tools (Copp, 2008; Kleinman & Copp, 1993).

Bracketing of the researcher's personal experiences—recognizing where the personal insight is separated from the researcher's collection of data—is important because it allows the researcher to perceive the phenomenon "freshly, as if for the first time" (Moustakas, 1994, p. 34). Still, it is difficult to fully bracket one's experiences as a qualitative researcher.

Anticipate Reviewers' Concerns

Researchers should anticipate proposal **reviewers' concerns**. Will this design work? Will this researcher be able to handle the anticipated **ethical dilemmas**? How will the researcher know where and how to collect data? Will he get people to speak and act authentically? Will he be able to make any meaningful sense of the voluminous data that will be amassed? One's research design section should draw supporting evidence for the decisions from the relevant quotations of researchers who have written about these issues, thereby allaying fears that dilemmas encountered in the field will be unmanageable. Making reference to particularly sensitive researcher ethics concerning participants, such as the experience of Krieger (1985) studying a lesbian community, is useful and compelling. Or the researcher can cite Chaudhry's (1997) example of handling complex **role dilemmas** as she studied Pakistani Muslim immigrants. Or the researcher can use the example of Lifton (1991) as he calculated how to approach survivors of the Hiroshima bombing. He demonstrates ethical sensitivity,

Figure 5.2 Reflexive Questions: Triangulated Inquiry

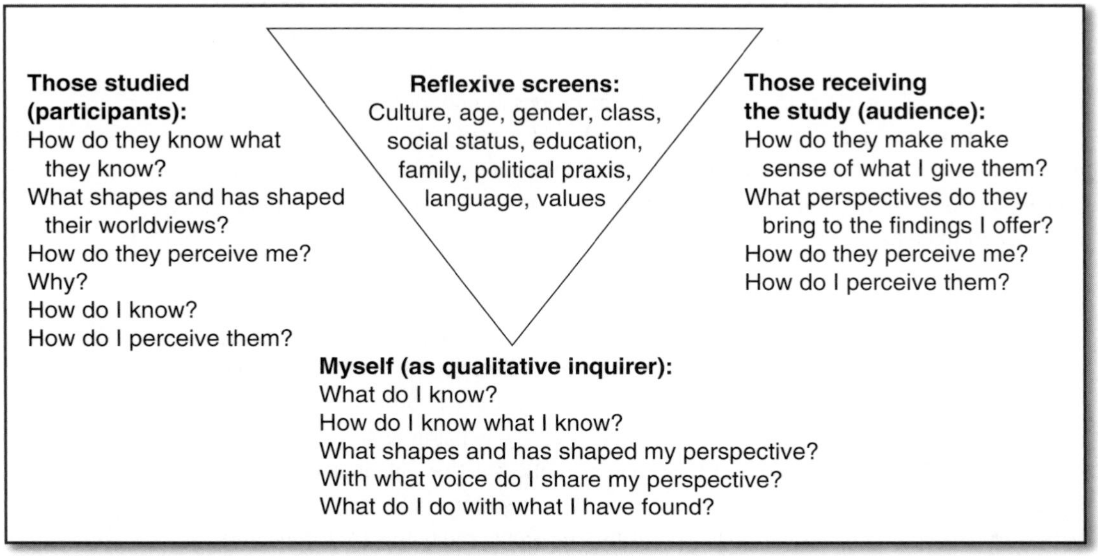

Those studied (participants):
How do they know what they know?
What shapes and has shaped their worldviews?
How do they perceive me? Why?
How do I know?
How do I perceive them?

Reflexive screens:
Culture, age, gender, class, social status, education, family, political praxis, language, values

Those receiving the study (audience):
How do they make make sense of what I give them?
What perspectives do they bring to the findings I offer?
How do they perceive me?
How do I perceive them?

Myself (as qualitative inquirer):
What do I know?
How do I know what I know?
What shapes and has shaped my perspective?
With what voice do I share my perspective?
What do I do with what I have found?

SOURCE: Patton (2002, p. 66). Reprinted with permission.

saying, "In making the arrangements for the interviews, I was aware of my delicate—even Kafkaesque—position as an American psychiatrist approaching people about their feelings considering the bomb" (p. 8). He continues with details of the excruciatingly careful and gradual negotiation of access, aided by intermediaries, and convincing people that

> rather than loose impressions and half-truths, systematic research was needed; and hope that such research might make some contribution to the mastery of these weapons and the avoidance of their use, as well as to our general knowledge of man. (p. 9)

Then researchers can use concepts from their conceptual framework and citations from their literature review to suggest possible categories or themes for data analysis. Finally, when possible, it is useful to include, in the research design section, a list of preliminary or tentative interview questions as well as observation and coding categories. Many IRB committees in universities require these. Funding agencies will find them useful in assessing the quality of the proposal. These can be developed from a pilot study or from the literature review. Such an outline demonstrates that the researcher has the ability to make connections between sensitizing concepts, from the literature review to the research design. It also emphasizes that the researcher understands how to start gathering data as he begins the study and that he has an initial approach to analyzing the data. As one illustration, Vignette 8 is derived from Basit's (2003) recounting of planning for data analysis in her study of the aspirations of British Muslim girls.

VIGNETTE 8 Anticipating the Initial Coding Categories

Anticipating the arduous, yet creative, dynamic process of inductive reasoning, thinking, and theorizing, Tehima Basit knew that prior planning for data coding was crucial. She read all the warnings and advice of Miles (1979), Gough and Scott (2000), and Delamont (1992), who cautioned against shortcuts. As she prepared to describe how she would handle "data condensation" and "data distillation" (Tesch, 1990), she knew that she must provide some concrete examples of how she would proceed. She recalled that "category names can come from the pool of concepts that researchers already have from their disciplinary and professional reading, or borrowed from technical literature, or are the words and phrases used by informants themselves" (Basit, 2003, p. 144). From her interviews with adolescent girls, parents, and teachers, she elicited 67 codes and themes: ethnicity, language, freedom, control, gender, family patterns, marriage and career, further education, homework, unrealistic aspirations, and so on. With these as a start, she referred to her literature review for concepts to elicit deeper connections. Thus, her evolving coding categories had evolved from her literature review but also from the interviews, which provided context and ways of altering, distilling, and refining themes.

Plunging into data collection and analysis with a good sense of **initial themes** and with a firm sense of the need to value the unstructured, nonnumerical nature of qualitative data provided Basit (and her reviewers) with needed guidance and reassurance. With confidence, she answered the questions "How are such voluminous rich data managed?" and "Which parts of your literature review frame your analysis?"

When a proposal is peppered with concrete plans for managing design decisions, it provides reassurance that the researcher has leaned on qualitative research traditions for advice, has anticipated a range of issues to be handled, and will be able to know what to do "in the field." One must include good statements of the overall approach in the proposal. Once this grounding is established, the proposal continues with the more focusing design decisions.

GETTING CONCRETE: THE SETTING, SITE, POPULATION, OR PHENOMENON

Unless a study is quite narrowly construed, researchers cannot study all relevant circumstances, events, or people intensively and in depth. Instead, they select samples. The first and most global decision—choosing the setting, site, population, or phenomenon of interest—is fundamental to the design of the study and serves as a guide for the researcher. This early, significant decision shapes all subsequent ones and should be clearly described and justified.

Some research questions are **site specific**. Other questions, however, can be pursued in many sites throughout the world. A study that asks, "By what processes do women's studies programs become incorporated into universities?" must focus on a setting where this takes place. In contrast, research that asks, "By what processes do innovative units become incorporated into educational organizations?" has a choice of many sites and many different substantive programs. There are many sites for studying "By what processes have Peace Corps volunteers been able to effect long-term health improvements in communities?" The decision to focus on a specific setting (e.g., the University of Massachusetts or a neighborhood in Cincinnati) is somewhat constraining; the study is defined by and intimately linked to that place. Choosing to study a particular kind of population (faculty in Women's Studies Programs in universities or urban street gangs) is somewhat less so: The study can be conducted in more than one place. Studying a phenomenon (the socialization of new faculty or adolescents' need for affiliation) is even less constrained by either place or population. In these latter instances, the researcher determines a sampling strategy that is appropriate, given the purpose of the study.

If the study is of a specific program, organization, place, or region, some detail regarding the setting must be provided. A rationale should outline why this specific setting is more appropriate than others for the conduct of the study. What is unique? What characteristics of this setting are compelling and unusual? Justify this early and highly significant decision. Where possible, identify "back-up" settings that could suffice if access is denied or delayed. The smart researcher will identify research questions in ways that allows choices. For example, when Kanter (1977) wanted to study "how consciousness and behavior are formed by positions in organizations, to show how both men and women are the product of their circumstances" (p. xi), she could have chosen from thousands of settings for her ethnography. She focused on one, pseudonymed Industrial Supply Corporation (Indsco), since she had access already and her prior observations and her ponderings about organizational theory had given her a sense that she would have plentiful opportunity for data collection from ranges of behaviors and positions, over time, in that site. Her questions, and her research design, were not limited to Indsco, or even to corporations. Still, her design and her site allowed her to discover and describe how people's behaviors, aspirations, and likely career mobility are shaped by their access to "opportunity positions."

What about **research in your own setting**, where you work or where you live? While access to the site is automatic, since you are native to it, the following concerns are associated with such access: the expectations of the researcher based on familiarity with the setting and the people, the transition to researcher from a more familiar role within the setting, ethical and political dilemmas, the risk of uncovering potentially damaging knowledge, and struggles with closeness and closure (Alvesson, 2003). There are also positive aspects: relatively easy access to participants, reduced time expenditure for certain aspects of data collection, a feasible location for research, the potential to build trusting relationships, and, as Kanuha (2000) says, "being drawn to study 'my own kind'" (p. 441). Closeness to the people and the phenomenon through intense interactions provides subjective understandings that can greatly increase the quality of qualitative data (Toma, 2000). A realistic site is where (a) entry is possible; (b) there is a high probability that a rich mix of the processes, people, programs, interactions, and structures of interest is present; (c) the researcher is likely to be able to build trusting relations with the participants in the study; (d) the study can be conducted and reported ethically; and (e) data quality and credibility of the study are reasonably assured. Although this ideal is seldom attained, the proposal nonetheless describes what makes the selection of a particular site especially sound. A site may be perfect for its representativeness and interest and for providing a range of examples of the phenomenon under study, but if the researcher cannot gain access to the site or to a range of groups and activities within it, the study cannot succeed. Likewise, if the researcher is very uncomfortable or endangered in the site, or if the data gathering or the findings of the research would do harm, then that site will be full of risk and the research process will be hampered. Gaining access where the researcher was previously employed creates advantages and disadvantages. The problem of access should be less difficult and the researcher should easily be able to establish **rapport** with the participants—the researcher can pass as a colleague and the interconnectedness between the researcher and the participants can contribute to a mutual understanding that can lead to more accurate interpretations (Yeh & Inman, 2007). Disadvantages include researcher bias and subjectivity and the inability to separate one's self from the research.

Entry Letters and Scripts

Asking someone, "May I watch you?" or "May I interview you?" is actually very difficult! Getting permission to ask people to open up to a researcher or to enter a setting to collect data often requires approaching the organization's gatekeepers, either in a letter, through e-mail, or by phone. When asking, the request should include the elements of who, what, when, where, and why, as well as what will be gained and what specifically is requested. Table 5.2 shows one e-mail example.

Recipients of this e-mail get a sense of whether they are right for the study and whether the benefits outweigh any discomfort if they participate. E-mail requests are cheap and simple but quite impersonal and so very easy to delete! More personalized requests will have larger and more committed responses from potential participants.

Table 5.2 An Example of an E-Mail Entry Letter

Do you suffer from a premenstrual mood disorder?
If you suffer during the week before menstruation from depression, anxiety, irritability, or mood swings, and these symptoms interfere with normal functioning or interpersonal relationships, then you may have severe premenstrual syndrome (PMS) and qualify for research studies conducted in the XXX University Center for Women's Health (researcher's name and credentials).
WE NEED WOMEN WHO
1. have mood symptoms only premenstrually but not after the onset of menstruation;
2. are medically healthy and not currently suffering from some other chronic psychiatric condition;
3. are 18–50 years of age with regular menstrual cycles; and
4. are not taking any medications, including antidepressants and birth control pills.
You may qualify for research studies that give you diagnostic feedback on your symptoms and medical evaluations. You may also qualify for treatment studies and studies providing up to $420 in compensation. If you would like to participate, call Trudy (phone number).

Large organizations may have review boards that will require much more information and even legal reviews of researchers' requests. Whether the gatekeepers are school superintendents or gang leaders, research cannot proceed without a good letter or script, prepared carefully to anticipate any hesitations or concerns. Writing a draft of such a script or letter helps researchers clarify their next steps. Later, this chapter addresses entry and role in greater depth.

What Site and How Many Sites?

One cannot study the universe—everything, every place, all the time. Instead, the researcher makes selections of sites and samples of times, places, people, and things to study. When the focus of the study is a particular population, the researcher should present a strategy for sampling that population. For example, in her study of forced terminations of psychotherapy, Kahn's (1992) strategy was to post notices in local communities asking for participants. Much discussion ensued at her proposal hearing about the feasibility of this strategy. Given assurances about the soliciting of participants using this method previously, the committee agreed; the strategy was ultimately successful.

Sample size in qualitative research depends on many complex factors. Case studies may be of a single person, like the classic *The Man in the Principal's Office* (Wolcott, 1973), or of one organization, as in Kanter's *Men and Women of the Corporation* (1977), where a typical or representative example was selected for long-term participant observation. Sampling over time in the same site reveals roles, interactions, and sentiments, for example, in a bar, as in *The Cocktail Waitress* (Spradley & Mann, 1975), and reveals much more than just that particular site. In health research (which is likely to be well funded), recent qualitative case studies and mixed-methods studies averaged one to four informants. Ten groups was the average in focus groups; 16 to 24 months of fieldwork was the norm in observational studies (Safman & Sobal, 2004). *Ambiguous Empowerment: The Work Narratives of Women School Superintendents* (Chase, 1995) is based on 92 tape-recorded interviews with policymakers, selection consultants, school board members, and superintendents, as well as observations in work settings.

While funding and time constraints affect sample size, the weightier concerns center on the question of research purpose. An unknown culture or profession studied in depth over time may be composed of one case study or ethnography. A study of new mothers' receptivity to training for breast-feeding could have a huge sample, in a vast array of settings and diversity of population, with good funding and a large research team. A small sample would be useful as thick cultural description. A large sample in disparate and varied settings with diverse participants would also be seen as more useful, since the ease of transferability would be enhanced.

In the proposal, the researcher should anticipate questions about the credibility and trustworthiness of the findings; poor sampling design decisions may threaten these findings. To justify a sample, one should know the universe of the possible population and its variability and then sample according to all of the relevant variables. Since this is an impossible task, the best compromise is to include a sample with reasonable variation in the phenomenon, settings, or people (Dobbert, 1982).

Long ago, scholars in community studies dealt with sampling issues. When the famous Yankee City study seemed to demand a parallel study of the Deep South, Warner (reported by Gardner in Whyte, 1984) pondered identifying a city representative of the Deep South. After selecting several cities that fit the criteria of size and history, he met with leaders and established contacts in the communities, eventually selecting Natchez, Mississippi, as the site for *Deep South: A Social Anthropological Study of Caste and Class* (Davis, Gardner, & Gardner, 1941). Natchez would work for negotiating access to various levels of the caste system. The use of two wife-husband teams, one black and one white, also eased access. Because they were all raised in the South and familiar with appropriate behavior within the caste system, they could observe, interview, and participate in activities, interactions, and sentiments representing all levels of the Natchez community.

The reports demonstrated that Natchez, although not exactly like all other southern communities, was not atypical. Setting abstract criteria, checking out sites in advance, and carefully planning entry ensured that (a) the research team could move throughout the community to gather data and (b) Natchez was not an unrepresentative pocket of the research universe. Researchers had identified the site that would maximize comparability and permit access to a wide range of behaviors and perspectives. Clearly, the selection of site and sample are critical decisions.

In another community study, of "Elmtown," a typical midwestern community, the ease of establishing contacts with civic leaders enabled the team to act as full members of the community. They then gained access to parents and institutional functionaries through their interest in adolescent character development. This interest brought them invitations to speak before a variety of community organizations, resulting in additional contacts. They spent a considerable amount of time in informal settings with young people as well. They were at a high school before classes started, at noon, and after school; they attended most school activities, church affairs, Scout meetings, dances, and parties; and they skated, bowled, shot pool, played poker, and generally "hung out" where youth were known to gather. "The observational technique of being with them as often as possible and not criticizing their activities, carrying tales, or interfering overcame the initial suspicion in a few weeks" (Hollingshead, 1975, p. 15). The researchers' ability to gain access to a range of groups and activities was enhanced by their ability to blend in. Site and sample selection should be planned around practical issues, such as the researcher's comfort level, ability to fit into some role during participant observation, and access to a range of subgroups and activities. In some proposals, particularly those for multisite studies conducted with several researchers or for studies of organizations, it is wise to make even finer-grained decisions about sampling. This is discussed next.

SELECTING A SAMPLE OF PEOPLE, ACTIONS, EVENTS, AND/OR PROCESSES

Once the initial decision has been made to focus on a specific site, a population, or a phenomenon, waves of subsequent sampling decisions are made. The proposal describes the plan, as conceived before the research begins, that will guide sample selection, the researcher being always mindful of the need to retain flexibility. As Denzin (1989) says, "All sampling activities are theoretically informed" (p. 73). Thus, the sensitizing concepts from the literature review and the research questions provide the focus for site and sample selection; if they do not, the researcher at the very least makes the procedures and criteria for decision making explicit.

Sampling Within a Population and Focusing Within a Site

Well-developed sampling decisions are crucial for any study's soundness. Making logical judgments and presenting a rationale for these decisions go far in building the overall case for a proposed study. Decisions about sampling people and events are made concurrently with decisions about the specific data collection methods to be used and should be thought through in advance. (Chapters 6 and 7 will provide an array of choices for data collection.) When faced, for example, with the complexity of studying the meaning that women managers attach to computer-mediated communications, Alvarez (1993) had to decide what individuals and events would be most salient for her study and, at the same time, decide what her data might be and the various ways she might collect the data.

VIGNETTE 9 Focusing on People and Events

The general question guiding Alvarez's (1993) study was in what ways computer-mediated communications, specifically electronic mail, alter human communications within an organizational context. She was interested in the power equalization potential of e-mail communications among persons of unequal status within the organization and in the socioemotional content of messages sent and received in a medium of reduced social cues.

The sampling strategy began as a search for information-rich cases (Patton, 1990) to study individuals who manifested the phenomenon intensely. A related concern was to have both men and women participants in the study, given that the theoretical literature suggested that there are significant differences between men and women in ease of computer usage. Once she had identified participants and they had agreed to engage in the study with her, Alvarez had to make decisions about which specific events she wanted to observe or learn more about. She reasoned that observing the sending or receiving of a message would yield little; she therefore asked participants to share sets of correspondence with her and to participate in two in-depth interviews. The first request proved quite sensitive because Alvarez was asking people to share their personal and professional mail with her. She reassured them of the confidentiality of the study and also showed them how to send copies of e-mail directly to her without revealing the direct recipient of the message. This reassured them sufficiently so that she was able to obtain a substantial set of messages that could then be content analyzed.

Logical and Systematic Sampling

Often, at the most exploratory phases of research, the sampling strategies can only be guessed. As mentioned earlier in this chapter, Geer demonstrated that, in the first days in the field, one does not know enough about the site, the people, the behaviors, the rhythms, or even the most interesting research focus. Then, the research design section is full of "**it depends** on . . ." and assertions of the need to maintain flexibility. When pressed, research designers provide best guesses of the locations where data will be collected, the duration and intensity of the study, and the data collection devices to be used.

However, once the research becomes more focused on particular sites, populations and questions, it becomes possible and important to collect data according to a logical and systematic schema. The research project's final credibility and transferability will be greatly enhanced if future readers can read, in the research report, an account of the sites and sampling procedures (more on this in Chapters 9 and 10). Also, in designing studies with multiple sites, with a team of researchers, or with both, plans for systematic sampling are crucial. Researchers who follow an agreed-on schema for collecting data can then increase the likelihood that, for example, when comparing observations from many sites or interviews with many people, their comparisons are logical. Miles and Huberman (1994) provide excellent examples of schemas and guidance for such planning. Vignette 10 and Table 5.3 illustrate a sound **multisite sampling** plan in a study involving more than one researcher. This plan is taken from a study of high school cultures (Rossman, Corbett, & Firestone, 1984) and depicts extensive thinking, first about the themes derived from the literature that focused the research that the researchers would have to consider. Then the plan directs researchers to the places, circumstances, and people.

VIGNETTE 10 Sampling People and Behaviors

To plan for the study, the researchers identified those events, settings, actors, and artifacts that would have the greatest potential to yield good data on each of five cultural domains: collegiality, community, goals and expectations, action orientation, and knowledge base for teaching. These cultural domains were derived from their literature review, thus framing the kinds of behaviors, interactions, and events they needed to view in naturalistic settings. Items within each category provided parameters to frame data collection. The researchers believed that this framing would yield observations of, for example, collegiality or community, where evidence of collegiality or community existed, and what it looked like in different settings. This framing allowed systematic sampling of behaviors. The researchers started with settings because these were the most concrete, as they were collecting data in public places (the main office, hallways, the parking lot), the teachers' lounge or lunchroom, classrooms, meeting rooms, private offices, department offices or workrooms, the gymnasium or locker room, and the auditorium.

In the disciplinarian's office, they expected the handling of routine infractions, suspensions, or expulsions; in the counselor's office, there might be crisis interventions. In general, the researchers expected that the events of importance would include those during which professionals interacted. These would include formal routines such as faculty and department meetings, evaluations, and union meetings; informal routines such as lunch or coffee breaks, preparation periods, recess, and morning arrivals; and events during which professionals interacted with students, including teaching acts, extracurricular activities, suspensions and expulsions, roster changes, crisis counseling, postsecondary counseling, and assemblies and pep rallies.

The first category—events during which professionals interact—would provide major data on collegiality, goals and expectations, and the knowledge base for teaching. Faculty and department meetings would be crucial. In these meetings, norms governing the local definition of teaching and norms regarding how teachers should relate to one another in a meeting setting would be evident. Morning routines and other informal encounters—requests for help, supportive gestures, queries about how a particular concept or skill is best taught—would also reveal these norms and reflect notions of collegiality but in less structured settings.

The second category—events during which professionals and students interact—would provide data about community, goals and expectations, and action orientation. Both in the classroom and outside it, when teachers and students interacted, they would reveal whether or not there was a sense of community, what their expectations were for one another regarding behavior and achievement, and whether teachers felt it was important to translate ideas and concepts into actions, such as lesson and courses.

As data collection progressed, the researchers planned to sample the perceptions of key actors both within and external to the school. Finally, the researchers planned to collect or to be able to describe certain artifacts that would provide data for each of the five domains. In the above plan, the emphasis was on observation, because many of the domains the researchers were trying to understand were implicit. Thus, they inferred norms and values from behavior patterns and from naturally occurring conversations. Interviews helped them understand the settings and reconstruct the history of change in the high schools.

Data Collection: Sampling Plan

The sampling plan shown in Vignette 10 and Table 5.3 tried to ensure that events, rituals, resources, and interactions would be observed at each site. Purposive and theoretical sampling, which is guided by the theoretical framework and concepts, is often built into qualitative designs. For example, research on professional cultures would suggest that the researcher should sample among individuals, events, and sentiments in the early stages of initiation into a profession. Often, however, researchers' site selection and sampling begin with accessible sites (convenience sampling) and build on insights and connections from the early data collection (snowball sampling).

Miles and Huberman (1994) usefully describe different approaches to sampling in Table 5.4. Although such plans are often subject to change, given the realities of field research, at the proposal stage, the wise researcher has thought through some of the complexities of the setting and has made some initial judgments about how to deploy his time. The researcher can assert, for example, that his initial sampling will be "maximum variation" when he is trying to see the variety of behaviors or types of people but that he will then proceed to "stratified purposeful" sampling once enough data have been analyzed to identify subgroups. Or the researcher may start with "theory-based" sampling (e.g., social justice leadership theory directs the researcher to interview two

(Text continued on p. 112)

Table 5.3 Data Collection: Sampling Plan

	Collegiality	Community	Goals and expectations	Action orientation	Knowledge base
Setting					
Public places (main offices, hallways)	X	X	X	X	X
Teachers' lounge or lunchroom	X	X			X
Classrooms		X	X	X	X
Meeting rooms	X		X	X	
Private offices					
Counselor's		X	X		
Disciplinarian's		X	X		
Vice principal's for scheduling			X		
Coaches'		X	X		
Principal's			X		
Department office or workroom	X		X	X	X
Gymnasium or locker room		X	X		
Auditorium		X			
Events					
Events during which professionals interact					
Faculty/department meetings	X		X		X
Lunch/coffee break/recess	X	X			X
In-service sessions	X				X
After school (local pub?)	X	X			

	Collegiality	Community	Goals and expectations	Action orientation	Knowledge base
Events during which professionals and students interact					
Teaching acts		X	X	X	X
Extracurricular activities		X	X	X	
Suspensions and expulsions		X	X	X	
Roster changes		X	X	X	
Crisis counseling		X	X	X	
Assemblies and pep rallies		X	X	X	
Actors					
Administrators					
Principal			X	X	X
Vice principal for discipline		X	X		
Vice principal for curriculum	X		X	X	X
Vice principal for schedule/roster		X	X	X	
Vice principal for activities					
Counselors		X	X	X	
Coaches		X	X	X	
Teachers					
Department heads	X	X	X	X	X
Different tenure in building	X	X	X	X	X
Different departments	X	X	X	X	X

(Continued)

Table 5.3 (Continued)

	Collegiality	Community	Goals and expectations	Action orientation	Knowledge base
Students					
Different ability levels		X	X	X	
Different visibility		X	X	X	
Artifacts					
Documents					
Newspapers		X	X		X
Policy statements			X	X	X
Attendance records		X	X		
Disciplinary records		X	X		
Achievement test scores			X		
Objects					
Logos	X	X			
Mascots	X	X			
Trophies			X		
Decorations		X			
Art work		X			
Physical arrangements	X	X			

SOURCE: Rossman, Corbett, and Firestone (1984, p. 54). Reprinted by permission.

Table 5.4 Typology of Sampling Strategies in Qualitative Inquiry

Type of Sampling	Purpose
Maximum variation	Documents diverse variations and identifies important common patterns
Homogeneous	Focuses, reduces, simplifies, facilitates group interviewing
Critical case	Permits logical generalization and maximum application of information to other cases
Theory based	Finds examples of a theoretical construct and thereby elaborates and examines it
Confirming and disconfirming cases	Elaborates initial analysis, seeks exceptions, looks for variation
Snowball or chain	Identifies cases of interest from people who know people who know what cases are information rich
Extreme or deviant case	Learns from highly unusual manifestations of the phenomenon of interest
Typical case	Highlights what is normal or average
Intensity	Involves information-rich cases that manifest the phenomenon intensely, but not extremely
Politically important cases	Attracts desired attention or avoids attracting undesired attention
Random purposeful	Adds credibility to the sample when the potential purposeful sample is too large
Stratified purposeful	Illustrates subgroups, facilitates comparison
Criterion	Includes all cases that meet some criterion, useful for quality assurance
Opportunistic	Follows new leads, takes advantage of the unexpected
Combination or mixed	Involves triangulation and flexibility, meets multiple interests and needs
Convenience	Saves time, money, and effort but at the expense of information and credibility

SOURCE: Miles and Huberman (1994, p. 28). Reprinted by permission.

people who fit) and then proceed to "snowball," sampling by seeking interviews with people suggested from those first two interviews. Such plans also indicate that the researcher has considered both the informational adequacy and the efficiency of these methods. Related to these considerations, however, are the ethical issues of the researcher's role with participants.

THE RESEARCHER'S ROLE: ISSUES OF ENTRY, RAPPORT, RECIPROCITY, PERSONAL BIOGRAPHY, AND ETHICS

In qualitative studies, the **researcher is the instrument**. Her presence in the lives of the participants invited to be part of the study is fundamental to the methodology. As mentioned in Chapters 1 and 2, the genre in which a study is situated may include postmodern or more traditional assumptions affecting the researcher's role and position. A more traditional qualitative researcher learns from participants' lives but maintains a stance of "empathic neutrality" (Patton, 2002, p. 49) to collect data and provide descriptive representations. Critical and postmodern genres, though, assume that all knowledge is political and that researchers are not neutral, since their ultimate purposes include advocacy and action.

Whether the presence of the researcher in the setting is sustained and intensive, as in long-term ethnographies, or relatively brief but personal, as in in-depth interview studies, the researcher enters the lives of the participants. Even the brief interview disrupts participants' daily routines. For qualitative research designs, then, this brings a range of strategic, ethical, and personal issues that do not attend quantitative approaches (Locke, Spirduso, & Silverman, 2000). The research proposal should include an extensive discussion of a plan for dealing with issues before they present dilemmas and also as they may arise in unanticipated ways in the field, using the advice and experience of previous scholars. The issues range from technical ones that address entry and efficiency in terms of role to interpersonal ones that capture the ethical and personal dilemmas that arise during the conduct of a study. Clearly, the considerations overlap and have reciprocal implications. For clarity, however, we address each set of issues in turn, and we recommend that proposal writers do the same.

Technical Considerations

At the proposal stage, technical considerations include decisions about the deployment of the researcher's time and other resources and about negotiating access.

Situating the Self

Patton (2002) develops a series of continua for thinking about one's role in planning the conduct of qualitative research. This section relies on that work considerably. First, the researcher may plan to have a role that entails varying degrees of **participantness**—that is, the degree of actual participation in daily life. At one extreme is the full participant, who goes about ordinary life in a role or set of roles constructed in the setting. At the other is the complete observer, who does not engage in social interaction and may even shun involvement in the world being studied. Of course, all possible complementary mixes of these roles along the continuum are available to the researcher. Our experience is that some sort of direct and immediate participation in the research environment usually becomes important to building and sustaining relationships. The researcher may help out with small chores (or large ones), learn more about a particular activity (and hence enter into that activity), or feel compelled to engage in daily activities to meet the demands of reciprocity. Such interaction is usually highly informative while remaining informal. Patton (2002) develops a series of continua for thinking about one's role in planning the conduct of qualitative research. Researchers should consider their degree of participantness.

Next, the researcher's role may vary as to its **revealedness**, or the extent to which the participants know that there is a study going on. Full disclosure lies at one end of this continuum, complete secrecy at the other. Patton (2002) advises "full and complete disclosure. People are seldom deceived or reassured by false or partial explanations—at least not for long" (p. 273). Still, revealing exact purposes tends to cue people to behave in unnatural ways, undermining qualitative purposes and principles. The researcher should discuss in the proposal the issues concerning revealing or concealing the purpose of the study and lay out a plan for making decisions. Those decisions are about initial entry, that is, getting permission to observe and collect data in a setting. But they are also decisions for later stages, as when people ask questions such as "Are you finding out about such and such scandal?" or "How much do you want to know about the other things you didn't ask me?"

The ethical issues surrounding covert research can be reduced to one fundamental question: Is the potential advancement of knowledge worth deceit? (See Taylor & Bogdan, 1984, Chap. 3, for a provocative discussion.) Many researchers follow Taylor and Bogdan's advice to be "truthful but vague" (p. 25) in portraying a research purpose to participants. The researcher should discuss in the proposal the issues concerning revealing or concealing the purpose of the study.

Third, the dimensions of a researcher's **role intensiveness** and **extensiveness** may vary—that is, the amount of time spent daily in the setting and the duration of the study. Various positions on both dimensions demand certain role considerations by the researcher. For example, an intensive and extensive study requires the researcher to devote considerable time early on to developing trusting relations with the participants. Gathering pertinent data is secondary at that point. On the other hand, when the researcher will be minimally intrusive and present for a short period of time, he will need to practice and find ways to quickly build bridges and create trusting relations, since this mostly occurs in the first minutes of an interview and is crucial for gathering good data. In our view, this is especially difficult for novice (or shy) researchers.

Finally, the researcher's role may vary depending on whether the focus of the study is specific or diffuse. When the research questions are well developed beforehand and data appropriate to address those questions have been identified, the researcher's role can be managed efficiently and carefully to ensure good use of the available time (both the researcher's and the participants'). Even when well specified, however, sound qualitative design protects the researcher's right to follow the compelling question, the nagging puzzle that presents itself once in the setting. When the research questions are more diffuse and exploratory, the plan for deploying the self should ensure access to a number of events, people, and perspectives on the social phenomenon chosen for study. We emphasize this, too: Leave yourself time and role flexibility to follow serendipitous leads (whether in an interview planned for 20 minutes but needing two hours or a setting planned for one day and ending up being a one-year-long study!)

Fortunately, some researchers who have used participant observation have provided extensive descriptions of their plans, rationales, and actual experiences. Notable among these are researchers who have engaged in significant reflection on the research endeavor and their lives as researchers. References to these works are listed under "Personal Reflections" at the end of this chapter.

Negotiating Entry, Easing Tensions, and Role Maintenance

The research design section of a proposal should contain plans for negotiating access to the site and/or participants through formal and informal gatekeepers in an organization, whether the organization is an urban gang or an Ivy League university. We recommend that, rather than trying to be inauthentic by adopting a contrived role, qualitative researchers be themselves, true to their social identities and their interests in the setting and/or topic. The energy that comes from a researcher's high level of personal interest (called bias in traditional research) is infectious and quite useful for gaining access. Entry, access, and role will be a continuous challenge when the researcher moves around in various settings within an organization. The researcher should reveal sensitivity to participants' testing of her and their reluctance to participate, unquestionably respecting their right not to participate in a study. Excellent discussions of access issues can be found in the general texts about qualitative research referenced at the end of this chapter. Of particular interest is Anderson's (1976) experience in becoming accepted for an ethnographic study of an urban cultural group, detailed in Vignette 11.

VIGNETTE 11 Negotiating Entry

A bleak corner of urban life. A bar and liquor store named Jelly's that also serves as a hangout for African American men in south Chicago. In such a place, an angry man pulls a knife on another, a wino sleeps off his last bottle, police cars cruise without stopping, all within the sight of children at play. Jelly's and its countless urban counterparts "provide settings for sociability and places where neighborhood residents can gain a sense of self-worth" (Anderson, 1976, p. 1).

Anderson determined that he was going to study this particular setting, but how was he to gain entry? His first observations indicated that "visitors" received special treatment, because the next person might prove to be "the police," "the baddest cat in Chicago," or someone waiting to follow another home and rip him off. In the words of the regular clientele at Jelly's, "unknown people bear watching" (p. 5).

Anderson accepted visitor treatment for several weeks, being unobtrusive yet sociable, acquainting himself with the unwritten social rules. Being African American was insufficient justification for immediate acceptance by the regulars. Enter Herman. Anderson cultivated a relationship with Herman that became a means for mutual protection of each other's "rep and rank" in the social status system at Jelly's. Anderson responded openly to Herman's persistent questioning, and several days later, Herman reciprocated by introducing Anderson to Sleepy, TJ, and Jake: "He all right. Hey this is the study I been tellin' you about. This cat getting his doctor's degree." With this introduction to the regulars, Anderson's place in the social system had been defined. In short, it provided Anderson with a license to be around. Herman used Anderson to gain credibility at his on-the-job Christmas party, introducing Anderson as a "cousin" and getting him to tell the regulars at Jelly's how well Herman got along with "decent folks and intelligent folks" (p. 20).

Anderson's role evolved naturally from the low-key, nonassertive role he initially assumed to prevent unwieldy challenges from those who might have felt threatened by a more aggressive demeanor, especially from a stranger. It is the kind of role any outsider must play—is forced into—if he is not to disrupt the "consensual definition of social order in this type of setting" (pp. 22–23).

Anderson's experience is typical of those proposing long-term ethnographic studies of particular groups. At times, the best entry is one, like this one, where there is an insider who provides sponsorship and helps the researcher seem nonthreatening. There are circumstances, however, when sponsorship can backfire, setting the researcher up for difficulties in accessing other groups within the organization. For those conducting studies of organizations, negotiating access may require perseverance and persistence with formal leaders within the organization, as Vignette 12 depicts.

VIGNETTE 12 Negotiating and Maintaining Access With a Transient, Vulnerable Population

A study of socially marginalized women (former crack cocaine users and sex workers who became politically active after contracting HIV/AIDS) required great sensitivity on the part of the researcher. Berger (2003) found that negotiating **access to such a vulnerable population** required conversations with people in agencies such as homeless shelters, courthouses, the Department of Health, and substance abuse facilities. Gatekeepers in these agencies didn't always agree readily to participate in the study. They were often protective of their clientele (as well they should be) and of their own views of the relevant issues. Thus, when Berger spoke of her desire to understand the complexities of drug-related behaviors and of the lives of sex workers, the gatekeepers were reluctant to cooperate. Their expressed views were that drugs explain most of the women's behaviors and that prostitution is dangerous and degrading. To them, learning about the subtleties and complexities of this social world had no immediate use. Although they were accustomed to survey research, they simply could not see the value (to them) of long hours of oral histories. Yet these gatekeepers' assistance was essential. What was Berger to do?

With a new approach and a new set of gatekeepers, Berger introduced her study thus: Eliciting the women's stories would confirm what the gatekeepers knew about the challenging lives of these women, who frequently felt victimized by larger social structures and often felt at the mercy of their drug addiction. As she recounts, "A hook is better when it is short and simple . . . it's helpful to try to categorize the type of rejection . . . [and to] plan ahead to counter or redirect assumptions" (p. 67).

Although they still regarded Berger as quite strange, the gatekeepers eventually perceived her as a "nice black girl" (p. 67) who reminded them of some distant cousin. This fictive kin status served well, so she began to purposefully incorporate the naive fictive kin performance to maintain access, to encourage participants to help her get the record straight and help her tell outsiders how their real stories differed from televised stereotypes.

Tensions do arise whether researchers are involved over the long term or the short term. We recommend that researchers anticipate such tensions and plan strategies for preventing or easing them if they arise from relationships with research participants. A few anthropologists have written amusing accounts of how they muddled through such tensions. A carefully guarded bottle of gin and planned retreats to the city helped Bowen (1964) maintain some status and stability as she dealt with mamba snakes in the outhouse and resistance of the chiefs to her presence in a village in West Africa. And Paul Rabinow's (1977) descriptions of maintaining access, within the intertwinings of marital traditions, linage, rank, and rituals he encountered in Moroccan culture, are probably quite informative for the researcher planning participant observation in any complex cultural setting.

Researchers need to devise strategies to maintain themselves (remember that the researcher is the research instrument). Research designs should include strategies to protect the physical and emotional health and safety of the researcher by providing plans for quiet places in which he can write notes, reassess roles, retreat from the setting, or question the directions of the research. Several strategies for dealing with sometimes overwhelming emotional involvement include journal writing, peer debriefing, and personal counseling, as these are ways to maintain balance when data collection "can break your heart" (Rager, 2005, p. 23). In some settings, the researcher's planning may go well beyond considerations of comfort and stress relief. In "street ethnography" one must set up plans to stay safe. Unfamiliar settings where strangers are unwelcome, where illegal activities may be observed, or where the researcher's race or gender makes her unwelcome require careful sensitivities (Lee, 1995; Warren, 2001). In anticipating such potential difficulties, proposals should cite the experiences of previous researchers and apply them to the current research to think through role strategies; some excellent sources are provided at the end of this chapter.

Gaining access to sites—receiving formal approval, like Herman's sponsorship or a principal's approval—requires time, patience, and sensitivity to the rhythms and norms of a group. At the proposal stage, the researcher should, at least, have a draft **entry letter** or script or, even better, demonstrate that negotiations have begun and formal approval is likely and that she has knowledge about the nuances of entry and a healthy respect for participants' likely concerns.

Efficiency

In qualitative studies, the researcher should think through how he will deploy the resources available for the study to ensure full responses to the research questions. Although this consideration overlaps directly with decisions about data gathering, issues of role also arise here. The researcher should think carefully about how he can deploy the self, as it were, to maximize the opportunities for gathering data. This consideration should be balanced against the resources available for the study—most notably, time and energy. One should design the study to be reasonable in size and complexity so that it can be completed with the time and resources available (Bogdan & Biklen, 2007, p. 51). In other words, one makes judgment calls. Researchers who are not well versed in qualitative traditions put aside three months and naively assert that they will conduct 10 one-hour interviews, collect some documents, analyze and write, and then finish. Such a proposal should not be approved, for oh so many reasons!

On the other hand, we caution the novice to create some boundaries. Once a study is begun, tantalizing puzzles and intriguing questions mushroom. Even though the researcher reserves the right to pursue them, she should remain mindful of the goal of the project. Doctoral students often need to be gently prodded back into a structure for the completion of the work. A priori but tentative statements about boundaries will help: A discussion of goals and limitations (e.g., five life histories; observations in one school for one year) and reminders of practical considerations (e.g., dwindling funds, the need to get a "real" job) serve as reminders that the research must be finite. In Chapters 9 and 10, we will also discuss the techniques for making sure that data collection and analysis go hand in hand and that the researcher knows how to progress with data analysis in ways that support the final report. One should design the study to be "reasonable in size and complexity so that it can be completed with the time and resources available" (Bogdan & Biklen, 2007, p. 51).

Interpersonal Considerations

One could argue that the success of qualitative studies depends primarily on the interpersonal skills of the researcher. In general qualitative research texts, this caveat is often couched as building **trust**, maintaining good relations, respecting norms of reciprocity, and sensitively considering ethical issues. These entail an awareness of the politics of organizations as well as sensitivity to human interaction. Because the conduct of the study often depends exclusively on the relationships the researcher builds with participants, interpersonal skills are paramount. We would go so far as to dissuade a would-be qualitative researcher from using a qualitative approach if he cannot converse easily with others—being an active, patient, and thoughtful listener and having an empathetic understanding of and a profound respect for the perspectives of others. Researchers can lose great opportunities for data if they feel compelled to fill in silences, offer their own opinions, or show off how much they know. It is important to acknowledge that it is difficult for some people to become good qualitative researchers, despite sensitive and thoughtful training in courses and through pilot studies.

Furthermore, some of the traditions of social science create a kind of **academic armor** that prevents the intimate emotional engagement often required in qualitative research (Lerum, 2001). The use of obscure academic language (linguistic armor), professional clothing and demeanor (physical armor), assumptions of theoretical privilege (ideological armor), and the effort to avoid "going native" (to be objective and detached), all create this academic armor. Dropping the academic armor allows richer, more intimate acceptance into the ongoing lives and sentiments of participants; it is a visceral way of moving beyond seeing to understanding (Denzin, 1997). In his study of college football, Toma (2000) found that in the give-and-take of interviews, **rapport** helped participants see new and deeper meanings as they responded to him. Closeness, engagement, and involvement can enhance the richness of the research.

Still, the researcher needs protection at times. Researchers planning their roles and their degree of engagement—whether for research on sex workers, on snake handlers, or on professions where sexual harassment is allowed—will want to plan for some deployment of academic armor at times (Lerum, 2001). Researchers' respect and caring for participants can, if unguarded, go so far that they lose their ability to separate from personal entanglements (Wolcott, 2002). (We discuss this notion of having an **exit strategy** later in the chapter.)

In the research design section, discussions of one's role in the setting and consideration of how participants' willingness to engage in thoughtful reflection may be affected help provide evidence that the researcher knows enough about the setting and the people, their routines, and their environments to anticipate how she will fit in. Researchers benefit from carefully thinking through their own roles, because most participants detect and reject insincere, inauthentic people.

In addition, research designs may need plans to educate the participants about the researcher's role. Participants may be uneasy about their presence, may see them as spies or evaluators or new volunteer help! Researchers should prepare to describe their likely activities while in the setting, what they are interested in learning about, the possible uses of the information, and how the participants can engage in the research. Norms of reciprocity suggest that the researcher cannot be simply a spongelike observer in some settings. For example, Thorne (1983) describes in compelling detail, in her reflections on studying war resistance in the 1960s, how many people will not respond to or trust someone who will not take a stand. Providing further illustration of these ideas, Vignette 13 describes how Rosalie Wax (1971) went about the complex task of building trust in her study of Native Americans.

VIGNETTE 13 Building Trust

The extensive writing of anthropologist Rosalie Wax (1971) has emphasized the importance of the researcher's initial contacts with members of the society or group chosen for study. The reciprocal relationship between host and field worker enables the latter to avoid foolish, insulting, and potentially dangerous behavior; to make valuable contacts; and to understand the acceptance and repayment of obligations. "The most egregious error that a field-worker can commit," according to Wax (p. 47), is assuming that tolerance by hosts also implies their high regard and inclusion.

In her ethnographic community study of Native American reservation society, Wax found the women embarrassed and hesitant to open their poor, bare homes to the scrutiny of a researcher. Their trust and cooperation were essential to her study because Wax sought to understand the relationship between cultural patterns expressed in the home and poor adjustment and underachievement by the children at school. In her account of the slow uncovering of answers, Wax reveals her method of making others comfortable with her presence. She permitted children to play with her typewriter. She employed some of the women as interviewers. Avoiding the social worker or Bureau-of-Indian-Affairs do-gooder image, Wax interacted as woman to woman, always exploring but doing so with an interest in the welfare of the women's children.

Vignette 13 demonstrates that researchers should allow time and be sensitive to the need for time to pass, for flexibility in their roles, and for patience, because confidence and trust emerge over time through complex interactions. Roles and relationships do emerge in the field. At the proposal stage, however, the researcher should demonstrate a logical plan that respects the need for time to build relationships. It is not enough to throw in a statement asserting that trust and relationships are important. The researcher should also display the skills and sensitivities to deal with complexities in the relationships that will inevitably emerge during his fieldwork.

Moving on to another site is another way to manage—politically and ethically—a difficult situation: There are times when, even with the best planning, the researcher cannot gain entry to a site, as Vignette 14 shows.

VIGNETTE 14 Moving On

Wanting to explore the interaction between the political demands of a community and access to leadership in a school district by women and people of color, Marshall (1992) designed comparative case studies and identified two sites—two cities in the same region of the country with similar political cultures, demographic composition, and comparatively large numbers of women and people of color in leadership positions. The sites were chosen for comparability along those dimensions but with one significant difference: "Change City" showed evidence of a political structure undergoing substantial change, whereas "Avondale" represented a more placid political climate.

At Avondale, Marshall encountered no more than the typical bureaucratic barriers to gaining access: letters to gatekeepers, meetings with district research directors, assurances of compliance with district monitoring of the research. Pleased with this response, she began the access process in Change City by subscribing to the local newspaper to learn about local politics and by placing phone calls to the superintendent, a newly hired African American man from another state. Weeks passed. Months passed. Her politely persistent calls resulted in a telephone relationship with the secretary! She devised other strategies: letters flattering to the superintendent, reassurances of the value of the research for the district, name-dropping, emphasizing the university letterhead in her written correspondence and the study's connection to a national center on school leadership. Still no response.

Searching for insights behind the scenes, Marshall learned that this new superintendent was extremely careful about controlling information as he dealt with an explosive dispute about resources, people of color in administrative positions, and political maneuvers to support incumbent white administrators. Intrigued, Marshall tried one last tactic: the "chance" meeting. With a little help from the superintendent's secretary, she got herself invited to a conference that the superintendent planned to attend and was able to engage him in conversation during a coffee break. In the context of conference-related talk, she mentioned casually that she hoped to talk with him about doing research in the district. Gracious, interested, and promising to talk at length at the next break, the superintendent appeared open. Much to Marshall's chagrin, however, his assistant apologized that the superintendent had been called back to the office to manage some emergency. Foiled again!

Marshall resumed the phone calls and letters, but the silence from his office was deafening. It was time to face facts. The political controversy about people of color in leadership positions—the very question that she wanted to study—was the tense and difficult issue that kept this superintendent from risking exposure in this political maelstrom. Marshall realized she should respect that and try to find another Change City.

Sometimes, sensitivities in one setting make entry, role, and ethics quite dilemma laden, so researchers should change the plan. At some point, they decide that the efforts to get around the barriers to entry are excessive, and they must respect the needs of key actors in the setting. With topics that are politicized and sensitive, the researcher should identify several potential sites so he can move to an alternative site with little delay if need be.

Reciprocity

A thorough research proposal also demonstrates the researcher's awareness of reciprocity issues. Qualitative studies intrude into settings as people adjust to the researcher's presence. People may be giving their time to be interviewed or to help the researcher understand group norms; the researcher should plan to reciprocate. When people adjust their priorities and routines to help the researcher, or even just tolerate the researcher's presence, they are giving of themselves. The researcher is indebted and should be sensitive to this. Reciprocity may entail giving time to help out, providing informal feedback, making coffee, being a good listener, or tutoring. Of course, reciprocity should fit within the constraints of research and personal ethics and of maintaining one's role as a researcher. Research design sections should include an array of possible tokens of appreciation: cookies, books, a gift card, an offer, perhaps, of an hour of leaf raking or babysitting. A word of caution: Think ahead about boundaries. Prior planning can ward off uncomfortable situations where the researcher is asked for an undeserved job recommendation letter or for a date.

Ethics

The qualities that make a successful qualitative researcher reveal themselves as an exquisite sensitivity to the ethical issues surrounding any moral act. As introduced in Chapter 3, ethical considerations are much more than just ensuring **informed consent** and protecting participants' anonymity. The research design anticipates the array of ethical challenges that will occur. As Lerum (2001) says, emotionally engaged researchers must continuously evaluate and construct their behavior. If anticipated ahead of entry into the field, especially addressing Chapter 3's Big E issues, then that emotional engagement is more manageable. When planned ahead, in the research design section, the challenges will be less dilemma laden in the field and may provide opportunities for ways of reasoning that may help negotiate such dilemmas when they do arise.

Several authors discuss ethical considerations in qualitative research, describing the dilemmas they have encountered. Role, reciprocity, and ethical issues must be thought through carefully in all settings but especially in those that are particularly sensitive or taboo. In developing the section of the proposal that addresses role and reciprocity issues, the qualitative researcher should draw on the advice and experience of her predecessors.

The competent research proposal, then, anticipates issues of negotiating entry, reciprocity, **role maintenance**, and receptivity and, at the same time, adheres to ethical principles. The researcher must demonstrate awareness of the complex ethical issues in qualitative research and show that the research is both feasible and ethical. If the researcher will be playing a deceptive role, he should demonstrate that this will not be harmful to the participants. If he will require people to change their routines or donate their time, doing so must be voluntary for them. What is routine and acceptable in one setting may be harmful in another; what is volunteered in one may be withheld in another. The researcher cannot anticipate everything, but he must reveal an awareness of, an appreciation for, and a commitment to ethical principles for research. Several authors have explored these issues in the general texts and articles referenced at the end of this chapter (especially in the "Personal, Political, and Ethical Dilemmas" section of the Further Reading list) as well as in the studies described in the following vignettes.

VIGNETTE 15 Ethics and Ethnographic Fieldwork

Ethnographic research has traditionally been undertaken in fields that, by virtue of the contrast between them and the researcher's own culture, could be described as exotic. The researcher's goal is to describe the symbols and values of such a culture without passing judgment based on his cultural context. Soloway and Walters (1977), however, point out that when a researcher studies those whose acts are considered criminal, profound ethical dilemmas arise: "When one decides to attempt to enter their world and to study it, the field-worker arrives at a true moral, ethical, and legal existential crisis" (p. 161).

One option is to carry out studies of criminal subcultures from within institutions such as prisons or treatment centers. Critical of such a procedure, Soloway and Walters note that "if addicts are studied at Lexington [a federal hospital], then the result is a study of patients. If addicts are studied in jail, the result is a study of prisoners" (p. 163).

To understand addiction, Soloway chose to enter the addicts' natural habitat. Entry was aided by his affiliation with a methadone treatment program and by the fact that he was doing his research within the neighborhood where he had spent his childhood. One of his contacts during observation of the weekly distribution of methadone was Mario, an old neighborhood friend and a patient at the treatment center.

Mario saw this relationship as a source of status both within the program and on the street. He chose to test this relationship at one point, coming in "high" for his weekly dose. When he was refused the methadone because of his condition, he sought out his friend the ethnographer to intercede with the nurses. Not only did the researcher refuse to intercede, he rebuked Mario, saying, "I'm no lame social worker from the suburbs; you're high and everybody knows it" (p. 165). Even though he risked jeopardizing the researcher-informant relationship, the risk paid off because Mario eventually introduced Soloway to other addicts. This involvement with urban heroin addicts enabled him to observe them in the context of their total social milieu, where junkie was only part of their identity.

Was Soloway taking advantage of his friendship with Mario? Is the participant observer a friend to participants? Can the researcher be both observer and friend? How does one juggle the objectivity of the stranger and the desire for the well-being of a friend? "The bind on the ethnographer's personal ethic," according to Soloway and Walters (1977), "is that his total integrity cannot be maintained in either role" (p. 166). What represents a researcher's ethical response when observing or possibly becoming involved in criminal activity? Polsky (1969) insists that to study adult criminals in their natural settings, one must "make the moral decision that in some ways he will break the law himself" (pp. 133–134). On the other hand, Yablonsky (1965) asserts that participant observation among the criminally deviant merely serves, by way of the researcher's interest in the subject, to reinforce the criminal behavior.

In the exchange with Mario, the researcher attempted to strike a balance by employing the principle of relativism. According to this principle, ethnographers are not expected to renounce their own culturally formed consciences, nor are they to project those values on their subjects. "Relativism operationally guards against two dangers, the ethnographer's own ethnocentrism and an equally dangerous inverted ethnocentrism—that is, going native and personally identifying with the studied value system" (Soloway & Walters, 1977, p. 168).

Manning (1972) recounted advising a student designing research on police. He noted that the student could walk the beat with the police officer, ride in the patrol car with the police officer, and even tag along when an arrest is about to be made. But he could not be a police officer, wear the uniform, take the risks, make the arrests, or adopt the police officer's perspective. How do researchers go about courting the cooperation of individuals whose social ecology is so very different from their own? Must researchers assume identities other than their own? According to Westley (1967), a critical norm among law enforcement personnel is the maintenance of secrecy:

> It is carefully taught to every rookie policeman. . . . The violator is cut off from vital sources of information and the protection of his colleagues in times of emergency. Secrecy means that policemen must not talk about police work to those outside the department. (p. 774)

Thus, he had to consider whether it is ethical to encourage police officers to talk about their work. He had to anticipate dilemmas if he should observe an incidence of police brutality. Complying with the law and turning the officer in would risk the destruction of the study. Remaining silent would gain the trust of those he was observing, along with some leverage. This student planned ahead, deciding to opt for the benefits of silence.

Not all qualitative studies present such extreme ethical dilemmas. It is, however, quite difficult to maintain the role of researcher when caught in the middle of events that seem to call for action. Researchers must anticipate more routine ethical issues and be prepared to make on-the-spot decisions that (one hopes) follow general ethical principles (see, especially, Christians, 2000, 2005; Punch, 1994; Welland & Pugsley, 2002). Reading other researchers' discussions of ethical problems and using case material to prepare for hypothetical situations can illuminate so-called standard ethical considerations and refine the researcher's abilities to reason through moral argument. Vignette 16 draws from the work of a Chicana ethnographer as she struggled with the challenges of conducting research to fulfill her own goals while respecting those with whom she had conducted the study. The political and ethical dilemmas she confronted were acute, as she found herself co-opted by the dominant Anglo leaders in the community where she conducted her research.

VIGNETTE 16 Ethics, Power, and Politics

In her work, Villenas (1996) describes being caught between her role as a Chicana ethnographer, the marginalized Latino community she studied, and the Anglo groups in power within the community. She examined the educational histories of Latina mothers who were recent immigrants in the small rural community of Hope City in North Carolina. She focused on telling the women's stories about how they created educational models for raising their children.

Villenas focused on how to overcome the Latino community's perception of her as a privileged ethnographer from an elite university. However, she found herself being co-opted by the dominant English-speaking community, who spoke of Latino family education and child-rearing practices as problematic and "lacking." By using and not challenging the language of the community leaders, she was complying with this negative representation.

Concerned about gaining access to community leaders, she censored herself when she spoke to the Anglo leaders and did not point out their racist language and demeaning depictions of the Latino community. In addition, the community leaders assumed that she shared their fear of poor persons and people of color and that she also saw the Latino community as a "problem." Because there were no Latinos/as in the community in leadership positions with whom Villenas could align herself, she became the sole Latina accepted by the community leaders. In this role, she was accepted as an insider in the Anglo community while, at the same time, being seen as an outsider by the Latino community.

To counter this co-opted role, she started "to engage in small subversive strategies and acts of resistance" (p. 725). For example, she used opportunities to speak at meetings to present a positive depiction of the Latino community and chose not to sit at the head table with the community leaders, sitting in the audience with friends she had made in the Latino community instead.

Vignette 16 shows that a researcher's role can be co-opted by people in positions of power. Although the intent of the research may be to show the positive aspects of a culture, it is easy for an inadequately self-reflexive researcher to be appropriated by and become complicit in the process by which marginalized groups are negatively depicted as a problem.

Potential dilemmas can be addressed at the proposal stage. For example, in a phenomenological study of gay, lesbian, and straight youth who participate in gay/straight alliances in high schools, Doppler (1998) described the issues involving ethics and human subjects in her study in some detail. To provide details of how to write about ethics, we include, below, excerpts from Doppler's proposal as well as her consent letter for students. Doppler's discussion of **informed consent** included the following:

> Because participants will be high school students, some of whom may be especially vulnerable because of being lesbian or gay or due to status as a heterosexual ally of lesbian and gay youth, it will be particularly important to protect them from any potential harm . . . Participants will have the opportunity to read transcripts of each interview in which they share their reactions and will be asked to modify the transcript.

Then Doppler's Appendix included the consent letter shown in Figure 5.3. (She constructed a similar informed consent letter to be signed by willing parents.)

Doppler's (1998) discussion of reciprocity included these reflections:

> [Participants] will have an opportunity to voice their experiences and feelings in a safe setting with someone who *will* validate the importance of their participation in a GSA [gay/straight alliance]. Lesbian or gay students may receive the greatest benefit because they will have an opportunity to voice feelings and thoughts about which they may usually remain silent. Also, interacting with a lesbian educator who is happy and well-adjusted to life as a lesbian can provide a positive role model. . . . On a cursory level, I will share power with participants by encouraging them to modify interview transcripts to make them fully accurate. Much more important is the power dispensed by providing opportunity for students to give voice to their experiences.

In the section titled "Right to Privacy," Doppler (1998) wrote,

> Pseudonyms will be used to protect the anonymity of participants. It is possible for this study, however, that some participants will want to have their names used as a rite of passage out of the closet. In that case, the implications of the use of actual names versus pseudonyms will be discussed with any participant who wants her or his name to be used. Participants will be promised every reasonable attempt to maintain confidentiality with the exception of self-reports of suicidality or abuse.

Doppler (1998) also included a section titled "Advocacy/Intervention," in which she wrote,

> I anticipate that ethical considerations around advocacy/intervention may create personal dilemmas during my fieldwork. During the course of interviews, it is likely

Figure 5.3 Informed Consent: Students

Informed Consent for Dissertation Research Project Participation: Gay/Straight Alliance Participants in Public High Schools

Dear Gay/Straight Alliance Member:

I am a graduate student in the School of Education at the University of Massachusetts, Amherst. I would like to invite you to participate in a research project about the benefits and costs of participating in a gay/straight alliance. I am interested in exploring the experiences of self-identified lesbian, gay, and heterosexual students who participate in GSAs.

Your participation will include being interviewed twice for 45 minutes to an hour each time. A third interview of the same length may be added if it seems necessary after the first two interviews.

You may be vulnerable to someone's determining who you are and what you've said, but I will protect you from this possibility as much as possible by using a pseudonym for your name and for the school you attend. I will give you a hard copy of the transcript of each of your interviews. You will be able to make any changes you want. You have the right to withdraw from the study any time up until March 1, 1999. At that point, I will be in the final stages of the writing process and will not be able to remove quotations from the document.

This study will be shared with my dissertation committee and other appropriate members of the University of Massachusetts community. The dissertation that results from this work will be published in hard copy and microfiche, which will be housed at the W. E. B. DuBois Library on campus.

I appreciate your giving time to this study, which will help me learn more about the effect of participation in a GSA. If you have any questions, please feel free to call me at _________. You may also contact my committee chairperson, Professor _________ at _________.

Thank you,

Janice E. Doppler (signed)

Please sign below if you are willing to participate in the dissertation research project outlined above.

Signature ____

Print name ____

Date _________________

SOURCE: Reprinted by permission of Janice Doppler.

> that I will hear about harassment and discrimination. My impulse may be to intervene in the situation. At this point, I believe that it will be appropriate to be sure students know what avenues they can take to deal with harassment or discrimination. When that sort of situation arises, I will continue the interview to keep the flow going, but at the end of the interview session, I can offer to discuss channels of possible support within their individual schools or provide phone numbers for supports outside their schools.

She then provided an example of her recent use of this strategy. These excerpts from Doppler's (1998) proposal demonstrate sensitivity. She went on to show how she would manage political independence, how she would protect her ownership of the data, and why potential benefits would outweigh any risks associated with conducting the study. As she illustrates, informed consent can be a complicated process. Simplistic, trite, and unreflective verbiage will not suffice.

Review Boards

To protect human subjects from unnecessary harm, universities and professional associations have created codes of ethics and research review boards. IRBs in universities and agencies receiving federal funds must review all research proposals to ensure that the research will proceed with appropriate protections against risk to humans and animals, as mandated by the National Research Act, Public Law 93-348. Standards and guidelines are most stringent in the United States and Canada, and less so in other countries. Universities and agencies vary in their interpretations of the guidelines, and sometimes board members are unfamiliar with qualitative proposals. Furthermore, IRBs' primary purpose—to avoid biomedical and physical experimentation and to avoid manipulation of humans without their consent—is less relevant for many qualitative social science proposals. (See the overview of IRB benefits and drawbacks in Brainard, 2001.)

Sometimes qualitative proposals undergo criticism and demands for revisions as IRBs expect them to conform to more conventional designs. This has recently been compounded by the National Research Council's (2002) report stipulating what should be considered scientific inquiry. In her commentary on these conservative trends in the research community, Lincoln (2005) notes,

> Currently there appear to be four ways in which the work of qualitative researchers and scholars who teach qualitative research philosophies and methods is constrained by the manner in which new paradigms encounter institutional review board regulation on campuses: (a) increased scrutiny surrounding research with

> human subjects (a response to failures in biomedical research), (b) new scrutiny of classroom research and training in qualitative methods involving human subjects, (c) new discourses regarding what constitutes "evidence-based research," and (d) the long-term effects of the recent National Research Council (2002) report on what should be considered to be scientific inquiry. (p. 166)

Nevertheless, the principles of ethical management of role, access, data collection, storage, and reporting serve as essential reminders. IRBs require answers to certain specific questions: Describe the research, sites, and subjects; how will you attain access? How will you provide for informed consent, and what will your entry letter and informed consent form look like? What kinds of interactions will you have with subjects? What risks will subjects take, and how will you reduce those risks? How will you guard your data and your informants' privacy? (Glesne, 2005)

Cultural Challenges to Informed Consent

The IRB, with its requirement of informed consent, is a uniquely Western practice. Informed consent is based on principles of individualism and free will—also uniquely Western cultural assumptions. Written informed consent forms also assume literacy, a skill that may not be present when doing fieldwork in countries with different cultural and legal traditions. When working in cross-cultural contexts, where cultural beliefs and values may be collectivist and hierarchical, how does the notion of informed consent play out? Putting one's name or mark on a piece of paper may seem dangerous to participants outside the United States or Europe. These issues must be engaged directly, especially as international students doing fieldwork in their countries of origin must complete appropriate forms and undergo the required human subjects review by the university. How do they meet the demands for the protection of human subjects required by U.S. universities and yet still respect the cultural norms operating in the settings for their research?

As we discussed in Chapter 3, formulaic completion of the required forms evades the deeper issues of cultural biases embedded in the documents and procedures. Observing the intent behind the protection of human subjects that is encoded in documents and procedures, though, means that students must address three key demands: that participants understand (have explained to them) (1) that this is a research study with specific parameters and interests, (2) that they are free to participate or not without prejudice (but this raises its own set of issues, as discussed below), and (3) that their identities will be masked (protected) as much as possible.

VIGNETTE 17 Talking Through Cultural Challenges

MacJessie-Mbewe (2004), a doctoral student from Malawi in Southern Africa, discussed with Rossman at length how he would approach the participants in his study, given that Malawi is a highly collectivist and hierarchical culture. In his human subjects review forms, he wrote, "According to Malawian rural culture, informed consent will be obtained orally. Getting them to sign a form will yield unpleasant reactions and many will fear to participate because of that. Permission will be taken from heads of school, district, and Ministry [of Education]. According to Malawian rules, once you take permission from the Ministry of Education and the district education manager, it is enough to use schools for research."

Although this rationale passed the review process, many ethical issues arose in their discussion. For example, what does consent mean when, if a higher official has approved the study, teachers and heads of schools—as civil servants—must comply and participate? Are they freely agreeing to participate? Can they withdraw without repercussions from higher officials? Discussions with MacJessie-Mbewe and other students from Malawi centered on these issues. While working on the required forms, Rossman engaged students in discussions of how culturally inappropriate a written informed consent may be and encouraged them to elaborate on the reasons why. One typical reason is that written forms, which one must sign or put one's mark on, are associated with the government, often with sinister connotations in repressive or highly corrupt regimes. Another is that the participant (subject) is not literate and hence cannot be fully informed as to what she is signing. A third is that, in more collectivist cultures than those of the United States or Europe, trust and good faith are observed through one's word rather than one's signature. Thus, asking someone to sign a form will be taken as a sign of disrespect. In the end, students agreed on ways to discuss how they will observe the intent of the procedures: informing participants about their research, engaging their willing participation, and protecting their identities as much as feasible. So now MacJessie-Mbewe had more guidance.

While no perfect solutions emerged in this vignette, the issues were engaged openly, using a cultural critique of Western practice for research conducted in very different cultural contexts.

Planning the Exit

The logical, but often forgotten, extension of entry, access, role, reciprocity, and ethics is the researcher's exit strategy. A plan is needed, whether it is the thank you and goodbye after a 20-minute interview or the array of separations from roles played in a one-year immersion in an organization. For all respondents, the initial negotiation of access should have, at the very least, some explanation of what the final product will look like and, by implication, the stated expectation that the relationship is temporary. Still, with intense interaction and over time, with sharing, proffering of assistance, gifts, and confessions, this exit expectation fades. Researchers must decide. Some choose to maintain some relationship in small ways, such as birthday cards, or more fully, as consultants, friends, and even employees.

Whether the researcher chooses to end the relationships or to continue them in some way, being respectful of people and relationships is essential for being an ethical researcher. One does not grab the data and run. At the very least, for participants who have provided access and have opened up their daily lives and their views, the researcher should plan a gradual exit, talking about the completion of the project, providing samples of how the report will look, and leaving gifts or offers of assistance as tokens that supplement words and notes of gratitude. Asking to be kept on a mailing list and taking time to send articles of interest or photos from the setting and other personal notes ease potential resentments or a sense of abandonment. Also, after intense commitments of time and focus, the researcher most likely will, on leaving the field, have strong feelings of separation, loneliness, and loss. Anticipating these feelings is especially important for researchers with very social, relationship-oriented natures. Some never get over the transition to the lonelier phases of analysis and writing. Finally, researchers' plans for role management have to include self-care strategies to deal with fatigue, "compassion stress," and other powerful emotions (Rager, 2005). Knowing how to anticipate the emotions of fieldwork is part of the research design, to be addressed in proposal sections on role, entry, and ethics. Knowing how to view one's own emotions as valuable researcher tools (rather than "bad subjectivity") is a leap ahead in qualitative thought. As Copp (2008) says, "abundant literature on obtaining and maintaining research rapport chronicles the critical importance of role-taking emotions, such as trust and empathy" (p. 251). Knowing how to reflect, in field notes, on a feeling of anger or dislike or a feeling of skepticism can increase the trustworthiness of data and ward off jumping to conclusions.

* * * * *

The preceding discussions have taken the reader through the recursive process of deciding on an overall approach to the study, building a rationale around it, discussing the sites and participants, and thinking about your role, your access, your ways of reciprocating for access and help, and the ethical issues in the conduct of the study. The next two chapters describe primary and secondary data collection methods. They provide choices to help find the concrete answers to the question "How will I actually collect data and what will my data look like?"

Dialogue Between Learners

Melanie,

Thanks for the reply. I like what you said about qualitative work as hopelessly intertwined (and the image of the Gordian knot is wonderful). This brings to mind conversations I've had about the self-reflexive nature of qualitative work. Good qualitative research, it seems, is continually aware of the processes that produce and analyze the data. (Here I mean "processes" in terms of the mechanisms and artifacts involved in data collection and analysis as well as those social processes that shade our daily actions, if that makes any sense.) This self-reflexiveness allows us to trace our often messy path through the Gordian knot of our research. So we begin the many kinds of work involved in qualitative research and then reflexively look back at that work, allowing our later endeavors to be affected by the reflexive act. If we fail to do this, it seems we could easily plunge through, gathering data and analyzing it without being attuned to the subtleties involved in qualitative work (and, oh man, are there ever so many subtleties!).

Let me know if any of this makes sense. Hope all is well,

Aaron

Aaron,

Oh, I completely agree! The self is an integral part of qualitative research—for better or worse—and without that self-reflectivity, a piece of the research is lost. I've been struggling with this lately, however (how timely this conversation is!), because I often found myself in the participant-observer role during my study. My issue at the moment isn't with my status or my engagement, though, but with my level of transparency in writing up this research. How self-reflective should I be? How much of myself do I include in this study? How do I divide "researcher self" from "former instructor self" or "friend self," and how do I present those selves legitimately in my work?

While I can accept—and embrace—the self-reflective component of qualitative research, I find myself confused as to its parameters. Perhaps I'm suffering from long years of quantitative approaches to research? Still, where does the self begin and end in our research? Yes, technically I know we infuse our research, but our research isn't about us (unless we're purposefully taking a phenomenological approach), it's about our question, our topic, and (most important) our people. I suppose this is another strand of the Gordian knot. I don't want to plunge right through without engaging the subtleties (as you so aptly said), but neither do I want to enmesh myself with my own reflectivity to the point of suffocation.

Now I'm rambling! This is what happens when I haven't had my dinner. Does any of this make sense?

Melanie

FURTHER READING

Rationale and Evolving Design

Becker, H. S., Geer, B., Hughes, E. C., & Strauss, A. L. (1961). *Boys in white: Student culture in medical school.* Chicago: University of Chicago Press.

Brantlinger, E. A. (1993). *The politics of social class in secondary schools* (1st ed.). New York: Teachers College Press.

Campbell, A. (1991). *The girls in the gang* (2nd ed.). Cambridge, UK: Blackwell.

Chase, S. E. (1995). *Ambiguous empowerment: The work narratives of women school superintendents.* Amherst: University of Massachusetts Press.

Dicks, B., Soyinka, B., & Coffey, A. (2006). Multimodal ethnography. *Qualitative Research, 6*(1), 77–96.

Janesick, V. J. (1994). The dance of qualitative research design. In N. K. Denzin & Y. S. Lincoln (Eds.), *The Sage handbook of qualitative research* (pp. 209–219). Thousand Oaks, CA: Sage.

Kanter, R. M. (1977). *Men and women of the corporation.* New York: Basic Books.

Lesko, N. (1988). *Symbolizing society: Stories, rites, and structure in a Catholic high school.* New York: Falmer.

Metz, M. H. (1978). *Classrooms and corridors: The crisis of authority in desegregated secondary schools.* Berkeley: University of California Press.

Olesen, V. L., & Whittaker, E. W. (1968). *The silent dialogue: A study in the social psychology of professional socialization.* San Francisco: Jossey-Bass.

Smith, L. (1971). *Anatomy of an educational innovation.* New York: Wiley.

Valli, L. (1986). *Becoming clerical workers.* Boston: Routledge & Kegan Paul.

Whyte, W. F. (1981). *Street corner society: The social structure of an Italian slum* (3rd ed.). Chicago: University of Chicago Press.

Site and Sample

Polkinghorne, D. E. (1989). Phenomenological research methods. In R. S. Valle & S. Halling (Eds.), *Existential-phenomenological perspectives in psychology* (pp. 41–60). New York: Plenum Press.

Personal Reflections

Brizuela, B. M., Stewart, J. P., Carrillo, R. G., & Berger, J. G. (Eds.). (2000). *Acts of inquiry in qualitative research* (Reprint Series No. 34). Cambridge, MA: Harvard Educational Review.

deMarrais, K. B. (Ed.). (1998). *Inside stories: Qualitative research reflections.* Mahwah, NJ: Lawrence Erlbaum.

Eisner, E. W. (1991). *The enlightened eye: Qualitative inquiry and the enhancement of educational practice.* New York: Macmillan.

Geertz, C. (1988). *Works and lives: The anthropologist as author.* Palo Alto, CA: Stanford University Press.

Gitlin, A. (Ed.). (1994). *Power and method: Political activism and educational research.* New York: Routledge.

Glesne, C., & Peshkin, A. (2005). *Becoming qualitative researchers: An introduction.* (3rd ed.). White Plains, NY: Longman.

Golde, P. (1970). *Women in the field.* Chicago: Aldine.

Jorgensen, D. L. (1989). *Participant observation: A methodology for human studies.* Newbury Park, CA: Sage.

Kanuha, V. K. (2000). Being native versus going native: Conducting social work research as an insider. *Social Work, 45*(5), 439–447.

McLaughlin, D., & Tierney, W. G. (1993). *Naming silenced lives: Personal narratives and processes of educational change.* New York: Routledge.

Piotrkowski, C. S. (1979). *Work and the family system: A naturalistic study of working-class and lower-middle-class families.* New York: Free Press.

Toma, J. D. (2000). How getting close to your subjects makes qualitative data better. *Theory into practice, 39*(3), 177–184.

Van Maanen, J. (1988). *Tales of the field: On writing ethnography.* Chicago: University of Chicago Press.

Weis, L., & Fine, M. (2000). *Speed bumps: A student-friendly guide to qualitative research.* New York: Teachers College Press.

Whyte, W. F. (1984). *Learning from the field: A guide from experience.* Beverly Hills, CA: Sage.

Negotiating Entry and Access

Bogdan, R. C., & Biklen, S. K. (2006). *Qualitative research for education: An introduction to theory and methods* (5th ed.). Boston: Allyn & Bacon.

Collins, M., Shattell, M., & Thomas, S. P. (2005). Problematic interviewee behaviors in qualitative research. *Western Journal of Nursing Research, 27*(2), 188–199.

Dewing, J. (2002). From ritual to relationship: A person-centered approach to consent in qualitative research with older people who have dementia. *Dementia, 1*(2), 157–171.

Donelson, R., & Rogers, T. (2004). Negotiating a research protocol for studying school-based gay and lesbian issues. *Theory Into Practice, 43*(2), 128–135.

Eisner, E. W. (1991). *The enlightened eye: Qualitative inquiry and the enhancement of educational practice.* New York: Macmillan.

Feldman, M. S., Bell, J., & Berger, M. T. (Eds.). (2003). *Gaining access: A practical and theoretical guide for qualitative researchers.* Walnut Creek, CA: AltaMira Press.

Lifton, R. J. (1991). *Death in life: Survivors of Hiroshima.* Chapel Hill: University of North Carolina Press.

Patton, M. Q. (2001). *Qualitative research and evaluation methods* (3rd ed.). Newbury Park, CA: Sage.

Schwartz, H., & Jacobs, J. (1979). *Qualitative sociology: A method to the madness.* New York: Free Press.

Symonette, H. (2008). Cultivating self as responsive instrument: Working the boundaries and borderlands for ethical border crossings. In D. M. Mertens & P. E. Ginsberg (Eds.), *The handbook of social research ethics* (pp. 279–294). Thousand Oaks, CA: Sage.

Taylor, S. J., & Bogdan, R. (1998). *Introduction to qualitative research: The search for meanings.* New York: Wiley.

Yeh, C. J., & Inman, A. G. (2007). Qualitative data analysis and interpretation in counseling psychology: Strategies for best practices. *The Counseling Psychologist, 35,* 369–403.

Personal, Political, and Ethical Dilemmas

Bowen, E. S. (1964). *Return to laughter.* Garden City, NY: Doubleday.

Brainard, J. (2001). The wrong rules for social science? *Chronicle of Higher Education, 47*(26), A21–A23.

Christians, C. G. (2000). Ethics and politics in qualitative research. In N. K. Denzin & Y. S. Lincoln (Eds.), *The Sage handbook of qualitative research* (2nd ed., pp. 133–155). Thousand Oaks, CA: Sage.

Copp, M. A. (2008). Emotions in qualitative research. In L. M. Given (Ed.), *The Sage encyclopedia of qualitative research methods* (pp. 249–252). Los Angeles: Sage.

Emerson, R. (2001). Introduction. In R. Emerson (Ed.), *Contemporary field research: A collection of readings* (pp. 255–268). Prospect Heights, IL: Waveland.

Everhart, R. B. (1977). Between stranger and friend: Some consequences of long-term fieldwork in schools. *American Educational Research Journal, 14,* 1–15.

Fine, M. (1994). Negotiating the hyphens: Reinventing self and other in qualitative research. In N. K. Denzin & Y. S. Lincoln (Eds.), *The Sage handbook of qualitative research* (pp. 70–82). Thousand Oaks, CA: Sage.

Galliher, J. F. (1983). Social scientists' ethical responsibilities to superordinates: Looking up meekly. In R. Emerson (Ed.), *Contemporary field research: A collection of readings* (pp. 300–311). Prospect Heights, IL: Waveland.

Glesne, C. (1989). Rapport and friendship in ethnographic research. *International Journal of Qualitative Studies in Education, 2,* 43–54.

Kleinman, S., & Copp, M. A. (1993). *Emotions and fieldwork.* Newbury Park, CA: Sage.

Krieger, S. (1985). Beyond subjectivity: The use of self in social science. *Qualitative Sociology, 8,* 309–324.

Lincoln, Y. S. (1997). Self, subject, audience, text: Living at the edge, writing in the margins. In W. G. Tierney & Y. S. Lincoln (Eds.), *Representation and the text: Re-framing the narrative voice* (pp. 37–55). Albany: State University of New York Press.

Lincoln, Y. S. (2005). Institutional review boards and methodological conservatism: The challenge to and from phenomenological paradigms. In N. K. Denzin & Y. S. Lincoln (Eds.), *The SAGE handbook of qualitative research* (3rd ed., pp. 165–181). Thousand Oaks, CA: Sage.

Lincoln, Y. S., & Tierney, W. G. (2004). Qualitative research and institutional review boards. *Qualitative Inquiry, 10*(2), 219–234.

Olesen, V., & Whittaker, E. (1967). Role-making in participant observation: Processes in the research-actor relationship. *Human Organization, 26,* 273–281.

Peshkin, A. (1988). In search of subjectivity: One's own. *Educational Researcher, 17,* 17–21.

Punch, M. (1986). *The politics and ethics of fieldwork.* Beverly Hills, CA: Sage.

Punch, M. (1994). Politics and ethics in qualitative research. In N. K. Denzin & Y. S. Lincoln (Eds.), *The Sage handbook of qualitative research* (pp. 83–97). Thousand Oaks, CA: Sage.

Rabinow, P. (1977). *Reflections on fieldwork in Morocco.* Berkeley: University of California Press.

Rist, R. (1981, April). *Is there life after research? Ethical issues in the study of schools.* Paper presented at the annual meeting of the American Educational Research Association, Los Angeles.

Smith, M. (1999). Researching social workers' experiences of fear: Piloting a course. *Social Work Education, 18*(3), 347–354.

Spradley, J. S. (1979). *The ethnographic interview.* New York: Holt, Rinehart & Winston.

Thorne, B. (2001). Political activist as participant observer: Conflicts of commitment in a study of the draft resistance movement of the 1960s. In R. Emerson (Ed.), *Contemporary field research: A collection of readings* (pp. 216–234). Prospect Heights, IL: Waveland.

Van Maanen, J. (2001). The moral fix: On the ethics of fieldwork. In R. Emerson (Ed.), *Contemporary field research: A collection of readings* (pp. 269–287). Prospect Heights, IL: Waveland.

Wax, M. L. (2001). On field-workers and those exposed to fieldwork: Federal regulations and moral issues. In R. Emerson (Ed.), *Contemporary field research: A collection of readings* (pp. 288–299). Prospect Heights, IL: Waveland.

Welland, T., & Pugsley, L. (2002). *Ethical dilemmas in qualitative research.* Hants, UK: Ashgate.

Wolcott, H. F. (2002). *Sneaky kid and its aftermath: Ethics and intimacy in fieldwork.* Walnut Creek, CA: Alta Mira Press.

On Institutional Review Boards

Boser, S. (2007). Power, ethics and the IRB: Dissonance over human participant review of participatory research. *Qualitative Inquiry, 13*(8), 1060–1074.

Cheek, J. (2007). Qualitative inquiry, ethics, and politics of evidence: Working within these spaces rather than being worked over by them. *Qualitative Inquiry, 13*(8), 1051–1059.

Koro-Ljungberg, M., Gemignani, M., Brodeur, C. W., & Kmiec, C. (2007). The technologies of normalization and self: Thinking about IRB's and extrinsic research ethics with Foucault. *Qualitative Inquiry, 13*(8), 1075–1094.

Lincoln, Y. S. (2005). Institutional review boards and methodological conservatism: The challenge to and from phenomenological paradigms. In N. K. Denzin & Y. S. Lincoln (Eds.), *The SAGE handbook of qualitative research* (3rd ed., pp. 165–181). Thousand Oaks, CA: Sage.

Lincoln, Y. S., & Tierney, W. G. (2004). Qualitative research and institutional review boards. *Qualitative Inquiry, 10*(2), 219–234.

Wiles, R., Charles, V., Crow, G., & Heath, S. (2006). Researching researchers: Lessons for research ethics. *Qualitative Research 6*(3), 283–299.

Role, Access, and Ethics Issues With Special Populations

Dewing, J. (2002). From ritual to relationship: A person-centered approach to consent in qualitative research with older people who have dementia. *Dementia, 1*(2), 157–171.

Holmes, R. (1998). *Fieldwork with children.* Newbury Park, CA: Sage.

Hood, Jr., R. W. (2000). A phenomenological analysis of the anointing among religious serpent handlers. *International Journal for the Psychology of Religion, 10*(4), 221–240.

Jackson, B. (1978). Killing time: Life in the Arkansas penitentiary. *Qualitative Sociology, 1,* 21–32.

McLarty, M. M., & Gibson, J. W. (2000). Using video technology in emancipatory research. *European Journal of Special Needs Education, 15*(2), 138–139.

Peek, L., & Fothergill, A. (2009). Using focus groups: Lessons from studying daycare centers, 9/11, and Hurricane Katrina. *Qualitative Research, 9*(1), 31–59.

Pepler, D. J., & Craig, W. M. (1995). A peek behind the fence: Naturalistic observations of aggressive children with remote audiovisual recording. *Developmental Psychology, 31*(4), 548–553.

Thomas, S. P., & Pollio, H. R. (2002). *Listening to patients: A phenomenological approach to nursing research and practice.* New York: Springer.

Turner, W. L., Wallace, B. R., Anderson, J. R., & Bird, C. (2004). The last mile of the way: Understanding caregiving in African American families at the end-of-life. *Journal of Marital & Family Therapy, 30*(4), 427–488.

Wenger, G. C. (2003). Interviewing older people. In J. A. Holstein & J. F. Gubrium (Eds.), *Inside interviewing: New lenses, new concerns* (pp. 111–130). Thousand Oaks, CA: Sage.

KEY CONCEPTS

Academic armor

Access

Access to vulnerable populations

Biases

Case study

Closeness of interaction

Complexity of design

Degree of preparedness

Discourse analysis

Efficiency

Emotions

Empathy

Entry

Entry letter

Ethical dilemmas

Ethics

Exit strategy

Field notes

First days in the field

Identity

In-depth interview strategy

Informational adequacy

Informed consent

Initial themes

Institutional review board

"It depends"

Microanalysis

Multisite sampling

Participantness

Pilot studies

Rapport

Rationale

Reciprocity

Researcher as instrument

Research in your own setting

Revealedness

Reviewers' concerns

Risk

Role

Role boundaries

Role dilemmas

Role extensiveness

Role intensiveness

Role maintenance

Sampling

Self-reflections

Site selection

Site specific

Textual analysis

Trust

Voice

6

Primary Data Collection Methods

Qualitative researchers typically rely on four primary methods for gathering information: (1) participating in the setting, (2) observing directly, (3) interviewing in depth, and (4) analyzing documents and **material culture**, with varying emphases. These form the core of their inquiry—the staples of the diet. This chapter provides a brief discussion of these primary methods considered in designing a qualitative study. Several secondary and somewhat more specialized methods of data collection supplement them; these are discussed in Chapter 7. This discussion does not replace the many excellent, detailed references on data collection (we refer to several at the end of this chapter). Its purpose is to guide the proposal writer in stipulating the methods of choice for his study and in describing for the reader how the data will inform his research questions. At the end of these discussions, as appropriate, we provide a short narrative on the salient **ethical issues** that may arise. How the researcher plans to use these methods, however, depends on several considerations.

Chapter 1 presented an introductory discussion of the assumptions that shape qualitative methods. As the grounding for a selection of methods, we extend that discussion here, using Brantlinger's (1997) useful summary of seven categories of crucial assumptions for qualitative inquiry. While the discussion below suggests that these are binary positions, this is not the case. These sets of assumptions are more usefully grappled with as continua, which is how they are depicted in Table 6.1.

The first assumption concerns the researcher's views of the *nature of the research*: Is the inquiry technical and neutral, intending to conform to traditional research within her discipline, or is it controversial and critical, with an explicit political agenda? Second, how does he construe his location, his *positioning relative to the participants*? Does he view himself as distant and objective or intimately involved in their lives?

Table 6.1 Dimensions of Assumptions in Qualitative Inquiry

Dimension	Assumptive Continua
What is the nature of the research?	Technical and neutral ↔ controversial and critical
What is the relationship with participants?	Distant and objective ↔ intimate and involved
What is the "direction of gaze"?	Outward, toward others ↔ inner contemplation and reflection
What is the purpose of the research?	Professional and private ↔ useful to participants and the site
Who is the intended audience?	Scholarly community ↔ the participants themselves
What is the researcher's political position?	Neutral ↔ explicitly political
What are the researcher's views on agency?	Passive ↔ engaged in local praxis

SOURCE: Adapted from Brantlinger (1997).

Third, what is the *"direction of her 'gaze'"*? Is it outward, toward others—externalizing the research problem—or does it include explicit inner contemplation?

Fourth, what is the *purpose of the research*? Does the researcher assume that the primary purpose of the study is professional and essentially private (e.g., promoting his career), or is it intended to be useful and informative to the participants at the site? Related to the fourth category is the fifth: Who is the *intended audience of the study*—the scholarly community or the participants themselves? Sixth, what is the researcher's *political positioning*? Does he view the research as neutral, or does he claim an explicitly political agenda? Finally, the seventh assumption has to do with how the researcher views the *exercise of agency*: Does he see himself and the participants as essentially passive or as "engaged in local praxis"? (Brantlinger, 1997, p. 4). Assumptions made in these seven categories shape how the specific research methods are conceived and implemented throughout a study. At the proposal stage, some judicious and explicit discussion of assumptions strengthens the overall logic and integrity of the proposal.

The many books and articles describing the various ways a qualitative researcher might use the four primary methods (as well as secondary ones) are typically silent about the researcher who may be deaf or have hearing loss; the researcher who may be visually challenged; the researcher who uses a wheelchair; and other researchers who have physical or sensory challenges. In the discussion below, we try to be sensitive to differences in the ways qualitative researchers might interact in a setting, as they draw on their perceptual and kinesthetic strengths. At this point, we emphasize that in the proposal, the researcher would have to outline the specific challenges in conducting the proposed research as well as strategies to build on her strengths to ensure that sound, reliable data are gathered.

OBSERVATION

Observation is central to qualitative research. The term captures a variety of activities that range from hanging around in the setting, getting to know people, and learning the routines to using strict time sampling to record actions and interactions and using a checklist to tick off pre-established actions. Whether enacted informally (as "hanging around" suggests) or formally (as using a checklist suggests), observation entails the systematic noting and recording of events, behaviors, and **artifacts** (objects) in the social setting. It is crucial that these observations be recorded—written down or talked into a tape recorder. This record is frequently referred to as **field notes**—detailed, nonjudgmental (as much as possible), concrete descriptions of what has been observed. Few studies rely exclusively on observation (but see the discussion of interaction analysis in Chapter 7), as researchers have come to appreciate how difficult it is to interpret actions and interactions and so seek insights from participants, often in the form of interviews (whether formal or informal). Qualitative researchers have also come to acknowledge the power inherent in proffering interpretations made from the researcher's ideological standpoint.

Observation can be accomplished not only visually (as the discussion above suggests) but also through the other senses. A researcher with visual challenges could draw on his considerable auditory skills, his sense of touch, and his sense of smell to provide new and insightful descriptions of a particular setting.

In the early stages of qualitative inquiry, the researcher may enter the setting with broad areas of interest but without predetermined categories or strict observational checklists. As noted in Chapter 3, this stance captures the degree to which the study is prefigured or open-ended. Through a more open-ended entry, the researcher is able to discover the recurring patterns of behavior and relationships. After these patterns are identified and described through early analysis of field notes, checklists might become more appropriate and context sensitive. Focused observation may then be used at later stages of the study, usually to see, for example, if analytic themes explain behavior and relationships over a long time or in a variety of settings.

Observation is a fundamental and highly important method in all qualitative inquiry. It is used to discover complex interactions in natural social settings. Even in studies using in-depth interviews, observation plays an important role, as the researcher notes the interview partner's body language and affect, tone of voice, and other paralinguistic messages, in addition to her words. When the researcher-as-observer depends on senses other than sight, observations about movement and tone of voice become generative sources of insights. It is, however, a method that requires a great deal of the researcher. Discomfort, uncomfortable ethical dilemmas, and even danger; the difficulty of managing a relatively unobtrusive role; and the challenge of identifying the big picture while finely attending to huge amounts of fast-moving and complex behavior are just a few of the challenges.

Focused observations go beyond just "hanging out." Planful and reflexive observers use observation systematically (DeWalt & DeWalt, 2001). At the proposal stage, the researcher should describe the purpose of the observing, the phase of the study in which it is likely to be most fruitful, and how data recorded in field notes might be analyzed to respond to the research questions.

Field notes are not scribbles, although they may begin that way. Emerson, Fretz, and Shaw (1995) use the term "jottings" (p. 19) to indicate the on-the-spot notes that a researcher might take. These are then elaborated into full field notes to be useful for subsequent analysis. To help in planning the observation process, the proposal writer should describe some explicit note-organizing and note management strategies, indicating to the reader that he is capable of noting events and interactions and transforming them into useable field notes. Figure 6.1 provides an example of edited and "cleaned up" field notes for a study of kindergarten teachers. O'Hearn-Curran (1997) has formatted descriptive notes in a column on the left while reserving a second column on the right for her comments. These include her emerging analytic insights about the observed behavior. Observers' comments are often a quite fruitful source of analytic insights and clues that focus data collection more tightly (more on this in Chapter 8). They may also provide important questions for subsequent interviews.

Participant Observation

Developed primarily from cultural anthropology and qualitative sociology, **participant observation** (as this method is typically called) is both an overall approach to inquiry and a data-gathering method. To some degree, it is an essential element of all qualitative studies. As its name suggests, participant observation demands firsthand involvement in the social world chosen for study—the researcher is both a participant (to varying degrees) and an observer (also to varying degrees). Immersion in the setting permits the researcher to hear, see, and begin to experience reality as the participants do. Should any of these senses be a challenge for the researcher, she can draw on others to

Figure 6.1 Sample Field Notes

Tuesday, November 13, 1997, 12:40 p.m. **Observation**	**Observer's Comments**
There are 17 children in the room. There are three adults: one teacher, one classroom assistant, and one student teacher (the student teacher is an older woman). The room is in the basement of the school. The school is a brick building approximately 90 to 100 years old. The room is about 40 feet by 30 feet. The room is carpeted and is sectioned off by furniture. There is an area with big books and a chart in the left-hand back corner of the room. Next to that is a shelf with a mixture of small books, tapes, and big books in baskets. Next to that is a small area with toy kitchen furniture and dolls. There is an area with several tables in front of the kitchen area. There are many small chairs pulled up to the table. In the front of the room is an area with a sand table. There is a semicircular table in the left-hand front corner of the room. The walls are colorful, covered with papers that have been made by the children. One wall has papers with apples on them. Another wall has papers with pictures of the children with their names. There are several small windows in the room, and the florescent lighting seems to be the major source of light.	*The teacher seems to have done a great job of making the room seem very inviting. The space itself is not optimal.*
The children have just come into the room. They have put their coats and backpacks onto their hooks in the hall outside.	*Most of the children appear to know the routine.*

describe, for example, a cacophony of sounds in a classroom, the subtle ways people seek approval from superiors through eye contact, and the like. Ideally, the researcher spends a considerable amount of time in the setting, learning about daily life there. This immersion offers the researcher the opportunity to learn directly from her own experience. Personal reflections are integral to the emerging analysis of a cultural group, because they provide the researcher with new vantage points and with opportunities to make the strange familiar and the familiar strange (Glesne, 2005).

This method of gathering data is basic to all qualitative studies and invites consideration of the role or stance of the researcher as a participant observer—his positionality. This consideration links back to the assumption articulated by Brantlinger (1997), presented in Table 6.1, regarding the researcher's relationship with participants. We have explored issues of role more fully in Chapter 3. We reiterate that, at the proposal stage, it is helpful to elaborate on the planned extent of participation: what the nature of that involvement is likely to be, how much will be revealed about the study's purpose to the people in the setting, how intensively the researcher will be present, how focused the participation will be, and how ethical dilemmas will be managed. In addition, it would be important for the researcher to describe how any physical differences would provide a unique perspective. The researcher should be specific as to how his participation will inform the research questions. Table 6.2 displays the relation between the researcher's chosen role and data collection methods.

Ethical Issues in Observation and Participant Observation

The ethical issues that arise in observation and participant-observation studies center on the principle of respect for persons. Are the research participants aware that a study is going on and that they are part of it? Are they agreeable to this? And, as the research unfolds, is their consent to participate continually renegotiated? The researcher must be diligent about being sure that the participants are aware and willing. The practice of informed consent can be complex and, as noted in Chapter 1, it is not an event, but a process. Other complexities can arise when the study focuses on a group setting. Rossman recalls a dissertation that was an action research project on human rights awareness in an elementary school classroom. All but one child's parents agreed that their children could participate. How should the researcher handle observations that, quite naturally, included the one child whose parents did not approve his or her participation? How should she write field notes focusing on interactions among the children when that one child was present? Also subsumed under the principle of respect for persons is the relationship that builds with participants. Ethical practice would suggest that these relationships be benign, nonmanipulative, and mutually beneficial. Such considerations would appropriately be discussed in the proposal.

IN-DEPTH INTERVIEWING

Qualitative researchers rely quite extensively on **in-depth interviewing**. Kvale (1996) describes qualitative interviews as "a construction site of knowledge" (p. 2), where two (or more) individuals discuss a "theme of mutual interest" (Kvale & Brinkmann, 2009, p. 2). In any qualitative study, this method may be the overall strategy or only one of several methods employed. To distinguish the qualitative interview from, for example, a journalist's or television talk show interview, we might speak of its width instead of its depth (Wengraf, 2001). However, interviewing's ubiquity in modern social life has prompted methodologists (and other social observers) to describe us as living in an "interview society" (see, e.g., Gubrium & Holstein, 2003; Holstein & Gubrium, 2003; Silverman, 2000).

Table 6.2 Data Collection Methods Related to Observation Role

	Role			
Method	**I—Participant as observer**	**II—Observer as participant**	**III—Observer as nonparticipant**	**Comment**
Observation and recording of descriptive data	+	+	+	Particularly useful to Role I in areas of guarded interaction and sentiment.
Recording direct quotations of sentiment	+	+	+	Same as above.
Unstructured interview	+	+	*	If the researcher is skillful, a structure emerges.
Structured interview guides	–	*	+	Most useful in survey work (e.g., census).
Detailed interaction guides	–	–	*	Most useful in small-group work.
Interaction frequency tallies	+	+	+	Meaning in leadership studies.
Paper-and-pencil tests				Very helpful in certain circumstances for certain purposes.
–Questionnaires	–	–	+	
–Scales	–	–	+	
–Achievement or ability	–	–	*	
Written records				Very important to Role I in checking reliability of observed data.
–Newspapers	+	+	*	
–Official minutes	+	+	*	
–Letters	+	+	*	
–Speeches	+	+	*	
Radio and television reports	+	+	*	Same as above.

SOURCE: Lutz and Iannaccone (1969, p. 113). Reprinted with permission.

NOTE: +, likely to be used; *, may occasionally be used; –, difficult or impossible to use.

Whether conducted on a television talk show, as part of a dating game, or as a research strategy, interviewing varies in terms of a priori structure and in the latitude the interview partner has in responding to questions or in creating them himself. In a sustained critique of the typical and historical stance that the researcher has control over the interview questions, Brown and Durrheim (2009) argue for "mobile interviewing," that is, interviewing "while on the move (walking and/or driving)" (p. 911). These less structured and less formal venues disrupt deeply ingrained norms about "how to conduct an interview," "what the interviewer's role is," and "what the interviewee's role is."

Consistent with this critique are the metaphors developed by Kvale and Brinkmann (2009), where they describe researchers' stances toward the interview as those of a miner or a traveler (pp. 47–50). The miner approach assumes that ideas and knowledge exist within the interview partner; the interviewer's responsibility is to "dig nuggets of knowledge out of a subject's pure experiences" (p. 48), identifying the kernels or seams of priceless ore and mining them. The traveler, in contrast, is on a journey "to a distant country" (p. 48) with interview partners, either into "unknown terrain or with maps" (p. 48). The miner tends to assume that her role is more distant and objective, while the traveler is more intimately involved in co-constructing knowledge (see Table 6.1).

Patton (2002) categorizes interviews into three general types: (1) the informal, conversational interview; (2) the interview guide or topical approach; and (3) the standardized, open-ended interview (pp. 341–347). To these we would add the co-constructed, or the dialogic, interview (Rossman & Rallis, 2003). The informal, conversational interview takes place on-the-spot, as casual conversations are entered into with individuals and/or small groups; it is spontaneous and serendipitous. The interview guide is a bit more structured: The interview is scheduled, and the interviewer comes prepared with a list of topics or questions (which may or may not have been shared with the interview partner beforehand); this is the most typically used type of interview in qualitative studies. Standardized interviews are more carefully "scripted," asking specific questions in a specific sequence, sometimes without follow-up. This type of interview is often used in multisite case studies or with larger sample sizes. Finally, dialogic interviews may be scheduled, but both the interviewer and the interview partner generate new meaning together. Think of these types in terms of "talk time" (which is revealed, often quite dramatically, in transcripts): Informal and dialogic interviews show shared talk time; interviews that are topical or guided show more "talk" from the interview partner, as do standardized interviews.

With the more typical type—the topical or guided interview—the researcher explores a few general topics to help uncover the participant's views but otherwise respects the way the participant frames and structures the responses. This method, in fact, is based on an assumption fundamental to qualitative research: The participant's perspective on the phenomenon of interest should unfold as the participant views it (the emic perspective), not as the researcher views it (the etic perspective). As noted previously, a degree of systematization—a tighter prefiguring with more structure—in questioning may be necessary, for example, in a multisite case study or when many participants are interviewed, or at the analysis and interpretation stage, when the researcher is testing findings in more focused and structured questioning.

One of the most important aspects of the interviewer's approach is conveying the attitude that the participant's views are valuable and useful. The generativity of the interview depends on both partners and their willingness to engage in a deep discussion about the topic of interest. As Kvale and Brinkman (2009) note, "An interview is literally an *inter view*, an inter change of views between two persons" (p. 2). However, the qualitative researcher should bring some skills and sensibilities to the interview. Preparation is crucial, as is anticipating how he may be received and what ethical issues may arise, as discussed in Chapter 3 and at the end of this chapter. Also crucial for a fruitful interview are the researcher's skills in asking follow-up, elaborating questions. We argue that the richness of an interview is heavily dependent on these follow-up questions (often called, quite infelicitously, "probes"). Rossman and Rallis (2003) discuss three main types: (1) open-ended elaborations, (2) open-ended clarifications, and (3) detailed elaborations (p. 188).

Interviews have particular benefits. An interview yields data in quantity quickly. When more than one person participates (e.g., **focus-group interviews**, discussed below), the process takes in a wider variety of information than if there were fewer participants—the familiar trade-off between breadth and depth. Immediate follow-up and clarification are possible. Combined with observation (looking, hearing, smelling, or touching), interviews allow the researcher to understand the meanings that everyday activities hold for people. When conducted by a person who has challenges with hearing, an interview can be accomplished through the use of a signing interpreter or through writing questions and responses—both of which allow for immediate and direct follow-up questions.

Interviewing has limitations, however. Interviews are often intimate encounters that depend on trust; building trust—albeit time bound—is important. In some cases, interview partners may be unwilling or may be uncomfortable sharing all that the interviewer hopes to explore, or they may be unaware of recurring patterns in their lives. Furthermore, the interviewer may not ask questions that evoke long narratives from participants because of a lack of fluency in or familiarity with the local language or because of a lack of skill in expressing themselves. By the same token, she may not sensitively understand and interpret responses to the questions or various elements of the conversation. And, at times, interview partners may have good reason not to be truthful (see Douglas, 1976, for a discussion).

Interviewers should have superb listening skills (or sign language skills) and be skillful at personal interaction, question framing, and gentle probing for elaboration. Volumes of data can be obtained through interviewing, but it is time-consuming to analyze them. Also worth considering is the issue of the quality of the data. When the researcher is using in-depth interviews as the sole way of gathering data, he should demonstrate in the conceptual framework of the proposal that the purpose of the study is to uncover and describe the participants' perspectives on events—that is, that the subjective view is what matters. Evoking the continua in Table 6.1 about the nature of research, studies making more neutral and technical assumptions might triangulate interview data with data gathered through other methods. Finally, because interviews, at first glance, seem so much like natural conversations, researchers sometimes use them thoughtlessly, in an undertheorized manner, as if the interview partner is surely providing "an unproblematic window on psychological or social realities" (Wengraf, 2001, p. 1).

Figure 6.2 provides elaborated notes from an interview conducted for a study of students of color in a community college. Koski (1997) was particularly interested in how these students identified and defined effective teachers. She was intrigued with the notion of culturally relevant pedagogy and conducted several in-depth interviews with teachers identified by students as especially effective. She has formatted the notes from the interview to provide space for her comments, as did O'Hearn-Curran in the field notes presented in Figure 6.1.

In addition to generic in-depth interviewing, there are several more specialized forms, including **ethnographic interviewing**, **phenomenological interviewing**, and focus-group interviewing, as well as **life histories**, **narrative inquiry**, and **digital storytelling**. There are also special considerations when interviewing specific populations, such as elites or children and youth and when interviewing across social group identities. (Emergent strategies for interviewing that include the Internet and computer applications are discussed in Chapter 7.) We describe each of these below.

Ethnographic Interviewing

Grounded in the genre of cognitive anthropology, ethnographic interviewing elicits the cognitive structures guiding participants' worldviews. Described in the classic work of Spradley (1979) as "a particular kind of speech event" (p. 18), ethnographic questions are used by the researcher to gather cultural data. Ethnographic interviewing is an elaborate system of a series of interviews structured to elicit participants' cultural knowledge. Spradley identifies three main types of questions: descriptive, structural, and contrast. Descriptive questions are often quite broad, allowing the researcher to learn about the participants' views on "their experiences, their daily activities, and the objects and people in their lives" (Westby, Burda, & Mehta, n.d.). Structural questions discover the basic ways the participants organize their cultural knowledge into categories that are important to them (rather than those important to the interviewer). The ones found to be most generative are "strict inclusion, rationale, and means-ends questions" (Westby et al., n.d.). Strict inclusion questions put boundaries around salient categories of meaning; rationale questions focus on the participants' reasons for certain events or circumstances; and means-ends questions capture what leads to what, from the participants'

Figure 6.2 Sample Interview Transcript

Interview with DC October 15, 1997, 1:30–4:30 p.m.	**DC is an adviser with an academic department. The interview was set up by the dean.**
Setting: DC's office in the academic department. It's bright and lively—colorful tapestry on one wall, posters on the other walls. A giant poster about "I am okay." Books and papers are everywhere. On the corner of the desk are some wood games: tic-tack-toe, pyramid, and others. DC is a small, dark-skinned woman with her hair in small but longish braids all over her head. She wears glasses and a pinkish shade of lipstick that complements her coloring. She is lively, with a ready smile and a quick laugh. She comments on her height: "I'm smaller than any of my advisees, so I'm not a threat to anyone."	
I (KK) explain what I'm interested in and what my project is about. I tell her that I would like three things from her: One is an idea of what she as an adviser thinks are the attributes of a good teacher and what her students of color say, which teachers might possess those attributes, and which students I might talk to for the project.	*DC listens very intently here.*
DC: "OK. Good. Well, ask me a question." KK: "Tell me a little bit about what you do."	*This is an awkward moment for me and for her. I wasn't sure what to do. This general question seems to surprise her.*
DC: "I'm an adviser here. We get them in fresh off the street. I sit down with them and make out an educational plan. I like it when they know what's expected of them." DC: "The educational plan lists not only courses to be taken but clubs and other student activities. It lists the advising events the student will attend." DC returns. KK: "How many students do you have?" DC: "About 100."	*She hands me a form that she has worked on with a student. Just then someone comes in and tells her she has an important phone call that they can't transfer. She leaves for about 10 minutes. I am able to look around.*
KK. "100! Are you able to have a relationship with so many?" DC: "I feel I'm an advocate for students. I do whatever needs to be done to get them through this. I tell them not to overload, to relax about this . . . I think being honest with students is important. If I don't know, I tell them. But we can always look it up on the 'Net!"	*I don't remember her exact answer here. Something about keeping in touch.*

perspectives. Finally, contrast questions provide the ethnographer with the meaning of various terms that elaborate what something is like and what it's not like.

The value of the ethnographic interview lies in its focus on culture—broadly construed—from the participants' perspectives and through firsthand encounters. This approach is especially useful for eliciting participants' meanings for events and behaviors and for generating a typology of categories of meaning, highlighting the nuances of the culture. The method is flexible in formulating working hypotheses and avoids oversimplification in description and analysis because of its rich narrative descriptions.

There are shortcomings to this method, however. As with any method, the ethnographer can impose her values through the phrasing of questions or the interpretation of data. If the member of the cultural group chosen to participate does not represent that culture well, the subsequent analysis might be impoverished. The generativity of this method, as in all interviewing, depends highly on the researcher's interpersonal skills.

Phenomenological Interviewing

Phenomenological interviewing is a specific type of in-depth interviewing grounded in the philosophical tradition of phenomenology, which is the study of lived experiences and the ways we understand those experiences to develop a worldview. It rests on the assumption that there is a structure and essence to shared experiences that can be narrated. The purpose of this type of interviewing is to describe the meaning of a concept or phenomenon that several individuals share.

As elaborated by Seidman (2006), three in-depth interviews compose phenomenological inquiry. The first focuses on past experience with the phenomenon of interest; the second focuses on present experience; and the third joins these two narratives to describe the individual's essential experience with the phenomenon. Prior to interviewing, however, the researcher using this method may have written a full description of his own experience, thereby bracketing off his experiences from those of the interview partners. This phase of the inquiry is referred to as *epoché.* The purpose of this self-examination is to permit the researcher to gain clarity from his own preconceptions, and it is part of the "ongoing process rather than a single fixed event" (Patton, 1990, p. 408).

The next phase is called *phenomenological reduction*; here, the researcher identifies the essence of the phenomenon (Patton, 1990). The researcher then clusters the data around themes that describe the "textures of the experience" (Creswell, 1998, p. 150). The final stage, *structural synthesis*, involves the imaginative exploration of "all possible meanings and divergent perspectives" (p. 150) and culminates in a description of the essence of the phenomenon and its deep structure.

The primary advantage of phenomenological interviewing is that it permits an explicit focus on the researcher's personal experience combined with those of the interview partners. It focuses on the deep, lived meanings that events have for individuals, assuming that these meanings guide actions and interactions. It is, however, quite labor intensive and requires a reflexive stance on the part of the researcher. Phenomenological interviews have been quite successfully used in studies of teacher socialization (Maloy, Pine, & Seidman, 2002) and of the challenges to identity development of refugees (Mosselson, 2006).

Focus-Group Interviews

The method of interviewing participants in focus groups comes largely from marketing research but has been widely adapted to include social science and applied research. The groups are typically composed of 7 to 10 people (although groups range from as small as 4 persons to as large as 12 persons) who are unfamiliar with one another and have been selected because they share certain characteristics relevant to the study's questions. The interviewer creates a supportive environment, asking focused questions to encourage discussion and the expression of differing opinions and points of view. These focus-group interviews may be conducted several times with different individuals so that the researcher can identify trends in the perceptions and opinions expressed, which are revealed through careful, systematic analysis (Krueger & Casey, 2008). As with many methods, focus-group discussions can be conducted on a dedicated Internet blog that, in effect, creates a "virtual" focus group, not limited by time or location, such that many participants, from all over the world, can participate.

This method assumes that an individual's attitudes and beliefs are socially constructed: They do not form in a vacuum. People often listen to others' opinions and understandings in forming their own. Often, the questions in a focus-group setting are deceptively simple; the trick is to promote the participants' expression of their views through the creation of a supportive environment.

The strengths of focus-group interviews are that this method is socially oriented, studying participants in an atmosphere more natural than artificial experimental circumstances and more relaxed than a one-to-one interview. When combined with participant observation, focus-group interviews can be especially useful for gaining access, focusing site selection and sampling, and even for checking tentative conclusions (Morgan, 1997). As with other types of interviews, the format allows the facilitator the flexibility to explore unanticipated issues as they arise in the discussion. The results have high "face validity": Because the method is readily understood, the findings appear believable. Furthermore, the cost of focus-group interviews is relatively low, they provide quick results, and they can increase the sample size of qualitative studies by permitting more people to be interviewed at one time (Krueger & Casey, 2008). In action research and in program design and evaluation, focus groups are especially useful. They were useful tools, for example, in data gathering to design a program for working on the employment issues of persons with HIV/AIDS, based on their answers to questions about specific needs ranging from stress and availability of health care to family, spirituality, and hopes for the future (O'Neill, Small, & Strachan, 1999).

Focus-group interviews have also been found to be especially useful for fostering social support networks. For their discussion of the benefits and challenges of focus-group interviewing strategies, Peek and Fothergill (2009) analyzed three distinct research projects: (1) a study of teachers, children, and parents in urban day care settings; (2) the responses of Muslim Americans (born in the United States of immigrant parents) to the events and aftermath of 9/11; and (3) a collaborative project on children and youth following Hurricane Katrina. In all three cases, the researchers found that focus-group interviewing eased access and, perhaps more important for the participants, fostered the development of social ties that superseded the research projects.

There are, however, certain challenges to this method as well. First and foremost is the issue of power dynamics in the focus-group setting. Should the researcher choose to use this method, she should be exquisitely aware of power dynamics and be able to facilitate well—these are crucial skills. In addition, the interviewer often has less control over a group interview than an over individual one. Time can be lost while irrelevant issues are discussed; the data are difficult to analyze because context is essential to understanding the participants' comments; the method requires the use of special room arrangements (or dedicated discussion sites) and highly trained facilitators; the groups can vary a great deal and can be hard to assemble; and logistical problems may arise from the need to manage a conversation while getting good-quality data.

We should also note that with relatively inexpensive and easy-to-use technology such as video recorders, focus-group discussions are increasingly videotaped. As with interaction analysis (see Chapter 7), using this technology creates a more or less "permanent record" of the data, which in turn facilitates analysis. Using video recorders (and any pictorial medium), however, raises important ethical issues about the protection of the identities of participants. This is discussed more fully in the next section.

Ethical Issues in Focus-Group Interviews

As just noted, the primary ethical issues that may arise in conducting focus-group interviews center on the dynamics of power and influence that may play out in any group (whether physically together or on an Internet blog). The researcher must be exquisitely sensitive to these dynamics (e.g., is Robert dominating the discussion?) and be skilled at facilitating the process. Should the discussion be videotaped, the privacy of individuals and protection of their identities become paramount. We are aware of IRBs that, quite appropriately, require additional statements on informed consent forms that specifically address using video clips or still photographs in any ensuing research reports. Their use can immediately identify participants and therefore requires a more complex statement about the use of the data to ensure that the participants are fully informed. In fact, we would argue that using photographs or video clips of individuals or groups abrogates the respect for persons' consideration of anonymity. This is a thorny ethical issue that, in this digital age, will continue to be debated.

These issues, and others, arise in life history methodologies. This family of methods focuses explicitly on the stories individuals tell about their lives and includes narrative inquiry, digital storytelling, and the use of memoires.

LIFE HISTORIES, NARRATIVE INQUIRY, AND DIGITAL STORYTELLING

Life histories and narrative inquiry are in-depth interview methods that gather, analyze, and interpret the stories people tell about their lives. They assume that people live "storied" lives and that telling and retelling one's story helps one understand and create a sense of self. The story is important, but so is how the story is told (Riessman, 1991). The researcher, working closely with the participant, explores a story and records it. Life histories and narrative inquiry are used across the social science disciplines and are particularly useful for giving the reader an insider's view of a culture or era in history; as such, they represent the application of the principles of biography to the social sciences. A related approach is digital storytelling, in which an individual (or possibly a group) tells a story using digital content—images, sound, and perhaps videos. Digital storytelling may or may not involve interviewing; we include it here because it fits well with the focus of life histories and narrative inquiry on narrating stories. Each is discussed below.

Life Histories

Life histories seek to "examine and analyze the subjective experience of individuals and their constructions of the social world" (Jones, 1983, p. 147). They assume a complex interaction between the individual's understanding of his world and that world itself. They are, therefore, uniquely suited to depicting and making theoretical sense of the socialization of a person into a cultural milieu (Dollard, 1935). Thus, one understands a culture through the history of one person's development or life within it, a history told in ways that capture the person's feelings, views, and perspectives. The life history is often an account of how an individual enters a group and becomes socialized into it. That history includes learning to meet the normative expectations of that society by gender, social class, or age peers. Life histories emphasize the experience of the individual—how the person copes with society rather than how society copes with the stream of individuals.

Life histories can focus on critical or fateful moments. Indecision, confusion, contradiction, and irony are captured as nuanced processes in a life (Sparks, 1994). These histories are particularly helpful in defining socialization and in studying aspects of acculturation and socialization in institutions and professions. Their value goes beyond providing specific information about events and customs of the past—as a historical account might—by showing how the individual creates meaning within the culture. Life histories are valuable in studying cultural changes that have occurred over time, in learning about cultural norms and transgressions of those norms, and in gaining an inside view of a culture. They also help capture the way cultural patterns evolve and are linked to the life of an individual. Often, this point of view is missing from standard ethnographies (Atkinson, 1998).

One strength of life history methodology is that because it pictures a substantial portion of a person's life, the reader can enter into those experiences. Another is that it provides a fertile source of intriguing research questions that may be generative for focusing subsequent studies. And yet a third strength is that life histories depict actions and perspectives across a social group that may be analyzed for comparative study. This kind of research requires sensitivity, caring, and empathy by the researcher for the researched (Cole & Knowles, 2001). Life histories are often used in feminist research as a way of understanding, relatively free of androcentric bias, how women's lives and careers evolve (Lawless, 1991).

Jones (1983, pp. 153–154) offers five criteria for life histories. First, the individual should be viewed as a member of a culture; the life history "describe[s] and interpret[s] the actor's account of his or her development in the common-sense world." Second, the method should capture the significant role that others play in "transmitting socially defined stocks of knowledge." Third, the assumptions of the cultural world under study should be described and analyzed as they are revealed in rules and codes for conduct as well as in myths and rituals. Fourth, life histories should focus on the experience of an individual over time so that the "processual development of the person" can be captured. And fifth, the cultural world under study should be continuously related to the individual's unfolding life story.

The major concerns with the life history are that generalizing is difficult, sample sizes are by definition quite small, and there are few concepts to guide analysis. Once the researcher acknowledges the possible challenges with the method, however, she can address them, perhaps by supplementing in-depth interviews—"storying"—with other sources. For example, official records may provide corroborating information or may illuminate aspects of a culture absent from an individual's account. In addition, the researcher might substantiate meanings presented in a history by interviewing others in a participant's life. Before publishing *The Professional Thief*, for example, Sutherland and Conwell (1983) submitted the manuscript to four professional thieves and two police detectives to assess possible bias and to ensure that their interpretations resonated with the understandings of other professional thieves and those who come in contact with them.

A life history account can add depth and evocative illustration to any qualitative study. As with any qualitative genre, however, the abundance of data collected in a life history should be managed and reduced so that analytic headway can be made. Instead of using chronological order to present the story, the researcher might focus on (a) critical dimensions or aspects of the person's life, (b) principal turning points and the life conditions between them, and (c) the person's characteristic means of adaptation (Mandelbaum, 1973).

Narrative Inquiry

Closely related to life history is narrative inquiry, an interdisciplinary method that views lives holistically and draws from traditions in literary theory, oral history, drama, psychology, folklore, and film philosophy (Connelly & Clandinin, 1990). The method assumes that people construct their realities through narrating their stories. The researcher explores a story told by a participant and records that story. Narrative inquiry can be applied to any spoken or written account—for example, to an in-depth interview. As noted on the homepage of the journal *Narrative Inquiry*, this method "give[s] contour to experience and life, conceptualize[s] and preserve[s] memories, or hand[s] down experience, tradition, and values to future generations" (www.clarku.edu/faculty/ mbamberg/narrativeINQ/, accessed March 2, 2009).

Narrative inquiry requires a great deal of openness and trust between participant and researcher: The inquiry should involve a mutual and sincere collaboration, a caring relationship akin to friendship that is established over time for full participation in the storytelling, retelling, and reliving of personal experiences. It demands intense and active listening and giving the narrator full voice. Because it is a collaboration, however, it permits both voices to be heard.

This method is criticized for its focus on the individual rather than on the social context. Like life histories, however, narrative inquiry seeks to understand sociological questions about groups, communities, and contexts through individuals' lived experiences. Like any method that relies on participants' accounts, narrative may suffer from recalling selectively, focusing on subsets of experience, filling in memory gaps through inference, and reinterpreting the past (Ross & Conway, 1986). Furthermore, narrative inquiry is also time-consuming and laborious and requires some specialized training (Viney & Bousefield, 1991). Several researchers have articulated criteria for good narrative inquiry (see Connelly & Clandinin, 1990; Jones, 1983; Riessman, 1993).

Narrative inquiry is a relative newcomer to the social sciences and applied fields, but it has a long tradition in the humanities because of its power to elicit voice. Narrative inquiry values the signs, the symbols, and the expression of feelings in language and other symbol systems, validating how the narrator constructs meaning. It has been particularly useful in developing feminist and critical theory (Eisner, 1988; Grumet, 1988; Riessman, 1993). And it is especially useful when exploring issues of social change, causality, and social identity (Elliott, 2005) and when studying participants' experiences of violence, trauma, or genocide (Keats, 2009).

Narrative inquiry may rely on journal records, photographs, letters, autobiographical writing, e-mail messages, and other data. Typically, the field notes or interview transcriptions are shared with the narrator, and the written analysis may be constructed collaboratively. In the conduct of narrative inquiry, there is open recognition that the researcher is not just passively recording and reporting the narrator's reality. Connelly and Clandinin (1990) assert that researchers need to "be prepared to follow their nose and, after the fact, reconstruct their narrative of inquiry" (p. 7). This becomes, in effect, the recounting of methodology.

Digital Storytelling

Digital storytelling is a new approach to narrating stories that draws on the power of digitized images to support the content of the story. Emerging in the mid-1990s, the method has been developed to enable ordinary people to tell their stories. It thus has an empowering and/or emancipatory ideology, seeking to encourage people to give voice (and image and sound) to their life experiences. As noted on the Educause Web site, "Digital storytelling is fundamentally the application of technology to the age-old experience of sharing personal narratives. What's new is the growing availability of sophisticated tools" (Educause, n.d.).

Supported by video-editing computer applications, such as iMovie™ (for Macs) or MovieMaker™ (for PCs), the storyteller first constructs a narrative (the story) by writing a script or outline, then enhances this with still images, video clips, sound clips, and the like. These digitized elements may come from the storyteller's own archives or could be taken from the Internet as publicly available. Blending the storyline with these other elements represents the craft and art of digital storytelling.

Digital storytelling has been widely used in community development projects and educational settings. It has great appeal to young people who are very comfortable with software and willing to "hack around" to figure out how to create a compelling story. However, the open-ended nature of this highly creative process can be intimidating to some, and the costs of equipment may be prohibitive. Several universities and community-based organizations offer workshops on digital storytelling, creating a supportive group environment for experimentation and learning. The final product—the digital story—is often quite short, typically between four and eight minutes long.

Ethical Issues in Life Histories, Narrative Inquiry, and Digital Storytelling

The ethical issues that may arise in life history research or narrative inquiry, as with many types of interviewing, center on the relationship with the participants. Especially when focusing on one individual, the researcher must be exquisitely sensitive to disclosing more about the person than he is comfortable with. This demands a more collaborative approach to the research, as noted previously, where the participant and the researcher co-construct the history or narrative. This stance will help avoid the ethical problems associated with revealing more than the participant cares to have revealed. A related ethical issue is the challenge to fully protect the individual's identity and facts of his private life. This is a delicate matter, one that should be fully addressed in the proposal.

Digital storytelling represents somewhat different ethical challenges, since the production of the story is under the control of the storyteller. The issues that may arise here center on unauthorized uploading of highly personal digital stories to the Internet. This is a challenge that anyone using this method should keep in mind.

We now turn to a discussion of specific populations that the qualitative researcher might want to gather data from, or with: elites, children, and those with different social identities than those of the researcher.

Interviewing Elites

Interviewing elites—individuals in positions of power and influence—has a long history in sociology and organizational studies. An interview with an "elite" person is a specialized case of interviewing that focuses on a particular type of interview partner. Elite individuals are considered to be influential, prominent, and/or well-informed in an organization or community; they are selected for interviews on the basis of their expertise in areas relevant to the research and for their perspectives on, for example, an organization, a community, or specialized fields such as the economy or health policy. Citing the work of several organizational scholars, Delaney (2007) identifies various types of elites: philanthropic elites—often quite wealthy and known for major contributions or endowments to individuals, organizations, or causes; political elites—those elected or appointed to political office; ultra-elites—for example, Nobel Laureates or Olympic athletes; and organizational elites—CEOs or presidents of companies, for example. Elites have attained that status through extreme wealth and social responsibility (philanthropists); through success in attaining political office (politicians); through recognition of their scientific or scholarly accomplishment or extreme athletic achievement (awardees); or through achieving senior positions in organizations. One can well imagine other types.

Elite interviewing has many advantages. Valuable information can be gained from these participants because of the positions they hold in social, political, financial, or organizational realms. Taking organizational elites as an example, these individuals can provide an overall view of a company or its relationship to other companies, albeit from their own experiences and standpoints. They may be quite familiar with legal and financial structures. Elites are also able to discuss an organization's policies, histories, and plans, again from a particular perspective, or have a broad view on the development of a policy field or social science discipline. Bennis and Nanus's (2003) study of 90 corporate executives is a strong example of the former; Stephens's study of macroeconomists and the changing conception of their field (2007) shows how elite and ultra-elite scholars understand their field. Many studies of political elites have been conducted. Other elites, such as religious leaders, could be generative participants, as could be leaders of gangs or cults, union bosses, or tribal chiefs.

Elite interviewing also presents challenges. It is often difficult to gain access to elites because they are usually busy people operating under demanding time constraints; they are also often difficult to contact initially. We should note that this is also a consideration in other circumstances: busy school teachers, rural village women who have substantial work responsibilities, health care workers, and so on. With elite individuals particularly, the interviewer may have to rely on sponsorship, recommendations, and introductions for assistance in making appointments.

Another challenge in interviewing elites is that the interviewer may have to adapt the planned structure of the interview, based on the wishes and predilections of the person interviewed. Although this is true with all in-depth interviewing, elite individuals who are used to being interviewed by the press and other media may well be quite sophisticated in managing the interview process. (Sophistication and political astuteness are not exclusively the domain of elites, and we do not mean to suggest that they are.) They may want an active interplay with the interviewer. Well practiced at meeting the public and being in control, an elite person may turn the interview around, thereby taking charge of it. When there are considerable (and obvious) status differentials between the interviewer and the elite interview partner, this may become more of an issue. As Delaney (2007) asks, under these circumstances, "who controls the interview?"; she offers the principle from *jiujitsu* of "using your opponent's momentum to your own advantage" (p. 215). Elites often respond well to inquiries about broad areas of content and to open-ended questions that allow them the freedom to use their knowledge and imagination.

Working with elites often places great demands on the ability of the interviewer to establish competence and credibility by displaying knowledge of the topic or, lacking such knowledge, by projecting an accurate conceptualization of the problem through thoughtful questioning. The interviewer's hard work usually pays off, however, in the quality of information obtained. Elites may contribute important insight about the topic of the study through their specific perspectives. On the other hand, elites (just like other interview partners) may well have only vague understandings of a setting that is limited by a narrow viewpoint.

Interviewing and Conducting Research With Children and Youth

We begin this section by noting, quite sadly, that most of the materials available from publishers and on the Internet about interviewing and conducting research with children and youth are written for counselors, psychologists, police, health care workers, forensic experts, and lawyers. The issues covered include sexual abuse, parental abuse, custody issues, and the like. This is a very sad commentary on U.S. society today. However, our focus here is neither pathological nor legalistic; we are interested in those circumstances when the qualitative researcher may be interested in **interviewing children and youth** to learn about how they see some aspect of their worlds—a considerably more beneficent focus than those just described.

Thus, children or youth may be the primary focus of a study or one of many groups the researcher wants to interview or learn from more broadly. Increasingly, there are calls for including children's and youth's perspectives as relevant and insightful in learning more about aspects of their worlds. These arguments draw support from the "new sociology of childhood" (Ajodhia-Andrews & Berman, 2009, referencing Greene & Hill, 2005), which calls for "listening to the voices of children when conducting research about their lives" (Ajodhia-Andrews & Berman, 2009, p. 931). This is especially true in education, where all too often, those most affected by educational policy and programmatic decisions—the students—are absent from inquiry. There are special considerations, however, when the qualitative researcher proposes a study that involves children and other young people.

One such consideration might be the children's or youth's dominant or preferred mode of communication. Children and youth who use sign language to communicate or whose medium of communication is pictures or music at times require specialized tools for communicating. In their study with "Ian," a child who communicates primarily through "physical movements, gestures, and vocalizations", Adjodhia-Andrews and Berman (2009, p. 933) found it generative to use tools with pictures to elicit Ian's perspectives on schooling. The demand here, whatever the circumstances, is that all attempts be made to respect the child or the youth—through whatever media—to better understand her life world.

Also important are age considerations. Interviewing preschoolers, for example, is quite different from interviewing early adolescents. Young children are often active; early adolescents are frequently very self-conscious. Three-year-olds, exploring their emerging language skills, can drive one to distraction with their incessant questions (often quite sophisticated ones!), whereas early adolescents may be taciturn. It is unrealistic to expect young children to sit still for long, but joining them in some activity can create a climate for focused talk. One might use the projective technique of "play" with younger children, as is often done in psychotherapeutic settings. In contrast, some adolescents may feel more comfortable with their peers in a focus-group interview, whereas others may prefer the intimacy of one-to-one interviews. Decisions about how to gather data with various age groups requires sensitivity to their needs and their developmental issues, and flexibility. As Eder and Fingerson note (2003), creating a natural context is crucial, but what constitutes "natural" will depend on the age of the participants.

Second are role considerations with associated power dynamics. Fine and Sandstrom (1988) note that the roles an adult researcher assumes when studying children vary along two dimensions: "(1) the extent of positive contact between adult and child, and (2) the extent to which the adult has direct authority over the child" (p. 14). They offer the roles of supervisor, leader, observer, and friend as appropriate. Of these, they find the role of friend the most fruitful, noting that the researcher then interacts with the children "in the most trusted way possible—without any explicit authority role" (p. 17). They caution, however, that age and power differences between adults and children are always salient.

Ethical Issues in Interviewing Children and Youth

The ethical issues in interviewing children and youth center on protecting them from harm as a result of participating in the study, protecting their identities and privacy, and being diligent to ensure that they are willingly participating in the study. The injunction of *primum non nocere*—first, do no harm—is especially important for the researcher to be scrupulous about. Children receive special consideration in the principles and practices for the protection of human subjects because of their relative vulnerability. Thus, the researcher proposing a study that involves children and youth must assure the reviewers of the proposal that he is exquisitely sensitive to the power dynamics between himself and the children, that he will make extra effort to protect the children from harm (physical or psychological), and that parents or guardians continuously support the children's participation (signing an informed consent form is necessary but not sufficient, as discussed in Chapter 3).

Interviewing Across Differences in Social Identities

Since the publication of the fourth edition of this book, much has been written about the complexities of conducting **research across differences in social identities** between researcher and participants. The research and theorizing about differences in race, ethnicity, first language, gender, sexual orientation, able-bodiedness, and so on have taken up a central place in the qualitative inquiry discourse. A few stances have emerged. There are those who take the position, for example, that only women should interview women and men just won't be effective. And there are others who argue that interviewing those with the same or similar social identities risks the researcher's assuming too much tacit knowledge. And there are yet others for whom this issue is complex and nuanced; taking a single position doesn't contribute to thoughtful qualitative research. This latter position is the one we take.

That said, there are considerations at the proposal stage that should be addressed. A short discussion of some of the issues that might be encountered in the proposed research, depending on the research participants, will strengthen the reader's view that the researcher is sensitive to and thoughtful about these issues. There are two circumstances to be particularly aware of. When the researcher shares an aspect of social identity—gender, for example—with participants, he should be cautious about assuming that he understands the interview partner's experience *just because he's a man, too.* And he should guard against the interview partner making the same assumptions. Conversely, he should not avoid research sites or participants just because he does *not* share some aspect of social identity. Both of these positions are problematic, in our view.

As an example of a related issue, sharing professional identity, Rossman recalls interviewing teachers about a reform effort in their school and shared that she, too, had been a classroom teacher. In response to a question about everyday work in the school, one teacher responded, "Well, you know what it's like. You've been here." Rossman had to think quickly and followed up with, "Yes, but each school is different, so tell me about what it's like here." If she had not followed up, she would have been left with few data.

Two examples are particularly illustrative of these issues. Foster's (1994) classic work explored issues of race, gender, geography, and age. She found that sharing the identity of being black Americans (her term) did not necessarily foster shared understandings. Gender, geography (living in the northern or southern United States), and age also shaped the ease—or difficulty—of conducting interviews with the participants. Thus, sharing one salient social identity—race—was not always sufficient for seamless interviews. The title of her chapter, "The Power to Know One Thing Is Never the Power to Know All Things," captures the issue that differing social identities may complicate an interview, especially when the researcher assumes that sharing blackness, in this case, would be sufficient. Similarly, Riessman's (1991) study, focusing on women's experiences of divorce, used long, life history interviews. While both the researchers and the participants shared the gender identity of being women, they varied in terms of social class, first language, and place of origin. The interviews with middle-class white women, conducted by middle-class white women, went relatively smoothly, while the interviews with working-class Latina women did not. Riessman's analysis focuses on the differing narrative styles that the women used in the interviews. The middle-class white researchers had difficulty understanding the narrative style of the Latinas, having assumed that gender would be enough (to paraphrase the title of the chapter). Recalling the discussion about queer theory, which articulates that identity is fluid, we cannot automatically assume being "in" with a certain population. The fact that two people drive the same type of car does not necessarily mean that their experiences are the same or even somewhat similar! Queer theory recognizes the multiplicity of identities and how they interact and affect one another, challenging simplistic notions of shared identity categories.

Ethical Issues in Interviewing

Perhaps the most obvious fact about interviewing is that it is an intervention. As Patton (2002) notes, "A good interview lays open thoughts, feelings, knowledge, and experience, not only to the interviewer but also to the interviewee" (p. 405). Thus, the ethical issues that may emerge in any interview center on the relationship between the researcher and the interview partner. Is that relationship nonmanipulative? Is there the potential for reciprocity? Is there the potential for pain and anguish when the person interviewed shares painful experiences? The ethical researcher would have to consider ways to manage such circumstances in her proposal. And, of course, the demand that the interview partner's identity be protected throughout the study and in its writing up is crucially important.

We turn now to a discussion of using artifacts of material culture—documents, objects, songs, pictures, and the like—as an integral part of a typical qualitative research study. At the proposal stage, the writer will need to argue why and how inclusion of such materials will help participants respond to his research questions and, ultimately, enrich his analyses and interpretations.

ARTIFACTS OF MATERIAL CULTURES: DOCUMENTS AND OTHER OBJECTS

The artifacts that individuals, organizations, families, agencies, townships, or larger social groups produce take multiple forms: Some are documents; others are objects—pictures, clothing, pottery, trash. Documents, in particular, often are drawn on in a qualitative study. Various kinds of documents can provide background information that helps establish the rationale for selecting a particular site, program, or population; this is very relevant for the proposal. For example, the researcher may gather demographic data or describe geographic and historical particulars to justify selection of a site for the research. When she reviews old property transactions, skims recent newspaper editorials, or obtains information from a Web site about an organization, she is collecting data, but these data are used in the proposal to demonstrate that a particular site or setting will be generative. A different use of documents may be proposed as part of the in-depth data gathering for a study. For example, records of meetings, transcriptions of court cases, or personal letters may be identified in the proposal as useful sources of data to be gathered. In addition, she may propose that participants generate documents: journal entries or writing samples. Both uses of documents are valuable. In addition to documents, however, the researcher may propose to gather and learn about objects in the setting.

Researchers often supplement participant observation, interviewing, and observation with gathering and analyzing documents produced in the course of everyday events or constructed specifically for the research at hand. As such, the **analysis of documents** is potentially quite rich in portraying the values and beliefs of participants in the setting. Minutes of meetings, logs, announcements, formal policy statements, letters, and so on are all useful in developing an understanding of the organization, setting, or group studied. Research journals and samples of writing, as mentioned above, can also be quite informative. For her dissertation research in Composition Studies, Rosenberg (2006) used writing samples of newly literate adults to guide her interviews; this was particularly evocative of deeper insights into the challenges of literacy for adults, some of whom were becoming literate in a second or third language.

Archival data—documents often recording official events—are the routinely gathered records of a society, community, or organization. These may further supplement other qualitative methods. For example, marital patterns among a group of Mexicans, discovered through fieldwork in a community, could be tested through marriage records found in the offices of the county seat or state capitol. Descriptions of articulated funding priorities by policymakers could be corroborated (or not) through an analysis of budgetary allocations. As with other methodological decisions, the decision to propose gathering and analyzing documents or archival records should be linked to the research questions developed in the conceptual framework for the study. Furthermore, the analysis and interpretation of documents should be approached cautiously because the inferential span is long; that is, the meaning of the documents is never transparent. In the proposal, if arguing to gather and analyze documents, the researcher would want to indicate how he would seek corroboration of the meaning of the documents through other methods.

An analysis of other artifacts—those not encoded in text—might also be fruitful for a qualitative study. In fact, classic ethnographic research focused on many such artifacts: religious icons, clothing, housing forms, food, and so on. The researcher may well determine that focusing on some artifacts in the setting would add richness to the corpus of data to be gathered. For example, O'Toole and Were (2008) found that examining space and material culture in their study of a technology company added greatly to their insights about "power, identity, and status" (p. 616). As a further example, studies in classrooms might include student artwork, the decoration of walls, or clothing, for example. Photographs (discussed below) might also be included.

The use of documents may entail the analytic approach called content analysis. The raw material for content analysis is typically text: textbooks, novels, newspapers, e-mail messages, political speeches. Historically, content analysis was viewed as an objective and neutral way of generating a quantitative description of the content of various forms of communication; thus, counting the number of times specific words and terms appeared was central to the method (Berelson, 1952). As this process has evolved, however, researchers now focus on "the presence, meanings and relationships of . . . words and concepts, then make inferences about the messages" (Busch et al., 2005). Thus today, the process is viewed more generously as a method for describing and interpreting the written productions of a society or social group.

Probably the greatest advantage of using documents and other artifacts is that it does not disrupt ongoing events: These materials can be gathered without disturbing the setting. The researcher determines where the emphasis lies after the data have been gathered. A potential weakness, however, is the span of inferential reasoning, as noted above. That is, the analysis of written materials or photographs or clothing, for example, entails interpretation by the researcher, just as in the analysis of interactively gathered data: Minutes of meetings and Nike sneakers do not speak for themselves. Care should be taken, therefore, in displaying the logic of interpretation used in inferring meaning from the artifacts.

Ethical Issues in Using Documents and Artifacts

The ethical issues in relying on documents and artifacts center on how publically available these materials are. Using public materials might seem harmless, but the researcher should nonetheless consider how using them might harm the organization or individuals (even though not specifically identified). Would analysis and writing about these materials denigrate those who produced them? In what ways? Could the researcher be viewed as an artifact "lurker"? A spy? More private materials should be subjected to even closer ethical reasoning. Even if a research participant agrees to write a journal (for research purposes), what if she discloses troublesome information? How should the researcher respond? The overall consideration here is for the researcher to ask, "Are the producers of these artifacts likely to feel exposed or that their privacy has been violated if these materials are used?"

* * * * *

Some combination of these primary research methods is typical for in-depth qualitative inquiry. In Vignette 18, Shadduck-Hernandez (1997) articulates a complex design that incorporates several. The vignette is adapted from her proposal for research about CIRCLE (Center for Immigrant and Refugee Leadership and Empowerment), a participatory project involving newcomer undergraduate students, graduate students, and members from refugee and immigrant communities.

VIGNETTE 18 Using Multiple Methods

Imagine 12 university students, on a chilly Saturday morning, sprawled out on a classroom floor formulating their thoughts for a proposal on scattered sheets of newsprint. Laughter, silence, and intense discussion highlight the writing process of these authors, who are first-generation refugee and immigrant (newcomer) students from China, Cambodia, Vietnam, Laos, and Korea participating in an undergraduate seminar on cross-cultural experiences in community development.

This dissertation research acknowledges the real tensions that exist in any qualitative research endeavor. Certain models can be rigid, one-way streets if they seduce participants into a process of inquiry in which the researcher alone is the analyzer and interpreter of data. This study consciously tried to counter such situations by applying participatory research as the guide of the inquiry (Maguire, 2000; Reardon, Welsh, Kreiswirth, & Forester, 1993). Study participants have been involved in this inquiry as researchers and valued members of a learning team to produce knowledge that may help stimulate social change.

Stemming from my commitment to participatory processes, the research I am conducting is collaborative in nature, emerging from the students and the communities I work with. Collaboration and participation in developing critical learning environments produce pooled resources and shared expertise leading to integrated and collective activities. Collaboration, action, and reflection enhance the legitimacy of each participant's knowledge (Brice Heath & McLaughlin, 1993) and set the stage for the sources of multilevel data collection employed in this study. These six sources of data have evolved as a complement to the development of CIRCLE courses and community outreach activities and support the concept of a pedagogy for affirmation, advocacy, and action. They include the following: (a) journal entries and self-reflection papers; (b) focus-group interviews with 8 undergraduate students; (c) in-depth interviews with 10 students; (d) video and photography documentation; (e) oral history interviews conducted by students and youth with each other; and (f) research field notes, reflections, and academic papers for courses and conferences over the four years of my involvement with and participation in the project. These latter data provide critical insights into my own theoretical development in relation to this research and my role as researcher in this study.

Shadduck-Hernandez's (1997) discussion of the various sources of qualitative data—some generated as part of the CIRCLE project, others to be generated specifically for the dissertation—is eloquently congruent with her assumptions about the nature of this work, its purpose and audience, and her political stance. Note that she plans to rely on several methods: documents in the form of journals, self-reflective writing, and papers written for courses or conferences (both her own and those of the student participants); a focus-group interview; in-depth interviews; and video and photography. (Videotaping and photography are discussed in Chapter 8 as secondary or specialized methods, although one could base an entire study on videos and pictures.)

With many of the primary methods, transcription and translation challenges must be addressed. Even in his own culture, a white, middle-class sociology scholar will encounter challenges in **transcribing** and **translating**, for example, in-depth interviews of adolescents' attitudes toward religion (Smith & Faris, 2002). We turn to a discussion of these important issues next.

Issues With Transcribing and Translating

Especially when using interviews in a study, transcribing and (perhaps) translating text are critically important tasks. Unfortunately, many introductory texts on qualitative research are silent on these issues, providing little guidance to the writers of proposals about how to handle them. We argue that neither is a *merely technical task*; both entail judgment and interpretation. When data have been translated and/or transcribed, they are not raw data any more—they are "processed data" (Wengraf, 2001, p. 7). And we agree with materials available on the RECOUP Web site that "all social research involves translation, if only from the 'language of the streets' into formal academic prose" (Singal & Jeffery, 2008, sec. 2). Thus, the methodological literature is now offering discussions about the issues in transposing the spoken word (from a tape recording) into a text (a transcription) or in transposing the spoken word in one language (from a tape recording) into another language (a translation) and then into a text (a transcription). We have further found that the ethical issues arising from transcribing and translating are now being discussed (we discuss some below).

Transcribing

If the researcher is fortunate enough to have interview partners who are comfortable with tape recordings, she leaves the research encounter with spoken words, dutifully and seemingly unproblematically recorded on tape. Those who have then sat down to transcribe the tapes, however, know well the pitfalls of assuming that the spoken word closely parallels the written one. We do not speak in paragraphs, nor do we signal punctuation as we speak. The judgments involved in placing something as simple as a period or a semicolon are complex and shape the meaning of the written word and, hence, of the interview itself. Similarly, the visual cues that we rely on to interpret another's meaning are lost when we listen to a tape; the transcriber no longer has access to those important paralinguistic clues about meaning. (See Tilley, 2003, for further discussion.)

For example, Rossman (1994) conducted interviews for an evaluation of a systemic school reform initiative. One interview partner used a discursive style that could be described as complex and dense. The interview partner would begin one topic, then loop to another midsentence, then on to another, finally saying, "Where was I?" and returning to the original topic after a prompt from the interviewer. Although this style is fascinating, it was extremely difficult to transcribe—sentences were interrupted by the speaker herself, topics were left unfinished, and overall clarity was difficult to ascertain. Rossman struggled with this transcription, finally sharing it with the interview partner to be sure that the meaning was accurately rendered in the transcribed account of her words. In another example, Chase's (1995) study of women school superintendents, responses to questions were replete with long pauses, in which the subject was changed. These gaps were, in the end, interpreted as indicators of a strong pattern of avoiding talking about and even denying experiences of sex discrimination—a major finding in her study. What if this researcher had made the mistake of simplistic transcription? But there is a cautionary note here: The meaning of pauses in conversation is not transparent; the researcher should use caution, as did Chase, in drawing inferences and offering interpretations of these linguistic patterns.

Experiences such as this are common. The implication is that the researcher needs to discuss the problematic nature of transcribing in the proposal and provide strategies for handling the judgments and interpretations inherent in such work. One valuable strategy is to share the transcriptions with the interview partners for their confirmation (or not) that the transcription captures their meaning and intent if not always their precise punctuation. We also note that the transcription of audio tapes is greatly facilitated by the use of software such as Olympus Digital Wave Player™, discussed below.

Translating

Clearly, the issues associated with translating from one language into another are much more complex than those concerning transcribing because they involve more subtle matters of connotation and meaning. As noted above, the methodological literature has recently grown to include essays discussing the difficult issues with translating (Esposito, 2001; Temple & Young, 2004). Of particular note, in light of a recurring theme in this edition, is the work of Temple and Young (2004), who raise issues in the context of translating from American Sign Language into standard written English. Writing in the context of the need for more sophistication in cross-language health research with refugee and immigrant populations, Esposito (2001) notes that translation is "the transfer of meaning from a source language . . . to a target language" and that the translator is "actually an interpreter who . . . processes the vocabulary and grammatical structure of the words while considering the individual situation and the overall cultural context" (p. 570). Thus, the focus on generating insightful and meaningful data through translation processes is paramount.

Note the use of the term *interpreter* in the above quote. This is a crucial insight, as it permits us to lift the burden of absolute accuracy from transcriptions and translations. Our position is that this goal is a chimera; what we should aim for is a reasonable approximation of the interview partner's words and intent. Subtle nuances in meaning are signaled by punctuation and paragraphing (as in transcribing), and phrases and concepts generated in one language rarely translate directly into another. Clearly, using another person, other than the researcher, to transcribe the recorded interviews and using an interpreter to gather data (as might arise when working across languages) complicate the processes immeasurably.

The work of Temple and Young (2004) raises three important questions: (1) whether to identify the translation act in the research report; (2) whether it matters if the researcher is also the translator; and (3) whether to involve the translator in analysis. It is especially intriguing that their analysis of translation issues focuses on a spatial language—American Sign Language. While their questions help move the field forward, Rossman's experience in her graduate teaching, working intensively with students whose first language (or even second or third) is not English, critiques their discussion. Each issue they identify is problematic. In response, we argue that there is an ethical imperative to inform the reader that translation has occurred and to address how this will be (in the case of a proposal) or has been (in the case of a final research report) managed. Second, more issues of meaning and interpretation arise when *someone other than* the researcher translates spoken or written words. Third, since translation entails the construction of meaning, we believe that analysis is happening whether or not it is acknowledged.

So what are the important issues with translating the spoken or written word? Most important are the processes and procedures that the researcher/translator has used (or will use, as should be discussed in the proposal) to construct meaning through multiple transpositions of the spoken or written word from one language into another. Rossman and Rallis (2003, p. 260) identify three others:

1. If you have translated from one language to another, which language constitutes the direct quotes?
2. Can you use translated words as a direct quote?
3. How do you signal that a translation is accurate and captures the subtle meanings of the original language?

There are no simple strategies or blueprints for addressing these and other issues associated with translation. What *is* simple and clear, however, is that the reader of the proposal must know that the researcher understands the issues, will take an ethical stance on translating, and will make clear in the final report just what he has done. Rossman insists that her students discuss the language for interviewing (and/or document review) in the proposal, indicating whether or not the student is fluent in the language. If the researcher is not, what strategies will he use to ensure accuracy and subtlety in translation? Rossman also recommends that students include phrases and key words from the original language from time to time in their final narratives. Translations or interpretations of those phrases can be put into parentheses with the caveat that there is no direct translation of the phrase's meaning into English. Including phrases or words in the original language (often italicized) also serves as a reminder to the reader that the interviews were originally conducted in a language other than English. This subtle reminder helps decenter the hegemony of an English-centered world.

Two examples are taken from the dissertation research of doctoral students who conducted research in Malawi and Guatemala. The first one, a doctoral student who proposed a mixed-methods study of a complex policy domain in Malawi (MacJessie-Mbewe, 2004), described how he would use the local language, Chichewa, for his interviews. Since he was fluent in this language, this posed no real problem for his dissertation committee. In his dissertation, he included several words and phrases that had evocative meaning in Chichewa but did not translate easily into English. The second student, Cohen-Mitchell (2005), studied the literacy and numeracy practices of market women in Quetzaltenango, Guatemala, for her dissertation. She was fluent in Spanish but not in Quiché, the local language of the women in her study. She had to convince her dissertation committee that she would work closely with Rosa, an educated literacy practitioner fluent in Quiché and Spanish, as a coresearcher and an interpreter to obtain strong data from the women. Cohen-Mitchell proposed, moreover, that she would take Quiché lessons during her fieldwork to improve her limited understanding of that language. She used both Quiché and Spanish phrases and words in her dissertation.

Issues of transcribing and translating are subtle and complex; they are not merely technical tasks. The writer of a qualitative research proposal has an ethical obligation to discuss these issues and how she will approach them, especially since qualitative research generates words—the primary symbol system through which meaning is conveyed and constructed. Not all of the issues can be solved at the proposal stage; in fact, we are quite skeptical of those who write that they have them all wrapped up. Instead, the proposal should have a thoughtful discussion of the more generic issues of transcribing and translating, as well as the ones specific to the research site and participants. These ideas harken back to the section on Cultural Studies, which highlights and deconstructs representations to uncover forms of power. The authority—the authorial voice—represents power to be used with respect!

Ethical Issues in Transcribing and Translating

The ethical issues that arise in transcribing and translating others' words center on how we represent our research participants, how we demonstrate respect for them in transposing their spoken words into text that we then manipulate and write up. Thus, in transcribing, what stance will the researcher take on "cleaning up" words, sentences, and phrases? Is it ethical to represent our interview partners who have spoken to us in incomplete sentences or used incorrect grammar *exactly* that way? Or are we doing them a disservice in presenting their imperfect speech to the world in dissertations or articles? When translating from one language to another, how do we ensure that we have shown respect for our research partners in representing their worldviews and thoughts? These issues center on respect for our participants that becomes more salient when we transform their words into analyzed categories and represent these publically.

Rossman conducted an evaluation of a school reform effort in a largely immigrant section of a northeastern city. The data that she and her evaluation team gathered consisted of interviews and samples of students' written work. Many of the latter were written as one would expect of an early English language learner (as well as any newly literate schoolchild), with misspellings, incorrect grammar, reversed letters, and the like. The principal of the school was shocked when she saw these in a draft report and asked that the evaluation team "clean them up," certainly before the report was submitted to the School Council. The team did so. Was this an ethical decision? What trade-offs did they have to make? What might have been sacrificed? What gained?

* * * * *

This chapter has provided an overview of several key methods that qualitative researchers typically use as well as salient ethical issues that may arise. We have also discussed considerations in transcribing tapes and translating from one language into another, whether tape-recorded interviews or field notes. At the proposal stage, the writer should consider how the selection of any particular method will inform the research questions, thereby extending and deepening knowledge on the topic. As a guide for assessing which primary methods will be useful, Tables 6.3 and 6.4 offer judgments about each method's strengths and challenges.

A solid rationale for the choice of methods is crucial, as it indicates to the reviewer of the proposal that the choice of methods is grounded in the conceptual framework and builds on previous theoretical, empirical, and methodological knowledge. These same considerations apply for the somewhat more specialized methods discussed in Chapter 8.

Table 6.3 Strengths of Primary Data Collection Methods

Strengths	PO	O	I	FG	MC	NI
Fosters face-to-face interactions with participants	X		X	X		X
Useful for uncovering participants' perspectives	X		X			X
Data collected in a natural setting	X	X	X	X	X	X
Facilitates immediate follow-up for clarification	X		X	X		X
Valuable for documenting major events, crises, conflicts	X	X		X	X	X
Useful for learning about participants' unconscious thoughts	X				D	D
Useful for describing complex interactions	X	X	X	X		X
Useful for obtaining data on nonverbal behavior and communication	X	X	D	D		D
Facilitates discovery of nuances in culture	X	X	X	X	X	X
Provides for flexibility in formulating working hypotheses	X	X	X	X	D	X
Provides information on context	X	X	X	X	X	
Facilitates analysis, validity checks, and triangulation	X	X	X	X	X	
Encourages cooperation and collaboration	X	D	D	X		X

Strengths	PO	O	I	FG	MC	NI
Data are easy to work with and categorize for analysis					X	
Obtains large amounts of data quickly		X		X		
Allows wide ranges of types of data and participants	X			D	D	
Easy and efficient to administer and manage					X	
Easily quantifiable and amenable to statistical analysis					X	
Easy to establish generalizability or usefulness for other settings					D	
May draw on established instruments					X	
Expands access to distant participants					X	

NOTE: X = strength exists; D = depends on use; PO = participant observation; O = observation; I = interview; FG = focus-group interview; MC = material culture, including documents; NI = narrative inquiry.

Table 6.4 Challenges in Using Primary Data Collection Methods

Challenges	PO	O	I	FG	MC	NI
Leads researcher to fixate on details	X	X		D	X	X
Possible misinterpretations due to cultural differences	X	X	X	X	X	X
Requires technical training		D				
Depends on cooperation of key individuals	X		X			X
Readily open to ethical dilemmas	X	X	X			X
Difficult to replicate	X	X	X	X	X	X

(Continued)

Table 6.4 (Continued)

Challenges	PO	O	I	FG	MC	NI
Data more affected by researcher presence	X	X	X	X		D
Expensive materials and equipment						
Can cause discomfort or even danger to researcher	X					
Too dependent on participant openness/honesty	X		X			X
Too artistic an interpretation undermines the research	X	X	X	X		X
Depends on power of initial research questions		X		X	D	
Depends on researcher's interpersonal skills	X	X	X	X	X	X

NOTE: X = challenges exists; D = depends on use; PO = participant observation; O = observation; I = interview; FG = focus-group interview; MC = material culture, including documents; NI = narrative inquiry.

FURTHER READING

Observation and Participant Observation

Adler, P. A., & Adler, P. (1994). Observational techniques. In N. K. Denzin & Y. S. Lincoln (Eds.), *Handbook of qualitative research* (pp. 377–392). Thousand Oaks, CA: Sage.

Bogdan, R. C., & Biklen, S. K. (2006). *Qualitative research in education: An introduction to theory and methods* (5th ed.). Boston: Allyn & Bacon.

Brock, K., & McGee, R. (2002). *Knowing poverty: Critical reflections on participatory research and policy.* Sterling, VA: Earthscan.

Cooke, B., & Kothari, U. (Eds.). (2001). *Participation: The new tyranny?* London: Zed Books.

Delamont, S. (2001). *Fieldwork in educational settings: Methods, pitfalls, and perspectives* (2nd ed.). London: RoutledgeFalmer.

DeWalt, K. M., & De Walt, B. R. (2001). *Participant observation: A guide for fieldworkers.* Walnut Creek, CA: AltaMira Press.

Emerson, R. M., Fretz, R. I., & Shaw, H. L. (1995). *Writing ethnographic fieldnotes.* Chicago: University of Chicago Press.

Hickey, S., & Mohan, G. (Eds.). (2004). *Participation: From tyranny to transformation?* London: Zed Books

Jorgensen, D. L. (1989). *Participant observation: A methodology for human studies.* Newbury Park, CA: Sage.

Lee, R. M. (1995). *Dangerous fieldwork.* Thousand Oaks, CA: Sage.

Lofland, J., & Lofland, L. H. (1995). *Analyzing social settings: A guide to qualitative observation and analysis* (3rd ed.). Belmont, CA: Wadsworth.

Nordstrom, C., & Robben, A. (1995). *Fieldwork under fire: Contemporary studies of violence and survival.* Berkeley: University of California Press.

Smith, C. D., & Kornblum, W. (Eds.). (1996). *In the field: Readings on the field research experience.* Westport, CT: Praeger.

Spradley, J. S. (1980). *Participant observation.* New York: Holt, Rinehart & Winston.

Wolcott, H. F. (2005). *The art of fieldwork* (2nd ed.). Walnut Creek, CA: AltaMira Press.

Wolcott, H. F. (2008). *Ethnography: A way of seeing* (2nd ed.). Walnut Creek, CA: AltaMira Press.

Generic In-Depth Interviewing

Gubrium, J. F., & Holstein, J. A. (Eds.). (2002). *Handbook of interview research.* Thousand Oaks, CA: Sage.

Gubrium, J. F., & Holstein, J. A. (2003). *Postmodern interviewing.* Thousand Oaks, CA: Sage.

Holstein, J. A., & Gubrium, J. F. (Eds.). (2003). *Inside interviewing: New lenses, new concerns.* Thousand Oaks, CA: Sage.

Kvale, S., & Brinkmann, S. (2009). *InterViews: Learning the craft of qualitative research interviewing* (2nd ed.). Thousand Oaks, CA: Sage.

Patton, M. Q. (2002). *Qualitative research and evaluation methods* (3rd ed.). Thousand Oaks, CA: Sage.

Peace, S. D., & Sprinthall, N. A. (1998). Training school counselors to supervise beginning counselors: Theory, research, and practice. *Professional School Counseling, 1*(5), 2–9.

Riessman, C. K. (2002). Analysis of personal narratives. In J. F Gubrium & J. A. Holstein (Eds.), *Handbook of interview research* (pp. 695–710). Thousand Oaks, CA: Sage.

Rubin, H. J., & Rubin, I. S. (2004). *Qualitative interviewing: The art of hearing data* (2nd ed.). Thousand Oaks, CA: Sage.

Weiss, R. S. (1994). *Learning from strangers: The art and method of qualitative interview studies.* New York: Free Press.

Ethnographic Interviewing

Bateman, B. E. (2002). Promoting openness toward culture learning: Ethnographic interviews for students of Spanish. *Modern Language Journal, 86*(3), 318–331.

Crivos, M. (2002). Narrative and experience: Illness in the context of an ethnographic interview. *Oral History Review, 29*(2), 13–15.

Edmondson, R. (2005). Wisdom in later life: Ethnographic approaches. *Ageing and Society, 25*(3), 339–356.

Montgomery, L. (2004). "It's just what I like": Explaining persistent patterns of gender stratification in the life choices of college students. *International Journal of Qualitative Studies in Education, 17*(6), 785–802.

Spradley, J. S. (1979). *The ethnographic interview.* New York: Holt, Rinehart & Winston.

Turner, W. L., Wallace, B. R., Anderson, J. R., & Bird, C. (2004). The last mile of the way: Understanding caregiving in African American families at the end-of-life. *Journal of Marital & Family Therapy, 30*(4), 427–488.

Westby, C., Burda, A., & Mehta, Z. (n.d.). Asking the right questions in the right ways: Strategies for ethnographic interviewing. *The ASHA Leader Online.* Retrieved February 25, 2009, from http://www.asha.org/publications/leader/archives/2003/q2/f030429b.htm

Wolcott, H. F. (1985). On ethnographic intent. *Educational Administration Quarterly, 3,* 187–203.

Phenomenological Interviewing

Collins, M., Shattell, M., & Thomas, S. P. (2005). Problematic interviewee behaviors in qualitative research. *Western Journal of Nursing Research, 27*(2), 188–199.

Holstein, J. A., & Gubrium, J. F. (1995). *The active interview.* Thousand Oaks, CA: Sage.

Hood, R. W., Jr. (2000). A phenomenological analysis of the anointing among religious serpent handlers. *International Journal for the Psychology of Religion, 10*(4), 221–240.

Lackey, N. R., Gates, M. F., & Brown, G. (2001). African American women's experiences with the initial discovery, diagnosis, and treatment of breast cancer. *Oncology Nursing Forum, 28*(3), 519–527.

Maloy, R., Pine, G., & Seidman, I. (2002). *Massachusetts teacher preparation and induction study report: First year findings* (National Education Association Professional Development School Research Project Teacher Quality Study). Washington, DC: National Education Association.

Mosselson, J. (2006). *Roots and routes: Bosnian adolescent refugees in New York.* New York: Peter Lang.

Seidman, I. E. (2006). *Interviewing as qualitative research: A guide for researchers in education and the social sciences* (3rd ed.). New York: Teachers College Press.

Thomas, S. P., & Pollio, H. R. (2002). *Listening to patients: A phenomenological approach to nursing research and practice.* New York: Springer.

Van Manen, M. (1990). *Researching lived experience: Human science for an action sensitive pedagogy.* Buffalo: State University of New York Press.

Focus-Group Interviewing

Allen, L. (2006). Trying not to think "straight": Conducting focus groups with lesbian and gay youth. *International Journal of Qualitative Studies in Education, 19,* 163–176.

Botherson, M. J. (1994). Interactive focus group interviewing: A qualitative research method in early intervention. *Topics in Early Childhood Special Education, 14*(1), 101–118.

Hennink, M. M. (2007). *International focus group research: A handbook for the health and social sciences.* Cambridge, UK: Oxford University Press.

Hennink, M. M. (2008). Emerging issues in international focus group discussions. In S. N. Hesse-Biber & P. Leavy (Eds.), *Handbook of emergent methods* (pp. 207–220). New York: Guilford Press.

Krueger, R. A., & Casey, M. A. (2008). *Focus groups: A practical guide for applied research* (4th ed.). Thousand Oaks, CA: Sage.

Linhorst, D. M. (2002). A review of the use and potential of focus groups in social work research. *Qualitative Social Work, 1*(2), 208–228.

Morgan, D. L. (1997). *Focus groups as qualitative research* (2nd ed.). Thousand Oaks, CA: Sage.

Peek, L., & Fothergill, A. (2009). Using focus groups: Lessons from studying daycare centers, 9/11, and Hurricane Katrina. *Qualitative Research, 9*(1), 31–59.

Stewart, D. W., & Shamdasani, P. N. (1990). *Focus groups: Theory and practice.* Newbury Park, CA: Sage.

Life Histories, Narrative Inquiry, and Digital Storytelling

Adams, T. E. (2008). A review of narrative ethics. *Qualitative Inquiry, 14*(2), 175–194.

Atkinson, R. (1998). *The life story interview.* Thousand Oaks, CA: Sage.

Bell, J. S. (2002). Narrative inquiry: More than just telling stories. *TESOL Quarterly, 36*(2), 207–213.

Center for Digital Storytelling [Web site]. Accessed October 24, 2009, at www.storycenter.org/index1.html

Clandinin, D. J., & Connelly, F. M. (2000). *Narrative inquiry: Experience and story in qualitative research.* San Francisco: Jossey-Bass.

Clandinin, D. J., Huber, J., Huber, M., Murphy, M. W., & Orr, A. M. (Eds.). (2006). *Composing diverse identities: Narrative inquiries into the interwoven lives of children and teachers.* New York: Routledge.

Conle, C. (2000). Narrative inquiry: Research tool and medium for professional development. *European Journal of Teacher Education, 23*(1), 49–54.

Conle, C. (2001). The rationality of narrative inquiry in research and professional development. *European Journal of Teacher Education, 24*(1), 21–33.

Digital Storytelling Association [Website]. Accessed April 8, 2009, at www.dsaweb.org/

Educause. (n.d.). *Educause learning initiative: 156 resources.* Accessed April 8, 2009, at www.educause.edu/Resources/Browse/EDUCAUSELearningInitiative/33152

Etter-Lewis, G., & Foster, M. (1996). *Unrelated kin: Race and gender in women's personal narratives.* New York: Routledge.

Gluck, S. B., & Patai, P. (Eds.). (1991). *Women's words: The feminist practice of oral history.* New York: Routledge.

Goldman, R., Hunt, M. K., Allen, J. D., Hauser, S., Emmons, K., Maeda, M., et al. (2003). The life history interview method: Applications to intervention development. *Health Education & Behavior, 30,* 564–581.

Hodgson, K. (2005). *Digital storytelling: Using technology to tell stories.* Retrieved April 8, 2009, from www.umass.edu/wmwp/DigitalStorytelling/Digital%20Storytelling%20Main%20Page.htm

iMovie™ [Computer software]. Retrieved October 29, 2009, from www.apple.com/ilife/imovie/

Josselson, R. (Ed.). (1996). *Ethics and process in the narrative study of lives.* Thousand Oaks, CA: Sage.

Josselson, R., & Lieblich, A. (Eds.). (1993). *The narrative study of lives.* Newbury Park, CA: Sage.

Lieblich, A., Tuval-Mashiach, R., & Zilber, T. (1998). *Narrative research: Reading, analysis, and interpretation.* Thousand Oaks, CA: Sage.

Mandelbaum, D. G. (1973). The study of life history: Gandhi. *Current Anthropology, 14,* 177–207.

Martin, R. R. (1995). *Oral history in social work: Research, assessment, and intervention.* Thousand Oaks, CA: Sage.
Miller, R. L. (1999). *Researching life stories and family histories.* Thousand Oaks, CA: Sage.
Mitchell, W. J. (Ed.). (1981). *On narrative.* Chicago: University of Chicago Press.
MovieMaker™ [Computer software]. Retrieved October 29, 2009, from www.microsoft.com/windowsxp/downloads/updates/moviemaker2.mspx
Narayan, K., & George, K. M. (2003). Personal and folk narratives as cultural representation. In J. F. Gubrium & J. A. Holstein (Eds.), *Postmodern interviewing* (pp. 123–139). Thousand Oaks, CA: Sage.
Narrative Inquiry: The Forum for Theoretical, Empirical, and Methodological Work on Narrative [Web site]. Accessed March 2, 2009, at www.clarku.edu/faculty/mbamberg/narrativeINQ/
Riessman, C. K. (1993). *Narrative analysis.* Newbury Park, CA: Sage.
Riessman, C. K. (2002). Analysis of personal narratives. In J. F. Gubrium & J. A. Holstein (Eds.), *Handbook of interview research* (pp. 695–710). Thousand Oaks, CA: Sage.
Slim, H., & Thompson, P. (1995). *Listening for a change: Oral testimony and community development.* Philadelphia: New Society.
Stanley, L., & Temple, B. (2008). Narrative methodologies: Subjects, silences, re-readings and analyses. *Qualitative Research, 8*(3), 275–282.
Thompson, P. R. (2000). *The voice of the past: Oral history* (3rd ed.). Oxford, UK: Oxford University Press.
Wengraf, T. (2001). *Qualitative research interviewing: Biographic narrative and semi-structured methods.* London: Sage.
Yow, V. R. (1994). *Recording oral history: A practical guide for social scientists.* Thousand Oaks, CA: Sage.

Interviewing Elites

Aberbach, J. D., & Rockman, B. A. (2002). Conducting and coding elite interviews. *PS: Political Science & Politics, 35(*4), 673–676.
Becker, T. M., & Meyers, P. R. (1974–1975). Empathy and bravado: Interviewing reluctant bureaucrats. *Public Opinion Quarterly, 38,* 605–613.
Bennis, W., & Nanus, B. (1985). *Leaders: The strategies for taking charge.* New York: Harper & Row.
Delaney, K. J. (2007). Methodological dilemmas and opportunities in interviewing organizational elites. *Sociology Compass, 1*(1), 208–221.
Hertz, R., & Imber, J. B. (1995). *Studying elites using qualitative methods.* Thousand Oaks, CA: Sage.
Marshall, C. (1984). Elites, bureaucrats, ostriches, and pussycats: Managing research in policy settings. *Anthropology and Education Quarterly, 15,* 235–251.
Odendahl, T., & Shaw, A. M. (2002). Interviewing elites. In J. F. Gubrium & J. A. Holstein (Eds.), *Handbook of interview research* (pp. 299–316). Thousand Oaks, CA: Sage.
Thomas, R. (1993). Interviewing important people in big companies. *Journal of Contemporary Ethnography, 22*(1), 80–96.

Interviewing and Studying (With) Children

Cappello, M. (2005). Photo interviews: Eliciting data through conversations with children. *Field Methods, 17*(2), 170–184.
Daniels, D. H., Beaumont, L. J., & Doolin, C. A. (2002). *Understanding children: An interview and observation guide for educators.* Boston: McGraw-Hill Higher Education.

Eder, D., & Fingerson, L. (2003). Interviewing children and adolescents. In J. A. Holstein & J. F. Gubrium (Eds.), *Inside interviewing: New lenses, new concerns* (pp. 33–53). Thousand Oaks, CA: Sage.

Faller, K. C. (2003). Research and practice in child interviewing. *Journal of Interpersonal Violence, 18(*4), 377–389.

Fine, G. A., & Sandstrom, K. L. (1988). *Knowing children: Participant observation with minors.* Newbury Park, CA: Sage.

Greene, S., & Hogan, D. (Eds.). (2005). *Researching children's experiences: Approaches and methods.* London: Sage.

Hart, R. A. (1997). *Children's participation: The theory and practice of involving young citizens in community development and environmental care.* London: Earthscan.

Kortesluoma, R. L., Hentinen, M., & Nikkonen, M. (2003). Conducting a qualitative child interview: Methodological considerations. *Journal of Advanced Nursing, 42*(5), 434–441.

Lewis, A., & Porter, J. (2004). Interviewing children and young people with learning disabilities. *British Journal of Learning Disabilities, 32*(4), 191–197.

Moore, T., McArthur, M., & Noble-Carr, D. (2008). Little voices and big ideas: Lessons learned from children about research. *International Institute for Qualitative Methodology, 7*(2), 77–91.

Smith, A. B., Taylor, N. J., & Gollop, M. M. (Eds.). (2000). *Children's voices: Research, policy and practice.* Auckland, NZ: Pearson Education.

Wilson, J. C., & Powell, M. (2001). *A guide to interviewing children: Essential skills for counsellors, police, lawyers and social workers.* New York: Routledge.

Interviewing Across Social Identities

Bell, J. S. (2002). Narrative inquiry: More than just telling stories. *TESOL Quarterly, 36*(2), 207–213.

Bloom, L. R., & Munro, P. (1995). Conflicts of selves: Non-unitary subjectivity in women administrators' life history narratives. In J. A. Hatch & R. Wisniewski (Eds.), *Life history and narrative* (pp. 99–112). London: Falmer Press.

Dunbar, C., Jr., Rodriguez, D., & Parker, L. (2003). Race, subjectivity, and the interview process. In J. A. Holstein & J. F. Gubrium (Eds.), *Inside interviewing: New lenses, new concerns* (pp. 131–150). Thousand Oaks, CA: Sage.

Edmondson, R. (2005). Wisdom in later life: Ethnographic approaches. *Ageing and Society, 25*(3), 339–356.

Foster, M. (1994). The power to know one thing is never the power to know all things: Methodological notes on two studies of Black American teachers. In A. Gitlin (Ed.), *Power and method: Political activism and educational research* (pp. 129–146). London: Routledge.

Kong, T. S. K., Mahoney, D., & Plummer, K. (2003). Queering the interview. In J. A. Holstein & J. F. Gubrium (Eds.), *Inside interviewing: New lenses, new concerns* (pp. 91–110). Thousand Oaks, CA: Sage.

Milner, H. R. (2007). Race, culture, and researcher positionality: Working through dangers seen, unseen, and unforeseen. *Educational Researcher, 36*(7), 388–400.

Reinharz, S., & Chase, S. E. (2003). Interviewing women. In J. A. Holstein & J. F. Gubrium (Eds.), *Inside interviewing: New lenses, new concerns* (pp. 73–90). Thousand Oaks, CA: Sage.

Riessman, C. K. (1991). When gender is not enough: Women interviewing women. In J. Lorder & S. A. Farrell (Eds.), *The social construction of gender* (pp. 217–236). Newbury Park, CA: Sage.

Ryen, A. (2003). Cross-cultural interviewing. In J. A. Holstein & J. F. Gubrium (Eds.), *Inside interviewing: New lenses, new concerns* (pp. 429–448). Thousand Oaks, CA: Sage.

Schwalbe, M. L., & Wolkomir, M. (2003). Interviewing men. In J. A. Holstein & J. F. Gubrium (Eds.), *Inside interviewing: New lenses, new concerns* (pp. 55–71). Thousand Oaks, CA: Sage.

Subedi, B., & Rhee, J. (2008). Negotiating collaboration across differences. *Qualitative Inquiry, 14*(6), 1070–1092.

Wenger, G. C. (2003). Interviewing older people. In J. A. Holstein & J. F. Gubrium (Eds.), *Inside interviewing: New lenses, new concerns* (pp. 111–130). Thousand Oaks, CA: Sage.

Wieder, A. (2003). White teachers/white schools: Oral histories from the struggle against apartheid. *Multicultural Education, 10*(4), 26–31.

Translating and Transcribing

Birbili, M. (2000). Translating from one language to another. *Social Research Update, 31.* Retrieved February 27, 2009, from http://sru.soc.surrey.ac.uk/SRU31.html

Edwards, R. (1998). A critical examination of the use of interpreters in the qualitative research process. *Journal of Ethnic & Migration Studies, 24*(1), 197–208.

Esposito, N. (2001). From meaning to meaning: The influence of translation techniques on non-English focus group research. *Qualitative Health Research, 11*(4), 568–579.

Maranhão, T., & Streck, B. (Eds.). (2003). *Translation and ethnography: The anthropological challenge of intercultural understanding.* Tucson: University of Arizona Press.

Maynard-Tucker, G. (2000). Conducting focus groups in developing countries: Skill training for local bilingual facilitators. *Qualitative Health Research, 10*(3), 396–410.

Poland, B. D. (2003). Transcription quality. In J. A. Holstein & J. F. Gubrium (Eds.), *Inside interviewing: New lenses, new concerns* (pp. 267–287). Thousand Oaks, CA: Sage.

Singal, N., & Jeffery, R. (2008). Transcribing and translating data. In *Qualitative research skills workshop: A facilitator's reference manual.* Cambridge, UK: RECOUP (Research Consortium on Educational Outcomes and Poverty). Retrieved February 27, 2009, from http://manual.recoup.educ.cam.ac.uk

Temple, B. (1997). Watch your tongue: Issues in translation and cross-cultural research. *Sociology, 31*(3), 607–618.

Temple, B. (2008). Narrative analysis of written texts: Reflexivity in cross language research. *Qualitative Research, 8*(3), 355–365.

Temple, B., & Young, A. (2004). Qualitative research and translation dilemmas. *Qualitative Research, 4*(2), 161–178.

Tilley, S. A. (2003). "Challenging" research practices: Turning a critical lens on the work of transcription. *Qualitative Inquiry, 9*(5), 750–773.

Using Documents and Material Culture

Busch, C., De Maret, P. S., Flynn, T., Kellum, R., Le, S., Meyers, B., et al. (2005). *An introduction to content analysis.* Retrieved March 2, 2009, from the Colorado State University Writing Center Web site at http://writing.colostate.edu/guides/research/content/pop2a.cfm

Hodder, I. (2000). The interpretation of documents and material culture. In N. K. Denzin & Y. S. Lincoln (Eds.), *Handbook of qualitative research* (2nd ed., pp. 703–716). Thousand Oaks, CA: Sage.

Neuendorf, K. A. (2002). *The content analysis guidebook.* Thousand Oaks, CA: Sage.

Neuendorf, K. A. (n.d.). *The content analysis guidebook online.* Retrieved March 2, 2009, from http://academic.csuohio.edu/kneuendorf/content

Rosenberg, L. (2006). *Rewriting ideologies of literacy: A study of writing by newly literate adults.* Unpublished PhD dissertation, University of Massachusetts, Amherst.

Storey, W. K. (2004). *Writing history: A guide for students.* New York: Oxford University Press.

KEY CONCEPTS

Analysis of documents

Artifacts

Digital storytelling

Ethical issues

Ethnographic interviewing

Field notes

Focus-group interviews

In-depth interviewing

Interviewing children and youth

Interviewing elites

Life histories

Material culture

Narrative inquiry

Observation

Participant observation

Phenomenological interviewing

Research across differences in social identities

Transcribing

Translating

7

Secondary and Specialized Methods

In addition to the primary data-gathering methods outlined in Chapter 6, the researcher can choose to incorporate several secondary and supplemental methods in the design of a study as he deems appropriate. Each of those described below is a full and complete method in and of itself and has a methodological literature explicating its nuances and subtleties. In some instances, the same terminology is used for data collection methods and for modes of reporting or presentation. For example, some speak of "doing case studies" as a way of collecting data, but, more often, an entire report, even a book, is a case study. Ethnographers talk of "doing an ethnography" to describe their approach to data collection, when, in fact, an ethnography is a written product—*ethno* = culture, *graphy* = writing—or an inscription. *Nisa: The Life and Words of a !Kung Woman* (Shostak, 1983) is a book that is the life history of one African woman, and the data-collection method is called life history, consisting of long-term participant observation and in-depth and ethnographic interviewing. Yes, this *is* confusing!

The discussions that follow are necessarily simplified and brief, as was the preceding, and the list is not exhaustive. The methods discussed below, if used, should always be used with the understanding that observation, participant observation, interviewing, and analyzing documents and artifacts are the primary data collection methods for discovering context-laden patterns and understandings. These might well be supplemented by a variety of secondary or specialized methods. Some of these are variations of the primary four. Below, we discuss five for consideration: (1) using computers and Internet technology; (2) using videos and photographs; (3) historical analysis; (4) interaction analysis; and (5) dilemma analysis. This is just a sampling; there are many others that qualitative researchers might include. However, at the proposal stage, the researcher considering the use of any of these would have to convince the reader that she is knowledgeable about the method and capable of implementing it thoughtfully and ethically in her study.

USING COMPUTER APPLICATIONS AND INTERNET TECHNOLOGIES

Since the publication of the fourth edition of this book, the social world and the research community have witnessed the continuing explosion of the potential uses of computer software and the Internet for research purposes. It remains true that there is no question that the Internet and its associated hardware (desktop and laptop computers, personal digital assistant [PDAs], iPods™, etc.) are continuing to at times radically change the methodologies of social science research. Searching the Internet for resources (now called Googling); using **software to assist in transcribing audiotapes**, to manage citations, and for data analysis; interviewing by means of e-mail, on Skype™, or in dedicated chat rooms; and using dialogues and interactions online as sites for study are all now part and parcel of much scholarship in the social sciences and applied fields, as is the integration of technology into narratives, noted in Chapter 6 under Digital Storytelling. In Chapter 2, we noted this emerging method as comprising three major strands: (1) the use of the Internet for gathering data; (2) the use of software packages that support transcribing tapes and analysis of data; and (3) the use of **Internet ethnography**, in which the Internet itself is a site for research.

These uses of computer software and the Internet are reflected in the three editions of the *Handbook of Qualitative Research* (Denzin & Lincoln, 1994, 2000, 2005), when one examines the chapters dedicated to the use of computers in qualitative research. The first edition (1994) included a chapter titled "Using Computers in Qualitative Research" (Richards & Richards, 1994), in which the authors described various software programs designed to assist in qualitative data management and analysis. The second edition contained a similar chapter, "Software and Qualitative Research" (Weitzman, 2000). The acronym for this developing field is QDA, for *qualitative data analysis.* The third edition of the *Handbook of Qualitative Research* (2005) includes no chapter on QDA. Instead, Markham's chapter focuses on *Internet ethnography*, illustrating the growing focus on the Internet itself as a site for identity representation and construction. Not mentioned in any edition is the use of the Internet for directly gathering data through e-mail or dedicated discussion blogs.

Gathering Data Using the Internet

The use of the powers of the Internet for gathering data has mushroomed in recent years. Surveying a large sample using applications such as SurveyMonkey™ is now commonplace.

While not typically the case, such applications could include only open-ended questions, as would be appropriate in a qualitative study. Following up interviews with e-mail questions for clarification or elaboration is frequently used, as are technologies that allow for asynchronous "conversations with participants, especially when they are distant from the researcher" (James & Busher, 2006, p. 403). In addition, dedicated discussion blogs or sites create "virtual" focus group discussions, as noted above.

All these uses of the Internet present challenges and questions: Are data collected from an Internet discussion blog as rich as, for example, in-person interviews or focus groups? What cues are missing when the data are gathered without actually seeing, sensing, or touching the participants? What intuitive inferences are lost? Furthermore, how can you protect the anonymity of your sources if you collect data online? And how do you justify a sample that is made up of only people who are computer literate, comfortable with the medium, and have computer access? Despite these challenges, computer-mediated **data gathering** may offer an alternative to face-to-face interviewing and be most appropriate for certain research projects. Because of its pervasiveness in today's society, Seymour (2001) explored the experiences of individuals with various disabilities (paralysis as a result of spinal cord injuries, cerebral palsy, visual impairment, and amputated arms or hands) in using technology, seeking to understand if and how they felt excluded from the communication channels embodied in the Internet.

As noted in Chapter 2, one major advantage in using the Internet to gather data is that one's sample can quite literally be global. Computers also provide access to populations uncomfortable with or unwilling to engage in face-to-face interactions. At the proposal stage, the researcher would have to provide a sound rationale for gathering data using the Internet, as with any method, arguing that this strategy flowed logically from the conceptual framework and research questions. He would also need to convince the readers that he was capable of using the medium successfully.

Software for Analyzing Data and Transcribing Tapes

The use of **software for analyzing qualitative data** has also mushroomed. Fifteen years ago, a handful of these applications were available commercially. Today, there is a multitude. The Web site of the American Evaluation Association (n.d.) lists 30 different software applications for assisting in analyzing text (from transcriptions or other sources), audio files, and video clips. This burgeoning industry has raised both hopes and fears among qualitative researchers.

In the second edition of the *Handbook*, Weitzman (2000) noted that computers can assist the analysis phase because they facilitate making and writing observational notes, editing, coding, storing, searching and retrieval, linking data, writing memos, analyzing content, displaying data, drawing and verifying conclusion, building theory, mapping graphics, and writing reports. He went on to note, however, that "software . . . cannot do the analysis for you, not in the same sense in which a statistical package such as SPSS or SAS can do, say, multiple regressions" (p. 805). Our experience is that novice qualitative researchers hope that software will do the hard work of analysis for them, somewhat magically. Unfortunately, just like life at times, qualitative research is not so easy. We caution that software is only a tool to help with some of the mechanical and management aspects of analysis; the hard analytic thinking must be done by the researcher's own internal hard drive!

While we make no specific recommendations here (and do not get a payment from the producers), we observe that perhaps the most commonly used applications are Atlas.ti™, Ethnograph™, and NVivo™ (we provide URLs for information or free trial copies at the end of this chapter). We do recommend, however, that the researcher proposing to use software to assist in analyzing data demonstrate, at the proposal stage, that she is familiar with the application, has used it before, and is capable of drawing on its strengths while ensuring that she understands that the hard analytic work must be her own.

Also growing exponentially in use is software to help with transcribing audiotapes. When interviews are conducted using a digital recorder, the files can be entered directly into a software application. Working at one's computer, the transcriber listens to the tapes and types the words into a word-processing program. Various key strokes permit slowing down, speeding up, or pausing the tape's playback. Again, while we make no specific recommendations, Express Scribe™ and Olympus Digital Wave Player™ are useful. Also increasing in use, although with extreme problems, are voice recognition software applications, which the researcher can "train" to recognize his voice, as well as the voices of those interviewed. Two examples are Dragon Naturally Speaking™ and e-Speaking™.

Internet Ethnography

As discussed in Chapters 2 and 6, scholars from a number of disciplines have focused on Internet sites and blogs as sites for their research, giving birth to a new genre of qualitative research—Internet ethnography. In particular, the fields of communication and cultural studies have contributed fascinating studies of the Internet and its wealth of opportunities to reflect changing social identities, communities, and cultures (see, e.g., Baym, 2000; Gatson & Zwerink, 2004; Hine, 2000; Kendall, 2002; Miller & Slater, 2000). Their fascination emerges in part from the postmodern turn that has examined and problematized the embodied construction of identity. The Internet provides a disembodied site where social identities (gender, social class, sexual orientation, etc.) are hidden. Thus emerges the possibility of studying the construction of identity solely through text. As Markham (2005) notes, "Although we recognize that reality is socially negotiated through discursive practice, the dialogic nature of identity and culture is thrown into high relief in computer-mediated environments" (p. 795). A qualitative study could be designed to focus exclusively on a particular blog, as did Gatson and Zwerink (2004) in their studies of sites dedicated to fans of *Buffy, the Vampire Slayer*.

Ethical Issues in Using Computers and Internet Technology

Gathering data using Internet technology poses one set of ethical issues; using various software applications poses others; and using the Internet as a site for the conduct of research brings its own considerations. When gathering data through this medium, there are particular concerns about protecting anonymity and privacy. As interviews are increasingly digitized, the researcher cannot claim, with strict confidence, that the data will be destroyed at the end of the study (a common requirement from institutional review boards). Files stored on a computer are easily hacked into; files that are backed up automatically onto a server are never "destroyed" and remain accessible, despite the researcher's best intentions. Considering these ethical issues at the proposal stage is critically important. Using software to transcribe tapes poses challenges similar to those discussed above, and they center on respecting one's interview partners in how their words are represented. This is not unique to using software but remains an important ethical concern.

Finally, conducting ethnographies of Internet sites poses a different set of ethical issues. Are all participants informed that research is going on? Have they willingly consented to participate? If they are on the site as avatars (a computer user's representation of herself, which can be three-dimensional or a photo or in text), can the researcher easily request that they be allowed to review the transcripts or analyses prior to publishing them? And does conducting research change the dynamics of interaction on the site such that the ethnography is really a study of online blog participants' engagement in a study? Just when it looked as if qualitative study was starting to make sense, the Internet emerged as a whole new world that provokes more confusing questions!

VIDEOS AND PHOTOGRAPHS

With the advent of digital cameras, which take not only pictures but also short videos, visually recording events at research sites and participants' interactions is quite easy. In parallel, the advent of the video-sharing Web site YouTube™ makes the uploading and sharing of videos commonplace. These recent developments bring opportunities and ethical risks (discussed below) and link to a long tradition in anthropology and other social science disciplines, as well as highly respected work in documentary filmmaking. Note their relationship to digital storytelling, discussed in Chapter 6.

Historically, using films and photography constituted the field of *visual anthropology* or *film ethnography*, where interactions and activities were systematically recorded to depict a cultural group or event. The Visual Anthropology Society now has a Web site to facilitate knowledge sharing within the discipline. The various forms of film can be used for data collection and for organizing, interpreting, and validating qualitative inquiry (Szto, Furman, & Langer, 2005). As Banks (2001) illustrates, films of marriage ceremonies in different social strata in contemporary India, coupled with historical photos and documents, raised key questions in his search for cultural understanding of the interconnections between economics and tradition in handicrafts, dowries, and trousseaux.

The tools of videos and photographs are now used in many disciplines: communication, cultural studies, anthropology, and many applied fields. Scholars focus on visual media as sites for analyses and use the production of visual representation to depict their analyses. From what can be argued as a cultural studies perspective, Hurdley (2007) studied photographs on living room mantelpieces as "domestic display" (p. 355), expressive of the "complexities of 'doing' home cultures" (p. 355). Videos and photographs have the unique ability to capture visible phenomena in a seemingly objective manner—yet always from the perspective of the filmmaker, just as with other forms of observation. The filmmaker—the observer—must decide what to focus on while recording and then decide on how to interpret the data in that recording (whether on film or in field notes). More recently, the method of photovoice has emerged, which has an explicit empowerment ideology (see Wang & Burris, 1997; Wang & Pies, 2004). Described as a "participatory action research methodology" (Wang & Pies, 2004, p. 95), the method is used by ordinary community members to document and describe their community by taking photographs. It blends photography with social action, encouraging community members to build awareness of and commitment to changes in their community's circumstances. Several Web sites describing this method are included at the end of this chapter.

Researchers choose to use photographs or videos for their obvious strengths. Visual representations are evocative and can be profoundly moving. Videos and photographs can document rituals and ceremonies, creating a visual record of cultural events to pass on to successive generations. It can document social conflicts (court proceedings, public speakers, Senate sessions, etc.). Videos can be especially valuable for documenting nonverbal behavior and communication patterns such as facial expressions, gestures, and emotions. These visual records can help preserve unique, disappearing, or rare events. However, interpretation of the images in film can be problematic, as with other forms of observation and in the use of documents and artifacts. One strategy could be to share the images with participants and invite them to share their interpretations as a form of member validation. Two excellent examples of classic ethnographic film are *Educating Peter* (Home Box Office Project Knowledge, 1992), the story of the experiences of a boy with severe cognitive challenges in a regular classroom, and *High School* (Wiseman, 1969), a depiction of life in a comprehensive high school in the early 1970s. A more recent example is *Intimidad* (Sabin, 2008), which presents a moving portrayal of the emotional challenges of a migrant family in Mexico.

However, the use of film, in its various forms, has certain challenges. Videos and pictures can appear to be "true" and "accurate" when the viewer is not mindful that the film was taken by an individual with his own positionality. What might be the professional subjectivity and the interests of the filmmaker? Moreover, good-quality equipment can be expensive, and most research budgets are quite modest. And production can be problematic, especially in creating a smooth final product—a flowing video or collage of photographs interspersed with text and, perhaps, music. The researcher may need technical expertise, although there is now software that helps even novice researchers produce high-quality videos, such as Pinnacle Studio 12™. Historically, videos and photographs were not easily included in a book, journal article, or dissertation, but the capacity to burn a CD for inclusion in a dissertation or book is becoming increasingly common, as is the inclusion of digitized illustrative photographs in a written report.

Ethical Issues With Videos and Photographs

Do the participants know that photos or videos are being made? Are they fully aware? And most important, have they given their consent to be represented in a photo or in a video? Especially problematic with visual representations of people is the recurring question of protecting their identities. Furthermore, these representations, once digitized, may spread without the researcher's knowledge. In the proposal, the researcher should indicate how she will protect the identities of the participants, scrupulously, and how well she is prepared to use these media ethically and sensitively.

HISTORICAL ANALYSIS

A history is an account of some event or combination of events that occurred in the past. Historical analysis is a method of analyzing and interpreting what has happened using records and accounts. It is particularly useful in qualitative studies for establishing a baseline or background prior to participant observation or interviewing. Sources of historical data are classified as either primary or secondary. Oral testimony of eyewitnesses, documents, records, and relics are primary. Reports of persons who relate the accounts of eyewitnesses and summaries, as in history books and encyclopedias, are secondary.

Historical analysis is particularly useful in obtaining knowledge about unexamined areas and in reexamining questions for which answers are not as definite as desired. It allows for systematic and direct classification of data. Historical research traditions articulate procedures to enhance the credibility of statements about the past, to establish relationships, and to determine possible cause-and-effect relationships. Many research studies have a historical base or context, so systematic historical analysis enhances the trustworthiness and credibility of a study.

There is a dialectical tension in this kind of analysis between contemporary and historical interpretations of events, even though texts representing either perspective are influenced by the social contexts in which they are produced. Historical analysis cannot use direct observation, and there is no way to directly test a historical hypothesis. Moreover, there are challenges in analyzing and categorizing historical data. The research should keep in mind that documents may be falsified deliberately and that words and phrases used in old records may now have very different meanings. The meanings of artifacts, as we have noted before, are perceived and interpreted by the researcher. The researcher should retain a modest skepticism about such data.

INTERACTION ANALYSIS

Interaction analysis is an interdisciplinary approach that focuses on the interactions among people and between people and their environments in naturally occurring settings. The focus of many interaction analysis studies is on "human activities, such as talk, nonverbal interaction, and the use of artifacts and technologies, identifying routine practices and problems and the resources for their solution" (Jordan & Henderson, 1995, p. 31). The approach has emerged from ethnography (with its focus on participant observation), sociolinguistics, ethnomethodology (the study of the methods people use to accomplish ordered social interactions), conversation analysis, **kinesics** (the study of how nonverbal gestures, posture, and movement send communicative messages), and **proxemics** (the study of how people interact in terms of their distance to one another). What distinguishes interaction analysis as a specialized method is its reliance on video and audio recording and a noninterventionist stance toward the collection of data. Thus, those employing interaction analysis seek to unobtrusively observe naturally occurring interactions, record them on tape, and subsequently analyze those recordings through a particular analytic lens. What typically does not occur in interaction analysis is direct talk—interviewing—with participants in the setting chosen for study. First used as a method for studying small groups in organizations in the 1920s, interaction analysis gained prominence as a method for observing classrooms (Rex & Green, 2008; Rex, Murnen, Hobbs, & McEachen, 2002; Rex, Steadman, & Graciano, 2006) and for aiding teacher training (Flanders, 1970). Recently, it has been used in research on couples to develop coding systems that can powerfully analyze an ongoing stream of dyadic behaviors (Baucom & Kerig, 2004). Power dynamics are revealed with interaction analysis in micropolitical studies of organizations such as school boards, state legislatures, employment agencies, and corporations, as well as street gangs and playgrounds. One can see how conflicts are resolved, how dominance is maintained, and how ideologies are imposed (Corson, 1995).

Because interaction analysis has been widely used in education, specifically in studies of classroom interaction, we discuss this strand and then briefly describe kinesics and proxemics because of their generative historical role in the development of interaction analysis.

Classroom Interaction Analysis

With a long history drawing on multiple disciplines, classroom interaction analysis has tended to focus on the language in use in classrooms and how these interactions reflect, reproduce, and shape wider social processes such as the power dynamics of class, race, and gender. While it has diverse strands, studies typically "examine behaviors and strategies used by teachers and students . . . [and how these] correlate with student performance measures or student learning indices" (Rex & Green, 2008, p. 571). Researchers typically rely on videotaping and audiotaping to produce a permanent record of the interactions of interest.

Representative of studies in this genre is the work of Rex et al. (2002), who studied the stories that teachers tell in classrooms using videotaping as the primary method for gathering data. They argue that

> the frequency, duration, and kinds of stories that teachers tell and the occasions on which they tell them shape the norms for how students think they need to present themselves, what students count as knowledge, and how students display achievement in their classroom. (p. 768)

Rex and her graduate assistant took daily videos of classroom "talk"; they then coded these, noting "teachers' use of narrative-like constructions when addressing their classes" (p. 773). The theoretical notions that this research was embedded in helped frame their analyses.

Another relatively new development in interaction analysis, broadly construed, is **gesture research** in classrooms. This research focuses on ways in which gestures contribute to meaning making in the teaching-learning interaction. The assumption here is that gestures and other paralinguistic movements convey substantial meaning that may enhance or detract from the explicit verbal message (also see the subsection on kinesics below). Work in this domain has focused on learning science concepts and skills among middle school students (Singer, Radinsky, & Goldman, 2008) and on learning algebra concepts (Alibali & Nathan, 2007).

One strength of interaction analysis is that a permanent record is obtained through video and audio recording; this helps preserve the original data but does raise ethical issues (discussed below). Depending on how tightly focused the analytic categories are, the method can produce quantifiable data, should this be desired. Interaction analysis may be particularly useful for testing out patterns that were identified in early participant observations or interviews.

Clearly, interaction analysis is only as generative as the categories used to focus the observations. When these are culturally biased, too reflective of the researcher's prejudgments, or not well designed for the setting, the categories may not be particularly fruitful.

Two well-developed "grandparents" of interaction analysis broadly construed—kinesics and proxemics—offer examples of finely focused analyses. We discuss these below.

Ethical Issues in Interaction Analysis

The ethical issues that arise when conducting interaction analyses center on protection of and respect for the persons participating in the research. In today's age, when digitized data are never fully deleted from a computer, disk, or jumpdrive, protecting participants from future unwarranted or even harmful use of the data is problematic. Hacking into computers is a daily event; therefore, the protection of the data—and, more important, the participants—is of paramount concern. Furthermore, the temptation to use video segments when presenting research findings is seductive but might well violate promises made to participants about ensuring their anonymity. This would be especially true for children—as in classroom interaction analysis—and other vulnerable populations.

We now turn to a brief discussion of kinesics and proxemics—two generative methods that are closely linked to interaction analysis.

Kinesics

Learning about society can be enhanced if we study not only what people say but also what their body movements and other subtle, nonverbal cues reveal; this is the working assumption behind kinesics, which is the study of body motion, including nonverbal gestures and postures, and their communicative messages. Movement is analyzed systematically so that researchers can identify and interpret significant patterns in communication events.

The classic work of Birdwhistell (1970) asserted that nonverbal body behaviors function like significant sounds and combine like words into single or relatively complex units. Body movements ranging from a single nod of the head to a series of hand and leg gestures can attach additional meaning to spoken words. (Remember these gestures when transcribing an interview, as discussed above.) Kinesics research rests on the assumption that individuals are unaware of being engaged constantly in adjustments to the presence and activities of other persons. People modify their behavior and react verbally and nonverbally. Their nonverbal behavior is influenced by culture, gender, age, and other factors associated with psychological and social development.

However, correctly understanding just what these body movements mean is the main challenge in using kinesics. Novice body readers who have a "pop-psych" understanding of the science of kinesics may make incorrect, and perhaps damaging, interpretations of behavior. But note the wide popularity of *Blink* (Gladwell, 2005). On his Web site, the author states that *Blink* is

> about rapid cognition, about the kind of thinking that happens in a blink of an eye. When you meet someone for the first time, or walk into a house you are thinking of buying, or read the first few sentences of a book, your mind takes about two seconds to jump to a series of conclusions. Well, "Blink" is a book about those two seconds, because I think those instant conclusions that we reach are really powerful and really important and, occasionally, really good. (Gladwell.com, n.d.).

We also note here the development since the 1960s of the method of "microexpression," developed and elaborated by Ekman and his colleagues (see, e.g., Ekman, Campos, Davidson, & De Waais, 2003; Ekman & Friesen, 1975). This extension and elaboration of the basic principles of kinesic analysis has focused on **microexpressions**, which are involuntary, fleeting facial expression that, the authors argue, occur when one is trying to conceal an emotion. As developed by Ekman and his colleagues (2003), analysis of these fleeting, microsecond expressions may reveal when the individual is lying. Their analyses formed the basis for the current Fox Television Network's *Lie to Me*, in which the central character is based on Ekman.

One strength of kinesics analysis is that it provides another perspective on interactions in specific settings. With caution, a researcher may be more confident about the integrity of the data provided by an interview partner if the speaker's body language is congruent with his words. Also, the researcher can monitor his own nonverbal behavior to clarify messages sent to the research participant and to stay in touch with his own feelings during data collection.

Kinesic analysis has limitations, however, because the meanings conveyed in specific body movements or gestures are certainly not universal; researchers must be aware of cultural differences. Gestures signal different meanings in different cultures. In some countries, moving the head up and down signifies *no*, and moving it from side to side means *yes*. Body movements should be interpreted very tentatively and with exquisite sensitivity to the context.

Proxemics

Another classic example of the analysis of interaction, proxemics, is the study of people's use of space in relation to their cultures and environments. The term was developed by Hall (1966), although he did not perform the original work in this area. Many studies have been conducted on human activities in bars, airports, subways, elevators, and other public places where individuals have to deal with one another in a limited space. Using proxemics, the researcher focuses on how space is defined and managed, from interpersonal distance to the arrangement of furniture and architecture. Anthropologists, for example, have used proxemics to determine the territorial customs of cultures. Proxemics has been useful in the study of the behavior of students in the classroom and of marital partners undergoing counseling.

There are several strengths to the use of proxemics. It is unobtrusive, and usually, it is difficult for a research participant to mislead the observer deliberately. As with kinesics, because proxemics focuses on nonverbal behavior, participants would have to be skillful to "lie" about their feelings. Proxemics is useful for studying the way individuals react to the invasion of their territory. Likewise, proxemics can be used in cross-cultural studies because people's use of personal space varies greatly from one culture to the next. Finally, proxemic analysis is useful for studies in areas such as the effect of seating arrangements on student behavior or the effect of crowding on workplace productivity.

The greatest challenge with proxemics as a data collection method is that the researcher must be cautious when interpreting the observed behaviors. If the researcher is observing a conference or a business meeting, the manner in which the participants take their seats can be of vital importance for shaping the decisions that emerge in the meeting, but the data must be interpreted carefully. When used exclusively, proxemics could be misleading because relationships that do not exist might be suggested by the researcher's analysis. Proxemics, however, can provide fresh insights into a social group or interactions when coupled with other methods.

Ethical Issues in Proxemics

The ethical issues that arise when using proxemics as a method of data gathering center on informed consent and representation. If researchers are observing people in large, public spaces, such as airports or shopping malls, is it ethical to do so without their informed understanding? Are public spaces "exempt" from the ethics of research with humans? And how does the researcher "represent" these individuals without making unwarranted assumptions about their social class, ethnicity, and the like? These are all considerations that need to be pondered at the proposal stage when using proxemics.

DILEMMA ANALYSIS

Dilemma analysis focuses on research participants' reactions to situations that have no right answers, that is, dilemmas. The method can be used as a focused part of interviewing, particularly to get at the core of the interview partner's processes of thinking, assessing, valuing, and judging. It has been refined primarily in developmental psychology. However, it can be adapted wherever the research focuses on moral issues and practical decision-making processes. We describe two common types.

The first, the *hypothetical, researcher-generated dilemma*, is the most common. Several research participants are given a standardized dilemma and asked what they would do and what would guide their decision making. The famous example devised by

Kohlberg (1981) elicited research participants' moral reasoning about the so-called Heinz dilemma. In this dilemma, Heinz's wife has a terminal illness, and the only way to obtain a life-saving drug is to break a biblical commandment: violate someone's property, commit a crime, or steal it. Kohlberg used this method to generate theory on moral development. Shortly afterward, Gilligan (1982) critiqued Kohlberg's (1981) theory and methodology, arguing that the theory was gender biased because his samples were college-age men. She devised data collection strategies that were more contextualized and more attuned to real lives, as well as ones that focused on women. As a result, she developed very different conclusions about moral development. The real-life, researcher-generated dilemma uses a real crisis—from history or from typical workplace or family life situations—and asks for research participants' choices and the thoughts and feelings surrounding those choices.

The second, the *real-life, respondent-generated dilemma*, encourages research participants to describe the most difficult or heart-wrenching choices they have made, for example, while growing up, at work, or in their families. Thus, the situations are generated in a more naturalistic fashion. Although they are focused, they are closer to a straightforward interview, allowing respondents, at least to some extent, to choose what to focus on. For example, Marshall (1992, 1993; Marshall, Patterson, Rogers, & Steele, 1996) asked assistant principals to describe a situation that, in the past two years, had created ethical dilemmas for them in their workplaces. She guided them through standard questions to probe the parameters affecting the choices they made. In the interviews, telling the stories in depth to a sympathetic, nonjudgmental ear seemed cathartic. The rich data included stories of denying services to students because of policy, firing teachers, turning down promotions to avoid upsetting their family stability, and so on. While the interviews were wonderfully rich with personal context, pulling them together in data analysis and reporting was no easy task.

Dilemma analysis can be fun. Commonly focusing on one interview partner at a time, it produces a thematic coherence that does not depend on academic theories or hunches of the researcher (Winter, 1982). It opens doors to the innermost thoughts and can be designed to collect standardized data. Real-life, researcher-generated dilemmas, if well constructed, using insights from previous research, can be very useful, especially for focusing and standardizing data collection, when that is appropriate. Gathering data through real-life dilemmas is often enjoyable. People like to recount poignant, heroic, and angst-provoking situations—when they are in the past and when they believe that they have created an adequate resolution. Dilemma analysis can be dilemma laden, too! As in the Heinz example, people may not take the situation seriously, and the data may well reflect this. Also, the choice of a dilemma and the interview questions may be skewed to shape the choices, producing "interesting" data. In addition, the very personalized data elicited from real-life but respondent-generated dilemmas may be difficult to interpret and to compare with other data.

Ethical Issues in Dilemma Analysis

The ethical issues that may arise using dilemma analysis center on the potential for reasoning through thorny circumstances to elicit strong emotional reactions. This may be particularly true for the respondent-generated dilemma when uncovering problematic circumstances—ones that may still be raw and sore—bring up tears or anger. At the proposal stage, the researcher should articulate how she might handle such situations, with respect for the persons and sensitivity to their emotional reactions.

* * * * *

The above discussions provide a mosaic of various methods that a qualitative researcher might choose to implement to generate useful and insightful data. As we have noted throughout, it is quite common for a qualitative study to draw on more than one method. Tables 7.1 and 7.2 offer criteria for assessing the usefulness and the challenges of building one of these methods into a proposal. We then discuss some key considerations in combining methods and use a vignette to illustrate the choices and decisions to be made at the proposal stage.

COMBINING DATA COLLECTION METHODS

Many qualitative studies combine several data collection methods over the course of the study, as seen in Shadduck-Hernandez's (1997) proposal discussed in Vignette 18. The researcher can assess the strengths and challenges of each method and then decide if that method will work with the questions and in the setting for a given study. In drafting a proposal, the researcher should consider whether the method will provide good, rich data and be cost-effective and feasible in terms of the subtleties of the setting and the resources available for the study (the do-ability). As we have noted, the relative emphasis on participation and direct interaction suggests an emphasis on the primary methods discussed above. Judicious use of the secondary and specialized methods might, however, be quite generative in responding to the research questions. The rationale for their use should be integral to the overall argument in the proposal.

When considering the use of various methods, the researcher might usefully consider three questions; these can be applied to the overall research questions but are crucial in developing the design and methods section of the proposal. The first question asks whether a specific method should be implemented in a more open-ended way or whether it should be more tightly prefigured. The second focuses on the sequencing of different methods throughout a study: the ebb and flow. And the third considers whether to focus more broadly or more in depth. Combining various methods encourages the proposal writer to consider these questions. He will be well served by developing a clear (albeit flexible) plan for implementing various methods (interviewing and

Table 7.1 Strengths of Secondary and Specialized Data Collection Methods

	I	F	HA	IA	DA
Fosters face-to-face interactions with participants					
Useful for uncovering participants' perspectives					D
Data collected in a natural setting	X	X		X	
Facilitates immediate follow-up for clarification	X			D	
Valuable for documenting major events, crises, and conflicts	X	X	X		X
Useful for learning about participants' unconscious thoughts		X		X	
Useful for describing complex interactions	X	X	X	X	
Useful for obtaining data on nonverbal behavior and communication		X		X	
Facilitates discovery of nuances in culture		X	X	X	
Provides for flexibility in formulating working hypotheses		X	X	X	
Provides information on context		X	X		D
Facilitates analysis, validity checks, and triangulation	X	X		X	X
Encourages cooperation and collaboration	X				
Data are easy to work with and categorize for analysis					
Obtains large amounts of data quickly	D	X	X		
Allows wide ranges of types of data and participants	X			D	
Easy and efficient to administer and manage	X		X	X	
Easily quantifiable and amenable to statistical analysis				X	
Easy to establish generalizability or usefulness for other settings			D	X	
May draw on established instruments	X			X	X
Expands access to distant participants	X				

NOTE: X = strength exists; D = depends on use; I = Internet use; F = film; HA = historical analysis; IA = interaction analysis; DA = dilemma analysis.

Table 7.2 Challenges in Using Secondary Data Collection Methods

	I	F	HA	IA	DA
Leads researcher to fixate on details	X	X		X	
Possible misinterpretations due to cultural differences		X	X	X	X
Requires technical training		X			
Depends on cooperation of key individuals					
Readily open to ethical dilemmas	X	X			X
Difficult to replicate		X	D		
Data more affected by researcher presence		D		D	X
Expensive materials and equipment	X	X		D	
Can cause discomfort or even danger to researcher					
Too dependent on participant openness/honesty	X				X
Too artistic an interpretation undermines the research		X	X		
Depends on power of initial research questions		X	X	X	X
Depends on researcher's interpersonal skills					

NOTE: X = challenges exists; D = depends on use; I = Internet use; F = film; HA = historical analysis; IA = interaction analysis; DA = dilemma analysis.

then observing or vice versa), for writing about whether the focus will be broad (many events, many participants) or more in depth (a few crucial events, a few individuals), and for making decisions about approaching interviews and observations, for example, with a wide-angle lens or a more focused one. Thinking through these issues of combining methods and articulating the reasoning behind his choices is important for demonstrating that he has thought through these issues and has a clear plan in mind. The reviewers of a proposal that provides a strong level of elaboration for design and implementation choices will likely be pleased.

We illustrate the above discussion with Vignette 19, which describes how a researcher selected data collection methods in a study about a long-term health care facility.

VIGNETTE 19 Choosing Data Collection Methods

How might one's view of life be shaped by residence in a long-term health care facility? A doctoral student in health care management (Kalnins, 1986) wanted to examine—in depth and in detail—the contexts, processes, and interactions that shaped patients' perspectives. She reasoned that a qualitative approach would be most fruitful in picking up everyday actions and interactions about complex social structures.

From the variety of data collection strategies, she proposed a combination of direct observation, participant observation, and semistructured interviewing. Her beginning point would be direct observation of residents and staff in various areas of the facility, "witnessing events which particularly preoccupied the hosts, or indicated special symbolic importance to them" (Schatzman & Strauss, 1973, p. 59). This would allow her to get a holistic view and to gather data that would inform the interview process.

Kalnins's (1986) plan as a participant observer would be to observe the residents and staff in the natural setting of the long-term health care facility, requiring her "commitment to adopt the perspective of those studied by sharing in their day-to-day experiences" (Denzin, 1970, p. 185). In her proposal, Kalnins (1986) anticipated that participant observation and interviewing would run concurrently, allowing data from each to be used to substantiate events, explore emerging hypotheses, and make further decisions about the conduct of the research. Her role as participant observer would mean that Kalnins would become immersed in the lives and activities of those she was studying. She understood the interactive-adaptive nature of participant observation, reflecting the complex relationship between field observation and emerging theory, and the impact of this relationship on decisions about further data collection. Her decisions about the data to be collected and methods for collecting those data would be guided by Wilson's (1977) list of five relevant types of data employed to get at meaning structures: (1) the form and content of verbal interaction between participants, (2) the form and content of their verbal interaction with the researcher, (3) nonverbal behavior, (4) patterns of actions and nonaction, and (5) traces, archival records, artifacts, and documents (p. 255).

To generate facts, opinions, and insights (Yin, 1984), Kalnins (1986) planned for open-ended structured interviews (using questionnaires) that would enable the exploration of many topics but that could focus on cultural nuances, firsthand encounters, and the perceptions, meanings, and interpretations of others. Information would also be gathered from various documents and archives, lending a historical perspective to the study.

Vignette 19 illustrates how a researcher chose an array of data collection methods, knowing that each method had particular strengths and that each would help elicit certain desired information. It shows that data collection strategies and methods cannot be chosen in a vacuum. Intensively examining the possible methods, trying them out, examining their potentials, and fitting them to the research question, site, and sample are important design considerations. In addition, researchers should consider their *own* personal abilities to successfully implement any particular overall approach or method. Thus, the proposal should convince the reviewer that the researcher is capable of selecting, refining, and implementing data collection methods that are appropriate, well thought out, and thorough. As discussed in Chapter 1, demonstrating competence with methods is a central part of the do-ability of a study. As we have noted throughout, however, a challenge at the proposal stage is retaining flexibility in the design and implementation of the study—one of the hallmarks of qualitative inquiry. The reality is that the research questions may change as the research progresses; in response, the specific methods used may need to change to pursue the intriguing new directions. The researcher is challenged to reserve this flexibility. Vignette 20 provides an example.

VIGNETTE 20 Design Flexibility

A graduate student wanted to explore the implementation of a state mandate for local school councils. Rodriguez first proposed participant observation of meetings and in-depth interviews with board members. The data collection plan showed a schedule for observing the meetings, goals for interviewing, and a time allowance for analysis of data and for follow-up data collection. But in the process of initial data collection and preliminary analysis, he discovered that teacher resentment of the councils was creating a pattern of unintended negative consequences. This discovery could have important implications for policy development. Did Rodriguez have to stay with the original question and data collection plan? Wouldn't a design alteration offer important insights?

Rodriguez reasoned that if he could describe the processes whereby well-intended policy is thwarted, policymakers could gain insight that might help them make timely alterations in policy development or implementation. Given this possible benefit to the study, he could choose to focus subsequent data collection on the conflicts between teacher needs and the mandate to school boards to implement councils. This would require him to turn to additional literatures on, for example, teacher needs, teacher participation in decision making, or teacher unions. He might also need to employ additional data collection methods (e.g., surveying teacher needs, observing teacher union meetings, and doing historical research on the reactions of teacher lobbies to mandates for school councils), or he might need to sample additional settings or people. As the research question became more focused, his initial research design and data collection strategy would most likely undergo some changes.

In the example in Vignette 20, the research proposal probably did not include a plan for analysis of lobbying efforts or observation of collective bargaining sessions. It would, however, be entirely appropriate—indeed, recommended—for the researcher to modify the research proposal if an exciting and significant focus emerges from early data collection. In fact, the primary strength of the qualitative approach is this very flexibility, which allows, even encourages, exploration, discovery, and creativity.

Along with choosing appropriate strategies for data collection, the researcher should address the complex processes of managing, recording, and analyzing data. These processes are not discrete, sequential events but occur dialectically throughout the conduct of a qualitative study: Analysis occurs as themes are identified, as the deeper structures of the social setting become clear, and as consequent modifications are made in the initial design. At the proposal stage, however, the researcher should present some initial ideas about how the data will be managed and stored and provide some preliminary discussion of the processes for analyzing those data. We discuss these issues in the next chapter.

Note: This vignette is fictitious.

Dialogue Between Learners

Melanie,

I really feel and appreciate your questions about the many selves that are infused within our research. I'm a former writing instructor, so I have a tendency to believe in writing through these types of difficulties. I wonder what would happen if you did a bit of writing on the same topic from your different perspectives: as researcher, former instructor, and friend. Would they each look differently at the same topic? Where would they overlap? What I'm getting at is if you were to consciously take on the persona of one of your selves and then took on an issue from three perspectives, you might get some wonderful insights into how your unique position creates an interpretation. Does that make any sense? My guess is that you'll find more points of overlap than not. It might, however, allow you to examine and honestly address your role in your research.

You've no doubt noted the number of different approaches in Chapter 4 of Catherine and Gretchen's book—it's a bit overwhelming to say the least! Sometimes it's a bit hard to not get caught up in the specifics of one particular approach—to not feel as though there were only one right way to complete an ethnographic interview or narrative analysis. I have a tendency to read up on different approaches and run the risk of losing sight of what I bring to the project—that there is perhaps a bit of a dialectical relationship between what I bring to the project and the effect the project has on me.

While I agree that, ultimately, our research might not be about us, I can't deny that it does, in no small way, reflect us and our experiences. We might say that our research is, in a very real sense, autobiographical. No

(Continued)

(Continued)

doubt you selected your area of research because in some way you connect with it. Imagine working so hard on something that you were distinctly separate from and neutral toward!

But there is something so very disconcerting or indulgent about the ongoing navel-gazing. Like you, I hedge at focusing too much on myself (or, my self). There are also the voices and selves of the students you work with and study. Hmmm . . . I suppose this is where we look to our mentors to read our work and say, "Hey, this is not all about you" or ask, "Where do you fall in all of this?" I suppose we can also turn to other graduate students! I get a lot out of our conversations; it's nice to have someone to chat with about these issues, and writing it down in an e-mail seems to help.

Hope all is well.

Aaron

Hi Aaron,

You make some good points, especially that our research does, in some way, revolve around us; otherwise, it wouldn't be our research. Thanks for the suggestions, too; I like the idea of writing from my different selves. (I'm a former English teacher—bring on the pen!) I think it's quite easy to get stuck at approaching our research in one specific way; remembering the flexibility in technique and presentation really opens up our options.

I really like thinking through these topics, too. Working through the tangles with a fellow grad student gives one the license to be ignorant! Even though we know so much about so many different things, we're still making sense in personal, practical ways. Conversations among grad students are more of a meaning-making experience—working together to create an understanding that applies to our personal situations. I get a lot out of seeing other grad students tackle different techniques, too. A few of my friends here are dedicated to life history and film ethnography. I'm more of an in-depth interview, computer interaction type of researcher. Even if I don't see myself taking on those specific types of techniques (yet!), I learn from seeing their use of different approaches. We might gain info like this faster by asking a professor or reading an article, but we don't absorb it or apply it the same way.

So, what else is on your mind?

Melanie

FURTHER READING

Computer Applications and Internet Technology

Anderson, T., & Kanuka, H. (2003). *E-research: Methods, strategies, and issues.* Boston: Allyn & Bacon.

Bagley, C. (2008). Educational ethnography as performance art: Towards a sensuous feeling and knowing. *Qualitative Research, 8*(1), 53–72.

Basit, T. N. (2003). Manual or electronic? The role of coding in qualitative data analysis. *Educational Research, 45*(2), 143–154.

Baym, N. K. (2000). *Tune in, log on: Soaps, fandom and online community.* Thousand Oaks, CA: Sage.

Best, S. J., & Krueger, B. S. (2004). *Internet data collection.* Thousand Oaks, CA: Sage.

Buchanan, E. A. (Ed.). (2004). *Readings in virtual research ethics: Issues and controversies.* Hershey, PA: Information Science.

Chen, S., Hall, G. J., & Johns, M. D. (Eds.). (2003). *Online social research: Methods, issues and ethics.* New York: Peter Lang.

Couper, M. P., & Hansen, S. E. (2003). Computer-assisted interviewing. In J. A. Holstein & J. F. Gubrium (Eds.), *Inside interviewing: New lenses, new concerns* (pp. 195–213). Thousand Oaks, CA: Sage.

Davidson, J., & Jacobs, C. (2008). The implications of qualitative research software for doctoral work. *Qualitative Research Journal, 8*(2), 72–80.

Gajjala, R. (2004). *Cyber selves: Feminist ethnographies of South Asian women.* New York: AltaMira Press.

Garcia, A. C., Standlee, A. I., Bechkoff, J., & Cui, Yan. (2009). Ethnographic approaches to the Internet and computer-mediated communication. *Journal of Contemporary Ethnography, 38*(1), 52–84.

Gatson, S. N., & Zwerink, A. (2004). Ethnography online: "Natives" practicing and inscribing community. *Qualitative Research, 4*(2), 179–200.

Gough, S., & Scott, W. (2000). Exploring the purposes of qualitative data coding in educational enquiry: Insights from recent research. *Educational Studies, 26,* 339–354.

Hewson, C., Yule, P., Laurent, D., & Vogel, C. (2003). *Internet research methods: A practical guide for the social and behavioral sciences.* Thousand Oaks, CA: Sage.

Hine, C. (2001). *Virtual ethnography.* London: Sage.

Hughey, M. W. (2008). Virtual (br)others and (re)sisters: Authentic black fraternity and sorority identity on the Internet. *Journal of Contemporary Ethnography, 35*(5), 528–560.

James, N., & Busher, H. (2006). Credibility, authenticity and voice: Dilemmas in online interviewing. *Qualitative Research, 6*(3), 403–420.

Kendall, L. (2002). *Hanging out in the virtual pub: Masculinities and relationships online.* Berkeley: University of California Press.

Lee, B. K., & Gregory, D. (2008). Not alone in the field: Distance collaboration via the Internet in a focused ethnography. *International Journal of Qualitative Methods, 7*(3), 30–46.

Leedy, P. D. (Ed.). (1997). *Practical research: Planning and design* (6th ed.). Upper Saddle River, NJ: Prentice Hall.

Mann, C., & Stewart, F. (2000). *Internet communication and qualitative research: A handbook for researching online.* London: Sage.

Mann, C., & Stewart, F. (2003). Internet interviewing. In J. F. Gubrium & J. A. Holstein (Eds.), *Postmodern interviewing* (pp. 81–105). Thousand Oaks, CA: Sage.

Markham, A. N. (2004). Internet communication as a tool for qualitative research. In D. Silverman (Ed.), *Qualitative research: Theory, method and practice* (pp. 95–124). London: Sage.

Markham, A. N. (2005). The methods, politics, and ethics of representation in online ethnography. In N. K. Denzin & Y. S. Lincoln (Eds.), *Handbook of qualitatative research* (3rd ed., pp. 793–820). Thousand Oaks, CA: Sage.

Miller, D., & Slater, D. (2000). *The Internet: An ethnographic approach.* New York: Berg.

Sade-Beck, L. (2004). Internet ethnography: Online and offline. *International Journal of Qualitative Methods, 3*(2), Article 4. Retrieved March 2, 2009, from www.ualberta.ca/~iiqm/backissues/3_2/ pdf/sadebeck.pdf

Seale, C. F. (2003). Computer-assisted analysis of qualitative interview data. In J. A. Holstein & J. F. Gubrium (Eds.), *Inside interviewing: New lenses, new concerns* (pp. 289–308). Thousand Oaks, CA: Sage.

Selwyn, N. (2002). Telling tales on technology: The ethical dilemmas of critically researching educational computing. In T. Welland & L. Pugsley (Eds.), *Ethical dilemmas in qualitative research* (pp. 42–56). Hants, UK: Ashgate.

Seymour, W. S. (2001). In the flesh or online? Exploring qualitative research methodologies. *Qualitative Research, 1*(2), 147–168.

Sixsmith, J., & Murray, C. D. (2001). Ethical issues in the documentary data analysis of Internet posts and archives. *Qualitative Health Research, 11*(3), 423–432.

Tesch, R. (1990). *Qualitative research: Analysis types and software tools.* New York: Falmer Press.

Ward, K. J. (1999). Cyber-ethnography and the emergence of the virtually new community. *Journal of Information Technology, 14,* 95–105.

Williams, M. (2007). Avatar watching: Participant observation in graphical online environments. *Qualitative Researcher, 7*(1), 5–24.

Software

Atlas.ti 6.0 for Windows [Computer software]. Trial copy available at the Atlas.ti Scientific Software Development Web site at www.atlasti.com

Dragon Naturally Speaking 10 for Windows [Computer software]. Retrieved March 3, 2009, from the Nuance Communications, Inc. Web site at www.nuance.com/naturallyspeaking

e-Speaking [Computer software]. Retrieved March 3, 2009, from www.e-speaking.com

The Ethnograph 6.0 for Windows [Computer software]. Retrieved February 27, 2009, from the Qualis Research Web site at www.qualisresearch.com

Express ScribeTranscription Playback Software for Windows [Computer software]. Retrieved March 2, 2009, from the NCH Software, Inc. Web site at www.nch.com.au/scribe

NViv08 for Windows [Computer software]. Trial copy available at the QRS International Web site. Accessed March 2, 2009 at www.qsrinternational.com

Olympus Digital Wave Player 2 [Computer software]. Retrieved October 26, 2009, from www.olympusvoice.com.au/products/digital/notetakers/vn240pc_specifications.html

Pinnacle Studi012 [Computer software]. Retrieved March 3, 2009, from www.pinnaclesys.com/PublicSite/us/Products/Consumer+Products/Home+Video/Studio+Family/ (Avid Technology, Inc.)

SurveyMonkey [Computer software]. Retrieved March 5, 2009, from www.surveymonkey.com

Sykpe [Computer software]. Retrieved October 26, 2009, from www.Skype.com

Historical Analysis

Barzun, J., & Graff, H. F. (2004). *The modern researcher* (6th ed.). Belmont, CA: Wadsworth.

Berg, B. L. (2004). *Qualitative research methods for the social sciences* (5th ed.). Boston: Pearson.

Brooks, P. C. (1969). *The use of unpublished primary sources.* Chicago: University of Chicago Press.

Crivos, M. (2002). Narrative and experience: Illness in the context of an ethnographic interview. *Oral History Review, 29*(2), 13–15.

Edson, C. H. (1998). Our past and present: Historical inquiry in education. In R. R. Sherman & R. B. Webb (Eds.), *Qualitative research in education: Focus and methods* (pp. 44–57). New York: Falmer Press.

Gottschalk, L. A. (1969). *Understanding history.* New York: Knopf.

Hodder, I. (2000). The interpretation of documents and material culture. In N. K. Denzin & Y. S. Lincoln (Eds.), *Handbook of qualitative research* (2nd ed., pp. 703–716). Thousand Oaks, CA: Sage.

Schutt, R. K. (2001). *Investigating the social world: The process and practice of research.* Thousand Oaks, CA: Pine Forge Press.

Storey, W. K. (2004). *Writing history: A guide for students.* New York: Oxford University Press.

Tuchman, G. (1994). Historical social science. In N. K. Denzin & Y. S. Lincoln (Eds.), *Handbook of qualitative research* (pp. 306–323). Thousand Oaks, CA: Sage.

Zinn, H. (2005). *A people's history of the United States: 1492-present.* New York: Harper.

Videos and Photographs

Asch, T. (Producer). (1970). *The feast* [Motion picture]. Washington, DC: U.S. National Audiovisual Center.

Beckman, K., & Ma, J. (Eds.). (2008). *Still moving: Between cinema and photography.* Durham, NC: Duke University Press.

Campbell, L. H., & McDonagh, D. (2009). Visual narrative research methods as performance in industrial design education. *Qualitative Inquiry, 15*(3), 587–606.

Cappello, M. (2005). Photo interviews: Eliciting data through conversations with children. *Field Methods, 17*(2), 170–184.

Collier, J., & Collier, M. (1986). *Visual anthropology: Photography as a research method.* Albuquerque: University of New Mexico Press.

Gardner, R. (1974). *Rivers of sand* [Motion picture]. New York: Phoenix Films.

Harper, D. (1994). On the authority of the image. In N. K. Denzin & Y. S. Lincoln (Eds.), *Handbook of qualitative research* (pp. 403–412). Thousand Oaks, CA: Sage.

Hockings, P. (Ed.). (1995). *Principles of visual anthropology.* New York: Mouton de Gruyter.

Kopal, M., & Suzuki, L. A. (Eds.). (1999). *Using qualitative methods in psychology.* Thousand Oaks, CA: Sage.

McLarty, M. M., & Gibson, J. W. (2000). Using video technology in emancipatory research. *European Journal of Special Needs Education, 15*(2), 138–139.

Noyes, A. (2004). Video diary: A method for exploring learning dispositions. *Cambridge Journal of Education, 34*(2), 193–209.

Pepler, D. J., & Craig, W. M. (1995). A peek behind the fence: Naturalistic observations of aggressive children with remote audiovisual recording. *Developmental Psychology, 31*(4), 548–553.

Photovoice.org [Web site]. Accessed April 8, 2009, at www.photovoice.org

Pink, S. (2001). More visualizing, more methodologies: On video, reflexivity and qualitative research. *Sociological Review, 49*(4), 586–599.

Prosser, J. (1998). *Image-based research: A sourcebook for qualitative researchers.* London: Falmer Press.

Raingruber, B. (2003). Video-cued narrative reflection: A research approach for articulating tacit, relational and embodied understandings. *Qualitative Health Research, 13*(8), 1155–1169.

Rollwagen, J. (Ed.). (1988). *Anthropological filmmaking.* New York: Harwood Academic.

Rose, G. (2008). *Visual methodologies: An introduction to the interpretation of visual methods* (2nd ed.). Thousand Oaks, CA: Sage.

Sabin, A. (Cinematographer). (2008). *Intimidad* [Motion picture]. Available at the Carnivales que Films Web site at www.carnivalesquefilms.com/intimidad.html

VisualAnthropology.net. Accessed March 3, 2009, at www.visualanthropology.net

Wang, C., & Burris, M. A. (1997). Photovoice: Concept, methodology, and use for participatory needs assessment. *Health Education & Behavior, 24*(3), 369–387.

Wang, C. C., & Pies, C. A. (2004). Family, maternal, and child health through photovoice. *Maternal and Child Health Journal, 8*(2), 95–102.

Wiseman, F. (Director). (1969). *High school* [Motion picture]. Boston: Zippora Films.

Wright, T. (2008). *Visual impact: Culture and meaning of images.* Oxford, UK: Berg.

Interaction Analysis, Proxemics, and Kinesics

Alibali, M., & Nathan, M. (2007). Teachers' gestures as a means of scaffolding students' understanding: Evidence from an early algebra lesson. In R. Goldman, R. Pea, B. Barron, & S. Derry (Eds.), *Video research in the learning sciences* (pp. 349–366). Mahwah, NJ: Lawrence Erlbaum.

Birdwhistell, R. L. (1970). *Kinesics and context: Essays on body motion communication.* Philadelphia: University of Pennsylvania Press.

Corson, D. (1995). Ideology and distortion in the administration of outgroup interests. In D. Corson (Ed.), *Discourse and power in educational organizations* (pp. 87–110). Cresskill, NJ: Hampton Press.

Edgerton, R. B. (1979). *Alone together: Social order on an urban beach.* Berkeley: University of California Press.

Ekman, P., Campos, J., Davidson, R. J., & De Waals, F. (2003). *Emotions inside out: 130 years after Darwin's "The Expression of the Emotions in Man and Animals."* New York: Annals of the New York Academy of Sciences.

Ekman, P., & Friesen, W. V. (1975). *Unmasking the face: A guide to recognizing emotions from facial clues.* Upper Saddle River, NJ: Prentice Hall.

Flanders, N. A. (1970). *Analyzing teaching behavior.* Reading, MA: Addison-Wesley.

Freedman, J. (1975). *Crowding and behavior.* New York: Viking Press.

Guerrero, L. K., DeVito, J. A., & Hecht, M. L. (Eds.). (1999). *The nonverbal communication reader: Classic and contemporary readings* (2nd ed.). Prospect Heights, IL: Waveland Press.

Hall, E. T. (1966). *The hidden dimension.* Garden City, NY: Doubleday.

Hall, E. T., & Hall, M. R. (1977). Nonverbal communication for educators. *Theory Into Practice, 16,* 141–144.

Jordan, B., & Henderson, A. (1995). Interaction analysis: Foundations and practice. *Journal of the Learning Sciences, 4*(1), 39–103.

Keegan, S. (2008). Projective techniques. In L. Given (Ed.), *The Sage encyclopedia of qualitative research methods* (pp. 686–688). Thousand Oaks, CA: Sage.

Kering, P. K., & Baucom, D. H. (Eds.). (2004). *Couple observational coding systems.* Mahwah, NJ: Lawrence Erlbaum.

Rex, L. A., & Green, J. L. (2008). Classroom discourse and interaction: Reading across the traditions. In B. Spolsky & F. Hull (Eds.), *Handbook of educational linguistics* (pp. 571–584). Wiley-Blackwell.

Rex, L. A., Murnen, T. J., Hobbs, J., & McEachen, D. (2002). Teachers' pedagogical stories and the shaping of classroom participation: The dancer and the graveyard shift at the 7–11. *American Educational Research Journal, 39*(3), 765–796.

Rex, L. A., Steadman, S., & Graciano, M. (2006). Researching the complexity of classroom interaction. In J. L. Green, G. Camilli, & P. E. More (Eds.), *Handbook of complementary methods in education research* (pp. 727–772). Mahwah, NJ: Lawrence Erlbaum.

Rutter, D. R. (1984). *Aspects of nonverbal communication.* Amsterdam: Swets & Zeitlinger.

Scherer, K. R., & Ekman, R. (Eds.). (1982). *Handbook of methods in nonverbal behavior research.* New York: Cambridge University Press.

Siegman, A. W., & Feldstein, S. (Eds.). (1987). *Nonverbal behavior and communication* (2nd ed.). Hillsdale, NJ: Lawrence Erlbaum.

Singer, M., Radinsky, J., & Goldman, S. R. (2008). The role of gesture in meaning construction. *Discourse Processes, 45*(4), 365–386.

Soley, L., & Smith, A. (2008). *Projective techniques for social sciences and business research.* Milwaukee, WI: Southshore Press.

Dilemma Analysis

Baron, R. S., & Kerr, N. L. (2003). Social dilemmas. In R. S. Baron & N. L. Kerr (Eds.), *Group process, group decision, group action* (2nd ed., pp. 139–154). Philadelphia: Open University Press.

Eek, D. (n.d.). *To work or not to work? A social dilemma analysis of health insurance.* Retrieved June 29, 2005, from www.psy.gu.se/download/gpr983.pdf

McCrea, H. (1993). Valuing the midwife's role in the midwife/client relationship. *Journal of Clinical Nursing, 2*(1), 47–52.

Simpson, B. (2003). Sex, fear, and greed: A social dilemma analysis of gender and cooperation. *Social Forces, 82*(1), 35–52.

Van Lange, P. A. M., Van Vugt, M., Meertens, R. M., & Ruiter, R. A. C. (1998). A social dilemma analysis of commuting preferences: The roles of social value orientation and trust. *Journal of Applied Social Psychology, 28*(9), 796–820.

Van Vugt, M. (1997). Concerns about the privatization of public goods: A social dilemma analysis. *Social Psychology Quarterly, 60*(4), 355–367.

Webb, J., & Foddy, M. (2004). Vested interests in the decision to resolve social dilemma conflicts. *Small Group Research, 35*(6), 666–697.

KEY CONCEPTS

Data gathering

Dilemma analysis

Gesture research

Historical analysis

Interaction analysis

Internet ethnography

Kinesics

Microexpressions

Photographs

Proxemics

Software for analyzing qualitative data

Software to assist in transcribing audiotapes

Videos

8

Managing, Analyzing, and Interpreting Data

Once the researcher has settled on a strategy, chosen a site, selected a sample, and determined the methods to be adopted for collecting data, she should discuss how she will record, manage, analyze, and interpret the data. She should also put forward preliminary ideas for writing up the analysis or representing it in some other format. At the proposal stage, this discussion can be brief, but it should present initial strategies for analysis and interpretation. In addition, it should provide the proposal reader with a sense that the data will be recorded efficiently and managed in ways that allow for easy retrieval. The writer should be prepared to provide examples of how the methods of data collection and analysis might proceed. Pilot studies or previous research are excellent sources for such examples.

RECORDING AND MANAGING DATA

The section of the proposal on research design should include plans for recording data in a systematic manner that is appropriate for the genre, the setting, and the participants, showing how the plans will facilitate analysis. The researcher should demonstrate an awareness that the techniques for recording observations, interactions, and interviews will not intrude excessively on the flow of daily events. In some situations, even taking notes interferes with, inhibits, or, in some way, acts on the setting and the participants. In the proposal, the researcher should delineate any plans to use tape recorders, cameras, and other mechanical devices and demonstrate that he will use data-recording strategies that fit the setting and the participants' sensitivities, but only with the participants' consent.

The genre of the research will have a bearing on the plans. For example, in the genre of participatory and action research, the researcher is integrated with the setting. Because these approaches are fundamentally interactive and include participants quite fully in framing questions and gathering data, the researcher's presence is not intrusive.

Whatever the qualitative approach, however, the researcher should cultivate the habits of labeling audiotapes, carrying extra batteries, and finding quiet places for taking notes. Such practices will pay off with data that are intact, complete, organized, and accessible. Imagine the horror of losing a precious three hours of a never-to-be-recaptured interview just because your batteries failed! And do you want to be one of those all-but-dissertation students with piles of scarily unorganized, unlabeled data? Over the years, researchers have developed a variety of data management strategies, ranging from color and number codings on index cards to computer programs. In the past, these techniques were mysterious, shared as part of the folklore of fieldwork, and, rarely, inserted as part of the appendices. Whatever method is devised, it must enable the researcher to organize and make data easily retrievable and manipulatable. Even if your routines are as funny as some used by baseball pitchers, if it works for you, just do it!

In more objectivist proposals, researchers may have lists of predetermined **categories** for data coding. Relying on such categories does facilitate retrieval and analysis, but to remain true to qualitative research assumptions, the researcher should plan decision rules for altering those categories during focused analysis. Furthermore, planning for the coding of notes to keep track of dates, names, titles, attendance at events, chronologies, descriptions of settings, maps, sociograms, and so on is invaluable. In piecing together patterns, in defining categories for data analysis, planning further data collection, and especially for writing the final product of the research, color coding is a useful tool. For researchers fascinated with details about the range of coding processes, see Saldana (2009).

Most introductory texts on qualitative methods provide extended discussions of the processes of analyzing data. Terminologies for qualitative data analysis include the following:

- Analytic induction
- Constant comparative method of analysis
- Developing grounded theory
- Template and editing

Through this chapter, we will provide examples that use the varied terminologies and techniques. The researcher must demonstrate not only knowledge of the terms but also application of the terms to his own research questions and conceptual frameworks. He must be able to say things such as "To begin my data coding, I will use the conceptual levers listed on page XX of my proposal when I observe YY kinds of behaviors." He must provide examples of how he will generate categories as the coded data accumulate and he sees patterns. He must speak of how he will create site or case summaries, make comparisons, and try out **clusters**, hierarchies, networks, linkages, **matrices** and **typologies**, data saturation, and search for **negative instances** so that he will sound convincing when he speaks of analytic induction.

GENERIC DATA ANALYSIS STRATEGIES

The process of bringing order, structure, and interpretation to a mass of collected data is messy, ambiguous, time-consuming, creative, and fascinating. It does not proceed in a linear fashion; it is not neat. At times, the researcher may feel like an eccentric and tormented artist; not to worry, this is normal! Qualitative data analysis is a search for general statements about relationships and underlying themes; it explores and describes and builds grounded theory (Strauss & Corbin, 1997). As described by Wolcott (1994), description, analysis, and interpretation—three somewhat distinct activities—are often bundled into the generic term *analysis.* He notes,

> By no means do I suggest that the three categories—description, analysis, and interpretation—are mutually exclusive. Nor are lines clearly drawn where description ends and analysis begins, or where analysis becomes interpretation. . . . I do suggest that identifying and distinguishing among the three may serve a useful purpose, especially if the categories can be regarded as varying emphases that qualitative researchers employ to organize and present data. (p. 11)

Wolcott (2009) even advises his doctoral students to write a tentative table of contents for the final report in their proposals! Acknowledging that it will be altered, he views this device as a tool for supporting the massive challenge of moving from proposal to analysis to writing up. The design section of the research proposal should describe initial decisions about data analysis and should convince the reader that the researcher's knowledge of qualitative analysis encompasses data organization, theme development and interpretation, and report writing. Although none of these can be given exhaustive consideration in the proposal itself, the researcher should convince the reader that thought and awareness have gone into planning the analysis phase of the study. What follows is a discussion of some considerations the researcher should bring to this section of the proposal.

Whether the researcher prefigures the analysis before collecting data, begins analyzing while collecting, or collects first and analyzes later depends on the qualitative genre and assumptions of the study. If he begins with a literature review on a conceptual framework that points directly to predetermined categories to use in analysis, he will be using a quasi-qualitative approach for testing hypotheses in context. He is not exploring to understand. His analysis is quite technical, almost statistical. Such focused, tightly structured, and highly organized data-gathering and data-analyzing schemes are efficient. However, they preclude the opportunity to explore and discover. Also, they often filter out the unusual and the serendipitous—the puzzle that if attended to and pursued would require a recasting of the entire research endeavor. Generating categories of data to collect, like defining cells in a matrix, can be an important focusing activity for the study. Thus, a balance must be struck between efficiency and design flexibility.

Crabtree and Miller (1992) propose a continuum of analysis strategies (see Figure 8.1), although they note that "nearly as many analysis strategies exist as qualitative researchers" (p. 17). At the extreme left end of their continuum are technical, scientific, and standardized strategies in which the researcher has assumed an objectivist stance relative to the inquiry and has stipulated the categories in advance. At the other end are the "immersion strategies," in which categories are not prefigured and which rely heavily on the researcher's intuitive and interpretive capacities. What they call "template" and "editing" analysis strategies stand along the continuum, with the template process more prefigured and stipulative than the editing processes (pp. 17–18). They begin with a template and gather context-laden data to fill in the contextual details. Still, template strategies can begin with sets of codes to apply to the data, but they may undergo revision as the analysis proceeds. Editing strategies, on the other hand, are less prefigured. "The interpreter engages the text naively, without a template" (p. 20), searching for segments of text to generate and illustrate categories of meaning. This method is closely allied with recent writing on grounded theory (Charmaz, 2000, 2005; Harry, Sturges, & Klingner, 2005; Strauss & Corbin, 1997).

In qualitative studies, data collection and analysis typically go hand in hand to build a coherent interpretation. The researcher is guided by initial concepts and developing understandings that she shifts or modifies as she collects and analyzes the data. Her overall strategy is closer to the interpretive/subjectivist end of the continuum than to the technical/objectivist end. In their classical work—still very useful—Schatzman and Strauss (1973) portray the process of qualitative data collection and analysis:

> Qualitative data are exceedingly complex and not readily convertible into standard measurable units of objects seen and heard; they vary in level of abstraction, in frequency of occurrence, in relevance to central questions in the research. Also, they vary in the source or ground from which they are experienced. Our model researcher starts analyzing very early in the research process. For him, the option represents an *analytic* strategy: he needs to analyze as he goes along both to adjust his observation strategies, shifting some emphasis towards those experiences which bear upon the development of his understanding, and generally, to exercise control over his emerging ideas by virtually simultaneous checking or testing of these ideas. . . . Probably the most fundamental operation in the analysis of qualitative data is that of discovering significant *classes* of things, persons and

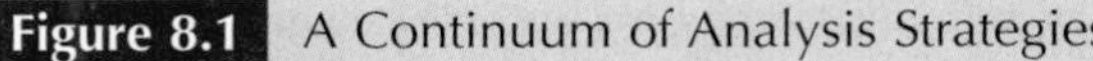

Figure 8.1 A Continuum of Analysis Strategies

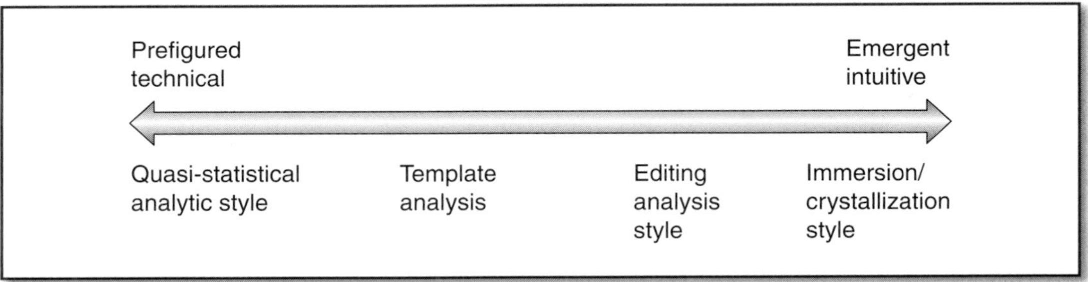

SOURCE: Adapted from Crabtree and Miller (1992, pp. 17–20).

> events and the *properties* which characterize them. In this process, which continues throughout the research, the analyst gradually comes to reveal his own "is's" and "because's": he names classes and links one with another, at first with "simple" statements (propositions) that express the linkages, and continues this process until his propositions fall into *sets*, in an ever-increasing density of linkages. (pp. 108–110)

The researcher should use preliminary research questions and the related literature developed earlier in the proposal as guidelines for data analysis. This early grounding and planning can be used to suggest several categories by which the data could initially be coded for subsequent analysis. These are theory-generated codes.

As a coherent interpretation, with related concepts and themes, emerges from the analysis, troublesome or incomplete data will lead to new collecting and analysis that will serve to strengthen the interpretation. Interpretation takes shape as major modifications become rare and concepts fall into established categories and themes. Analysis will be sufficient when critical categories are defined, relationships between them are established, and they are integrated into an elegant, credible interpretation.

ANALYTIC PROCEDURES

Typical analytic procedures fall into seven phases: (1) organizing the data, (2) immersion in the data, (3) generating categories and themes, (4) coding the data, (5) offering interpretations through **analytic memos**, (6) searching for alternative understandings, and (7) writing the report or other format for presenting the study. Each phase of data analysis entails the following: (a) **data reduction,** as the reams of collected data are brought into manageable chunks, and (b) *interpretation*, as the researcher brings meaning and insight to the words and acts of the participants in the study. At the proposal stage, the researcher should project what this process will entail, in preliminary ways. The procedures to be followed, the initial guides for categories, and the potential coding schemes all indicate to the reader that this crucial phase of the research will be managed competently.

The interpretive act remains mysterious in both qualitative and quantitative data analysis. It is a process of bringing meaning to raw, inexpressive data that is necessary, whether the researcher's language is standard deviations and means or a rich description of ordinary events. Raw data have no inherent meaning; the interpretive act brings meaning to those data and displays that meaning to the reader through the written report. As Patton (2002) notes, "Qualitative analysis transforms data into findings. No formula exists for that transformation. Guidance, yes. But no recipe. . . . [T]he final destination remains unique for each inquirer, known only when—and if—arrived at" (p. 432). With this caution in mind, we offer some general stages to guide the analysis section of the proposal.

Organizing the Data

When beginning analysis, it is important that the researcher should spend some time organizing the data. The researcher can list on note cards the data that have been gathered, perform the minor editing necessary to make field notes retrievable, and generally clean up what seems overwhelming and unmanageable. The researcher should also log the types of data according to the dates and times when, the places where, and the persons with whom they were gathered. This should be done all along, revisiting the "huge piles" of data periodically. An example is provided Table 8.1.

Nowadays, researchers often enter the data into one of the several software programs designed for the management or analysis of qualitative data (Richards & Richards, 1994; Tesch, 1990; Weitzman, 2000; Weitzman & Miles, 1995). (Recall the discussion in Chapter 7 outlining these examples of software.)

Immersion in the Data

There is no substitute for intimate engagement with your data. Researchers should think of data as something to cuddle up with, embrace, and get to know better. Reading, rereading, and reading through the data once more force the researcher to become intimate with the material. People, events, and quotations sift constantly through the researcher's mind. As Patton (2002) notes,

> The data generated by qualitative methods are voluminous. I have found no way of preparing students for the sheer mass of information they will find themselves

Table 8.1 Log of Data-Gathering Activities

Date	Place	Activity	Who	What
3/21/05	Fort River School	Focus group	Three teachers—Joe, Maria, Marcella	Strategies for including students
3/25/05	Fort River School	Observation	Maria's classroom—Amy	Seeing how Amy does math
3/25/05	Amy's home	Interview	Amy's parents	Challenges, supports

> confronted with when data collection has ended. Sitting down to make sense out of pages of interviews and whole files of field notes can be overwhelming. Organizing and analyzing a mountain of narrative can seem like an impossible task. (p. 440)

He then underscores how much of qualitative reporting consists of descriptive data, the purpose of which is to display the daily events of the phenomenon under study. Careful attention to how the data are being reduced is necessary throughout the research endeavor. In some instances, direct transfer onto predeveloped data-recording charts is appropriate, as with the template strategies. Miles and Huberman (1994) suggest several schemas for recording qualitative data. Such techniques streamline data management, help ensure reliability across the efforts of several researchers, and are highly recommended for large, complex studies such as multisite case studies (Yin, 2003). In using graphics and schemas, however, the researcher should guard against losing the serendipitous finding. For researchers relying on editing or immersion strategies, this phase of data analysis is the most difficult, complex, ambiguous, creative, and fun.

The proposal itself should, at least, provide a listing of likely themes, derived from the literature review—that is, *theory-generated codes*. It may also provide codes that will likely emerge in the real-life data—that is, **in vivo codes**. For example, in Table 8.2 the list of themes was generated from a research project that explored how educators could be social movement activists in spite of their conservative profession. Most themes and codes were derived from reading social movement theory and research on educators' careers, but many of them were derived from the researchers' insider sense of the issues that would occur in real life.

Often, such themes are displayed in a conceptual framework, as we showed in Chapter 4, so the researcher is sensitized to the likely relationships among themes and will see them in the data. At the same time, they will also be sensitized to exploring to understand when those expected and hypothesized relationships do *not* appear in the data.

Table 8.2 Codes From the Activist Educator

Theory-Generated Codes	In Vivo Codes
Social movement themes	**Potential themes likely from first look at data**
Social networks	Recruitment into activism versus inheritance
Adversary: confronting elites, fear of injury, death, and harm	Educational background/family background
Identity, vision, or goal: common purpose	Level of involvement/activities
Collective action, social solidarity	Critical events/catalysts
Sustained interaction and mobilization	Current political space
Slogans, music, and symbols	Resources
Educators' dilemmas	Denial/"closet" activism
Career	Public/private activism
Personal	Personal/political
Fear of career harm	Coming out/owning movement
Fear of backlash	Aha moments
Fear of imposing values	

SOURCE: Adapted from Marshall and Anderson (2008).

Coding the Data

Coding data is the formal representation of analytic thinking. The tough intellectual work of analysis is in generating categories and themes. The researcher then applies some coding scheme to those categories and themes and diligently and thoroughly marks passages in the data using the codes. Codes may take several forms—abbreviations of key words, colored dots, **numbers**—the choice is up to the researcher. The codes come from varied sources, including the literature review, the actual words and behaviors in the data, and the creative insight of the researcher. As coding progresses, the researcher sees the ways in which data/codes group or cluster together and behaviors and sentiments appear concomitantly or in some patterned sequence. He may write a memo that is a draft of an emerging definition of a key concept, with reference to bits of data to illustrate it (e.g., "a good marriage"). He may write a memo that is a draft of a kind of hierarchy or ordering that comes from participants' talk (e.g., "valuable qualities in a spouse"). Gradually, using both the readings of the data, and the conceptual framework for indications, the researcher sees how the data function or nest in their context and what varieties appear and how frequently the different varieties appear. As analysis progresses, he will search for clusters, starting with a main topic and pulling anything that is related, perhaps seeing how some things are **subclusters**. Ideas about codes can happen just about anytime and anywhere—in front of the computer, on a dinner napkin at a restaurant, creating designs in the sand while at the beach, in the shower, and more!

Writing Analytic Memos

In **thematic** and **theoretical memos**, the researcher writes his thoughts about how the data are coming together in clusters or patterns or themes he sees as the data accumulate. The original literature review provides stimuli that give some direction to his wondering, so some memos may read like this: "I wonder if my data are falling into a pattern that would be explained somewhat by such and such theory?" or "I think there is an emerging set of themes that are increasingly evident as I collect my data."

Throughout the analytic process—the transformational process, according to Wolcott (1994)—we strongly encourage the researcher to write. Writing notes, reflective memos, thoughts, and insights is invaluable for generating the unusual insights that move the analysis from the mundane and obvious to the creative. Several recent scholars underscore the value of writing early and often throughout the research process, especially during more focused analysis. For example, in *Small-Scale Research*, Knight (2002) begins with a chapter not on designing small-scale research or with an overview of research methods but on writing. He notes that this chapter is about "the interplay of writing and thinking *from the beginning* of the small-scale inquiry . . . writing as a part of the research process" (p. 1). Private writing and more public writing are great stimuli—to foster creativity and push one's thinking (Knight, 2002; Richardson, 2000; Richardson & St. Pierre, 2005). As Richardson and St. Pierre (2005) note, "Language is a constitutive force, creating a particular view of reality and of the Self" (p. 961). So choosing the language while writing brings codes to a conceptual level in data analysis. Writing prompts the analyst to identify categories that subsume a number of initial codes. It helps identify linkages among coded data. It helps identify gaps and questions in the data. It forces the analyst to stay thoughtfully immersed in her study, even when pulled away by tempting distractions. Distractions—cute dogs wanting a walk, friends suggesting a movie, your boss—may be useful breaks and may even provide "think time," but writing provides a structure for the constant thinking the researcher *will* be doing as she is propelled forward by the richness and intrigue of her data.

Authors have described specific forms of analytic writing—analytic memos. Schatzman and Strauss's (1973) classic suggestions on observational notes, methodological notes, theoretical notes, and analytic memos are quite useful, as is Maxwell's (1996) discussion of analytic memos. The same kinds of strategies, with different names, are ***methodological memos***, *thematic memos*, and *theoretical memos* (Rossman & Rallis, 2003). By keeping notes about what works (or not) in one's methods (e.g., "This interview respondent was distracted, so the data are probably incomplete" or "In the next observations, I will focus on the nurse-practitioners' caregiving"), the researcher has an account of design decisions made in the field. By writing thematic memos, he assembles thoughts about how a story of events, behaviors, or sentiments seems to have meanings, and he will use these as building blocks in his analysis. With his theoretical memos, he plays with the ways his theory and the related literature do or do not explain and lend meaning to his emerging data.

Patton (2002) describes the processes of inductive analysis as "*discovering* patterns, themes, and categories in one's data," in contrast with deductive analysis, where the analytic categories are stipulated beforehand "according to an existing framework" (p. 453). The researcher may generate "indigenous typologies" (p. 457) or "analyst-constructed typologies" (p. 458) to reflect the understandings expressed by the participants. Indigenous typologies are those created and expressed by participants and are generated through analyses of the local use of language.

Generating Categories, Themes, Typologies, Matrices, and Clusters

Although researchers often devise their own strategies, this phase is best described through examples. The analytic process demands a heightened awareness of the data, a focused attention to those data, and an openness to the subtle, tacit undercurrents of social life. Identifying salient themes, recurring ideas or language, and patterns of belief that link people and settings together is the most intellectually challenging phase of data analysis—one that can integrate the entire endeavor. Through the process of questioning the data and reflecting on the conceptual framework, the researcher engages the ideas and the data in significant intellectual work.

Open coding that is related to conceptual categories is the first step. Moving from that first step happens as the researcher constantly compares her codes of events and behaviors and words and "soon starts to generate theoretical properties of the category" (Glaser & Strauss, 1967, p. 106). Thus, data could be sorted for initial coding. A next step might be grouping the codes according to conceptual categories that reflect commonalities among codes—**axial coding** (Fielding & Lee, 1998; Strauss & Corbin, 1998). The codes are clustered around points of intersection, or axes.

Another device for analysis is called clustering. *Clustering* is creative work in which the researcher creates diagrams of relationships—outlines according to what is most overarching. He is doing conceptual or situational mapping, playing with construction pictures of how the data fit together. We say playing because it should be seen as drafting and experimentation. Still, it can lead to preliminary sketches that move along the analysis.

For editing and immersion strategies, the researcher generates the categories through prolonged engagement with the data—the text. Many of the categories will be modifications of concepts derived from her conceptual framework and literature review. These categories then become buckets or baskets into which segments of text are placed. As she generates ideas about the interconnections among concepts and categories from the intensive reading and rereading of her data, her analysis progresses. In Figure 8.2, we provide one example of themes and categories from a literature review for a study exploring to understand that identity, family life, schooling, career aspirations, and marriage were interconnected for British Muslim girls (Basit, 2003). Wanting to ascertain how British Muslim girls' aspirations were shaped, Basit's literature review helped her devise questions about identity, family life, marriage, social and academic aspects of schooling, and career aspirations. Gradually, through immersion with her data, she could see expanded dimensions of these categories. This then could demonstrate the need to see this complexity, so that future researchers, practitioners, and policymakers would avoid simplistic assumptions that could blunt opportunities for these girls.

The process of category generation involves noting patterns evident in the setting and expressed by participants. As categories of meaning emerge, the researcher searches for those that have internal convergence and external divergence (Guba, 1978). That is, the categories should be internally consistent but distinct from one another. Here, the researcher does not search for the exhaustive and mutually exclusive categories of the statistician but, instead, identifies the salient, grounded categories of meaning held by participants in the setting.

Analyst-constructed *typologies* are those created by the researcher that are grounded in the data but not necessarily used explicitly by participants. In this case, the researcher applies a typology to the data. As with all analysis, this process entails uncovering patterns, themes, and categories, but it may well run the risk of imposing "a world of meaning on the participants that better reflects the observer's world than the world under study" (Patton, 2002, pp. 459–460). In a related strategy, through logical reasoning, classification schemes are crossed with one another to generate new insights or typologies for further exploration of the data. Usually presented in matrix format, these cross-classifications suggest holes in the already

Figure 8.2 Themes and Categories on British Muslim Girls' Choices

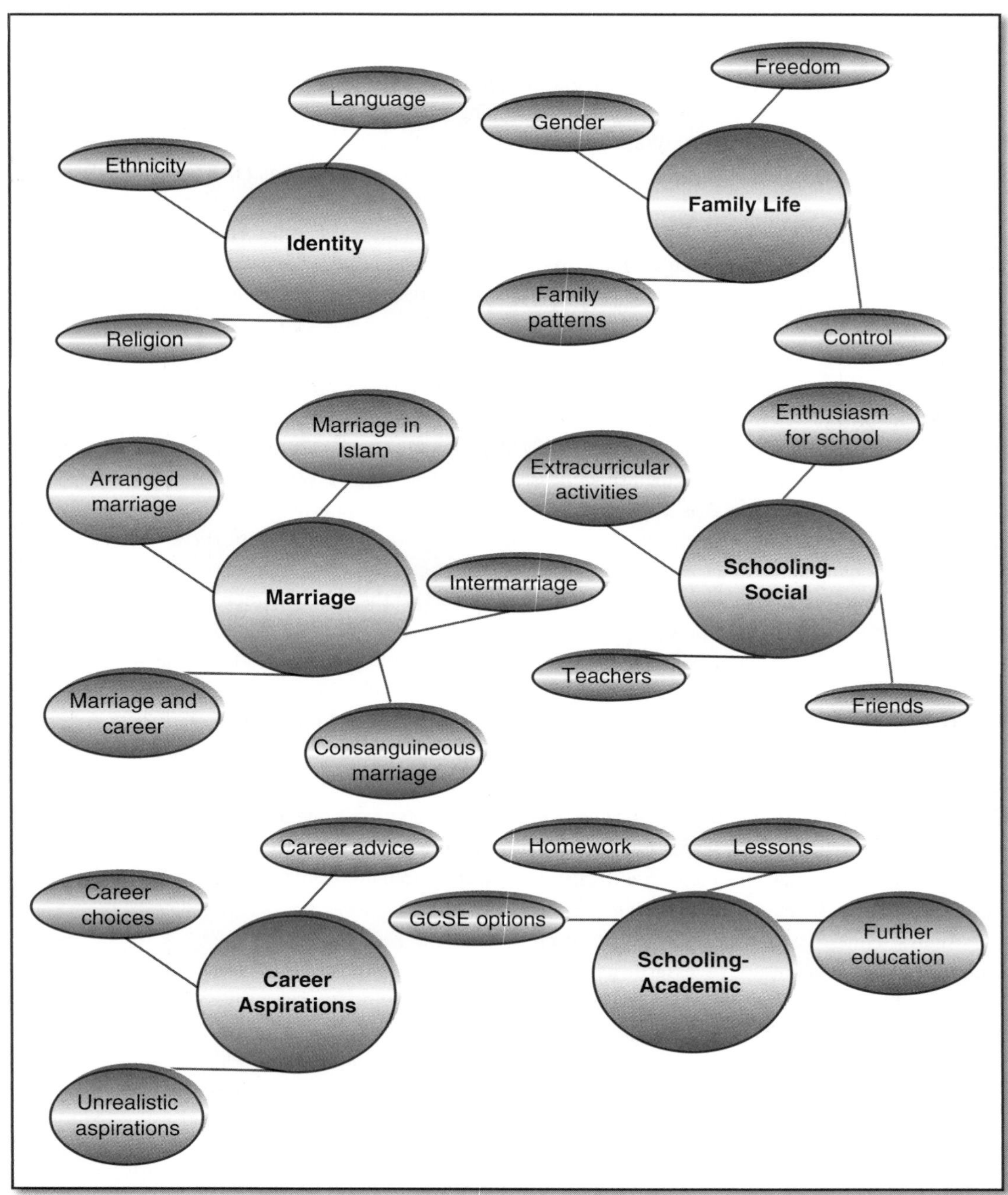

SOURCE: Basit (2003, p. 148). Reprinted with permission.

analyzed data, suggesting areas where the data might be *logically* uncovered. Patton (2002), however, cautions the researcher not to allow these *matrices* to lead the analysis but, instead, to generate **sensitizing concepts** to guide further explorations: "It is easy for a matrix to begin to manipulate the data as the analyst is tempted to force data into categories created by the cross-classification to fill out the matrix and make it work" (pp. 469–470). An example of a logically constructed matrix is presented in Figure 8.3.

Any of these devices, and any other creative analytic strategies, can be managed with the aid of computer programs. For smaller projects, and for more intimate immersion in one's data, we still like being computer free. As Vignette 21 shows, there was no choice before computers.

Figure 8.3 An Empirical Typology of Teacher Roles in Dealing With High School Dropouts

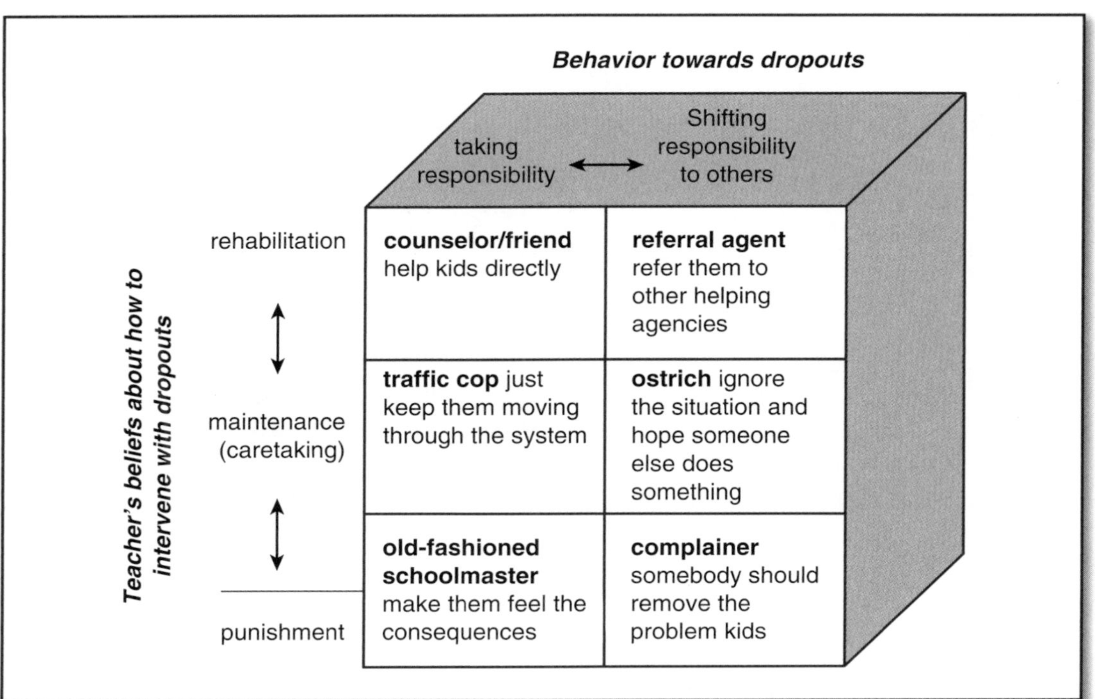

SOURCE: Patton (1990, p. 413). Reprinted by permission.

VIGNETTE 21 Data Management Before Computers

In her dissertation research on women's socialization in school administration, Marshall (1979) developed an efficient process by which data transcription, organization, and analysis were combined in a single operation. Neither word-processors nor programs for computer-assisted qualitative data management were available. Now, for those who are technology averse, and for small projects, her process may still be instructive. Observational notes and prefieldwork mapping of sites or subjects were recorded on hardback legal pads that could be held in the lap or used on the run. Following each interview, Marshall partially transcribed the field notes of audiotaped conversations, selecting conceptually intriguing phrases that either connected with previous literature or suggested patterns emerging from the analysis of previous data.

Preserving the data and meanings on tape and combining the transcription with preliminary analysis greatly increased the efficiency of data analysis. The researcher's transcription, done with the literature review, previous data, and earlier analytic memos in mind, became a useful part of data analysis and not a mere clerical duty.

Marshall's data analysis was guided by a conceptual framework and a set of guiding hypotheses. By trying out conceptual levers such as Goode's (1960) role strain theory to code interview data revealing conflicts experienced by women entering male sex-typed careers, she began devising grounded theory of a career-role strain that included feminine identity and sexuality crises prompted by the demands of working in a male-normed profession.

Employing constant comparative data analysis, she discovered in her data a period of transition. During this period, women resist the pull of aspiration, resent the exclusion, get angry about the double demands, and yet simultaneously create new ways to fill the roles.

Data collection, management, and analysis went hand in hand. The work of transferring data to index cards, writing codes on those cards, sorting cards to identify the overlapping categories, and placing the cards into piles eventually led to identifying more inclusive, overarching, and abstract domains. Methodological notes, analytic memos, and theoretical notes were used to create case summaries, charts, and dummy tables, all of which were steps in analysis. This was time-consuming, but it allowed Marshall to combine the initial transcription with analysis, it avoided the intrusiveness of the computer program, and it moved the study forward efficiently and without threat to the exploratory value of qualitative research or to data quality.

Vignette 21, above, describes the old-fashioned way of managing thick, complex data.

Computer-Assisted Analysis

No mechanism can replace the mind and creativity of the researcher. Still, computers can serve as tools. Software programs for data analysis typically rely on abbreviations of key words for coding. For example, in a dissertation proposal, Tucker (1996) discussed how she might use the following codes for her data:

TCARE.LIS: Teacher's caring as demonstrated through listening

TCARE.Q'S: Teacher's caring as demonstrated through honoring questions

TDIS.RACISMO: Teacher's disrespect as demonstrated through overt racism

Were she not using software, she might have planned to use differently colored dots to place on the interview transcripts and field notes or she might have underlined passages with different colored highlighting pens. Whatever system the researcher plans to use, he should know that the scheme will undergo changes—*coding is not a merely technical task.* As the researcher codes the data, new understandings may well emerge, necessitating changes in the original plan. Computer software can assist with axial coding, clustering, and writing analytic memos, and it can also help the researcher ask questions of his coded data. If, in his thematic memo, a researcher develops the thought that "contribution to economic security" is very high in his respondents' views of the valuable spouse, he can query his data, perhaps finding that (1) it is true for 44% of the participants and (2) that there are new questions to ask about the other 56%. This may lead to neat new avenues of inquiry in the analysis or even to new data collection questions.

Offering Interpretations

As categories and themes are developed and coding is well under way, the researcher begins a process whereby she offers integrative interpretations of what she has learned. Often referred to as "telling the story," interpretation brings meaning and coherence to the themes, patterns, and categories, developing linkages and a story line that makes sense and is engaging to read. As Patton notes (2002), "Interpretation means attaching significance to what was found, making sense of the findings, offering explanations, drawing conclusions, extrapolating lessons, making inferences, considering meanings, and otherwise imposing order" (p. 480). Part of this phase is concerned with evaluating the data for their usefulness and centrality. The researcher should select the most useful data segments to support the emerging story to illuminate the questions being explored and to decide how they are central to the story that is unfolding about the social phenomenon. Eventually, these may become the section of final reports, as we will show in Chapter 10.

Searching for Alternative Understandings

What if the descriptions, inferences, interpretations, and explanations are nothing but exactly what the researcher set out to find? How do the processes of data management and data quality assessment guard against this? Scrupulous qualitative researchers are on guard from the beginning, having been explicit about their voice, their biases, and how their identities have shaped their research questions. This caution, then, guides the researcher during his data analysis. Our scrupulous researcher is scrutinizing his data and his field notes, checking where data were undermined by a faulty approach, a less than forthcoming participant, and his early mistakes in the field. He looks suspiciously at his own observations, asking where he might have applied his own biases and interpretations instead of those generated from the actual behaviors, interactions, words, and sentiments of his participants.

As the researcher develops categories and themes, with her use of coding well under way, with numerous analytic memos written that summarize key "chunks" of the findings, she is constantly evaluating the plausibility of her developing understandings. She is constantly searching through the data. She is constantly challenging the very explanations and interpretations that she is putting forward. We have used terms such as *analytic induction, constant comparative analysis*, and *building grounded theory*. That is what our researcher is doing here. She is writing case summaries. She is comparing the viability of themes and explanations, checking them against the data she has, and seeing whether she needs to collect more or different data. She is comparing her emerging themes and explanations with those in her literature review and looking for any new variations or surprises. She is playing with creating matrices, clusters, and hierarchies with the goal of constructing a credible explanation that provides significant knowledge from her new study. She is reviewing her original conceptual framework and guiding hypotheses with great curiosity about the ways in which her own new data and analyses fit, and do not fit, with her earlier premises. These are the activities of the scrupulous yet creative qualitative researcher—that is, doing constant comparative analysis and analytic induction and also constructing grounded theory. She notices when she sees or hears the same patterns repetitively, and so she senses that little more can be gained by further data collection, since there is *saturation* of data (Saumure & Given, 2008). She then tests the themes, typologies, and patterns as she searches in her data for *negative instances* of the patterns. This may lead to new data collection. Just as likely, it will lead to refinement of her analysis as she incorporates the negative instances into expanded constructs, as necessary.

We used to speak of **theoretical saturation** as meaning the sense that any additional data collection will only result in more of the same findings. Dey (1999) calls saturation an "unfortunate metaphor" (p. 257), suggesting that we now should speak of **theoretical sufficiency**, whereby we have categories well described by and fitting with our data. This acknowledges the fact that we can never know everything and that there is never one complete Truth.

As the researcher discovers categories and patterns in the data, he should engage in critically challenging the very patterns that seem so apparent. He should search for other plausible explanations for these data and the linkages among them. Alternative explanations *always* exist, and the researcher must identify and describe them and then demonstrate how the explanation that he offers is the most plausible. This recalls the discussion in Chapter 1 concerning *the proposal as an argument* that offers assertions about the data, provides substantial evidence for those assertions, builds a logical interrelationship among them, and finally presents a summation of how the assertions relate to previous and future research.

We have discussed earlier, especially in Chapters 3 and 5, the ways to design a qualitative study so that it is credible and so that the study progresses to zero in on the findings. Over the decades, in their search for ways to decide whether their research is complete and credible, qualitative researchers have developed useful terms and strategies. Some of these strategies are **triangulation**, **member checking**, **peer debriefing**, **intercoder reliability**, **audit trails**, and theoretical sufficiency.

Triangulation, discussed earlier in Chapters 3 and 5, needs to be built into the setup of data collection, early on. Still, it is projected as a strategy that will help the researcher assert that her data interpretations are credible. She will have ways of showing that she got the participants' real views and authentic behavior.

In *member checking*, the researcher devises a way to ask the participants whether he "got it right." Most often, he gives summaries before writing up his study and asks for reactions, corrections, and further insights.

In *peer debriefing*, the researcher makes arrangements with knowledgeable and available colleagues to get reactions to the coding, the case summaries, the analytic memos written during data analysis, and the next-to-final drafts. *Audit trails* will be discussed in more detail in Chapter 9. Briefly, they provide a transparent way to show how data were collected and managed—to account for all data and for all design decisions made in the field so that anyone could trace the logic.

Intercoder reliability borrows terminology from quantitative research. As the researcher begins and proceeds through coding, she develops definitions for each code and asks "blind" review coders to apply the definitions to data to check for consistency in meanings and application. She also may uncover interesting nuances of interpretation as she puzzles over any differences between her coding and her blind coders' work. In the next chapter, we discuss more about strategies for managing the voluminous data in ways that will make the research process transparent and also enhance its credibility.

Numbers Are Useful

Yes, the qualitative researcher can use numbers. First, he may wonder how frequently themes and categories or patterns appear in the data as he asks himself questions about his emerging analysis. Numbers serve nicely for identifying frequencies and distributions. An analysis revealing contribution to economic security is strongly related to people's definition of "the good spouse," and it can be tested and pushed further when the researcher asks, "How often and according to what patterns among my population of participants?" This kind of testing can be used in a qualitative report as long as readers remember that this is quite different from the ways numbers are used in quantitative research. Thus, the report may say, "In this research, the pattern indicated that the spouses' economic contribution was much more likely to be reported as valuable by people with longer marriages. This pattern offers interesting insights for future research."

Writing the Report or Representing the Inquiry

Writing about qualitative data cannot be separated from the analytic process, as noted above in the section on writing analytic memos. In fact, it is central to that process, for in choosing words to summarize and reflect the complexity of the data, the researcher is engaging in the interpretive act, lending shape and form—meaning—to mountains of raw data. Then, in Chapter 10, we revisit the idea that the proposal is an argument that makes sense and that will gradually lead to *writing*—to a final product. Many aspects of data analysis processes are intertwined with managing the research process (see Chapter 9) and lead logically to the final product (see Chapter 10).

Into the various phases of data analysis and report writing are woven considerations of the soundness, usefulness, and ethical conduct of the qualitative research study. Some consideration should be given to the value, truthfulness, and soundness of the study throughout the design of the proposal. Considerations of role, for example, should address the personal biography of the researcher and how that might shape events and meanings. In what ways is the research, whether participatory or more objectivist, altering the flow of daily life? Selection of the setting and sampling of people and behaviors within that setting should be based on sound reasoning, and a clear rationale should guide those choices. Chapter 10 continues this discussion of writing, with consideration of planning for demonstrating the soundness, transparency, and credibility of the procedures of data analysis.

* * * * *

Previous chapters have brought the researcher through the complex, sometimes tedious, process of building a design and choosing data collection for the research study. The design section of the proposal should demonstrate that the researcher is competent to conduct the research; knowledgeable about the issues, dilemmas, choices, and decisions to be made in the conduct of the research; and immersed in the literature that provides guidance for the qualitative methodology and for the particular questions in the proposal. The research design should be well written and should reveal sensitivity to various issues, the capacity to be reflective about the nature of inquiry and the substantive questions at hand, and willingness to tolerate some ambiguity during the conduct of the study. These qualities will stand the researcher in good stead over the course of the research. In addition, however, the researcher should demonstrate some knowledge of the management of resources in the design of a qualitative study. This is the focus of the next chapter.

Dialogue Between Learners

Melanie,

OK, on to the next topic! Gretchen and I were talking yesterday about the "everydayness" of qualitative research practices. That is, those practices that some would find the most laborious and tedious (i.e., making sure you have fresh batteries in your recorder, the right notebook for note taking, ink in your pen, etc.). If I'm obsessive about anything, I suppose it's these little things. My worst fear is sitting in an interview or focus group and my recorder runs out of batteries, or reaching the place where the interview is to occur 20 minutes late (or on the wrong day). As a result, I have a drawer full of half-used batteries because I replace them so often, and I often arrive at my interview sites incredibly early. I suppose I just want to be able to focus on the task at hand when I'm interviewing, and so on. I mentioned to Gretchen that it was like going on a trip with the gas tank three fourths empty. I start out on the road, and inevitably my eye begins to fixate a bit on the gas gauge as I look for signs of it moving toward the red line. I begin to wonder when I should stop, how much farther I can make it. Meanwhile, I miss all the sights and sounds that make up the trip.

OK, admittedly, this might just be me and my strange fear of running out of gas/batteries. However, I do think that sometimes we talk so earnestly about the philosophy or theory behind qualitative work that we forget that there are these everyday events that actually make up the research project. For example, I have terrible handwriting. Yet when I'm taking field notes or conducting interviews I have a tendency to speed up my writing, to scribble. Not a good thing. There's nothing worse than returning to your field notes a few hours later and having to attempt a lengthy translation of your own handwriting. I try to get around this by being very thorough in my preparations, yet there is always something that comes up.

The latest chapter I've read, Chapter 5, deals quite a bit with writing up the report (whether it be a dissertation proposal or otherwise). Of course, to write the report, you have to know when you've finished collecting and analyzing your data. This is a problem for me. There's no final answer in qualitative research, it seems like you can keep going back for more. When do you know you're done? Sometimes I worry that my fear of actually writing the report will keep me in the data collection/analysis stage forever! I suppose I'll need to jump off that bridge when I come to it . . .

Hope things are well with you. Enjoy the weekend,

Aaron

Hi Aaron,

So, back after a weekend reprieve. I can't argue with much that you said in your last e-mail. There are so many little tasks to take into account before an interview, for example, that the tasks overwhelm the actual purpose of the interview! My handwriting falls apart during an interview, too—thank goodness for my little digital recorder.

To me, the everydayness is the result of detail-oriented work. I double-check my supplies before I go teach a class; I scribble illegible notes while I'm skimming journal articles; I obsess about asking worthless questions before a job interview. Attention to detail has to play a part in the research process, or we would miss much of the research we're trying to collect! There's a fine line, as you point out, between obsession and natural cautiousness—the battery thing does hinge on obsession—but that obsessive tendency may save us later down the road when we come up against questions in the analysis and can actually refer to our notes or our carefully transcribed interview to find the answer.

As for knowing when we're finished, I think you have to put your best effort forward but recognize that it's always a process. One of my professors really helped me with this when he reminded me that the data are always mine and I can always return to them with a fresh approach, a new idea, and/or a different lens. One of the reasons I'm drawn to qualitative research is the ability to present an answer instead of the one answer—so that gives me permission to move on, knowing that my research isn't a one-way trip.

Thanks bunches—must plan my lesson for tomorrow!

Melanie

FURTHER READING

On Data Analysis

Anfara, V. A., Jr., Brown, K. M., & Mangione, T. L. (2002). Qualitative analysis on stage: Making the research process more public. *Educational Researcher, 31*, 28–38.

Atkinson, P., & Delamont, S. (2005). Analytic perspectives. In N. K. Denzin & Y. S. Lincoln (Eds.), *The SAGE handbook of qualitative research* (3rd ed., pp. 821–840). Thousand Oaks, CA: Sage.

Charmaz, K. (2006). *Constructing grounded theory: A practical guide through qualitative analysis.* Thousand Oaks, CA: Sage.

Coffey, A. (1996). *Making sense of qualitative data: Complementary research strategies.* Thousand Oaks, CA: Sage.

Cohen, L., Manion, L., & Morrison, K. (2007). *Research methods in education.* New York: Routledge.

Dey, I. (1999). *Grounding grounded theory: Guidelines for qualitative inquiry.* San Diego, CA: Academic Press.

Emerson, R. M., Fretz, R. I., & Shaw, L. L. (1995). *Writing ethnographic fieldnotes.* Chicago: University of Chicago Press.

Fielding, N. G., & Lee, R. M. (1998). *Computer analysis and qualitative research.* London: Sage.

Goetz, J. P., & LeCompte, M. D. (1981). Ethnographic research and the problem of data reduction. *Anthropology & Education Quarterly, 12*(1), 51–70.

Harry, B., Sturges, K. M., & Klingner, J. K. (2005). Mapping the process: An exemplar of process and challenge in grounded theory analysis. *Educational Researcher, 34*(2), 3–13.

Katz, J. (2001*). Analytic induction revisited.* In R. M. Emerson (Ed.), *Contemporary field research* (2nd ed., pp. 331–334). Prospect Heights, IL: Waveland Press.

Kerig, P. K., & Baucom, D. H. (Eds.). (2004). *Couple observational coding systems.* Mahwah, NJ: Lawrence Erlbaum.

Krippendorf, K. (2004). *Content analysis: An introduction to its methodology* (2nd ed.). Thousand Oaks, CA: Sage.

Madison, D. S. (2005). *Critical ethnography: Method, ethics, and performance.* Thousand Oaks, CA: Sage.

Marshall, C., & Anderson, A. L. (Eds.). (2008). *Activist educators: Breaking past limits.* New York: Routledge.

Miles, M. B., & Huberman, A. M. (1994). *Qualitative data analysis: An expanded sourcebook* (2nd ed.). Thousand Oaks, CA: Sage.

Mills, G. E. (1993). Levels of abstraction in a case study of educational change. In D. J. Flinders & G. E. Mills (Eds.), *Theory and concepts in qualitative research: Perspectives from the field* (pp. 103–116). New York: Teachers College Press.

Morse, J. M., & Richards, L. (2002). *Read me first for a user's guide to qualitative methods.* Thousand Oaks, CA: Sage.

Neuendorf, K. A. (2002). *The content analysis guidebook.* Thousand Oaks, CA: Sage.

Patton, M. Q. (2002). *Qualitative research and evaluation methods* (3rd ed.). Thousand Oaks, CA: Sage.

Richards, L. (2005). *Handling qualitative data: A practical guide.* Thousand Oaks, CA: Sage.

Ryan, G. W., & Bernard, H. R. (2000). Data management and analysis methods. In N. K. Denzin & Y. S. Lincoln (Eds.), *Handbook of qualitative research* (2nd ed., pp. 769–802). Thousand Oaks, CA: Sage.

Saldana, J. (2009). *The coding manual for qualitative researchers.* Thousand Oaks, CA: Sage.

Sandelowski, M., & Barroso, J. (2003). Writing the proposal for a qualitative research methodology project. *Qualitative Health Research, 13*, 781–820.

Sanjek, R. (1990). On ethnographic validity. In R. Sanjek (Ed.), *Fieldnotes: The makings of anthropology* (pp. 385–418). Ithaca, NY: Cornell University Press.

Saumure, K., & Given, L. M. (2008). Data saturation. In L. M. Given (Ed.), *The SAGE encyclopedia of qualitative research methods* (Vol. 1, pp. 195–196). Thousand Oaks, CA: Sage.

Silverman, D. (1993). *Interpreting qualitative data: Methods for analyzing talk, text and interaction.* London: Sage.

Silverman, D. (2000). Analyzing talk and text. In N. K. Denzin & Y. S. Lincoln (Eds.), *Handbook of qualitative research* (2nd ed., pp. 821–834). Thousand Oaks, CA: Sage.

Silverman, D. (2005). *Doing qualitative research* (2nd ed.). Thousand Oaks, CA: Sage.

Silverman, D. (2007). *A very short, fairly interesting and reasonably cheap book about qualitative research.* Thousand Oaks, CA: Sage.

Strauss, A., & Corbin, J. (Eds.). (1997). *Grounded theory in practice.* Thousand Oaks, CA: Sage.

Tanaka, G. (1997). Pico college. In W. G. Tierney & Y. S. Lincoln (Eds.), *Representation and the text: Re-framing the narrative voice* (pp. 259–304). Albany: State University of New York Press.

Thornton, S. J. (1993). The quest for emergent meaning: A personal account. In D. J. Flinders & G. E. Mills (Eds.), *Theory and concepts in qualitative research: Perspectives from the field* (pp. 68–82). New York: Teachers College Press.

Wolcott, H. F. (1994). *Transforming qualitative data: Description, analysis, and interpretation.* Thousand Oaks, CA: Sage.

Yeh, C. J., & Inman, A. G. (2007). Qualitative data analysis and interpretation in counseling psychology: Strategies for best practices. *The Counseling Psychologist, 35,* 369–403.

On Data Quality and the Quality of the Analysis

Cho, J., & Trent, A. (2006). Validity in qualitative research revisited. *Qualitative Research, 6*(3), 319–340.

Cho, J., & Trent, A. (2009). Validity criteria for performance-related qualitative work: Toward a reflexive, evaluative, and coconstructive framework for performance in/as qualitative inquiry. *Qualitative Inquiry, 15*(6), 1013–1041.

Kvale, S. (1995). The social construction of validity. *Qualitative Inquiry, 1*(1), 19–40.

On the Continuum between Creativity and Control

Coffey, A. (1996). *Making sense of qualitative data: Complementary research strategies.* Thousand Oaks, CA: Sage.

Janesick, V. J. (2000). The choreography of qualitative research design. In N. K. Denzin & Y. S. Lincoln (Eds.), *Handbook of qualitative research* (pp. 1–29). Thousand Oaks, CA: Sage.

Janesick, V. J. (2004). *Stretching exercises for qualitative researchers* (2nd ed.). Thousand Oaks, CA: Sage.

van den Hoonard, D. K., & van den Hoonard, W. C. (2008). Data analysis. In L. M. Givens (Ed.), *The SAGE encyclopedia of qualitative research methods* (Vol. 1, pp. 185–186). Thousand Oaks, CA: Sage.

Wolcott, H. F. (2009). *Writing up qualitative research.* Thousand Oaks, CA: Sage.

On Analysis Using Computer Software

Auerbach, C., & Silverstein, L. B. (2003). *Qualitative data: An introduction to coding and analysis.* New York: NYU Press.

Basit, T. N. (2003). Manual or electronic? The role of coding in qualitative data analysis. *Educational Research, 45*(2), 143–154.

Bazeley, P. (2007). *Qualitative data analysis with NVivo.* Thousand Oaks, CA: Sage.

Kelle, E. (Ed.). (1995). *Computer-aided qualitative data analysis.* Thousand Oaks, CA: Sage.

Lewins, A., & Silver, C. (2007). *Using software in qualitative research.* Thousand Oaks, CA: Sage.

Piety, P. (2009, April). *The network model case study: A research method for studying educational practice across organizations.* Paper presented at the annual meeting of the American Educational Research Association, San Diego, CA.

Richards, T. J., & Richards, L. (1994). Using computers in qualitative research. In N. K. Denzin & Y. S. Lincoln (Eds.), *Handbook of qualitative research* (pp. 445–462). Thousand Oaks, CA: Sage.

Seale, C. F. (2003). Computer-assisted analysis of qualitative interview data. In J. A. Holstein & J. F. Gubrium (Eds.), *Inside interviewing: New lenses, new concerns* (pp. 289–308). Thousand Oaks, CA: Sage.

Tesch, R. (1990). *Qualitative research: Analysis types and software tools.* New York: Falmer Press.

Weitzman, E. A. (2000). Software and qualitative research. In N. K. Denzin & Y. S. Lincoln (Eds.), *Handbook of qualitative research* (2nd ed., pp. 803–820). Thousand Oaks, CA: Sage.

Weitzman, E. A., & Miles, M. B. (1995). *Computer programs for qualitative data analysis.* Thousand Oaks, CA: Sage.

Audience

Barone, T. (2008). Audience. In L. M. Givens (Ed.), *The SAGE encyclopedia of qualitative research methods* (Vol. 1, pp. 37–38). Thousand Oaks, CA: Sage.

KEY CONCEPTS

Analytic induction

Analytic memos

Audit trails

Axial coding

Categories

Clusters

Computer-assisted analysis

Constant comparative

Data reduction

In vivo codes

Intercoder reliability

Matrices

Member checking

Methodological memos

Negative instances

Open coding

Peer debriefing

Sensitizing concepts

Subclusters

Taxonomies

Thematic memos

Theoretical memos

Theoretical saturation

Theoretical sufficiency

Triangulation

Typologies

9

Planning Time and Resources

The process of planning and projecting the resource needs for a qualitative study is an integral aspect of proposal development. In general, the resources most critical to the successful completion of the study are **time**, **personnel**, and **financial support**. The last of these is not always readily available, especially in dissertation research; serious consideration, however, must be given to time and personnel. Many hidden costs associated with the study may become apparent only after the researcher has carefully analyzed and reflected on the study's demands. Convincing potential funding agencies that the expenses are worthwhile may also be a challenge.

This chapter provides the researcher with strategies for projecting the resource demands of qualitative research in particular, but the principles and reasoning processes can be applied to any study or project proposal. Using three vignettes as illustrations, we provide general guidelines for consideration in the development and projection of resource needs. Vignette 22 shows the process of planning resource needs for a multiresearcher, multisite study developed with ample financial resources and a long time frame for completion of the project. In contrast, Vignette 23 reveals the planning process of a solo doctoral student proposing a study with few financial supports to back it up. The contrast between Vignettes 22 and 23 is intended to display how each proposal must address difficult resource questions. Finally, Vignette 24 demonstrates the need to teach reviewers about the labor intensity of qualitative analysis. Careful, detailed consideration of the resource demands of a study is critical in demonstrating that the researcher is knowledgeable about qualitative research, understands that its inherent flexibility will create resource difficulties at some point, has thought through the resource issues, and recognizes the demands that will be made.

To begin with, many resource decisions cannot be made until basic design decisions are in place. The researcher, however, should consider resources as she struggles with the conceptual framework and design issues. For example, a researcher cannot decide to conduct a multisite, multiperson project unless she has some prospect of financial resources in sight, nor can she prudently plan to conduct a long-term, intensive, participant-observation study when she knows she must continue to work full time and cannot possibly devote the necessary time to the study. Thus, general decisions about resources and design are often made in parallel and are major criteria for the do-ability of the study.

In the narrative structure of the proposal, after discussing the design of the study, the researcher should address resource needs specifically. These include time demands and management, personnel needs and staffing, and financial support for the entire endeavor. The two vignettes presented below are followed by a discussion of the major resource needs of each. The vignettes are intended to display the strategies for resource allocation in two quite different studies.

PLANNING RESOURCES FOR A LARGE STUDY

Although the resource needs for a long-term, complex study are substantially more elaborate than those for dissertation research, the processes of projecting those resources remain very similar. Careful and explicit plans regarding resource allocation need to flow from the overall design of the study. The challenges are exacerbated in multisite comparative research conducted over several years. Sometimes these studies are collaborations among researchers in several institutions or with practitioners. The larger the scope, the more resources are necessary to ensure that there are (a) adequate time (sufficient to describe and analyze practices in detail), (b) personnel (capable of thoroughly and efficiently gathering the needed data), and (c) other supports for personnel, such as travel, data analysis, and report writing.

The first task in projecting resource needs for a large-scale study is to organize its activities into manageable tasks. These typically consist of (a) planning, (b) meetings of the research team, (c) meetings among principal investigators, (d) advisory committee meetings, (e) site visits in the field for data gathering, (f) data analysis, (g) report writing, (h) conference attendance for dissemination, and (i) preparation for and management of a final policy forum or other means for public dissemination.

For some large-scale studies, especially those funded by the U.S. government, the funding agency may require an outside "auditor" to review the data, analyses, and reports, essentially "certifying" that the research was conducted well and the data support the analyses and findings. Marshall had this experience. Called in to serve as an external auditor for a large study, she reviewed data files, inspected analyses, and examined reports. This function was required by the funding agency. The implication of this for projecting resources is that the researchers must diligently manage their data and analyses, creating an "audit trail" that an external reviewer (or other legitimately interested parties) can examine. And there are resource implications for this. Recall the discussions in

Chapters 3 and 8 about how planning for an audit trail helps convince a proposal's reviewers that the study will be conducted systematically and in ways amenable to "outside inspection."

In working through the details of a large-scale study, a research team typically iteratively refines its initial projections of time as members are able to make associated cost projections. That is, the team can first plan an ideal study, one in which resources are virtually infinite. Creative insights often emerge through imagining such an ideal study before tempering these with the realities of ceilings on funding, limited availability of researchers, and other considerations of feasibility—the do-ability criterion discussed in Chapter 1. Often, such ideal plans call for immersion in the setting, with many site visits. Refinements must be made when realistic costs in terms of time, personnel, and travel are estimated.

Vignette 22 details how resource decisions were made in planning for a two-state qualitative study of successful leadership in multicultural schools. It paraphrases the research proposal and details the final allocation of resources to each research task.

VIGNETTE 22 Projecting Resources for a Large-Scale Study

"Leading Dynamic Schools for Newcomer Students: Studies of Successful Cross-Cultural Interaction" (Rossman & Rallis, 2001) proposed a collaborative research project between the Center for International Education at the University of Massachusetts and the Neag School of Education of the University of Connecticut. The purpose of the study was to create grounded depictions of how leadership is enacted in multicultural schools. The principal investigators wanted to learn how successful school principals—and leadership more broadly—interact across cultural differences with empathy and respect. They posed the following broad research questions:

1. In what ways are school leaders savvy and attuned to the multiple cross-cultural dynamics in schools that serve migrant, refugee, and immigrant children particularly well?
2. How do they mediate the cultural differences that can be confusing, emotional, humorous, hurtful, and inspirational?

In designing a proposal to respond to the call for field-initiated research from the Office of Educational Research and Improvement of the U.S. Department of Education, Rossman and Rallis had to make a series of decisions to support their multisite, multiresearcher, multiyear case studies of leadership practices in 12 schools in Connecticut and Massachusetts. As the principal investigators (PIs) identified important aspects of the study that would require time and effort (i.e., more data), the study grew and grew. But ideal projections then had to be grounded in real considerations of the total budget allocated for the study. Using the study's conceptual framework and the requirements of the RFP, the

(Continued)

VIGNETTE 22 (Continued)

researchers ensured sound adherence to the initial research questions. Table 9.1 shows the final allocation of staff days to tasks.

In the text of the proposal, Rossman and Rallis explained that the project would (a) identify the leadership strategies used successfully in dynamic schools that serve large populations of newcomer students (migrants, immigrants, and refugees); (b) analyze and synthesize the research to develop prototype strategies that can be used in professional development; and (c) disseminate these prototypes to practitioners (administrators, teacher groups, administrator preparation programs, and community groups), policymakers, and the scholarly community.

They then proposed using a multisite case study design to describe and analyze the leadership in 12 such schools in Massachusetts and Connecticut that serve newcomer students particularly well. The findings of the research project would be disseminated to practitioners, policymakers, and the scholarly community through a project Web site, presentations at conferences, articles in journals, and two policy forums. Furthermore, these findings would be communicated to the National Institute for the Education of At-Risk Students and the National Institute on Educational Governance, Finance, Policymaking, and Management.

The research design section proposed a multisite case study. The PIs explained,

> The local school and the community it serves will be the unit for analysis. . . . Case studies, in-depth explorations of a single phenomenon, seek to understand that larger phenomenon through close examination of a specific instance. . . . The case studies in this project will generate grounded depictions of leadership. Observations and interviews will yield rich descriptions that illustrate the complexities of the settings: their structures, politics, cultures, and moral principles. Six sites will be selected in each state, yielding a total of 12 schools. Yearlong fieldwork will be conducted at each site, generating qualitative data descriptive of leadership in context. Cross-case analysis to generate prototype leadership strategies will be performed in Year Two of the project. The key activities for each year, focusing on data gathering, data analysis, Site Researcher responsibilities, and Advisory Committee roles, are described below.

To justify the resource requests, the proposal provided details for data gathering:

> We envision yearlong fieldwork in the 12 schools for the first year of the project. The design will deploy the Site Researchers to the schools for one day per week per school. Thus, each Site Researcher will focus on two schools, providing the depth of knowledge necessary for constructing prototypes of leadership. Typical fieldwork strategies will be employed: informal and formal observations coupled with conversations (both informal and structured interviews) and the review of key documents. Observations of interactions between the principal and other key leaders in the school and community members will occur. Interviews with these key individuals will be scheduled. In addition, focus group interviews with community members and teachers

will be conducted. Activities for the project are summarized in Table 9.1. The proposal also explained the resources allocated for data analysis:

Preliminary data analysis will be ongoing, as the Site Researchers gather information, conduct initial analyses of it, and share those analyses in analytic memos and in the Research Team meetings. During Year Two, the Site Researchers, supervised by the Project Director and Co-Director, will engage in detailed data analysis to build the prototypes of leadership in the 12 dynamic schools. During this process, they will return to the sites on a twice-monthly basis to share emergent conclusions with principals and other participants and gather additional data as needed. This will ensure that the conclusions and prototypes are grounded in the realities of the schools and the perspectives of participants.

Next, the proposal explained the duties of site researchers, who would conduct the yearlong fieldwork for the project and be actively involved in data analysis and the development of products during the second year. The proposal then presented the makeup and duties of the advisory committee, which would meet semi-annually to provide feedback to the project and to ensure that the emerging results were incorporated into policy and practitioner dialogues.

The explanation of products and dissemination of information called for a Web site devoted to the project to share emergent findings and relevant literature. The Web site would link to the Institute for the Education of At-Risk Students. Dissemination strategies also included two policy forums, presentations to scholarly audiences at national conferences, articles submitted to research journals, and dissertations by the site researchers.

Next, the proposal attempted to justify the time and resources of personnel. It requested salary support for the directors, the principal investigators, the community liaisons, a fiscal administrator, six full-time site researchers (research associates), and four half-time research assistants. Time allocations of 20% for directors, who were responsible for the management of the project, were justified for production of reports and supervision of staff and finances. The principal investigators would devote 10% of their time to provide management support and supervision of the site researchers. The community liaisons would devote 15% of their time, and the fiscal administrator would work half-time on the project. The responsibility of the six research associates, three in each university, was to conduct the field research; the four half-time research assistants would develop and maintain the Web page and support the software for advanced data analysis. Table 9.2 summarizes the key budget features of the proposal.

Once Rossman and Rallis had determined the scope of the study, they were able to plan its implementation, presented in Table 9.1. This, in turn, had implications for staffing the research (discussed above in the vignette), which, in turn, had a direct effect on the overall budget. The final decisions that are represented in Tables 9.1 and 9.2 are the end result of many iterations in projections about the scope of the study, the personnel needed, and the costs of personnel, travel, and data analysis.

Table 9.1 Schedule of Work

Schedule	Aug	Sep	Oct	Nov	Dec	Jan	Feb	Mar	Apr	May	June	Jul
Year 1 (August 2001–July 2002): Planning and site research												
Planning	→	→										
University-based research team meetings			X	X	X	X	X		X	X	X	X
Full-research-group meetings	X		X		X		X		X		X	
Director and codirector meetings		X		X		X		X		X		X
Data gathering in schools		→	→	→	→		→	→	→			
Data gathering in communities	→		→					→		→		
Preparation for/attendance at conference						→	→	X				
Planning for/conduct of policy forum						→	→	→	X			
Deliverables						RPI					RDG	
Year 2 (August 2002–July 2003): Data analysis and product development												
Planning	→	→										
University-based research team meetings												
Full-research-group meetings												
Director and codirector meetings												
Advisory committee meetings												

Schedule	Aug	Sep	Oct	Nov	Dec	Jan	Feb	Mar	Apr	May	June	Jul
Year 2 (August 2002–July 2003): Data analysis and product development												
Site visits for verification	→	→	→	→	→	→						
Summarizing interviews	→	→	→		→		→					
Summarizing field observations	→	→	→		→		→					
Writing analytic memos			→	→		→	→					
Writing interim summaries	→	→	→									
Preparation for/attendance at conferences	→	→	X			→	→	X				
Preparation for/conduct of policy forum						→	→	→	→	X		
Writing final report								→	→	→	→	→
Deliverables			RFS									FR

SOURCE: Rossman and Rallis (2001). Adapted with permission.

NOTE: FR = final report; RDG = report of preliminary data gathering; RFS = report of feedback from schools; RPI = report of planning and implementation in schools.

Table 9.2 Budget Summary

Budget Item	Requested From ED	In-Kind Support	Total
Year 1			
Direct costs			
1. Salaries ($)	134,201	3,343	137,544
2. Employee benefits	15,678	40,740	56,418
3. Employee travel	12,340		12,340
4. Equipment	11,590		11,590
5. Materials and supplies	1,250		1,250
6. Consultants and contracts	318,629		318,629
7. Other	13,550		13,550
Total direct costs	507,238	44,083	551,321
Indirect costs	124,981		124,981
Total	632,219	44,083	676,302
Year 2			
Direct costs			
1. Salaries ($)	101,672	3,444	105,116
2. Employee benefits	19,571	40,740	60,311
3. Employee travel	15,940		15,940
4. Equipment	0		0
5. Materials and supplies	850		850
6. Consultants and contracts	325,087		325,087
7. Other	13,550		13,550
Total direct costs	476,670	44,184	520,854
Indirect costs	109,436		109,436
Total	586,106	44,184	630,290
Total budget request			1,306,592

SOURCE: Rossman and Rallis (2001). Adapted with permission.

Time

As Vignette 22 illustrates, projecting sufficient time to undertake a richly detailed study that also remains "do-able" is a difficult task but one that can be rewarding. Thinking through the time necessary for various research activities can be sobering even for experienced researchers; the novice learns a great deal from this discipline. For example, each of the research tasks described in this vignette required a certain number of days for its successful completion. The first step was to determine the optimal number of days for each site visit. Although this depended on the year of the study, the research team was able to estimate days by deciding on the number of interviews possible in each school, the hours to allocate for observations, as well as the amount of time necessary to talk with community members and to gather documents and other archival data.

In qualitative proposals, the number of days allocated to data gathering becomes a metric for estimating the time required for other tasks, such as data management, analysis, and report writing. That is, the amount of data gathered dictates the amount of time needed to manage and analyze them. Once the researcher has projected time for fieldwork, a management plan can be developed. The projections developed for Table 9.1 helped construct a framework for estimating costs, discussed below.

The researcher should also use this kind of framework to address practical concerns. A time management chart, research agenda, calendar of research events, description of research phases, or some other concrete plan shows a funding agency or dissertation committee with which the researcher has discussed the feasibility of involving specific people, settings, events, and data in the research. This demonstrates that the research is feasible. But the researcher should remind the reader that this plan is a guide; it is a tentative road map that will most likely undergo some modifications as data are collected and analyzed and as new patterns for more focused data collection become apparent. The chart serves as a guide for initial contacts and reminds the reader of the inherently flexible nature of qualitative research. It also serves as an important reminder—sometimes an anchor—for the researcher herself once she becomes immersed in the study.

Personnel

The allocation of time to tasks also shapes decisions about personnel needs. In Vignette 22, as the scope of the study developed (number of school sites, single- or multiple-person research teams), personnel decisions could be made. Principal investigators with university contracts can allocate the equivalent of the summer months and one day per week to the effort. Their time can be supplemented by a cadre of graduate students who can be awarded research assistantships to work on the project for limited hours per week for the academic year, with additional summer funding budgeted into the proposal. These kinds of "person loadings" are illustrated in the budget summarized in Table 9.2.

Financial Resources

For dissertation research or sole-investigator studies, analyzing tasks can help the researcher decide to purchase certain services—for example, audiotape transcription or data processing. This analysis can also introduce the novice to the variety of tasks associated with the project. Determining the resources necessary for the study must often wait until fundamental design decisions have been made. Those design choices, however, must be made with some knowledge of the finances available. In the preceding vignette, the evaluators knew that they were constrained by a total budget of approximately $1 million for the two-year study.

Although this sum may seem considerable to the novice proposal writer, planning a multisite, multiyear study with intensive data gathering as a primary design goal became quite difficult within this budget. Travel and personnel costs increased with inflation and rising salaries, and they represented a substantial proportion of the total budget.

The other major costs associated with the evaluation activities included (a) local travel; (b) equipment (computers, fax machine); (c) office supplies, telephones, and postage; (d) books and subscriptions; (e) printing and duplicating; and (f) contracted services (tape transcription, data analysis, consultants). Because the costs of data analysis specialists vary considerably, the proposal writer would consult local costs and time allocations in developing that portion of a qualitative proposal. The time required for thorough transcription also varies. Each hour of tape requires from three or four to seven or eight hours for transcription. Thus, transcription costs, which are always high, could vary enormously.

PLANNING DISSERTATION RESEARCH

Many of the same issues confronted in the large-scale evaluation project are apparent in Vignette 23, a proposal for dissertation research. Although the scope is considerably smaller, similar resource challenges emerged in planning the study.

VIGNETTE 23 Feasibility and Planning for Dissertation Research

"Should I do a study that is clean, relatively quick, limited, and do-able so as to finish and get on with my professional life, or should I do something I really want to do that may be messy and unclear but would be challenging and new enough to sustain my interest?" (S. Hammonds-White, personal communication, August 5, 1987),

A doctoral student, finding any number of stumbling blocks standing between her and the completion of her dissertation project, was asked to reflect on the process through which the research plan had been developed. Her response indicated that, as with any kind of major investment, a preliminary notion of how to proceed should be tempered by a comparison of anticipated costs and available resources. In this student's case, she had to weigh energy (her physical and emotional stamina), time, and finances.

The demands of the student's chosen research methods were many. Seeking to explore a process, she chose naturalistic inquiry, which would encourage her to search for multiple views of reality and the ways in which such views were constructed. Her training, experience, and interest in counseling psychology, coupled with a positive assessment of her knowledge and competence in this field, constituted excellent sources of personal energy. This was an area of particular interest (the want-to-do-ability); methods were elegantly suited to that substantive focus. The researcher realized, however, that personal energy and a deep commitment to the topic were not going to be sufficient.

She looked to the university for two types of support, which she described as "risk-taking support" and "learning support." The first would encourage someone attempting to go beyond the conventional in his or her research. The second was offered by faculty members who possessed the interests and the skills necessary to advise her.

In addition to personal energy and commitment and faculty support, a third source of energy was a support group made up of others who were engaged in dissertation research. Of that group she wrote, "We meet every other week, set short-term goals for ourselves, and help each other with the emotional highs and lows of the process."

The commitment in time required of an individual doing qualitative research is substantial. This particular researcher was quick to advise that those following similar research plans would do well to build into their proposals more time than they thought would be required in order to make allowances for the unexpected. In her case, a change in her family situation necessitated a return to full-time employment, thus having to suspend her research when it was only two-thirds complete.

Financial resources need to be equal to the financial demands of a study. When it appeared unlikely that grant monies would be available, the student opted for a smaller-scale study that she could finance personally.

Vignette 23 illustrates the importance of being practical and realistic. Although it is impossible to anticipate all the potential stumbling blocks, a thoughtful and thorough research proposal will address the issue of feasibility by making an honest assessment of available energy, time, and financial resources and requirements.

While the researcher was planning for and conducting the above study, several resource issues became apparent. First, the commitment to a graduate student's dissertation research differs from that required of the researchers in Vignette 22. A dissertation, often one's first major, independent scholarly work, carries more professional and personal significance than subsequent research projects. Furthermore, the project described in Vignette 22 had built-in supports for the researchers. As a team project funded by an external agent, commitments to colleagues and professional responsibilities to the funding agent were adequate to rebuild interest when it began to wane. A dissertation demands different kinds of supports; the most important are those of mentors and peers.

Mentors and Peers

In planning qualitative dissertation research, the judgments of university faculty about the adequacy of the proposal are crucial. At least one committee member, preferably the chair, should have had experience conducting qualitative studies. Such experience enables the faculty to help in making decisions about how to allocate time realistically to various tasks, given the all-important idea that qualitative research often takes much more time than one might predict. The support and encouragement of faculty are critical for developing research proposals that are substantial, elegant, and do-able and for advocating in the larger university community the legitimacy of a particular study and of qualitative research generally.

The experiences of our graduate students suggest that the support of peers is also crucial for the personal and emotional sustenance that students find so valuable in negotiating among faculty whose requests and demands may be in conflict with one another. Graduate seminars or advanced courses in qualitative methods provide excellent structures for formal discussions as students deal with issues arising from role management or plan how to build grounded theory in their dissertations. Student support groups also build in a commitment to others not unlike that found in the team project described in Vignette 22. By establishing deadlines and commitments to one another, students become more efficient and productive. These groups bridge the existential aloneness of dissertation research. Finally, rereading literature on qualitative inquiry is both a support and a reminder of the traditions and challenges faced by all of us. It helps to know that William Foote Whyte (1980) managed ethical dilemmas in the field, too.

Time on a Small Scale

Developing a dissertation proposal for qualitative research demands sensitivity to the time necessary for the thorough completion of the project. This is where the experience of mentors on the university faculty becomes crucial. As noted in Chapter 3, complying with institutional review board requirements for proceeding ethically takes time. Gaining access to a setting can take six months or more and may require the skills of a diplomat. As in Vignette 23, personal circumstances may intervene to alter dramatically the student's available time and energy to conduct the study. Thus, even though not all critical events can be anticipated, planning for more time than initially appears necessary is prudent. As Locke et al. (2000) note, "Relatively few research studies finish on schedule, and *time requirements invariably are underestimated* [italics added]. Frequent setbacks are almost inevitable" (p. 44). We have both had the experience of advanced doctoral students needing to find jobs. The economic necessity often has to take priority over completing their degrees, at least in a timely manner. This most often delays completion and, in a few cases, means that students don't finish at all. Though unfortunate, this is the reality of doctoral-level work.

Financing

In some fields (notably mental health, urban planning, anthropology, and international education), financial support for dissertation research may be available through federal agencies or private foundations. Unfortunately, this is not typically the case in most social science fields, in education, or in other applied fields. Opportunities do sometimes become available, however, to work on a university professor's funded grant as a research assistant. This was the case in Vignette 22. Several graduate students would have been supported annually, and several of them could have dovetailed their research interests with those of the project.

Much more common, especially in education, is the case in Vignette 23. The student had to modify the proposed research to conform to the personal financial resources she was able to devote to the project. Recall that the proposal for funded research described in Vignette 22 suffered the same fate. The researchers planned an ideal study based on design considerations and the purposes of the study and then had to modify that ideal design based on the real budgetary constraints imposed by the funding agency.

For dissertation research, many costs, some obvious and some hidden, will arise over the course of the study. Planning ahead for these makes them a bit more manageable. These costs are clustered into three categories: materials, services, and personal costs.

Materials. The materials necessary for the completion of a dissertation may include word-processing equipment and materials, computer **software for data analysis**, computer disks, note cards and filing systems, tape recorders and tapes, video equipment and cameras, books, articles, and copies of completed dissertations. The student should project the costs in each category, being sure to include the costs of photocopying journal articles, drafts of the work as it proceeds, and the final document.

Costs associated with materials may also be necessary for ensuring that committee members can examine the data, analyses, and interim findings. As discussed in terms of ensuring an audit trail for a large-scale study, small-scale researchers must also be diligent about documenting their work such that a committee member could go through the data and analyses and find evidence to support the final results and interpretations.

Services. The services necessary for the completion of the dissertation vary depending on the skills of the student. Typical services, however, might include tape transcribing, word processing, statistical data analysis consulting, and professional proofreading and editing. The student often wants to have copies of the work professionally bound; this is an additional service that might be important for the student to consider as well.

Personal costs. Personal costs are the most difficult to specify but may also be the most important in terms of perceived costs to the individual student. Dissertation work is unlike any scholarly work the student has ever undertaken (and, most likely, any the

student will do in the future). It is not like a large course or like reading for exams. It is of a quite different magnitude than those. The sustained effort necessary to complete the project takes time away from all other commitments in the student's life, whether these are work, family, friends, or professional associations and volunteer groups. Students who are the most successful in moving through the phases of the dissertation build support networks for themselves within their families or through friends and colleagues. Dissertation proposal sections discussing researcher role (see Chapter 3) should include assessments of the researcher's ability to manage the personal costs. Even though not all the costs associated with personal sacrifice can be anticipated, knowledge that the undertaking is not trivial and will require sacrifices on the part of the student can make the entire process more manageable.

Sometimes, researchers seek new funds to continue a project that uncovered interesting data. It is difficult to convince funding agency reviewers that a reworking of data analysis is a worthwhile venture. Vignette 24 describes a researcher trying to convince funding agency reviewers that a secondary analysis of qualitative data is worthy of financial support.

VIGNETTE 24 Walking the Reviewers Through Qualitative Analysis

The data collected were voluminous, comparative, qualitative, and quantitative from key state education policy makers in six states. From a study funded by the National Institute of Education, Mitchell, Wirt, and Marshall (1986) developed a taxonomy of state mechanisms for influencing school programs and practices and showed the effect of political culture and the relative power of policymakers to affect the choices made in state capitals about education. Captivated by the richness of the interview data, Marshall began to develop a grounded theory of assumptive worlds—the understandings that policymakers have about the way things are done, as demonstrated in their stories. Although this theory had been published (Marshall, Mitchell, & Wirt, 1985, 1986), the next step required funds. Her proposal to the National Science Foundation's political science program promised a secondary analysis of the interview data from six states, assisted by a computer program for data analysis to elaborate the theory. The funding could be minimal because no new data collection was required.

Months later, the reviewers came back. One of them wrote, "This proposal breaks fresh and important ground in the political field." Another noted that "using qualitative data in a systematic way and employing computers in data management are innovative techniques well worth development." A third, however, objected, "The proposal is to apply qualitative analysis to the interview materials. Perhaps that term has some [other] understood connotation in other research traditions, but so far as I could fathom, what it means is the investigator would read/listen to interview materials and file them on a micro computer." The proposal was rejected.

Overcoming frustration, Marshall revised and resubmitted her proposal with important changes. First, for the theoretical framework, related literature, and significance, she created a chart, tracing the precise place where assumptive worlds fit with other political science and education policy theory and literature. Second, after explaining the traditions of qualitative research, she cited political scientists' calls for more theory building with comparable case studies and calls to get behind the scenes to find out how the values of the policy culture affect policy outcomes. Third, with Table 9.3, she demonstrated the promise of the theory. Narratively, she described its significance for understanding the policy culture. Finally, and perhaps most important, following a section on the philosophy of qualitative methodology and a section on the use of microcomputers with qualitative data, she wrote the following step-by-step description:

> Qualitative data analysis seems to be a mystical process to those accustomed to statistical analysis. However, the goal of both methodologies is the same: to identify clear and consistent patterns of phenomena by a systematic process. I will follow the following steps:
>
> 1. Transcribe data in Ethnograph files, using categories from preliminary analysis. Analyze field notes and taped interviews from Wisconsin, Illinois, Arizona, and California.
> 2. Expand assumptive world rules by examining all computer files with relevant descriptors. For example, when identifying patterns of behavior in legislative–state board relations, call up all files under the descriptor "state board" or, when identifying constraints on legislative staffers, call up all field notes and quotations under that label.
> 3. Do content analysis of all six states' data to (a) identify any additional patterns of behavior or belief, and (b) redefine domains and operational principles.
> 4. Reanalyze the file data using the alterations of assumptive world domains and operational principles.
> 5. Reorder the six states' files until clear, mutually exclusive, and exhaustive categories of behavior and belief systems are identified that organize the data descriptions of the policy environment.
> 6. Identify assumptive world effects on policy outcomes from field notes and interview data based on analytic notes regarding assumptive worlds (already started with West Virginia and Pennsylvania data).

Vignette 24 demonstrates the tasks involved in convincing funding agencies of the labor intensiveness of qualitative data analysis. It requires time and money and is not as simple as sitting in a comfy chair and reading over interview data. Those more attuned to traditional research, however, may need explicit details before they will provide support for that labor. Charts, diagrams, timelines, examples of precedents from highly regarded publications, and explicit delineation of the procedures will be convincing when tied to text. Funding agencies, pressed by the needs of many eager researchers and guided by the peer review process, will not provide resources unless everyone involved can see clearly how the

Table 9.3 Functions of the Operative Principles of Assumptive Worlds

Action Guide Domains and Operational Principles	Maintain Power and Predictability	Promote Cohesion
Who has the right and responsibility to initiate?		
The prescription for the CSSO role	x	
The prescription for the SDE role	x	
Legislative-SDE role	x	
Variations in initiative in legislature	x	
What policy ideas are deemed unacceptable?		
Policies that trample on powerful interests		x
Policies that lead to open defiance		x
Policies that defy tradition and dominant interests		x
Policy debates that diverge from the prevailing value		x
Untested, unworkable policy		x
What uses of power in policy-making activities are appropriate?		
Know your place and cooperate with the powerful	x	
Something for everyone	x	
Touch all the bases	x	
Bet on the winner	x	
Limits on social relationships	x	
Constraints on staffers	x	
Work with constraints and tricks	x	
Policy actors' sponsorship of policy issue network		x

Action Guide Domains and Operational Principles	Maintain Power and Predictability	Promote Cohesion
Uses of interstate comparison		x
What are the special-state conditions affecting policy?		
Cultural characteristics		x
Geographic, demographic characteristics		x

SOURCE: C. Marshall, grant proposal to National Science Foundation (1988).
NOTE: CSSO = Chief State School Officer; SDE = State Department of Education.

money will be converted into knowledge. Even small requests for a graduate assistant or a computer program will be denied if the research sounds like a mystical process or if it sounds like simple filing. Anyone who has ever done qualitative data analysis knows better, but those with the funds need explicit guidance so they can see how the expenditure is justified. Vignette 24 shows the need to fit explanations to the knowledge bases and predilections of reviewers by walking them through the steps to be followed and thereby providing assurances that the researcher can produce something meaningful on their terms.

* * * * *

This chapter has displayed the recursive processes of planning sufficient resources to support the conduct of a qualitative research project. Vignette 22 could aptly be retitled "Planning in a Context of Largesse," because the study was proposed to a funding agency with substantial financial resources. The major problem for that study was paring down the ideal design to conform to those budget parameters.

Vignette 23 portrays some of the unique problems associated with planning dissertation research, in which financial resources are largely unavailable and where time and personal support systems become critical. Each type of project has unique challenges when the researcher is designing the proposal. Consideration of these issues strengthens the proposal by demonstrating that the researcher is aware of and sensitive to the many challenges that may arise during the conduct of the study. Finally, Vignette 24 reminds us that even low-budget studies will be criticized if they cannot lead the reviewers to an understanding of the resources needed for qualitative analysis. Attention to these considerations helps strengthen the overall proposal and makes its positive evaluation more likely.

Throughout this book, we have presented considerations for building clear, thorough, and thoughtful proposals for qualitative research. In the final chapter, we make these considerations more explicit by describing them as a set of criteria.

Dialogue Between Learners

Hi Aaron,

Okay, my next topic of choice is (drumroll, please) time. How do you maximize your research time, especially for analysis and writing? Do you set aside a few hours each day, a specific day a week, work only on the weekends, grab chunks of time as they come? In the past, when I was working on a lengthy paper, I set aside whole afternoons and evenings, even several days in a row, and just pounded out the work. That isn't possible with qualitative research: There are too many tasks and too many levels of complexity. I question working in small segments of time. Can you immerse yourself deeply enough to produce anything of quality in short amounts of time? Don't you need lengthy involvement to appreciate the subtleties found in your data? When I'm truly interested in something, it's easy for me to push aside other demands and concentrate on that particular issue. While that may benefit the task I'm working on, other things fall by the wayside. Suddenly, my time has become a resource I have to allocate, just like the gas in my car! Anyway, I'm curious as to how you approach this particular part of the research process.

One question I haven't asked you: How did you narrow your study down to a manageable question?! My questions always begin so broadly, and I really struggle to narrow my interests down to functional bits. I didn't expect the research question to be one of the hardest parts of the research process. After all, you have a question, you answer the question. How naive! Crafting a good research question is very difficult, but just narrowing down the general to the specific is a sweat-inducing task for me. And it takes so much time! What techniques do you use to help in the process? Are you working with one encompassing question or several, more focused ones? Do you also struggle with this?!

Hope things are going well in Amherst! I have to hit the pile of papers now. . . .

Melanie

Hi Melanie,

In terms of your questions about time—I try to break my day into chunks for reading and chunks for writing. I'm the type that would be quite happy strolling around the library (material or virtual) for the rest of my life. I find that I have to be very disciplined about setting aside my reading and actually putting pen to paper. So I tend to get up early in the morning and read and/or make notes about what I'm reading. I love mornings, so this seems like a satisfying way to begin my day. At night, I try to write (if I read I fall asleep). Keeping this schedule also has a tendency to keep me on task. I've found that writing small bits of analysis (almost like little letters to myself) throughout the process of data collection and analysis helps quite a bit. There's no pressure to perform when writing these short bits, there's just a sense of trying to get an early read on what I've encountered. If nothing else, it can, at times, make me feel as though I've produced something.

I don't want to be a student forever (no matter what the perks!), so the issue of the time it takes to adequately take on qualitative research is pretty big for me. Time is a resource that I don't want to take for granted. I know that dissertations can sometimes take years to finish; however, I've also been told that "the best dissertation is a done dissertation." Knowing my tendency to dig deeper and deeper into the papers I write, I worry a bit about how long it will take me to produce the dissertation. From defining the research question to entering the field, collecting data, analysis, and writing the actual dissertation, I can easily understand why people are perpetually ABD [all but dissertation].

You've asked about how to narrow down the research questions, and my friends here would laugh, as I'm the last person they would ask. I, like you, also begin with a very broad question and then try and try to get it more and more specific. My writing teachers used to tell me to write the introductions to my papers last, after the paper has been written. This way you get a sense of what the introduction will actually be introducing. Often, I find that the research question doesn't come to me until I'm out there in the field and have interactions with a variety of people. Not that it's inspired stuff, mind you, just that it sort of evolves into a more specific question as time wears on. I've become OK with that practice, and I'm lucky to have an adviser who is very patient and kind enough to humor me along the way. Yes, concision and precision are issues that I need to work on. However, at some point, I need to trust that I will figure it out. After all, someone let me into this program; they must have felt that I could pull something off. . . .

Hope all is well. We're hoping for a break in the weather here. I'm tired of sweating while brushing my teeth.

Take care,

Aaron

FURTHER READING

Cheek, J. (2000). An untold story? Doing funded qualitative research. In N. K. Denzin & Y. S. Lincoln (Eds.), *Handbook of qualitative research* (2nd ed., pp. 401–420). Thousand Oaks, CA: Sage.

Cheek, J. (2008). Funding. In L. M. Given (Ed.), *The SAGE encyclopedia of qualitative research methods* (pp. 360–364). Thousand Oaks, CA: Sage.

Coley, S. M., & Scheinberg, C. A. (2000). *Proposal writing* (2nd ed.). Thousand Oaks, CA: Sage. (See Appendix A on estimating time)

Locke, L. F., Spirduso, W. W., & Silverman, S. J. (2000). *Proposals that work: A guide for planning dissertations and grant proposals* (4th ed., chap. 9 & 10). Thousand Oaks, CA: Sage.

Morse, J. M. (1994). Designing funded qualitative research. In N. K. Denzin & Y. S. Lincoln (Eds.), *Handbook of qualitative research* (pp. 220–235). Thousand Oaks, CA: Sage.

Penrod, J. (2003). Getting funded: Writing a successful qualitative small-project proposal. *Qualitative Health Research, 13*(6), 821–832.

Tripp-Riemer, T., & Cohen, M. Z. (1991). Funding strategies for qualitative research. In J. M. Morse (Ed.), *Qualitative nursing research: A contemporary dialogue* (pp. 243–256). Newbury Park, CA: Sage.

KEY CONCEPTS

Data analysis software

Financial support

Personnel

Time

10

Revisiting Proposal as Argument and Forecasting Final Representations

In Chapter 1 and throughout this book, we have provided guidance for the preparation of a well-documented argument to convince readers that the study should and can be done. As should be clear by now, all the elements of a proposal intertwine. Identifying the genre and the ways in which the study will fill gaps in knowledge, policy, and practice intertwine with the researcher as a person. Considerations of role, for example, should address the personal biography of the researcher and how that might shape events and meanings. In what ways is the research, whether participatory or more objectivist, altering the flow of daily life? Selection of the setting and sampling of people and behaviors within that setting should be based on sound reasoning, and the rationale that has guided those choices should be presented, indicating how they will inform the research questions. Just as the proposal addresses issues of the value, truthfulness, and soundness of the study, it also addresses the various phases of data analysis and report writing. Considerations of the ethical conduct of the study are woven throughout the proposal.

Writers of any research proposal must develop a sound rationale for the choice of methodology. In qualitative proposals, a crucial task is developing the logic and argument for the interpretive paradigm—the idea of conducting research in a natural setting with the researcher as the primary means for gathering and interpreting data. Qualitative research involves a series of choices: "These choices and the theoretical reasons for them need to be presented explicitly" (Sanjek, 1990, p. 395). Qualitative research is generally no longer tossed aside as simply an alternative or merely the pilot study. However, as noted in the Preface to this edition and discussed below, the qualitative researcher needs to be mindful of strong countervailing conservative forces, which is especially pronounced in the United States with the federal government's calls for "**scientifically based research.**" When facing debates and challenges about the soundness, validity, utility, and generalizability of qualitative methods, the researcher can draw on the deep conversations in the literature that address these issues.

Many social sciences have put aside the old doubts and mistrusts of qualitative inquiry. Arguments and concerns about quantitative versus qualitative can now be recast. The research community now generally recognizes that the rationales and the supporting criteria for various approaches to inquiry will differ. In general, qualitative research proposals can move on to the current methodological scene with discussions of criteria for judging the soundness of any research and with discussions about choices of genres. While such proposals may encounter debates and challenges from those with a more traditional take and from those with concerns about postmodern, feminist, action, and emancipator stances in research, still, the more naturalistic and explicitly interpretive approach of qualitative research has gathered momentum and support in research communities.

In the **politics of knowledge**, certain research is seen as the "gold standard"—the most dependable, the conventional and privileged way. Powerful and dominant groups work to maintain those conventions, sometimes marginalizing other forms or sources of knowledge (Lather, 1991; Marshall, 1997a; Scheurich, 1997). To promote traditional designs, the U.S. Department of Education requests and supports studies by "qualified scientists" that "address causal questions" and that "employ randomized experimental designs" (Flinders, 2003, p. 380) as the way to transform the field. This focus on quantitative inquiry means that expanded exploration of issues does not qualify as research under these new restrictions.

We, however, put aside these realities of knowledge politics for the moment. Instead, we concentrate on ways for the proposal and for the researcher to be ready and articulate about the interpretive paradigm. The essential considerations are articulated well by Patton (2002), who notes that the **credibility** of a qualitative report depends on the use of rigorous methods of fieldwork, on the credibility of the researcher, and on the "fundamental appreciation of naturalistic inquiry, qualitative methods, inductive analysis, purposeful sampling, and holistic thinking" (pp. 552–553). Developing a logic that will solidly defend a proposal entails three large domains: (1) responding to criteria for the overall soundness of the project; (2) demonstrating the usefulness of the research for the particular conceptual framework and research questions; and (3) demonstrating the sensitivities and sensibilities to *be* the research instrument. Careful consideration of each will help the proposal writer develop a logic in support of the proposal.

This chapter revisits points made throughout Chapters 1 to 9 and helps the researcher think ahead about the final product or report. As he moves toward the big leap of submitting his proposal, the qualitative researcher must revisit and be ready to answer questions and point to specific sections in the proposal that address those questions. He should, as an exercise, pretend to be a mere reader, not the writer of the proposal, and see what questions still need to be answered for the reader. Whether he is sending a proposal for funding or prepping for a dissertation **proposal defense** or not, he should give one last look at his proposal and have one last practice session so that he can calmly answer questions. To make it fun, he might gather together a few fellow researchers and have them play roles of professors or funding agencies doling out the third degree on the proposal!

CRITERIA OF SOUNDNESS

Where and how well does the researcher address soundness, credibility, and trustworthiness? Recall our discussion, particularly in Chapters 3 and 8, about the criteria against which the trustworthiness of the project can be evaluated. These canons can be phrased as questions to which all social science research must respond (Lincoln & Guba, 2000). First, how credible are the particular findings of the study? And by what criteria can we judge them? Second, how transferable and applicable are these findings to another setting or group of people? Third, how can we be reasonably sure that the findings would be replicated if the study were conducted with the same participants in the same context? And fourth, how can we be sure that the findings reflect the participants and the inquiry itself rather than a fabrication from the researcher's biases or prejudices? Postmodern and feminist challenges to traditional research assert that all discovery and truths emerge from the researcher's prejudgments and predilections. Those espousing these positions argue that such predispositions should be used "as building blocks . . . for acquiring new knowledge" (Nielson, 1990, p. 28).

Recall Lincoln and Guba's (1985) strategies for establishing the "**truth value**" (p. 290) of the study, its applicability, consistency, and neutrality. Every systematic inquiry into the human condition must address these issues. Strategically, it may be useful to at least be prepared to discuss how these terms have parallels to the conventional positivist paradigm—internal validity, external validity, reliability, and objectivity and then the ways in which Lincoln and Guba and others demonstrated the need to rework these constructs for interpretive qualitative inquiry. Be ready to discuss their, or others', alternative constructs that have given qualitative researchers new terms with different connotations—ones that more accurately reflect the assumptions of the qualitative paradigm. Discuss *credibility*, in which the goal is to demonstrate that the inquiry was conducted in such a manner as to ensure that the subject was appropriately identified and described. The inquiry should then be "credible to the constructors of the original multiple realities" (p. 296). The credibility/believability of a qualitative study that aims to explore a problem or describe a setting, a process, a social group, or a pattern of interaction will rest on its validity. An in-depth description showing the complexities of processes and interactions will be so embedded with data derived from the setting that it is convincing to readers. Within the parameters of that setting and population and the limitations of the theoretical framework and design, the research will be credible. A qualitative researcher should therefore adequately state those parameters, thereby placing boundaries around and limitations on the study.

Be prepared to discuss **transferability**, ways in which the study's findings will be useful to others in similar situations, with similar research questions or questions of practice. The burden of demonstrating that a set of findings applies to another context rests more with the researcher who would make that transfer than with the original researcher. Kennedy (1979) refers to this as the **second decision span in generalizing**. The first decision span allows the researcher to generalize the findings about a particular sample to the population from which that sample was drawn (assuming adequate population specification and random selection of the sample). The second decision span occurs when another researcher wants to apply the findings about a population of interest to a second population believed or presumed to be similar enough to the first to warrant that application. This entails making judgments about and an argument for the relevance of the initial study to the second setting.

However, a qualitative study's transferability or generalizability to other settings may be problematic, at least in the probabilistic sense of the term. Generalizing qualitative findings to other populations, settings, and treatment arrangements—that is, its *external* validity—is seen by traditional canons as a weakness in the approach. To counter the challenges, the researcher can refer to the original theoretical framework to show how data collection and analysis will be guided by concepts and models. By doing so, the researcher states the theoretical parameters of the research. Then, those who make policy or design research studies within those same (or sufficiently similar) parameters can determine whether the cases described can be generalized for new research policy and transferred to other settings. In addition, the reader or user of specific research can see how research ties itself into a body of theory.

For example, a case study of a new staff development program in a high school can be tied to theories of the implementation of innovations in organizations, leadership, personnel management, and adult career socialization. The research can then be used in planning program policy and further research in a variety of settings—not just the high school, school organizations, and staff development. It can be included with research about organizations and can contribute to the literature on organizational theory.

Be prepared to discuss strategic choices that can enhance a study's generalizability, such as triangulating multiple sources of data. **Triangulation** is the act of bringing more than one source of data to bear on a single point. Derived from navigation science, the concept has been fruitfully applied to social science inquiry (see Richards, 2005; Rossman & Wilson, 1994). Data from different sources can be used to corroborate, elaborate, or illuminate the research in question (Rossman & Wilson, 1994). Designing a study in which multiple cases, multiple informants, or more than one data-gathering method is used can greatly strengthen the study's usefulness for other settings.

Be prepared to discuss **dependability**—showing the ways by which the researcher plans to account for changing conditions in the phenomenon chosen for study and changes in the design created by an increasingly refined understanding of the setting. This represents a set of assumptions very different from those shaping the concept of reliability. Positivist notions of reliability assume an unchanging universe where inquiry could, quite logically, be replicated. This assumption of an unchanging social world is in direct contrast with the qualitative/interpretative assumption that the social world is always being constructed and the concept of replication is itself problematic.

Be prepared to discuss **confirmability**—the ways in which qualitative researchers can parallel the traditional concept of objectivity. Discuss ways to ask whether the findings of the study could be confirmed by another person or another study and demonstrate the impossibility and foolishness of doing so. But still, be ready to discuss ways to show that the logical inferences and interpretations of the researcher can make sense to someone else. Does that reader or **critical friend** see how the inferences were made? Do they make sense? Be prepared to argue that the logic and interpretive nature of qualitative inquiry can be made (somewhat) transparent to others, thereby increasing the strength of the assertions.

Be prepared to respond to concerns about the natural subjectivity of the researcher shaping the research. Again, the researcher should assert the strengths of qualitative methods by showing how she will develop an in-depth understanding of, even empathy for, the research participants to better understand their worlds. The researcher's insights increase the likelihood that she will be able to describe the complex social system being studied. She should, however, build into the proposal strategies for limiting bias in interpretation. Be ready with strategies such as the following:

- Plan to use a research partner or a person who plays the role of a critical friend who thoughtfully and gently questions the researcher's analyses.
- Build in time for cross-checking, peer debriefing, and time sampling to search for negative instances.
- Describe how analysis will use, but not be limited by, previous literature and how it will include checking and rechecking the data and also a purposeful examination of possible alternative explanations.
- Provide examples of explicitly descriptive, nonevaluative note taking: planning to take two sets of notes, one with description and another with tentative categories and personal reactions.
- Cite previous researchers who have written about bias, subjectivity, and data quality.
- Plan to conduct an audit trail of the data collection and analytic strategies. (See Lincoln & Guba, 1985; Richards, 2005.)

Clearly, criteria of goodness for qualitative research differ from the criteria developed for experimental and positivist research. Still, it is helpful to articulate the parallels and differences. Qualitative research does not claim to be replicable. The researcher purposely avoids controlling the research conditions and concentrates on recording the complexity of situational contexts and interrelations as they occur naturally. The researcher's goal of discovering this complexity by altering research strategies within a flexible research design, moreover, cannot be replicated by future researchers, nor should it be attempted to do so.

However, qualitative researchers can respond to the traditional social science concern for **replicability** by taking the following steps: First, they can assert that qualitative studies by their nature (and, really, all research) cannot be replicated because the real world changes. Second, by planning to keep thorough notes and a journal or log that records each design decision and the rationale behind it, researchers allow others to inspect their procedures, protocols, and decisions. Finally, by planning to keep all collected data in a well-organized, retrievable form, researchers can make them available easily if the findings are challenged or if another researcher wants to reanalyze the data.

For works emphasizing the interpretive strengths of qualitative inquiry, though, it is more important to embrace subjectivity. *Triangulation* is not so much about getting the "truth" but rather about finding the multiple perspectives for knowing the social world. Another set of criteria derives from the assumption that research is good if it helps promote *emancipatory* change; this is derived from feminist theory and critical theory. Such goodness criteria support the value of research that highlights oppressive power relations and that empowers the participants, often with collaborative action research. Finally, and relatedly, we see an emerging trend toward judging research value through its presentation or its performance. Thus, one values the research effort for the aesthetics of its narrative, the theater, the poetry, or other performance aspects (McCall, 2000). Whichever philosophical assumptions ground one's proposal, the researcher should have good responses to the important question: How can you make sure that your earthy, thick, evocative finding is not, in fact, wrong? The traditional, realist responses will be very different from those of the proposal writer doing critical ethnography. Each response must be convincing in the arguments and strategies it proposes for ensuring goodness.

For some descriptive studies aimed at presenting a thick description of reality, traditional scientific standards can be paralleled, as in using comparative analysis and in emphasizing rigor in data collection, in cross-checking, and in intercoder consistency, as explicated in, for example, Miles and Huberman's (1994) guidelines and Anfara, Brown, and Mangione's (2002) demonstration. However, continuing discussions of criteria for assessing the value and trustworthiness of qualitative research are quite persuasive. Qualitative inquiry, moving to a kind of "non-naïve realism" (Smith & Deemer, 2000), recognizes that understanding is relative and there are ***multiple understandings*** and that, at best, we present a report that is likely to be true given our existing knowledge. As Smith and Deemer (2000) put it,

> Relativism is nothing more or less than the expression of our human finitude: we must see ourselves as practical and moral beings, and abandon hope for knowledge that is not embedded with our historical, cultural, and engendered ways of being. (p. 886)

Finally, "criteria should not be thought of as an abstraction, but as a list of features that we think, or more or less agree at any given time and place, characterize good versus bad inquiry" (p. 894).

Planning ahead, thinking about how one's final research product will be judged as "good," is a useful exercise for proposal writers. Marshall (1985a, 1990) developed criteria to apply to written reports of qualitative research; we have adapted them here for proposal development. Attention to these issues ensures a sound and convincing research proposal.

The Design and Methods Should Be Explicitly Detailed

The researcher explicates the design and methods so that the reader can judge whether they are adequate and make sense. He includes a rationale for qualitative research generally and also the specific genre in which the study is situated. He discusses the anticipated methods for attaining entry and managing role, data collection, recording, analysis, ethics, and exit. He describes how the site and the sample will be selected. Data collection and analysis procedures will be made public, not remain magical.

The researcher states clearly any assumptions that may affect the study. Biases are expressed, and the researcher engages in some preliminary self-reflection to uncover personal subjectivities. She articulates, often drawing on the work of others, how she will be a finely tuned research instrument whose personal talents, experiential biases, and insights will be used consciously. She argues that she will take care to be self-analytical and will recognize when she is becoming overly subjective and not critical enough of her interpretations. As part of this process, she analyzes the conceptual framework for theoretical biases. Furthermore, the researcher articulates how she will reflexively engage with and discuss the value judgments and personal perspectives that are inherent in data collection and in analysis. She will, for example, exercise caution in distinguishing between descriptive field notes ("The roofs had holes and missing tiles") and judgmental ones ("Many houses were dilapidated").

The researcher writes about his tolerance for ambiguity, how he will search for alternative explanations, check out negative instances, and use a variety of methods to ensure that the findings are strong and grounded (e.g., with triangulation). Methods are proposed for ensuring data quality (e.g., informants' knowledgeability, subjectivities, and candor) and for guarding against ethnocentric explanations by eliciting cross-cultural perspectives.

The researcher describes preliminary observations—a pilot study—or her first days in the field, demonstrating how the research questions have been generated from observation, not merely from library research. The researcher is careful about the sensitivity of those being researched: Ethical standards are maintained. She argues that people in the research setting will likely benefit in some way (ranging from an hour of sympathetic listening, to feeling empowered to take action in order to alter some facet of their lives).

Research Questions and the Data's Relevance Should Be Explicit and Rigorously Argued

The researcher discusses how there will be abundant evidence from raw data to demonstrate the connection between those data and his interpretations. He shows how data will be presented in a readable, accessible form, perhaps aided by graphics, models, charts, and figures. He states the preliminary research questions clearly and argues that the data collected will allow him to respond to those questions and generate further questions. The relationship between the proposed study and previous studies is explicit. The researcher discusses how the study will be reported in a manner accessible to other researchers, practitioners, and policymakers. He argues that he will be able to make an adequate translation of findings so that others will be able to use them in a timely way.

The Study Should Be Situated in a Scholarly Context

The researcher's proposal acknowledges the limitations of qualitative inquiry vis à vis generalizability. A more important task is assisting proposal readers in seeing the potential transferability of findings and showing how the study is tied into the big picture. The researcher has to be convincing about looking holistically at the setting to understand the linkages among systems and about the need to trace the historical context to understand how institutions and roles have evolved.

She may argue that, while defining central concepts, with reference to previously identified phenomena, her research will go beyond established frameworks, challenging old ways of thinking (as Rosalie Wax sought to do in her study of Native Americans). She may argue that her highly descriptive ethnographic account will reveal unknown realities that matter for creating effective programs and policies (as an ethnography or case studies of teenage parents might). Chapter 4 details ways to use the literature review to situate the study in previous research and in the need for information for policy and practice. Chapter 5, too, points to sections in research design that must articulate the reasons why the qualitative approach is needed for the questions being pursued.

Records Should Be Kept

The researcher describes how the data will be preserved and available for other analyses. He documents any infield analysis. Furthermore, there is an explicit mention of a **running record** of procedures, perhaps an audit trail that will be included in an appendix to the final written report. Chapters 8 and 9 provide details of how that can be managed.

Attention to these criteria ensures a solid qualitative proposal that displays concern for issues of trustworthiness and shows how knowledgeable the proposal writer is regarding these issues. Many issues are addressed in the body of the proposal; others may be discussed in the meeting to defend the proposal or in response to the queries of funding agencies. (See Marshall, 1985b, 1990, for a discussion of the evolving set of "criteria of goodness" that cuts across scholarly and political debates.)

Finally, researchers need to allay fears (both their own and those of their reviewers) that they might stay in the field or become stalled when faced with analyzing the data. They need to demonstrate their ability to move from data collection to analysis and from interpretation to writing. Again, a pilot study, a hypothesized model, or an outline of possible data analysis categories can be appended to the proposal. Qualitative researchers should always caution that such models, outlines, and categories are primarily heuristic—they are tentative guides to begin observation and analysis. They are reassuring, however, to those who are uncomfortable with the flexibility and ambiguity. Such guides assist in demonstrating that qualitative researchers are, indeed, guided by concrete and systematic processes in collecting and analyzing the data. Chapter 8 provided numerous strategies for moving the analysis along. Still, qualitative research cannot get bogged down by what Schwandt (1996) calls **criteriology**: lists that are too restrictive and preordained.

Clarity Should Be Balanced With Academic Credibility

Audience matters. Some assessors of proposals are quite impressed with the deeply philosophical treatises and the loads of jargon-laden, quote-laden, long-winded backgrounding of issues. Others impatiently skim through this, asking, "Where's the beef?" or saying, "OK fine, just tell me what you want to do and why and how?" Dissertation students should calculate how to balance their proposals and their answers to questions, having planned ahead, given what they know of their professors. Proposers seeking funding should sleuth to find anything available about their audience—the foundation's previous projects, their likely reviewers' styles and preferences. All proposers can benefit from Silverman's (2007) "anti-bullshit agenda" (p. 139). He advises qualitative researchers to consider clarity, reason, economy, beauty, and truth as guides to their plan for their proposal as well as for their plan for final reports. How long should the proposal be? How long should the final report be? Perhaps the answer is "It depends" or "Long enough to balance clarity with adequate academic credibility."

DEMONSTRATING THE ESSENTIAL QUALITATIVENESS OF THE QUESTIONS

Many discussions about criteria of goodness for qualitative research emphasize the transparency of the data collection and analysis and the "systematization" of procedures for gathering and presenting evidence. Other standards matter as well. The real-world significance of the questions asked, the practical value of potential findings, and the degree to which participants in the study may benefit are emerging criteria. Frequently still, in attempting to make a proposed design efficient and conform to traditional research, reviewers recommend alterations in the original design. They may argue that the time for exploration is wasteful, or they might just propose a pilot study; they may try to change the nature of the study from ethnographic exploration and description to a more traditional design. They may worry that the design is not "tight." Researchers' explanations, therefore, must sway their audiences with the power of their methodologies for the kinds of unanswered questions they will explore. Also, they must allay fears about design "looseness," the immersion in the natural setting, and the time expended in exploration.

THE VALUE OF THE QUALITATIVE APPROACH

In Chapter 1, and throughout this book, we discuss the matching of methodology with research questions. When presenting a proposal, this kind of matching constitutes the most essential and potentially convincing argument. *It is not enough to give a nod to this by citing Denzin and Lincoln (2005) and Rallis and Rossman (in press)!*

The researcher must be eloquent about the need for research methodologies that are culturally sensitive and that, in the real world, can identify contextually generated patterns. She must be able to speak and write effectively about why nonmeasurable soft data are so valuable. Her extensive critique of previous research that left unanswered questions, which made clear the need to observe naturally or to elicit **emic perspectives**, substantiates her assertions. Demonstrating how persistent problems continue unresolved can substantiate her proposal to toss aside the survey with the wrong questions and to instead explore the narratives of people involved with the problems. Demonstrating the value of qualitative inquiry's "toolbox that enables researchers to develop concepts" (Morse, 2004) in fields with inadequate conceptualizing and theory building can buttress her proposal. Using humorous analogies and wit can be effective, if done judiciously. For example, she might use Morse's (2004) criticism of medical research's insistence on the use of quantitative methods even for qualitative questions as "trying to put in a nail using a chainsaw" (p. 1030).

Feminist, postmodern, and critical theorists invite us to engage in research that does not "otherize" participants and has **liberatory potential**. They seek to discover and create, often collaboratively, knowledge that benefits those usually marginalized from the mainstream. Thus, emerging criteria lend special credence and value to proposals that challenge dominant (and *dominating*) practice or that include participants whose meaning making was overlooked in previous policy and research (Carspecken, 1996; Harding, 1987; Lather, 1991; Marshall, 1997b; Scheurich, 1997). And increasingly, the practical utility of research is becoming a valued criterion, especially for action research and when immediate pressing problems need research-based recommendations (Hammersley, 1990).

Thus, the value to be derived from using a qualitative approach needs to be convincingly explicated. Proposal writers need to anticipate reviewers' concerns and walk them through with rationales and examples. Vignettes 25 and 26 show how two researchers developed rationales for their work. Vignette 25 describes how a proposal writer anticipated a funding agent's challenge to the usefulness of qualitative research. Vignette 26 shows how a doctoral student successfully withstood challenges to his right to alter the design during fieldwork if it became necessary or prudent.

VIGNETTE 25 Justifying Time for Exploration

A proposal to conduct three in-depth case studies of high schools undergoing change (Rossman et al., 1984) had received favorable internal review, although one administrator had quite a few worries about the value of qualitative research. The proposal had been transmitted to a federal agency where it would receive close scrutiny as a major portion of the group's work over the next five years.

As the research team sat on a train heading south, they pondered the type of questions they would be required to answer. Surely their sampling plan would be challenged: The criterion of "improvement" would have to be quite broadly construed to locate the kinds of high schools they wanted. The notion of studying a school's culture was new to many in the research community, never mind the Washington bureaucrats. The team anticipated questions about the usefulness of that concept, as well as the presentation of theoretical ideas on cultural change and transformation.

It struck the researchers as prudent to develop a rationale grounded in the applied research of others rather than relying on anthropological constructs. As they reviewed that logic, three points seemed most salient. First, the research proposal assumed that change in schools could not be adequately explored through a snapshot approach. Rather, the complexity of interactions among people, new programs, deeply held beliefs and values, and other organizational events demanded a long-term, in-depth approach. Second, at that time, little was known about change processes in secondary schools. Most of the previous research focused on elementary schools and had been generalized, perhaps inappropriately, to secondary schools. The proposed research was intended to fill the gap. Finally, much had been written about teachers' resistance to change. The rationale for and significance of the study

(Continued)

VIGNETTE 25 (Continued)

would be in uncovering some of that construct, in delving beneath the surface and exploring the meaning perspectives of teachers involved in profound change.

The proposal called for long-term engagement in the social worlds of the three high schools selected for study. The team anticipated a challenge to their time allocation and decided to defend it through the rationale presented above as well as with the idea that complex processes demand adequate time for exploration—that is, interactions and changes in belief systems occur slowly.

After the two-hour hearing, the team felt that it had done a credible job but realized that the funding agent had not yet come to accept the longer time frame of qualitative research. In the negotiations, the research team had to modify the original plan to engage in participant observation over the course of a single school year. To save the project from rejection, they had agreed to 6 months of data collection, over the winter and spring terms.

In this vignette, the researchers developed a sound logic for the major aspects of the study. Justification for the substantive focus grew from the conceptual framework and the significance of the study. The major research approach—long-term engagement in the social world—could best be justified through demonstrating the need for exploration.

The quest for cultural understandings requires intense and lengthy involvement in the setting and design flexibility. For example, in their research on Fijian communities, Laverack and Brown (2003) discuss their need to adapt, given the different cultural styles of group dynamics, facilitative, spatial arrangements; gender dynamics; and protocols and perceptions of time. Without making adaptations of traditional Western assumptions, their research would have flopped. Convincing the uninitiated critic that design flexibility is crucial can be a tough hurdle for the proposer of qualitative research. Vignette 26 shows how a fictitious doctoral student in economics successfully countered challenges to the need for design flexibility.

VIGNETTE 26 Defending Flexibility

Katz had been fascinated with families' financial decisions long before he first took a course in microeconomics as a college sophomore. That exposure to theory crystallized his interest and gave it an intellectual home. During his doctoral course work, however, he had pursued this interest from a cross-cultural perspective, enrolling in as many anthropology courses as his adviser would permit.

Katz's interest grew as he read case studies of families in other cultures. Quite naturally, he became interested in the methods anthropologists used to gather their data; they seemed so different from econometrics or even economic history methods. As he immersed himself in these methods, his fascination grew. Now, about to embark on his dissertation, he had convinced one committee member to support his proposal to engage in a long-term, in-depth study of five families in very different socioeconomic circumstances. As he prepared for a meeting with the other two committee members, he reviewed the strengths of his proposal.

First, he was exploring the inner decision-making processes of five families—something no economics research had done. The value of the research would rest, in part, on the contribution this would make to understanding of the beliefs, values, and motivations of certain financial behaviors. Second, he was contributing to methodology because he was approaching a topic using new research methods. He could rely on the work of two or three other qualitative economists, well-established scholars in their fields, to demonstrate that others had undertaken such risky business and survived!

Third, he had thoroughly combed the methodological literature for information that would demonstrate his knowledge of many of the issues that would arise: The design section of the proposal was more than 60 pages long and addressed every conceivable issue. He had not attempted to resolve them all but, rather, to show that he was aware that they might arise, knowledgeable about how others had dealt with them, and sensitive to the trade-offs represented by various decisions.

During the committee meeting, the thoroughness and richness of the design section served him well. The fully documented topics and sensitive discussion revealed a knowledge and sophistication not often found in doctoral students. What Katz had not anticipated, however, was the larger question brought up by one committee member: With such a small sample, how could the research be useful?

Fortunately, Katz recalled the argument developed by Kennedy (1979) about generalizing from single case studies. He had conceptualized his study as a set of family life histories from which would be drawn analytic categories, with relationships among them carefully delimited. Not unlike a multisite case study, Katz's proposal could be evaluated from that perspective. This logic proved convincing enough for Katz's committee to approve his proposal.

In the Vignettes 25 and 26, each proposal demanded a well thought out, thorough, and logical defense. When the proposal is considered as an argument, the need to provide a clear organization, document major design decisions, and demonstrate the overall soundness of the study becomes clear. Following the advice we provide here will help the qualitative research proposal writer think through the conceptual and methodological justifications and rationales for the proposed study. In planning a defense of the proposal, we suggest that the researcher anticipate the questions that may come from a funding agency or from a dissertation committee.

Having well-prepared and well-rehearsed answers will facilitate the defense. Tables 10.1 and 10.2 present the types of questions that we have encountered. Those in Table 10.1 come from reviewers with little experience with qualitative methods; those in Table 10.2 are from those who are familiar with the methods and seek justifications for the decisions in the proposal.

Table 10.1 Questions From Reviewers With Little Qualitative Experience

I'm not used to this; could you explain this qualitative approach you're taking?
Why don't you include any surveys in this research study?
I don't see any numbers here—how is this real research?
What is your control group?
How can this be generalized?
If you're the one collecting and analyzing the data, how will we know you're right?
How can you be objective?
How can you verify your findings?
Can you explain this idea of "grounded theory"?
Explain this concept of emergent sampling (or emergent data analysis).
It looks like you're using stories as part of your data collection. Are stories really data?
How can you start this research without knowing what you're looking for?
How will you use any of these findings? How will you explain how this small sample can be OK?
I think this will be a fun study, but I worry about whether you'll be able to publish it in a journal.
I don't see how you can have findings that give real answers for policymakers.

Table 10.2 Questions From Reviewers Attuned to Qualitative Methodology

I like your research design, but what's the significance of your findings?
How have you made a good match of topic and qualitative or quantitative approaches?
Is it feasible to believe that you can finish this study in a year?
What processes will you go through to categorize your data?
How will you talk about and handle validity and reliability in this qualitative research?
Could you give me an example of going from concepts to data collection? Going from interpretations to generalizable findings? What about other naturalistic inquiries or dealing with negative instances?
What if you don't get access to your study population? What if people won't talk to you?
How can you justify, ethically, your plan to muck around in peoples' lives?
What is the final product going to look like?

Can you give me some examples of comparable work?

How can you condense your qualitative research to a publishable 12-page journal article? How will you make time in your life to focus on this research?

Are you going to go out "in the field," never to be seen again?

How will you know when to stop collecting data?

How will policymakers or practitioners make use of your findings?

What philosophical assumptions guide you in your efforts to ensure the "goodness" of your research?

Shouldn't you try some of those neat new things, such as performance ethnography?

Although some of these questions may never be articulated, they may be present in the minds of foundation officials or dissertation committee members. Building a logic in support of the proposed qualitative study will help reassure skeptics and strengthen the argument. And to ease worries and tense questioning, the proposer can tell stories. For example, to explain the flexibility and reflectiveness of the human research instrument, he might read a bit from Narayan's (1993) account of fieldwork in the Himalayan foothills—of how she was variously identified as being from her mother's village, from Bombay, a native, and an outsider. But when she appeared at weddings, "where a splash of foreign prestige added to the festivities, I was incontrovertibly stated to be 'from America'... she came *all* the way from there for this function, yes, with her camera and her tape recorder" (p. 674). Thus, she was viewed as an honored guest, even though many people present thought that Americans were savages because television revealed that they didn't wear many clothes.

DEMONSTRATING PRECEDENTS

Now, in the 21st century, with academic journals and handbooks devoted to qualitative inquiry and with doctoral programs sometimes requiring qualitative skills, researchers have plentiful resources to draw on. While we honor old traditions, like that of Margaret Mead and other classical ethnographers going into the field and inventing strategies, the budding researcher now can, and should, draw on the wisdom gleaned from those inventions. Furthermore, she can often cite scholars in her own field whose use of qualitative methodology has led to important new understandings.

Qualitative research has **respectability** and has proliferated in the practice disciplines such as nursing and those dealing with health, illness, and life transitions (Sandelowski & Barroso, 2003). In psychology, a field traditionally associated with the controlled experiment and the statistical analysis creating mathematical models of psychological processes, some scholars recognize the need for qualitative inquiry as a way to delve into "the personal 'lifeworlds'... and the range of social interpretations of events" (Ashworth, 2003, p. 4). The fields of social work and journalism are naturals for qualitative inquiry and are developing literatures and courses to hone skills and goodness criteria (Morse, 2003; Shaw, 2003; Shaw & Ruckdeschel, 2002). Ninety-five percent of the articles submitted to an English-teaching journal in a five-year period were qualitative in nature (Smagorinsky, 2007). Other fields may still see only the rare one-per-year qualitative publication.

Probably the best strategy for demonstrating the value of one's proposed qualitative study is to share copies of important qualitative books and journal articles from one's own or similar fields with a possibly skeptical committee member or reviewer. While some (quantitative) sociologists might still challenge the understandings of professional enculturation in *Boys in White* (Becker, Geer, Hughes, & Strauss, 1961) or *The Silent Dialogue* (Olesen & Whittaker, 1968) or see little value in the methodological carefulness demonstrated in the detailed appendices of *Work and the Family System* (Piotrkowski, 1979) or Lareau's (1989) *Home Advantage*, others would be open to learning. While some might wonder how Kanter (1977) would want to spend so much time studying one business, others would find her representation of the effects of stunted career mobility in *Men and Women of the Corporation* valuable for individuals, for women and minorities, and for personnel managers, too. Citing such books and even showing copies of such well-managed and significant qualitative studies may impress and reassure evaluators and reviewers.

Being well-read in qualitative methodological approaches and in final research reports, in one's own discipline and in the books and articles of prestigious and well-known scholars, provides excellent support for arguing the value of a proposal and reassuring those who worry about whether it can be done. Precedents are useful, too, for demonstrating that conducting qualitative inquiry is a viable career choice for a budding academic. Wolcott (2009) finds that academic presses are more likely to be open to qualitative publications in the following fields: African studies, anthropology, art history, Asian studies, classical studies, cultural studies, European history, film, fine arts, gender studies, geography, Jewish studies, Latin American studies, law, linguistics, literary studies, Middle Eastern studies, music, natural history, philosophy, photography, political science, religious studies, science, sociology, and women's studies. Ironically, even as the federal government devalues qualitative genres, universities are advertising professorial positions for teaching them!

ENVISIONING THE FINAL REPORT, THE DISSERTATION, OR THE BOOK

As we showed in Chapter 8, data analysis and writing are intertwined. "Writing gives form to the researcher's clumps of carefully categorized and organized data" Glesne says (2006, p. 173). We suggest that the researcher consider at the proposal stage what modalities he will use for the final reporting. For dissertations, this is typically done by outlining the chapters to be included in the final document. For funded research proposals, reporting may entail periodic written reports as well as conferences, newsletters, documentary films, or exhibitions. Researchers working in the genres of performance ethnography and autoethnography often present alternative, experimental formats for presenting and re-presenting their findings. Thus, theater skits, poetry, and multimedia presentations could all form the "final product" of work in these genres. Despite interest in alternative dissemination strategies and reporting formats, however, the written report remains the primary mode for reporting the results of research.

There are several models for report writing. Wolcott (2009) describes various ways of balancing description, analysis, and interpretation. Patton (2002) discusses balancing description and interpretation, noting that "endless description becomes its own muddle. . . . Description provides the skeleton frame for analysis that leads to interpretation" (p. 503).

In their classic work, Taylor and Bogdan (1984, Chap. 8–12) suggest five different approaches. First, in the purely descriptive life history, the author presents one person's account of his or her life, framing that description with an analysis of the social significance of that life. Second is the presentation of data gathered through in-depth interviews and participant observation, where the participants' perspectives are presented and their worldviews structure the report. The third approach attempts to relate practice (the reality of social phenomena) to theory. Descriptive data are summarized and then linked to more general theoretical constructs. Taylor and Bogdan's fourth approach is the most theoretical. To illustrate it, they refer to a study of institutions for individuals with severe cognitive challenges. The report addresses the sociological theory on institutionalization and the symbolic management of conditions in total institutions. Their final approach tries to build theory with data from several types of institutions gathered under a variety of research conditions. They cite a report that addresses issues of the presentation of the self under various difficult circumstances and attempts to draw theoretical conclusions across types of institutions, persons, and circumstances.

In his well-known work *Tales of the Field*, Van Maanen (1988) identifies three different genres in qualitative writing. *Realist tales*, the most easily recognized, display a realistic account of a culture and are published in journals or as scholarly monographs in a third-person voice with a clear separation between researcher and the researched. Established by the grandparents of ethnography—Margaret Mead, William Foote Whyte, Howard Becker, and Branislaw Malinowski—this tradition set the standards and criteria for credibility, quality, and respectability in qualitative work. Van Maanen views these as frequently "flat, dry and sometimes unbearably dull" (p. 48).

Confessional tales are highly personalized accounts with "mini-melodramas of hardships endured in fieldwork" (Van Maanen, 1988, p. 73). This genre aims to display the author's powers of observation and the discipline of good field habits to call attention to the ways in which building cultural description is part of social science. Powdermaker's *Stranger and Friend* (1966) is a classic example of this genre.

In *impressionist tales*, the field worker displays her own experiences as a sort of autoethnography. Bowen's work (1964) provides a classic example; more current ones include Krieger (1985) and Thorne (1983). The separation of the researcher from the researched is blurred in this genre, and the tale is told through the chronology of fieldwork events, drawing attention not only to the culture under study but also to the experiences that were integral to the cultural description and interpretation.

Considerations of one's positionality, ethics, and political stance affect report writing. One may choose to present many truths, or multiple perspectives, or claim to identify a single truth. Choosing to say, "I interpreted this event" rather than "The data revealed" must be a clear decision. Postmodern and feminist discussions help researchers clarify such decisions. Writing *your* truth about others' lives is an assertion of power and can violate earlier assertions about working ethically and sensitively with participants (Lather, 1991; Tierney & Lincoln, 1997).

A useful listing of criteria for judging well-done and well-written dissertations is provided by Piantanida and Garman (1999) and includes the following:

- Integrity—"a well-reasoned connection between how the inquiry was conducted and the knowledge generated from it" (p. 147)
- Verité—"evidence that the researcher has . . . a mind-set conducive to an authentic enquiry" (p. 147)
- Rigor—"carefulness, precision and elegance of the researcher's thinking" (p. 149)
- Utility—"presented in ways that are useful to the intended audience" (p. 152)
- Vitality—creates "a vicarious sense of the phenomenon and context of the study" (p. 152)
- Aesthetics—makes connections to universals—to the spiritual
- Ethics—shows a strong, intimate bond of trust and ethical sensibility

Some dissertation writers will be excused if they have difficulty with aesthetics, admittedly, but the other criteria are essential elements in a worthy dissertation report.

Another useful guide comes from the guidelines for reporting interview quotes, by Kvale and Brinkmann (2009, pp. 279–281). In anticipating the "look of a final report, thinking ahead to ways data will be interspersed with explanation and context," their guidelines are useful:

- Quotes should be related to the general text.
- Quotes should be contextualized.
- Quotes should be interpreted.
- There should be a balance between quotes and text.
- The quotes should be short.
- Use only the best quotes.

- Interview notes should generally be rendered into a written style.
- There should be a simple signature system for the editing of quotes.

While this refers to interviews, the guidelines help the writer consider how to present any kind of data. There are many styles of presentation, so the researcher needs to develop his own, as appropriate to his genre, his audience, and his abilities.

On a very different note, the insights of Flyvbjerg (2001) urge research report writers to push toward pragmatic and action-oriented writing and to consider his values with reference to praxis. He draws from Aristotle's **phronesis**, which requires an "interaction between the general and the concrete; it requires consideration, judgment, and choice . . . experience" (p. 57) and is about intellectual virtue, above and beyond technical know-how. It requires deep pondering of questions such as "Where are we going?", "Is this desirable?", and "What should be done?" so that the researcher's reporting is much more than a straightforward objective social science report. Such pondering is especially poignant when, for example, conducting research on marginalized or colonized communities, where, too often, research is conducted that benefits the researcher but where there are few positive outcomes for the researched. Dunbar (2008) reported a quote from a research on Aboriginals: "Every time research is done a piece of my culture is erased" (p. 91).

Four genres of qualitative research and their attendant reporting are worthy of special mention—(1) case studies, (2) action research, (3) performance ethnography, and (4) autoethnography. All begin with the assumption that research must begin in natural settings and must incorporate sociopolitical contexts, they may use the full array of data collection strategies, and their typical reporting formats are quite different.

Case Study Reports

Reports of research on a specific organization, program, or process (or some set of these) are often called case studies (Yin, 2003). Case studies rely on historical and document analysis, interviewing, and, typically, some forms of observation for data collection. A rich tradition of community studies, organizational research, and program evaluations documents the illustrative power of research that focuses in depth and in detail on specific instances of a phenomenon. Case studies take the reader into the setting with a vividness and detail not typically present in more analytic reporting formats.

Action Research Reporting

Research with practitioners, and often by practitioners, who want to improve their own situation and that of others and discover and solve problems is called action research. Research questions are defined collaboratively with participants; the researcher's role is often that of a facilitator who expands the questions through consultation, problem posing, and knowledge of existing literature. Although action research follows the traditions of systematic inquiry, innovative and evolving data collection strategies may shift as the inquiry proceeds (Noffke & Somekh, 2009; Selener, 1997; Stringer, 1999). Reporting from action research may take several forms. A written report may be collaboratively produced, depending on the interests and needs of participants. Frequently, short oral reports or displays of lessons learned in photo montages, exhibitions, or documentary films are preferred.

Because action research is fundamentally determined by participants—for their own uses—rather than by the scholarly needs of the researcher, the reporting should be true to that guiding principle. Reporting, whatever form it takes, has a built-in relevance. Usefulness to participants may be more important than methodological rigor (Argyris & Schön, 1991). The researcher, as participant, may become a trusted insider with access seldom possible in more traditional observer roles (Cole, 1991). Often, action researchers take an activist, critical, and emancipatory stance, using the research process as an empowering process in an organization or a community (Cancian & Armstead, 1992; Fals-Borda & Rahman, 1991; Freire, 1970; Kemmis & McTaggart, 2005; Reason, 1994).

Researchers hope that their reports will contribute to societal improvement, either directly in action and participatory approaches or indirectly by enhancing policy or programmatic decisions. (See the discussion of a study's potential significance in Chapter 2.) Choosing participatory action research, however, can be an ideological stance—a determination to try to change the world in direct ways—as Vignette 27 illustrates.

VIGNETTE 27 Planning Reporting for Qualitative Participatory Evaluation

Research design and data collection strategies can be structured to facilitate the active participation of the individuals being researched. An example of this is the work of Paul Castelloe, a graduate student in social work who designed a participatory evaluation study of the Learning Together program in North Carolina (Castelloe & Legerton, 1998). The program was designed to serve two purposes: (1) to increase the school preparation of children, from ages 3 to 5, with no other preschool experience and (2) to strengthen their caregivers' capacity to provide education and development support.

Drawing on the work of Fraser (1997) as well as that of Mouffe and LeClau (1985), Castelloe designed his research project with a radical democratic philosophy to create an evaluation process committed to sharing power with the research participants. Although traditional research designs place the researcher(s) in the sole position of determining research design and creating research questions, participatory action research brings the individuals being studied into the research process. With his interest in grassroots change and democratic processes, Castelloe democratically structured his study to collect data in a way that would include the participants. This approach led to data collection techniques designed to include individuals at all levels (including those traditionally silenced in a study, the individuals whom a policy is supposed to help—caregivers and students).

Castelloe designed his study to teach the program staff and community members the skills required to conduct an evaluation. In this role, he decided to serve as facilitator and "colaborer" in the collaborative evaluation process. The direction, plan, questions, and goals of the evaluation were designed to be done collaboratively by Castelloe and the program staff, the program participants, and the community in which the program was located.

The primary data collection techniques selected were in-depth interviews, observational methods, and focus-group interviews. He created several strategies to include participants in the research decision-making process. For example, he developed interview questions in collaboration with program administrators, program staff, and community members and asked them to provide feedback on data transcripts.

His philosophy and rationale concerning the democratic process served to guide his overall approach to include participants in the research process and examine whether the Learning Together program was democratic, participatory, and inclusive. Collectively, Castelloe and the participants determined how and when reporting would take place. These deliberations strengthened the democratic principles of their work together.

Performance Ethnography Representation

Performance ethnography is the "staged re-enactment of ethnographically derived notes" (Alexander, 2005, p. 411) in which culture is represented in performed, embodied ways rather than exclusively textual ones. The notion of performance comes from the idea that cultural materials and understandings can be presented as drama, with the attendant scripts, props, sets, costumes, and movement (McCall, 2000). Thus, representation in performance ethnography is not only a text (the ethnography, the script) but also an embodied, transient depiction of cultural knowledge in a performative or dramatic form, such as a staged production, art, dance, storytelling, street theater, or film (Conrad, 2008). Recent writing about performance ethnography, however, asserts its critical, liberatory potential. As Alexander (2005) notes, some, but not all, of the work in this genre is politically and practically allied with the principles of critical pedagogy (p. 424).

The Autoethnography

Autoethnography takes up some of the challenges offered by performance ethnography to disturb and challenge traditional notions of representation in qualitative research. Holman Jones (2005), who expresses her work and politics primarily through poetry, writes that autoethnography "overlaps with, and is indebted to, research and writing practices in anthropology, sociology, psychology, literary criticism, journalism, and communication . . . to say nothing of our favorite storytellers, poets, and musicians" (p. 765). Representation in autoethnography may take a traditional form such as text, often closely resembling a research report in which the author and her voice are central to the narrative. Other forms may be poetry or a theatrical performance or musical production. Representation in autoethnography is presenting one's own story with the implied or explicit assertion that the personal narrative instructs, disrupts, incites to action, and calls into question politics, culture, and identity.

Vignette 28 is taken directly from an autoethnography written by Tassaporn (Pan) Sariyant (2002). Her literature review is extraordinarily creative and theoretically interesting. Although "performed" differently than most literature reviews, it holds true to the precepts of autoethnography and is engaging to read.

VIGNETTE 28 Pan in (Academic) Wonderland: Discourse Review

Knowing requires a knower. Enter any great library, and one is surrounded by so much waste paper until the texts collected there are decoded. The "knowledge" of the library collection is underwritten by bodies of knowers, those who can interpret, evaluate, or, in a word, read (MacIntyre, 1981, quoted in Steedman, 1991, p. 53).

I don't know how long I have been sitting here. I must have dozed off on that chair for a long time. My back aches. My eyes are burning. When I look around, I notice that the few people who sat reading not far from me are not there anymore. The early afternoon sunlight that was shining through the window near the table where I sat reading is already gone. The atmosphere of the room at this moment gives me a creepy, uneasy feeling. The room looks quite dim. Rows and rows of gigantic bookshelves look spooky, like the walls of a mysterious dungeon. It makes me think that some unexpected things might be lurking behind any of them. However, I don't want to leave this library room before I finish reading a couple of books that I had taken from the shelves when I came in. I quickly brush those silly images out of my head.

After standing and stretching my weary body for a moment, I walk toward the light switch that I remember seeing on a wall at the opposite corner. As I walk toward the wall, out of the corner of my eye I suddenly notice several silhouette figures sitting quietly around a table in that very corner. Who are these people? Why do they sit talking in the dark? Ghosts of the library? A sudden cold fear runs down my spine. Goose bumps cover my whole body. I cannot decide whether I should run out of that room or go to the light switch and turn it on as quickly as possible. Before I can do anything, I hear a gentle voice from the table calling, "Are you coming to join us?" I stand frozen. Another figure waves a hand, beckoning me to the table and saying, "Please turn the light on and come and join us here." Although I am horrified by the thought that those figures will vanish as soon as the light is on, I quickly flick the light on.

To my relief, they do not disappear. Under the soft fluorescent light from the ceiling above them, those silhouette figures turn out to be seven scholarly looking women and men—precisely five women and two men—who sit smiling at me. They are not ghosts as I initially thought. Although their faces look familiar, I cannot recall where I have seen them. . . . A Caucasian man, sitting on the right of a white-bearded old man, urges me, "Come and join the dialogue with us." Dialogue with these people? Oh, my word! They look so scholarly, so knowledgeable. What am I going to say or discuss with them? "Come, sit next to me. There is a chair here." A kind, motherly woman, who sits on the left of the white-bearded old man, points at an empty chair beside her. . . .

I quickly introduce myself as I sit down. "My name is Pan, a Thai doctoral student at the Center for International Education. I am at the stage of writing my dissertation. I work in the Department of Nonformal Education in Thailand. Generally, my work revolves around education for community development. I am interested in exploring the relationships among the discourses on development, nonformal education, and pedagogy for empowerment, especially for rural Thai women, and I want to . . . "

"Wait." Before I finish my sentence, the white-bearded old man interrupts. "You are not going to do your dissertation research on all those subjects, are you?" I shake my head and say no. The short-haired woman asks the question that I am afraid to face. "What is really your focus?" I drop my eyes to the table and admit with a great shame, "I am not quite sure yet." When I look up, I see sympathetic looks on every face. I hear a quickly whispered phrase, "rookie academician," which makes my ears turn red with embarrassment. Before I can think of how to defend myself, the woman with dark hair on my right suggests, "Why don't we begin by asking her why she wants to know about those subjects, what she wants to get from those discourses, and how those discourses have anything to do with her dissertation topic. Then, we can give her some suggestions later." She turns to me and says, "Could you elaborate on that for us?" My face suddenly turns pale with intimidation as every pair of questioning eyes fixes on me.

In a somewhat more traditional vein, the Vignettes 29 and 30 depict the challenges and considerations that the researchers brought to writing up their reports. Vignette 29 shows how analysis and writing are interwoven throughout a study,,and Vignette 30 comes from a study of incest in which the challenges of writing were substantial.

VIGNETTE 29 Interspersing Reporting and Analysis

Often, data analysis and writing up the research are thought of and portrayed as two discrete processes. Increasingly, however, researchers are using the writing up of research as an opportunity to display, in the body of the report, how data analysis evolved. Gerstl-Pepin (1998) accomplished this quite elegantly in her study of educational reform.

Gerstl-Pepin constructed a theoretical framework to critically examine whether an arts-based educational reform movement in North Carolina functioned as a counterpublic sphere (Fraser, 1997)

(Continued)

VIGNETTE 29 (Continued)

and led to democratically structured educational policy and reform. Although interested in examining theoretical issues concerning the prospects for democratically structured reform, she was also interested in telling the story of the reform movement.

To balance these two interests, Gerstl-Pepin decided to take an approach similar to that of Lather and Smithies (1997) and weave her shifts in thinking about research questions into the body of the text. Her interest in including the researcher's evolving thought processes arose out of an awareness of the shifting research paradigms that highlight the subjectivity of the researcher. While analyzing the data, Gerstl-Pepin encountered teachable moments in the research process in which her conceptualization and understanding of the research developed and shifted. She included these pieces within the narrative story about the reform movement as separate boxes of text and titled these pieces "Interludes: Reflections on the Research." They were included at various points in the narrative, depicting shifts in her thinking process and research focus. These pieces served as stories within the story and were intended to allow the reader to participate not only in the story of the reform process but also in the discovery process for the researcher.

Although we have discussed ethics frequently, we must revisit it now, while discussing the plan for the final report. Even while managing the entry and data collection with deep concern about ethics, new issues arise as one plans the report format. But plan you must: No researcher should get toward the end of her project and then be shocked with the realization that, in the act of publishing, she will do harm. Our last vignette for this last chapter, Vignette 30, presents the ethical dilemmas of reporting about taboo topics.

VIGNETTE 30 Talking Taboo: Continuing the Research Relationship

During analysis and reporting of the data, Kiegelmann (1997) was inventive with methods to protect her research participants. This is always important, but for her research on brother-sister incest she was particularly attuned to how the participants had trusted her with emotion-laden and highly sensitive aspects of their lives. One had even shared her childhood journal, in which she had written just minutes after the incest occurred. Kiegelmann and the participants had become a support group, continuing to meet after the research was completed.

As the data analysis proceeded, Kiegelmann identified themes and noted the range of nuances in the study participants' talk. Previous literatures guided her, especially writings about girls' views of femininity, of "good girls," and of girls' ways of knowing. Three voice clusters emerged: (1) silent voices, (2) embodied voices, and (3) naming voices. Anticipating the need to report, to have validity checks, and to regain permission for using their words, Kiegelmann created biographies of each woman participant and sent them to them, inviting their comments. She received feedback and commentary from them, which she incorporated into her writing. As the research neared completion, she sent a draft of the full study to all of them. Each participant used this opportunity to offer more details but not to change the interpretations. Furthermore, she invited the participants to write statements directly to the readers of the research, giving the women the final word. Thus, the trusting relationships were maintained beyond the time of the study, the study's truthfulness was increased, and she avoided taking away power and control over the representation of their lives from the participants.

Vignette 30 reveals a highly ethical sensitivity to the participants of the study. Kiegelmann (1997) honored their life stories and voices throughout the process. This involved several iterations: writing biographies, sending them to the participants for commentary, incorporating their feedback, sending the full draft for further commentary, and incorporating the women's final comments in the final document. Although this process was time-consuming, it expressed Kiegelmann's deep commitment to the women and to the ethical conduct of her study.

* * * * *

Philosophical inquiry and shifting paradigms highlight the subjectivity of the researcher and his relationship to the research process. Placing analytic memos, methodological notes, or interludes in the report makes these processes transparent. Traditions of science, in the past, dictated a rather lifeless final report. Qualitative inquiry, however, usually full of earthy evocative quotes and titles and subtitles derived from some combination of scholarly with colloquial quotes, allows researchers to be creative. Thus, a final report on the care of elderly veterans might be titled *Veteran Care: "Who Cares About Us?"* and thus provoke more curiosity than would a typical report.

Doctoral advisors do not relish constant advising on multiple drafts and constant **handholding** through the analysis and writing by their doctoral candidates. Among Wolcott's (2009) many hints, we like the one where he tells his students to write as if he were looking over their shoulder.

As researchers ponder over the "look" of their final report, they should consider what to include and what format to use, based on how the report will be used. Studies funded by a foundation, a government agency, or a business probably have prescribed formats. Final dissertations usually mimic formats derived from positivist traditions but altered so that the "Findings" chapters are lengthy, and there may be numerous chapters named to represent five or six themes. Studies written with an intention to find a publisher will use formats that publishers think will be appealing—whether for airport kiosk marketing or for scholarly libraries. Scholars with long track records may be more playful and creative. Robert Coles's (1977) series on children of crisis include children's crayon drawings, along with rich description. He managed to convince the publishers that these data were crucial to the report and also that the 500-page books were worth the cost. He even said, in writing about his method of writing, "I tried to embrace, within my limits, the tradition of the social essay. . . . I suppose this book is a mixture of clinical observation, narrative description, oral history, psychological analysis, social comment" (Coles, 1977, p. 59). With his scholarly track record, he could get away with this, but few dissertation students can do the same. Regarding the format for reporting, our bottom line advice is that it depends on what works best for your desired audience and for the original purpose and passion that drove your research intentions from the beginning!

It may seem presumptuous, at the proposal stage, to be planning for the "look" of the final report. However, all aspects of the proposal have implications for the final report. Decisions about the genre, the do-ability, the role, the ethics, the setting, the data collection, the management, and the analysis strategies, all affect the final report. To plan for that writing, think ahead—using how you will begin for making the big leap from doing research to the actual writing. Wolcott's (2009) simple advice is still useful: Begin with description, or begin with method, but *do* begin!

A FINAL WORD

The process of developing a qualitative research proposal—the revisions necessitated by the interrelatedness of the sections—will create a final product that convinces readers and develops a rationale for the researcher's own guidance. It will justify the selection of qualitative methods and demonstrate the researcher's ability to conduct the study. The writing and creating processes will help the researcher develop a logic and a plan that will guide and direct the research. The time, thought, and energy expended in writing a proposal will reap rewards. A proposal that is theoretically sound, methodologically ethical, efficient, and thorough will be impressive. A proposal that demonstrates the researcher's capacity to articulate the arguments for "goodness" to conduct the fieldwork and to find sound, credible, and convincing ways to analyze and present the research will truly prepare you for your research endeavor.

Prepare a great proposal, and get ready to plunge into your research. You will be ready for your journey into the delightful and challenging "disciplined messiness" (Lather, 2009) of qualitative inquiry.

Dialogue Between Learners

Melanie,

I thought I'd raise another issue that relates to the focus question that I responded to this morning. When people ask me what I do, I often respond that I'm a professional student. As much as I enjoy the freedoms of being a full-time student, one cannot stay this way forever. I want my dissertation to be a strong one (after all,

I'm only planning on writing one). I like the idea of creating a dissertation work group with friends who are working on their dissertations at the same time. This seems like a good way to create a support group and help each other along through this process. However, I'm also finding that the more I move into the process of the dissertation, the more isolated I am from my peers. If it weren't for my assistantships, I might not be on campus at all. I could easily be in the field for a prolonged period of time and lose contact with the people I used to take classes with. What do you think? Anything to be concerned about?

Hope all is well,

Aaron

Hi Aaron,

I think isolation is a huge issue for graduate students (possibly professors, as well). In fact, this is one issue I've been conscious of since day one of graduate school. How can I specialize in my own interests while staying generalizable enough to my peers?

I'm with you on dissertation support groups. I have tried to establish writing groups or reading groups or just plain support groups through my years here, but I've had very little success. Everyone is so busy, with so many other claims on their time; without a true commitment to group meetings, it just falls by the wayside. I wonder if a dissertation group would meet with the same fate. It does carry more weight than a reading group, after all, and there's a definite product to introduce into the meetings. I feel like I need that human connection during this process. In some ways, research is very dehumanizing to the researcher. You can spend days on end with audio files, articles, scraps of field notes, computer printouts but yet have no actual human contact. Surrounded by people on paper but none in physical actuality! As much as I would like someone to read through my drafts and question my methods, I also want someone to talk to about the daily issues, issues such as writer's block, writing for a committee, work locations, and/or forgetting to eat dinner. I really value the human connection, which is why my research interests so often hinge on relationships, and I would like that connection as a support throughout the research process.

So there's my two cents. Talk to you soon,

Melanie

FURTHER READING

On the Proposal Hearing

Bloomberg, L. D., & Volpe, M. (2008). *Completing your qualitative dissertation: A roadmap from beginning to end.* Thousand Oaks, CA: Sage.

Meloy, J. M. (1994). *Writing the qualitative dissertation: Understanding by doing.* Hillsdale, NJ: Lawrence Erlbaum.

Piantanida, M., & Garman, N. B. (1999). *The qualitative dissertation: A guide for students and faculty.* Thousand Oaks, CA: Corwin Press.

On Forms of Writing, Presentation, and Representation

Conrad, D. H. (2008). Performance ethnography. In L. M. Given (Ed.), *The SAGE encyclopedia of qualitative research methods* (pp. 607–611). Thousand Oaks, CA: Sage.

DeCuir, J. T., & Dixson, A. D. (2004). "So when it comes out, they aren't that surprised that it is there": Using critical race theory as a tool of analysis of race and racism in education. *Educational Researcher, 33,* 26–31.

Denzin, N. K., Lincoln, Y. S., & Smith, L. T. (Eds.). (2008). *Handbook of critical and indigenous methodologies.* Thousand Oaks, CA: Sage.

Dunbar, C., Jr., Rodriguez, D., & Parker, L. (2003). Race, subjectivity, and the interview process. In J. A. Holstein & J. F. Gubrium (Eds.), *Inside interviewing: New lenses, new concerns* (pp. 131–150), Thousand Oaks, CA: Sage.

Ellis, C., & Bochner, A. P. (Eds.). (1996). *Composing ethnography: Alternative forms of qualitative writing.* Walnut Creek, CA: AltaMira.

Flyvbjerg, B. (2001). *Making social science matter: Why social inquiry fails and how it can succeed again.* Cambridge, UK: Cambridge University Press.

Flyvbjerg, B. (2004). Five misunderstandings about case study research. In C. Seale, G. Gabo, J. F. Gubrium, & D. Silverman (Eds.), *Qualitative research practice* (pp. 420–434). Thousand Oaks, CA: Sage.

Furman, R., Langer, C. L., Davis, C. S., Gallardo, H. P., & Kulkarni, S. (2007). Expressive, research and reflective poetry as qualitative inquiry: A study of adolescent identity. *Qualitative Research, 7*(3), 301–315.

Gitlin, A. (Ed.). (1994). *Power and method: Political activism and educational research.* New York: Routledge.

Glesne, C. (2006). *Becoming qualitative researchers: An introduction.* Boston: Allyn & Bacon.

Kvale, S., & Brinkmann, S. (Eds.). (2009). *Interviews: Learning the craft of qualitative research interviewing* (2nd ed.). Thousand Oaks, CA: Sage.

Narayan, K., & George, K. M. (2003). Personal and folk narratives as cultural representation. In J. F. Gubrium & J. A. Holstein (Eds.), *Postmodern interviewing* (pp. 123–139). Thousand Oaks, CA: Sage.

Noffke, S. E., & Somekh, B. (Eds.). (2009). *The SAGE handbook of educational action research.* London: Sage.

Richardson, L. (1990). *Writing strategies: Reaching diverse audiences.* Newbury Park, CA: Sage.

Richardson, L. (1994). Writing: A method of inquiry. In N. K. Denzin & Y. S. Lincoln (Eds.), *Handbook of qualitative research* (pp. 516–529). Thousand Oaks, CA: Sage.

Richardson, L., & St. Pierre, E. A. (2005). Writing: A method of inquiry. In N. K. Denzin & Y. S. Lincoln (Eds.), *The SAGE handbook of qualitative research* (3rd ed., pp. 959–978). Thousand Oaks, CA: Sage.

Silverman, D. (2007). *A very short, fairly interesting and reasonably cheap book about qualitative research.* Thousand Oaks, CA: Sage.

Stake, R. (1995). *The art of case study research.* Thousand Oaks, CA: Sage.

Tierney, W. G., & Lincoln, Y. S. (Eds.). (1997). *Representation and the text: Re-framing the narrative voice.* Albany: State University of New York Press.

Van Maanen, J. (1988). *Tales of the field: On writing ethnography.* Chicago: University of Chicago Press.

Van Maanen, J. (Ed.). (1995). *Representation in ethnography.* Thousand Oaks, CA: Sage.

Wolcott, H. F. (2009). *Writing up qualitative research* (3rd ed.). Thousand Oaks, CA: Sage.

Zinsser, W. (1990). *On writing well: An informal guide to writing nonfiction* (4th ed.). New York: Harper.

KEY CONCEPTS

Confirmability

Credibility

Criteriology

Critical friend

Dependability

Emic perspectives

Forms of writing, presentation, and representation

Handholding

Liberatory potential

Multiple understandings

Phronesis

Politics of knowledge

Proposal defense

Replicability

Respectability

Running record

"Scientifically based research"

Second decision span in generalizing

Transferability

Triangulation

"Truth value"

REFERENCES

Ajodhia-Andrews, A., & Berman, R. (2009). Exploring school life from the lens of a child who does not use speech to communicate. *Qualitative Inquiry, 15*(5), 931–951.

Alexander, B. K. (2005). Performance ethnography: The reenacting and inciting of culture. In N. K. Denzin & Y. S. Lincoln (Eds.), *The SAGE handbook of qualitative research* (3rd ed., pp. 411–441). Thousand Oaks, CA: Sage.

Alibali, M. W., & Nathan, M. J. (2007). Teachers' gestures as a means of scaffolding students' understanding: Evidence from an early algebra lesson. In R. Goldman, R. Pea, B. Barron, & S. J. Derry (Eds.), *Video research in the learning sciences* (pp. 349–365). Mahwah, NJ: Erlbaum.

Altman, D. (2001). Rupture or continuity? The internationalization of gay identities. In J. Hawley (Ed.), *Postcolonial, queer: Theoretical intersections* (pp. 19–41). Albany: State University of New York Press.

Alvarez, R. (1993). *Computer mediated communications: A study of the experience of women managers using electronic mail.* Unpublished manuscript, University of Massachusetts Amherst.

Alvesson, M. (2003). Methodology for close up studies: Struggling with closeness and closure. *Higher Education, 46,* 167–193.

American Evaluation Association. (n.d.). *Qualitative data analysis software.* Retrieved March 1, 2009, from www.eval.org/Resources/QDA.htm

Anderson, E. (1976). *A place on the corner.* Chicago: University of Chicago Press.

Anderson, G. (1989). Critical ethnography in education: Origins, current status, and new directions. *Review of Educational Research, 59,* 249–270.

Anderson, G. L., & Herr, K. (1993). The micro-politics of student voices: Moving from diversity of voices in schools. In C. Marshall (Ed.), *The new politics of race and gender* (pp. 58–68). Washington, DC: Falmer Press.

Anfara, V. A., Jr., Brown, K. M., & Mangione, T. L. (2002). Qualitative analysis on stage: Making the research process more public. *Educational Researcher, 31,* 28–38.

Argyris, C., & Schön, D. A. (1974). *Theory in practice.* San Francisco: Jossey-Bass.

Argyris, C., & Schön, D. A. (1991). Participatory action research and action science compared: A commentary. In W. F. Whyte (Ed.), *Participatory action research* (pp. 85–96). Newbury Park, CA: Sage.

Ashcroft, B., Griffiths, G., & Tiffin, H. (2000). *Post-colonial studies: The key concepts.* London: Routledge.

Ashworth, P. (2003). The origins of qualitative psychology. In J. A. Smith (Ed.), *Qualitative psychology: A practical guide to research methods* (pp. 4–24). London: Sage.

Atkinson, P., Delamont, S., & Hammersley, M. (1988). Qualitative research traditions: A British response to Jacob. *Review of Educational Research, 58,* 231–250.

Atkinson, R. (1998). *The life story interview.* Thousand Oaks, CA: Sage.

Atlas.ti 6.0 for Windows. [Computer software]. Atlas.ti Scientific Software Development. Trial copy available at www.atlasti.com. Accessed March 2, 2009.

Bahna, D. (2005). What matters to girls and boys in a black primary school in South Africa. *Early Child Development and Care, 175*(2), 99–111.

Banks, M. (2001). *Visual methods in social research.* London: Sage.

Bargar, R. R., & Duncan, J. K. (1982). Cultivating creative endeavor in doctoral research. *Journal of Higher Education, 53,* 1–31.

Barone, T., & Eisner, E. (2006). Arts-based educational research. In J. L. Green, G. Camilli, & P. B. Elmore (Eds.), *Handbook of complementary methods in education* (3rd ed., pp. 95–108). London: Routledge.

Barthes, R. (1972). *Mythologies.* London: Cape.

Basit, T. (2003). Manual or electronic? The role of coding in qualitative data analysis. *Educational Research, 45*(2), 143–154.

Baucom, D. H., & Kerig, P. K. (2004). Coding couples' interactions: Introduction and overview. In P. K. Kerig & D. H. Baucom (Eds.), *Couple observational coding systems* (pp. 3–10). Mahwah, NJ: Lawrence Erlbaum.

Baym, N. (2000). *Tune in, log on.* Thousand Oaks, CA: Sage.

Becker, H. S., Geer, B., Hughes, E. C., & Strauss, A. L. (1961). *Boys in white: Student culture in medical culture.* Chicago: University of Chicago Press.

Bell, D. A., Jr. Guide to the Derrick A. Bell, Jr. Papers. Retrieved January 26, 2010 at http://dlib.nyu.edu/findingaids/html/archives/bell.html

Benbow, J. T. (1994). *Coming to know: A phenomenological study of individuals actively committed to radical social change.* Unpublished doctoral dissertation, University of Massachusetts Amherst.

Bennis, W. G., & Nanus, B. (2003). *Leaders: Strategies for taking charge.* New York: Harper & Row.

Berelson, B. (1952). *Content analysis in communication research.* Glencoe, IL: Free Press.

Berger, M. T. (2003). Dealing with difficult gatekeepers, vulnerable populations, and hooks that go awry. In M. S. Feldman, J. Bell, & M. T. Berger (Eds.), *Gaining access* (pp. 65–68). Walnut Creek, CA: AltaMira Press.

Bernal, D. D. (2002). Critical race theory, Latino critical theory, and critical raced-gendered epistemologies: Recognizing students of color as holders and creators of knowledge. *Qualitative Inquiry, 8*(1), 105–126.

Bhattacharya, K. (2007). Consenting to the consent form: What are the fixed and fluid understandings between the researcher and the researched? *Qualitative Inquiry, 13*(8), 1095–1115.

Bhana, D. (2005). Violence and gendered negotiation of masculinity among young black school boys in South Africa. In L. Ouzgane & R. Morrell (Eds.), *African masculinities: Men in Africa from the late 19th century to the present* (pp. 205–220). New York: Palgrave Macmillan.

Birdwhistell, R. L. (1970). *Kinesics and content: Essays on body motion communication.* Philadelphia: University of Pennsylvania Press.

Bishop, R. (2005). Freeing ourselves from neocolonial domination in research: A Kaupapa Maori approach to creating knowledge. In N. K. Denzin & Y. S. Lincoln (Eds.), *The SAGE handbook of qualitative research* (3rd ed., pp. 109–138). Thousand Oaks, CA: Sage.

Bloomberg, L., & Volpe, M. (2008). *Completing your qualitative dissertation.* Thousand Oaks, CA: Sage.

Boal, A. (1997). *Theater of the oppressed.* London: Pluto Press.

Boal, A. (2002). *Games for actors and non-actors* (2nd ed.). London: Routledge.

Bogdan, R. C., & Biklen, S. K. (2007). *Qualitative research in education: An introduction to theory and methods* (5th ed.). Boston: Allyn & Bacon.

Bowen, E. S. (1964). *Return to laughter.* Garden City, NY: Doubleday.

Brainard, J. (2001). The wrong rules for social science? *Chronicle of Higher Education, 47*(26), A21–A23.

Brantlinger, E. A. (1997, April). *Knowledge, position, and agency: Activism and inward gaze as a natural next step in local inquiry.* Paper presented at the annual meeting of the American Educational Research Association, San Diego, CA.

Brice Heath, S., & McLaughlin, M. (1993). *Identity and inner-city youth: Beyond ethnicity and gender.* New York: Teachers College Press.

Briggs, J. (2000). *Fire in the crucible: Understanding the process of creative genius.* Grand Rapids, MI: Phanes.

Bronfenbrenner, U. (1980). Ecology of childhood. *School Psychology Review, 9,* 294–297.

Brown, L., & Durrheim, K. (2009). Different kinds of knowing: Generating qualitative data through mobile interviewing. *Qualitative Inquiry, 15*(5), 911–930.

Browne, A. (1987). *When battered women kill.* New York: Free Press.

Burrell, G., & Morgan, G. (1979). *Sociological paradigms and organizational analysis.* London: Heinemann.

Busch, C., De Maret, P. S., Flynn, T., Kellum, R., Le, S., Meyers, B., et al. (2005). *An introduction to content analysis.* Retrieved March 2, 2009, from the Colorado State University Writing Center Web site at http://writing.colostate.edu/guides/ research/content/pop2a.cfm

Butler, J. (1999). *Gender trouble: Feminism and the subversion of identity.* New York: Routledge.

Campbell-Nelson, K. (1997). *Learning the land: A local hermeneutic for indigenous education in West Timor, Indonesia.* Unpublished research proposal to the U.S. Information Agency, Fullbright-Hays Doctoral Support Program, University of Massachusetts Amherst.

Cancian, F. M., & Armstead, C. (1992). Participatory research. In E. F. Borgatta & M. Borgatta (Eds.), *Encyclopedia of sociology* (Vol. 3, pp. 1427–1432). New York: Macmillan.

Cannella, G. S., & Manuelito, K. D. (2008). Feminisms from unthought locations: Indigenous worldviews, marginalized feminisms, and revisioning an anticolonial social science. In N. K. Denzin, Y. S. Lincoln, & L. T Smith (Eds.), *The handbook of critical and indigenous methodologies* (pp. 45–59). Thousand Oaks, CA: Sage.

Capra, F. (1975). *The Tao of physics.* Berkeley, CA: Shambhala.

Capra, F. (1982). *The turning point: Science, society and the rising culture.* New York: Simon & Schuster.

Capra, F. (1996). *The web of life.* New York: Doubleday.

Carspecken, P. F. (1996). *Critical ethnography in educational research: A theoretical and practical guide.* New York: Routledge & Kegan Paul.

Castelloe, P., & Legerton, M. (1998). *Learning together: Children and caregivers getting ready for school* (A two-year report and evaluation for the Learning Together Project). Lumberton, NC: Center for Community Action.

Center for Digital Storytelling [Web site]. Accessed October 30, 2009, from www.storycenter .org/index1.html

Charmaz, K. (2000). Grounded theory: Objectivist and constructivist methods. In N. K. Denzin & Y. S. Lincoln (Eds.), *Handbook of qualitative research* (2nd ed., pp. 509–535). Thousand Oaks, CA: Sage.

Charmaz, K. (2005). Grounded theory in the 21st century: Applications for advancing social justice studies. In N. K. Denzin & Y. S. Lincoln (Eds.), *The SAGE handbook of qualitative research* (3rd ed., pp. 507–535). Thousand Oaks, CA: Sage.

Chase, S. E. (1995). *Ambiguous empowerment: The work narratives of women school superintendents.* Amherst: University of Massachusetts.

Chase, S. E. (2005). Narrative inquiry: Multiple lenses, approaches, voices. In N. K. Denzin & Y. S. Lincoln (Eds.), *The SAGE handbook of qualitative research* (3rd ed., pp. 651–679). Thousand Oaks, CA: Sage.

Chaudhry, L. N. (1997). Researching "my people," researching myself: Fragments of a reflexive tale. *Qualitative Studies in Education, 10*(4), 441–453.

Cho, J., & Trent, A. (2006). Validity in qualitative research revisited. *Qualitative Research, 6*(3), 319–340.

Christians, C. G. (2000). Ethics and politics in qualitative research. In N. K. Denzin & Y. S. Lincoln (Eds.), *Handbook of qualitative research* (2nd ed., pp. 133–155). Thousand Oaks, CA: Sage.

Christians, C. G. (2005). Ethics and politics in qualitative research. In N. K. Denzin & Y. S. Lincoln (Eds.), *The SAGE handbook of qualitative research* (3rd ed., pp. 139–164). Thousand Oaks, CA: Sage.

Clarricoates, K. (1987). Child culture at school: A clash between gendered worlds? In A. Pollard (Ed.), *Children and their primary schools* (pp. 26–41). London: Falmer.

Cohen-Mitchell, J. B. (2005). *Literacy and numeracy practices of market women in Quetzaltenango, Guatemala.* Unpublished doctoral dissertation, University of Massachusetts at Amherst.

Cole, A. L., & Knowles, J. G. (2001). *Lives in context: The art of life history research.* Walnut Creek, CA: AltaMira Press.

Cole, R. E. (1991). Participant observer research. In W. F. Whyte (Ed.), *Participatory action research* (pp. 159–166). Newbury Park, CA: Sage.

Coles, R. (1977). *Eskimos, Chicanos, Indians: Children of crisis* (Vol. 4). Boston: Little, Brown.

Collins, P. H. (1990). *Black feminist thought: Knowledge, consciousness, and the politics of empowerment.* New York: Routledge & Kegan Paul.

Conrad, D. H. (2008). Performance ethnography. In L. M. Given (Ed.), *The SAGE encyclopedia of qualitative research methods* (pp. 607–611). Thousand Oaks, CA: Sage.

Connelly, F. M., & Clandinin, D. J. (1990). Stories of experience and narrative inquiry. *Educational Researcher, 19,* 2–14.

Connor, S. (1989). *Postmodernist culture: An introduction to theories of the contemporary.* Oxford, UK: Blackwell.

Cooper, H. M. (1988). Organizing knowledge syntheses: A taxonomy of literature reviews. *Knowledge in Society, 1,* 104–126.

Copp, M. A. (2008). Emotions in qualitative research. In L. M. Given (Ed.), *The SAGE encyclopedia of qualitative research methods* (pp. 249–252). Los Angeles: Sage.

Corbin, J., & Strauss, A. (2007). *Basics of qualitative research: Techniques and procedures for developing grounded theory* (3rd ed.). Thousand Oaks, CA: Sage.

Corson, D. (1995). Ideology and distortion in the administration of outgroup interests. In D. Corson (Ed.), *Discourse and power in educational organizations* (pp. 87–110). Cresskill, NJ: Hampton Press.

Crabtree, B. F., & Miller, W. L. (Eds.). (1992). *Doing qualitative research: Multiple strategies.* Newbury Park, CA: Sage.

Creswell, J. W. (1998). *Qualitative inquiry and research design: Choosing among five traditions.* Thousand Oaks, CA: Sage.

Creswell, J. W. (2002). Educational research: Planning, conducting, and evaluating quantitative and qualitative research. Upper Saddle River, NJ: Merrill-Prentice Hall.

Creswell, J. W., & Miller, D. L. (2000). Determining validity in qualitative inquiry. *Theory into Practice, 39*(3), 124–130.

Davies, D., & Dodd, J. (2002). Qualitative research and the question of rigor. *Qualitative Health Research, 12*(2), 279–289.

Davis, A., Gardner, B. B., & Gardner, M. R. (1941). *Deep South: A social anthropological study of caste and class.* Chicago: University of Chicago Press.

Delamont, S. (1992). *Fieldwork in educational settings: Methods, pitfalls and perspectives.* London: Falmer Press.

Delaney, K. J. (2007). Methodological dilemmas and opportunities in interviewing organizational elites. *Sociology Compass, 1*(1), 208–221.

Denzin, N. K. (1970). *The research act: A theoretical introduction to sociological methods.* New York: McGraw-Hill.

Denzin, N. K. (1989). *The research act: A theoretical introduction to sociological methods* (3rd ed.). Englewood Cliffs, NJ: Prentice Hall.

Denzin, N. K. (1997). *Interpretive ethnography: Ethnographic practices for the 21st century.* Thousand Oaks, CA: Sage.

Denzin, N. K. (2005). Indians in the park. *Qualitative Inquiry, 5*(1), 9–33.

Denzin, N. K., & Lincoln, Y. S. (Eds.). (1994). *Handbook of qualitative research.* Thousand Oaks, CA: Sage.

Denzin, N. K., & Lincoln, Y. S. (Eds.). (2000). *Handbook of qualitative research* (2nd ed.). Thousand Oaks, CA: Sage.

Denzin, N. K., & Lincoln, Y. S. (Eds.). (2005). *The SAGE handbook of qualitative research* (3rd ed.). Thousand Oaks, CA: Sage.

Denzin, N. K., Lincoln, Y. S., & Smith, L. T. (Eds.). (2008). *Handbook of critical and indigenous methodologies.* Thousand Oaks, CA: Sage.

DeWalt, K. M., & DeWalt, B. R. (2001). *Participant observation: A guide for fieldworkers.* Walnut Creek, CA: AltaMira Press.

Dey, I. (1999). *Grounding grounded theory: Guidelines for qualitative inquiry.* San Diego, CA: Academic Press.

Dixson, A. D. (2005). Extending the metaphor: Notions of jazz in portraiture. *Qualitative Inquiry, 11*(1), 106–137.

Dixson, A. D., Chapman, T. K., & Hill, D. A. (2005). Research as an aesthetic process: Extending the portraiture methodology. *Qualitative Inquiry, 11*(1), 16–26.

Dixson, A. D., & Rousseau, C. K. (2005). And we are still not saved: Critical race theory in education ten years later. *Race, Ethnicity, and Education, 8*(1), 7–27.

Dixson, A. D., & Rousseau, C. K. (Eds.). (2007). *Critical race theory in education: All God's children got a song.* New York: Routledge.

Dobbert, M. L. (1982). *Ethnographic research: Theory and application for modern schools and societies.* New York: Praeger.

Dollard, J. (1935). *Criteria for the life history.* New Haven, CT: Yale University Press.

Donmoyer, R. (2001). Paradigm talk reconsidered. In V. Richardson (Ed.), *Handbook of research on teaching* (4th ed., pp. 174–197). Washington, DC: American Educational Research Association.

Doppler, J. (1998). *The costs and benefits of gay-straight alliances in high schools.* Unpublished doctoral dissertation proposal, University of Massachusetts Amherst.

Douglas, J. D. (1976). *Investigative social research: Individual and team field research.* Beverly Hills, CA: Sage.

Dragon Naturally Speaking 10 for Windows [Computer software]. Burlington, MA: Nuance Communications, Inc.

Dunbar, C. (2008). Critical race theory and indigenous methodologies. In N. K. Denzin, Y. S. Lincoln, & L. T. Smith (Eds.), *Handbook of critical and indigenous methodologies* (pp. 85–100). Los Angeles: Sage.

Eder, D., & Fingerson, L. (2003). Interviewing children and adolescents. In J. A. Holstein & J. F. Gubrium (Eds.), *Inside interviewing: New lenses, new concerns* (pp. 33–53). Thousand Oaks, CA: Sage.

Educause. (n.d.). *Educause learning initiative: 156 resources.* Retrieved April 8, 2009, from www.educause.edu/Resources/ Browse/EDUCAUSE LearningInitiative/33152

Eisner, E. W. (1988). The primacy of experience and the politics of method. *Educational Researcher, 20,* 15–20.

Ekman, P., & Friesen, W. V. (1975). *Unmasking the face: A guide to recognizing emotions from facial clues.* Upper Saddle River, NJ: Prentice Hall.

Ekman, P., Campos, J., Davidson, R. J., & De Waais, F. (2003). *Emotions inside out.* New York: Annals of the New York Academy of Sciences.

Ellingson, L. L. (2009). *Engaging crystallization in qualitative research.* Thousand Oaks, CA: Sage.

Elliott, J. (2005). *Using narrative in social research: Qualitative and quantitative approaches.* Thousand Oaks, CA: Sage.

Ellis, C., & Bochner, A. P. (2000). Autoethnography, personal narrative, reflexivity. In N. K. Denzin & Y. S. Lincoln (Eds.), *Handbook of qualitative research* (2nd ed., pp. 733–768). Thousand Oaks, CA: Sage.

Emerson, R. M., Fretz, R. I., & Shaw, L. L. (1995). *Writing ethnographic fieldnotes.* Chicago: University of Chicago Press.

e-Speaking [Computer software]. Pittsburgh, PA: e-Speaking.com.

Esposito, N. (2001). From meaning to meaning: The influence of translation techniques on non-English focus group research. *Qualitative Health Research, 11*(4), 568–579.

The Ethnograph 6.0 for Windows [Computer software]. Colorado Springs, CO: Qualis Research.

Everhart, R. B. (2005). Toward a critical social narrative of education. In W. T. Pink & G. W. Noblit (Series Eds.) & G. W. Noblit, S. Y. Flores & E. G. Murillo, Jr. (Book Eds.), *Understanding education and policy: Postcritical ethnography.* Cresskill, NJ: Hampton Press.

Express ScribeTranscription Playback Software for Windows [Computer software]. Greenwood Village, CO: NCH Software, Inc.

Fals-Borda, O., & Rahman, M. A. (1991). *Action and knowledge: Breaking the monopoly with participatory action-research.* New York: Apex Press.

Fan Yihong. (2000). *Educating to liberate: Cross-boundary journeys of educators toward integration and innovation.* Unpublished doctoral dissertation proposal, University of Massachusetts Amherst.

Fielding, N. G., & Lee, R. M. (1998). *Computer analysis and qualitative research.* London: Sage.

Fine, G. A., & Sandstrom, K. L. (1988). *Knowing children: Participant observation with minors.* Newbury Park, CA: Sage.

Flanders, N. A. (1970). *Analyzing teaching behavior.* Reading, MA: Addison-Wesley.

Flick. U. (2006). *An introduction to qualitative research* (3rd ed.). London: Sage.

Flick, U. (2009). *An introduction to qualitative research* (4th ed.). Thousand Oaks, CA: Sage.

Flinders, D. J. (2003). Qualitative research in the foreseeable future: No study left behind? *Journal of Curriculum and Supervision, 18*(4), 380–390.

Flyvbjerg, B. (2001). *Making social science matter: Why social inquiry fails and how it can succeed again.* Cambridge, UK: Cambridge University Press.

Foster, M. (1994). The power to know one thing is never the power to know all things: Methodological notes on two studies of Black American teachers. In A. Gitlin (Ed.), *Power and method: Political activism and educational research* (pp. 129–146). London: Routledge.

Fraser, N. (1997). *Justice interruptus: Critical reflections on the "postsocialist" condition.* New York: Routledge & Kegan Paul.

Freire, P. (1970). *Pedagogy of the oppressed.* New York: Continuum.

Friend, R. A. (1993). Choices, not closets: Heterosexism and homophobia in schools. In L. Weis & M. Fine (Eds.), *Beyond silenced voices: Class race and gender in the United States* (pp. 209–235). Albany: State University of New York Press.

Gall, M. D., Borg, W. R., & Gall, J. P. (1996). *Educational research: An introduction* (6th ed.). White Plains, NY: Longman.

Gannon, S. (2006). The (im)possibilities of writing the self-writing: French poststructural theory and autoethnography. *Cultural studies: Critical methodologies, 6*(4), 474–495.

Garcia, A. C., Standlee, A. I., Bechkoff, J., & Cui, Y. (2009). Ethnographic approaches to the Internet and computer-mediated communication. *Journal of Contemporary Ethnography, 38*(1), 52–84.

Gatson, S. N., & Zwerink, A. (2004). Ethnography online: "Natives" practising and inscribing community. *Qualitative Research, 4*(2), 179–200.

Geer, B. (1969). First days in the field. In G. McCall & J. L. Simmons (Eds.), *Issues in participant observation* (pp. 144–162). Reading, MA: Addison-Wesley.

Geertz, C. (1973). Thick description: Toward an interpretive theory of culture. In C. Geertz (Ed.), *The interpretation of culture: Selected essays* (pp. 3–30). New York: Basic Books.

Gelman, S. A., Taylor, M. G., & Nguyen, S. (2004). Mother-child conversations about gender: Understanding the acquisition of essentialist beliefs. *Monographs of the Society for Research in Child Development, 69*(1).

Gerstl-Pepin, C. I. (1998). *Cultivating democratic educational reform: A critical examination of the A+ schools program.* Unpublished doctoral dissertation, University of North Carolina at Chapel Hill.

Gilligan, C. (1982). *In a different voice: Psychological theory and women's development.* Cambridge, MA: Harvard University Press.

Gladwell, M. (2005). *Blink: The power of thinking without thinking.* New York: Little, Brown.

Gladwell.com. (n.d.). *What is Blink about?* Retrieved November 1, 2009, from www.gladwell.com/blink/index.html

Glaser, B., & Strauss, A. (1967). *The discovery of grounded theory.* Chicago: Aldine.

Glazier, J. A. (2004). Collaborating with the "other": Arab and Jewish teachers teaching in each other's company. *Teachers College Record, 106*(3), 611–633.

Glesne, C. (2005). *Becoming qualitative researchers: An introduction* (3rd ed.). New York: Longman.

Glesne, C. (2006). Becoming qualitative researchers: An introduction. Boston: Allyn & Bacon.

Goode, W. J. (1960). A theory of role strain. *American Sociological Review, 25*(4), 483–496.

Gough, S., & Scott, W. (2000). Exploring the purposes of qualitative data coding in educational enquiry: Insights from recent research. *Educational Studies, 26*, 339–354.

Gray, A. (2003). *Research practices for cultural studies: Ethnographic methods and lived cultures.* London: Sage Publications.

Greenwald, J. (1992). *Environmental attitudes: A structural development model.* Unpublished doctoral dissertation, University of Massachusetts Amherst.

Griffin, C. (1985). *Typical girls?* London: Routledge & Kegan Paul.

Grumet, M. R. (1988). *Bitter milk: Women and teaching.* Amherst: University of Massachusetts Press.

Guba, E. G. (1978). *Toward a methodology of naturalistic inquiry in educational evaluation* (Monograph 8). Los Angeles: UCLA Center for the Study of Evaluation.

Gubrium, J. F., & Holstein, J. A. (2003). *Postmodern interviewing.* Thousand Oaks, CA: Sage.

Guillemin, M., & Gillam, L. (2004). Ethics, reflexivity, and "ethically important moments" in research. *Qualitative Inquiry, 10*(2), 261–280.

Gunzenhauser, M. G. (2006). A moral epistemology of knowing subjects: Theorizing a relational turn for qualitative research. *Qualitative Inquiry, 12*(3), 621–647.

Gunzenhauser, M. G., & Gerstl-Pepin, C. I. (2006). Engaging graduate education: A pedagogy for epistemological and theoretical diversity. *The Review of Higher Education, 29*(3), 319–346.

Hall, E. T. (1966). *The hidden dimension.* Garden City, NY: Doubleday.

Hammersley, M. (1990). *Reading ethnographic research: A critical guide.* London: Longman.

Haraway, D. (1988). Situated knowledges: The science question in feminism and the privilege of partial perspective. *Feminist Studies, 14*, 575–599.

Harding, S. (Ed.). (1987). *Feminism and methodology.* Bloomington: Indiana University Press.

Harry, B., Sturges, K. M., & Klingner, J. K. (2005). Mapping the process: An exemplar of process and challenge in grounded theory analysis. *Educational Researcher, 34*(2), 3–13.

Herr, R. S. (2004). A third world feminist defense of multiculturalism. *Social Theory & Practice, 30*(1), 73–103.

Hine, C. (2000). *Virtual ethnography.* Thousand Oaks, CA: Sage.

Hodgson, K. (2005). *Digital storytelling: Using technology to tell stories.* Retrieved April 8, 2009, from www.umass.edu/wmwp/DigitalStorytelling/Digital%20 Storytelling%20Main%20Page.htm

Hoffman, B. (1972). *Albert Einstein: Creator and rebel.* New York: Viking.

Hollingshead, A. B. (1975). *Elmtown's youth and Elmtown revisited.* New York: Wiley.

Hollingsworth, S. (Ed.). (1997). *International action research: A casebook for educational reform.* London: Falmer Press.

Holman Jones, S. (2005). Autoethnography: Making the personal political. In N. K. Denzin & Y. S. Lincoln (Eds.), *The SAGE handbook of qualitative research* (3rd ed., pp. 763–791). Thousand Oaks, CA: Sage.

Holstein, J. A., & Gubrium, J. F. (Eds.). (2003). *Inside interviewing: New lenses, new concerns.* Thousand Oaks, CA: Sage.

Home Box Office Project Knowledge. (1992). *Educating Peter* [Motion picture]. New York: Ambrose Video Publishing (Distributors).

hooks, b. (1994). *Teaching to transgress.* New York: Routledge.

hooks, b. (2004). Culture to culture: Ethnography and cultural studies as critical intervention. In S. N. Hesse-Biber & P. Leavy (Eds.), *Approaches to qualitative research: A reader on theory and practice* (pp. 149–158). New York: Oxford University Press.

hooks, b. (2008). Representations of Whiteness in the Black imagination. In P. S. Rothenberg (Ed.), *White privilege: Essential readings on the other side of racism* (3rd ed., pp. 19–24). New York: Worth.

Hurdley, R. (2007). Focal points: Framing material culture and visual data. *Qualitative Research, 7*(3), 355–374.

iMovie™ [Computer software]. Retrieved October 30, 2009, from www.apple.com/ilife/imovie

Jacob, E. (1987). Qualitative research traditions: A review. *Review of Educational Research, 51,* 1–50.

Jacob, E. (1988). Clarifying qualitative research: A focus on traditions. *Educational Researcher, 17,* 16–24.

Jagose, A. (1996). *Queer theory: An introduction.* Washington Square: New York University Press.

James, N., & Busher, H. (2006). Credibility, authenticity and voice: Dilemmas in online interviewing. *Qualitative Research, 6*(3), 403–420.

Jones, D. M. (2004). *Collaborating with immigrant and refugee communities: Reflections of an outsider.* Unpublished doctoral dissertation, University of Massachusetts Amherst.

Jones, M. C. (1983). *Novelist as biographer: The truth of art, the lies of biography.* Unpublished doctoral dissertation, Northwestern University, Evanston, IL.

Jones, S. H. (2005). Autoethnography: Making the personal political. In N. K. Denzin & Y. S. Lincoln (Eds.), *The SAGE handbook of qualitative research* (3rd ed., pp. 763–791). Thousand Oaks, CA: Sage.

Jordan, B., & Henderson, A. (1995). Interaction analysis: Foundations and practice. *The Journal of the Learning Sciences, 4*(1), 39–103.

Kahn, A. (1992). *Therapist initiated termination to psychotherapy: The experience of clients.* Unpublished doctoral dissertation, University of Massachusetts Amherst.

Kalnins, Z. G. (1986). *An exploratory study of the meaning of life as described by residents of a long-term care facility.* Project proposal, Peabody College of Vanderbilt University, Nashville, TN.

Kanter, R. (1977). *Men and women of the corporation.* New York: Basic Books.

Kanuha, V. K. (2000). "Being native" versus "going native": Conducting social work research as an insider. *Social Work, 45*(5), 339–447.

Kaplan, A. (1964). *The conduct of inquiry.* San Francisco: Chandler.

Keats, P. A. (2009). Multiple text analysis in narrative research: Visual, written, and spoken stories of experience. *Qualitative Research, 9*(2), 181–195.

Keddie, N. (1971). Classroom knowledge. In M. F. D. Young (Ed.), *Knowledge and control* (pp. 133–160). London: Collier-Macmillan.

Kelly, D., & Gaskell, J. (Eds.). (1996). *Debating dropouts: Critical policy and research perspectives.* New York: Teachers College Press.

Kemmis, S., & McTaggart, R. (2005). Participatory action research: Communicative action and the public sphere. In N. K. Denzin & Y. S. Lincoln (Eds.), *The SAGE handbook of qualitative research* (3rd ed., pp. 559–603). Thousand Oaks: CA: Sage.

Kemmis, S., & McTaggart, R. (Eds.). (1982). *The action research reader.* Geelong, Victoria, Australia: Deakin University Press.

Kendall, L. (2002). *Hanging out in the virtual pub: Masculinities and relationships online.* Berkeley: University of California Press.

Kennedy, M. M. (1979). Generalizing from single case studies. *Evaluation Quarterly, 12,* 661–678.

Kiegelmann, M. (1997). *Coming to terms: A qualitative study of six women's experiences of breaking the silence about brother-sister incest.* Ann Arbor: University of Michigan Press.

Kirkhart, K. E. (1995). Seeking multicultural validity: A postcard from the road. *Evaluation Practice, 16,*(1), 1–12.

Kleinman, S., & Copp, M. A. (1993). *Emotions and fieldwork.* Newbury Park, CA: Sage.

Knight, P. T. (2002). *Small-scale research: Pragmatic inquiry in social science and the caring professions.* Thousand Oaks, CA: Sage.

Kohli, R. (2009, April). *Breaking the cycle of racism in the classroom: Critical race reflections from future teachers of color.* Paper presented at the meeting of the American Educational Research Association, San Diego, CA.

Kohlberg, L. (1981). *Essays on moral development: The philosophy of moral development* (Vol. I). San Francisco: Harper & Row.

Kong, T. S., Mahoney, D., Plummer, K. (2002). Queering the interview. In J. F. Gubrium & J. A. Holstein (Eds.), *Handbook of interview research: Context and method* (pp. 239–258). Thousand Oaks, CA: Sage Publications.

Koro-Lundberg, M. (2008). Validity and validation in the making in the context of qualitative research. *Qualitative Health Research, 18*(7), 983–989.

Koski, K. (1997). *Interviewing.* Unpublished manuscript, University of Massachusetts Amherst.

Krieger, S. (1985). Beyond subjectivity: The use of self in social science. *Qualitative Sociology, 8,* 309–324.

Krueger, R. A., & Casey, M. A. (2008). *Focus groups: A practical guide for applied research* (4th ed.). Thousand Oaks, CA: Sage.

Kvale, S. (1996). *InterViews: An introduction to qualitative research interviewing.* Thousand Oaks, CA: Sage.

Kvale, S., & Brinkmann, S. (2009). *InterViews: Learning the craft of qualitative research interviewing* (2nd ed.). Thousand Oaks, CA: Sage.

Ladson-Billings, G. J. (1997). *The dreamkeepers: Successful teachers of African-American children.* San Francisco: Jossey-Bass.

Ladson-Billings, G. (2000). Racialized discourses and ethnic epistemologies. In N. K. Denzin & Y. S. Lincoln (Eds.), *Handbook of qualitative research* (2nd ed., pp. 257–277). Thousand Oaks, CA: Sage.

Ladson-Billings, G., & Donnor, J. (2005). The moral activist role of critical race theory scholarship. In N. K. Denzin & Y. S. Lincoln (Eds.), *The SAGE handbook of qualitative research* (3rd ed., pp. 279–301). Thousand Oaks, CA: Sage.

Ladson-Billings, G., & Tate, W. F. (2006). Toward a critical race theory of education. In A. D. Dixson & C. K. Rousseau (Eds.), *Critical race theory in education: All God's children got a song* (pp. 11–30). New York: Routledge.

Ladson-Billings, G. J. (2001). *Crossing over to Canaan: The journey of new teachers in diverse classrooms.* San Francisco: Jossey-Bass.

Ladson-Billings, G. J. (2005). *Beyond the big house: African American educators on teacher education.* New York: Teacher College Press.

Laible, J. (2003). A loving epistemology: What I hold critical in my life, faith, and profession. In M. D. Young & L. Skrla (Eds.), *Reconsidering feminist research in educational leadership* (pp. 179–192). Albany: State University of New York Press.

Lareau, A. (1989). *Home advantage: Social class and parental intervention in elementary education.* New York: Falmer Press.

Lather, P. (1991). *Getting smart: Feminist research and pedagogy with/in the postmodern.* London: Routledge & Kegan Paul.

Lather, P. (1993). Fertile obsession: Validity after poststructuralism. *Sociological Quarterly, 34*(4), 673–693.

Lather, P. (2001). Validity as an incitement to discourse: Qualitative research and the crisis of legitimation. In V. Richardson (Ed.), *Handbook of research on teaching* (4th ed., pp. 241–250). Washington, DC: American Educational Research Association.

Lather, P. (2009, April). *Discussing validity.* Unpublished presentation at the annual conference of the American Educational Research Association, San Diego, CA.

Lather, P., & Smithies, C. (1997). *Troubling the angels: Women living with HIV/AIDS.* Boulder, CO: Westview.

Laverack, G. R., & Brown, K. M. (2003). Qualitative research in a cross-cultural context: Fijian experiences. *Qualitative Health Research, 13,* 333–342.

Lawless, E. J. (1991). Methodology and research notes: Women's life stories and reciprocal ethnography as feminist and emergent. *Journal of Folklore Research, 28,* 35–60.

LeCompte, M. D. (1993). A framework for hearing silence: What does telling stories mean when we are supposed to be doing science? In D. McLaughlin & W. G. Tierney (Eds.), *Naming silenced lives: Personal narratives and processes of educational change* (pp. 9–27). New York: Routledge & Kegan Paul.

Lee, R. M. (1995). *Dangerous fieldwork.* Thousand Oaks, CA: Sage.

Lee, T. S. (2006). "I came here to learn how to be a leader": An intersection of critical pedagogy and indigenous education. *InterActions: UCLA Journal of Education and Information Studies, 2*(1), 1–24.

Lees, S. (1986). *Losing out.* London: Hutchinson.

Lerum, K. (2001). Subjects of desire: Academic armor, intimate ethnography, and the production of critical knowledge. *Qualitative Inquiry, 7,* 466–483.

Levinas, E. (1979). *Totality and infinity: An essay on exteriority.* London: Springer-Verlag. (Originally published in French)

Libby, W. (1922). The scientific imagination. *Scientific Monthly, 15,* 263–270.

Lifton, R. J. (1991). *Death in life: Survivors of Hiroshima.* Chapel Hill: University of North Carolina Press.

Lightfoot, S. L. (1983). *The good high school: Portraits of character and culture.* New York: Basic Books.

Lightfoot, S. L. (1985). The good high school: Portraits of character and culture. New York: Basic Books.

Lightfoot, S. L., & Davis, J. H. (1997). *The art and science of portraiture.* San Francisco: Jossey-Bass.

Lincoln, Y. S. (2005). Institutional review boards and methodological conservatism: The challenge to and from phenomenological paradigms. In N. K. Denzin & Y. S. Lincoln (Eds.), *The SAGE handbook of qualitative research* (3rd ed., pp. 165–181). Thousand Oaks, CA: Sage.

Lincoln, Y. S., & Guba, E. (1985). *Naturalistic inquiry.* Beverly Hills, CA: Sage.

Lincoln, Y. S., & Guba, E. G. (2000). Paradigmatic controversies, contradictions, and emerging confluences. In N. K. Denzin & Y. S. Lincoln (Eds.), *Handbook of qualitative research* (2nd ed., pp. 163–188). Thousand Oaks, CA: Sage.

Locke, L. F., Spirduso, W. W., & Silverman, S. J. (2000). *Proposals that work: A guide for planning dissertations and grant proposals* (4th ed.). Thousand Oaks, CA: Sage.

Lutz, F., & Iannaccone, L. (1969). *Understanding educational organizations: A field study approach.* Columbus, OH: Charles Merrill.

MacJessie-Mbewe, S. (2004). *Analysis of a complex policy domain: Access to secondary education in Malawi.* Unpublished doctoral dissertation, University of Massachusetts Amherst.

Madison, D. S. (2005). *Critical ethnography: Method, ethics, and performance.* Thousand Oaks, CA: Sage.

Maguire, P. (2000). *Doing participatory research: A feminist approach.* Amherst, MA: Center for International Education.

Maloy, R., Pine, G., & Seidman, I. (2002). *Massachusetts teacher preparation and induction study report on first year findings.* National Education Association Professional Development School Research Project Teacher Quality Study.

Mandelbaum, D. G. (1973). The study of life history: Gandhi. *Current Anthropology, 14,* 177–207.

Mann, C., & Stewart, F. (2002). Internet interviewing. In J. Gubrium & J. A. Holstein (Eds.), *Handbook of interview research: Context and method* (pp. 603–627). Thousand Oaks, CA: Sage.

Mann, C., & Stewart, F. (2004). Introducing online methods. In S. N. Hesse-Biber & P. Leavy (Eds.), *Approaches to qualitative research: A reader on theory and practice* (pp. 367–401). New York: Oxford University Press.

Manning, P. K. (1972). Observing the police: Deviants, respectables, and the law. In J. Douglas (Ed.), *Research on deviance* (pp. 213–268). New York: Random House.

Markham, A. N. (2004). Internet communication as a tool for qualitative research. In D. Silverman (Ed.), *Qualitative research: Theory, method, and practice* (pp. 95–124). Thousand Oaks, CA: Sage.

Markham, A. N. (2005). The methods, politics, and ethics of representation in online ethnography. In N. K. Denzin & Y. S. Lincoln (Eds.), *The SAGE handbook of qualitative research* (3rd ed., pp. 793–820). Thousand Oaks, CA: Sage.

Marshall, C. (1979). *Career socialization of women in school administration.* Unpublished doctoral dissertation, University of California at Santa Barbara.

Marshall, C. (1981). Organizational policy and women's socialization in administration. *Urban Education, 16,* 205–231.

Marshall, C. (1985a). Appropriate criteria of trustworthiness and goodness for qualitative research on education organizations. *Quality and Quantity, 19,* 353–373.

Marshall, C. (1985b). The stigmatized woman: The professional woman in a male sex-typed career. *Journal of Educational Administration, 23,* 131–152.

Marshall, C. (1987). *Report to the Vanderbilt Policy Education Committee.* Nashville, TN: Vanderbilt University.

Marshall, C. (1988). *State education politics.* Grant proposal to the National Science Foundation.

Marshall, C. (1990). Goodness criteria: Are they objective or judgment calls? In E. Guba (Ed.), *The paradigm dialog* (pp. 188–197). Newbury Park, CA: Sage.

Marshall, C. (1991). Educational policy dilemmas: Can we have control and quality and choice and democracy and equity? In K. M. Borman, P. Swami, & L. D. Wagstaff (Eds.), *Contemporary issues in U.S. education* (pp. 1–21). Norwood, NJ: Ablex.

Marshall, C. (1992). School administrators' values: A focus on atypicals. *Educational Administration Quarterly, 28,* 368–386.

Marshall, C. (1993). *The unsung role of the career assistant principal* [Monograph]. Reston, VA: National Association of Secondary School Principals.

Marshall, C. (1997a). Dismantling and reconstructing policy analysis. In C. Marshall (Ed.), *Feminist critical policy analysis: A perspective from primary and secondary schooling* (Vol. 1, pp. 1–34). London: Falmer Press.

Marshall, C. (Ed.). (1997b). *Feminist critical policy analysis: A perspective from primary and secondary schooling.* London: Falmer Press.

Marshall, C. (2008). *Making the impossible job possible.* Unpublished grant proposal, University of North Carolina at Chapel Hill.

Marshall, C., & Anderson, A. L. (Eds.). (2008). *Activist educators: Breaking past limits.* New York: Routledge.

Marshall, C., & Rossman, G. B. (2006). *Designing qualitative research* (4th ed.). Thousand Oaks, CA: Sage.

Marshall, C., & Young, M. D. (2006). Gender and methodology. In C. Skelton, B. Francis, & L. Smulyn (Eds.). *The SAGE handbook of gender and education* (pp. 63–78). Thousand Oaks, CA. Sage.

Marshall, C., Mitchell, D., & Wirt, F. (1985). Assumptive worlds of education policy makers. *Peabody Journal of Education, 62*(4), 90–115.

Marshall, C., Mitchell, D., & Wirt, F. (1986). The context of state level policy formulation. *Educational Evaluation and Policy Analysis, 8,* 347–378.

Marshall, C., Patterson, J., Rogers, D., & Steele, J. (1996). Caring as career: An alternative model for educational administration. *Educational Administration Quarterly, 32,* 271–294.

Matsuda, M. J., Delgado, R., Lawrence, C. R., & Crenshaw, K. W. (1993). *Words that wound: Critical race theory, assault speech, and the First Amendment.* Boulder, CO: Westview.

Maxwell, J. A. (1996). *Qualitative research design: An interactive approach.* Thousand Oaks, CA: Sage.

Maxwell, J. A. (2005). *Qualitative research design: An interactive approach* (2nd ed.). Thousand Oaks, CA: Sage.

McCall, M. M. (2000). Performance ethnography: A brief history and some advice. In N. K. Denzin & Y. S. Lincoln (Eds.), *Handbook of qualitative research* (2nd ed., pp. 421–433). Thousand Oaks, CA: Sage.

McNiff, J., & Whitehead, J. (2003). *Action research: Principles and practice.* London: Routledge.

Miles, M. B. (1979). Qualitative data as an attractive nuisance: The problem of analysis. *Administrative Science Quarterly, 24,* 590–601.

Miles, M. B., & Huberman, A. M. (1994). *Qualitative data analysis: An expanded sourcebook* (2nd ed.). Thousand Oaks, CA: Sage.

Miller, D., & Slater, D. (2000). *The Internet: An ethnographic approach.* Oxford, UK: Berg.

Milner, H. R. (2007). Race, culture, and researcher positionality: Working through dangers seen, unseen, and unforeseen. *Educational Researcher, 36*(7), 388–400.

Mishna, F. (2004). A qualitative study of bullying from multiple perspectives. *Children & Schools, 26*(4), 234–247.

Mitchell, D., Wirt, F., & Marshall, C. (1986). *Alternative state policy mechanisms for pursuing educational quality, equity, efficiency, and choice* (Final report to the U.S. Department of Education, Grant No. NIE-G-83 0020). Washington, DC: U.S. Department of Education.

Mooney, R. L. (1951). Problems in the development of research men. *Educational Research Bulletin, 30,* 141–150.

Morgan, D. L. (1997). *Focus groups as qualitative research* (2nd ed.). Thousand Oaks, CA: Sage.

Morse, J. M. (2003). A review committee's guide for evaluating qualitative proposals. *Qualitative Health Research, 13,* 833–851.

Morse, J. M. (2004). Using the right tool for the job [Editorial]. *Qualitative Health Research, 14,* 1029–1031.

Morse, J. M., & Richards, L. (2002). *Read me first for a user's guide to qualitative methods.* Thousand Oaks, CA: Sage.

Mosselson, J. (2006). *Roots and routes: Bosnian adolescent refugees in New York.* New York: Peter Lang.

Mouffe, C., & LeClau, E. (1985). *Hegemony and socialist strategy: Towards a radical democratic politics.* New York: Verso.

Moustakas, C. E. (1994). *Phenomenological research methods.* Thousand Oaks, CA: Sage.

MovieMaker [Computer software]. Retrieved October 31, 2009, from www.Microsoft.Com/Windowsxp/Downloads/Updates/Moviemaker2.Mspx

Narayan, K. (1993). How native is a "native" anthropologist? *American Anthropologist, 95*(3), New Series, 671–686.

Narrative Inquiry: The Forum for Theoretical, Empirical, and Methodological Work on Narrative. Retrieved March 2, 2009, from www.clarku.edu/faculty/mbamberg/ narrativeINQ

National Research Council, Center for Education, Division of Behavioral and Social Sciences and Education. (2002). *Scientific research in education. Committee on Scientific Principles for Education Research* (R. J. Shavelson & L. Towne, Eds.). Washington, DC: National Academies Press.

Nielson, J. (Ed.). (1990). *Feminist research methods: Exemplary readings in the social sciences.* Boulder, CO: Westview.

Noblit, G. W., Flores, S. Y., & Murillo, E. G., Jr. (Eds.). (2005). *Postcritical ethnography: Reinscribing critique.* Cresskill, NJ: Hampton Press.

Noffke, S. E., & Somekh, B. (Eds.). (2009). *The SAGE handbook of educational action research.* London: Sage.

NVivo8 for Windows [Computer software]. UK: QRS International. Trial copy available from www.qsrinternational.com Retrieved March 2, 2009.

Ochiel, M. (2009). Child-headed households and orphans: Exploring the nexus of poverty, politics, and HIV and AIDS in Kenya. Unpublished manuscript, University of Massachusetts Amherst.

O'Hearn-Curran, M. (1997). *First days in the field: Lessons I learned in kindergarten.* Unpublished manuscript, University of Massachusetts Amherst.

Olesen, V. (2000). Feminisms and qualitative research into the new millennium. In N. K. Denzin, & Y. S. Lincoln (Eds.), *Handbook of qualitative research* (2nd ed., pp. 215–255). Thousand Oaks, CA: Sage.

Olesen, V. L., & Whittaker, E. W. (1968). *The silent dialogue: A study in social psychology of professional socialization.* San Francisco: Jossey-Bass.

O'Neill, J., Small, B. B., & Strachan, J. (1999). The use of focus groups within a participatory action research environment. In M. Kopala & L. A. Suzuki (Eds.), *Using qualitative methods in psychology* (pp. 199–209). Thousand Oaks, CA: Sage.

Olympus Digital Wave Player 2. Retrieved October 31, 2009, from www.olympusvoice.com.au/products/digital/notetakers/vn240pc_specifications.html

O'Toole, P., & Were, P. (2008). Observing places: Using space and material culture in qualitative research. *Qualitative Research, 8*(5), 616–634.

Park, P., Brydon-Miller, M., Hall, B., & Jackson, T. (Eds.). (1993). *Voices of change: Participatory research in the United States and Canada.* Toronto, Ontario, Canada: Ontario Institute for Studies in Education Press.

Patton, M. Q. (1990). *Qualitative research and evaluation methods* (2nd ed.). Thousand Oaks, CA: Sage.

Patton, M. Q. (2002). *Qualitative research and evaluation methods* (3rd ed.). Thousand Oaks, CA: Sage.

Peek, L., & Fothergill, A. (2009). Using focus groups: Lessons from studying daycare centers, 9/11, and Hurricane Katrina. *Qualitative Research, 9*(1), 31–59.

Peräkylä, A. (2005). Analyzing talk and text. In N. K. Denzin & Y. S. Lincoln (Eds.), *The SAGE handbook of qualitative research* (3rd ed., pp. 869–886). Thousand Oaks, CA: Sage.

Phaik-Lah, K. (1997). The environments of action research in Malaysia. In S. Hollingsworth (Ed.), *International action research: A casebook for educational reform* (pp. 238–243). London: Falmer Press.

Photovoice.org [Web site]. Accessed April 8, 2009, at www.photovoice.org

Piantanida, M., & Garman, N. B. (1999). *The qualitative dissertation: A guide for students and faculty.* Thousand Oaks, CA: Corwin Press.

Pinnacle Studi012 [Computer software]. Mountain View, CA: Avid Technology, Inc. Retrieved March 3, 2009, from_www.pinnaclesys.com/PublicSite/ us/Products/onsumer+Products/ Home+Video/Studio+Family

Piotrkowski, C. S. (1979). *Work and the family system: A naturalistic study of working-class and lower-middle-class families.* New York: Free Press.

Polsky, N. (1969). *Hustlers, beats, and others.* Garden City, NY: Doubleday Anchor.

Poovey, M. (1995). *Making a social body: British cultural formation 1830–1864.* Chicago: University of Chicago Press.

Powdermaker, H. (1966). *Stranger and friend.* New York: W. W. Norton.

Prior, L. (2004). Following Foucault's footsteps: Text and context in qualitative research: In S. N. Hesse-Biber & P. Leavy (Eds.), *Approaches to qualitative research: A reader on theory and practice* (pp. 317–333). New York: Oxford University Press.

Punch, M. (1994). Politics and ethics in qualitative research. In N. K. Denzin & Y. S. Lincoln (Eds.), *Handbook of qualitative research* (pp. 83–97). Thousand Oaks, CA: Sage.

Rabinow, P. (1977). *Reflections on fieldwork in Morocco.* Berkeley: University of California Press.

Rager, K. B. (2005). Self-care and the qualitative researcher: When collecting data can break your heart. *Educational Researcher, 34*(4), 23–27.

Rallis, S. F., & Rossman, G. B. (in press). Reflexive research practitioners. In G. B. Rossman & S. F. Rallis (Guest Editors), Research ethics in the everyday. *International Journal of Qualitative Studies in Education, 23*(3).

Reardon, K., Welsh, B., Kreiswirth, B., & Forester, J. (1993). Participatory action research from the inside: Community development practice in East St. Louis. *American Sociologist, 24,* 69–91.

Reason, P. (Ed.). (1994). *Participation in human inquiry.* Thousand Oaks, CA: Sage.

Reason, P., & Rowan, J. (1981). *Human inquiry: A sourcebook of new paradigm research.* New York: Wiley.

Rex, L. A., & Green, J. L. (2008). Classroom discourse and interaction: Reading across the traditions. In B. Spolsky & F. Hull (Eds.), *Handbook of educational linguistics* (pp. 571–584). Malden, MA: Wiley-Blackwell.

Rex, L. A., Murnen, T. J., Hobbs, J., & McEachen, D. (2002). Teachers' pedagogical stories and the shaping of classroom participation: "The dancer" and the "graveyard shift at the 7–11." *American Educational Research Journal, 39*(3), 765–796.

Rex, L. A., Steadman, S., & Graciano, M. (2006). Researching the complexity of classroom interaction. In J. L. Green, G. Camilli, & P. Elmore (Eds.), *Handbook of complementary methods in education research* (pp. 727–772). Mahwah, NJ: Lawrence Erlbaum.

Rhyne, R. (2000). Foucault, Michel (1926–1984). In G. E. Haggerty (Ed.), *Gay histories and cultures: An encyclopedia* (Vol. 2, pp. 337–338). New York: Garland.

Richards, L. (2005). *Handling qualitative data: A practical guide.* Thousand Oaks, CA: Sage.

Richards, T. J., & Richards, L. (1994). Using computers in qualitative research. In N. K. Denzin & Y. S. Lincoln (Eds.), *Handbook of qualitative research* (pp. 445–462). Thousand Oaks, CA: Sage.

Richardson, L. (1997). *Fields of play: Constructing an academic life.* New Brunswick, NJ: Rutgers University Press.

Richardson, L. (2000). Writing: A method of inquiry. In N. K. Denzin & Y. S. Lincoln (Eds.), *Handbook of qualitative research* (2nd ed., pp. 923–948). Thousand Oaks, CA: Sage.

Richardson, L., & St. Pierre, E. A. (2005). Writing: A method of inquiry. In N. K. Denzin & Y. S. Lincoln (Eds.), *The SAGE handbook of qualitative research* (3rd ed., pp. 959–978). Thousand Oaks, CA: Sage.

Riessman, C. K. (1991). When gender is not enough: Women interviewing women. In J. Lorder & S. A. Farrell (Eds.), *The social construction of gender* (pp. 217–236). Newbury Park, CA: Sage.

Riessman, C. K. (1993). *Narrative analysis.* Newbury Park, CA: Sage.

Rogers, R. (Ed.). (2004). *An introduction to critical discourse analysis in education.* Mahwah, NJ: Lawrence Erlbaum.

Rosenau, P. M. (1992). *Post-modernism and the social sciences: Insights, inroads, and intrusions.* Princeton, NJ: Princeton University Press.

Rosenberg, L. (2006). *Rewriting ideologies of literacy: A study of writing by newly literate adults.* Unpublished doctoral dissertation, University of Massachusetts Amherst.

Ross, M., & Conway, M. (1986). Remembering one's own past: The construction of personal histories. In R. Sorrentino & E. T. Higgins (Eds.), *Handbook of motivation and cognition: Foundations of social behavior* (pp. 122–144). New York: Guilford Press.

Rossman, G. B. (1994, November). *External evaluation report: Designing schools for enhanced learning.* Unpublished report. Andover, MA: Regional Laboratory for New England and the Islands.

Rossman, G. B., Corbett, H. D., & Firestone, W. A. (1984). *Plan for the study of professional cultures in improving high schools.* Philadelphia: Research for Better Schools.

Rossman, G. B., & Rallis, S. F. (2001). *Leading dynamic schools for newcomer students.* Proposal submitted to the U.S. Department of Education, Office of Educational Research and Improvement.

Rossman, G. B., & Rallis, S. F. (2003). *Learning in the field: An introduction to qualitative research* (2nd ed.). Thousand Oaks, CA: Sage.

Rossman, G. B., & Rallis, S. F. (in press). Everyday ethics: Reflections on practice. *International Journal of Qualitative Studies in Education, 23*(3).

Rossman, G. B., & Wilson, B. L. (1994). Numbers and words revisited: Being shamelessly eclectic. *Quality and Quantity, 28,* 315–327.

Rossman, G. B., Rallis, S. F., & Kuntz, A. M. (in press). Standards of proof in qualitative inquiry: Reliability, validity, and related evidentiary issues. In E. Baker, B. McGaw, & P. Peterson (Eds.), *International encyclopedia of education* (3rd ed.). London: Elsevier.

Ryen, A. (2003). Cross-cultural interviewing. In J. A. Holstein & J. F. Gubrium (Eds.), *Inside interviewing: New lenses, new concerns* (pp. 429–448). Thousand Oaks, CA: Sage.

Sabin, A. (Cinematographer). (2008). *Intimidad* [Motion picture]. Carnivales que Films. Available at www.carnivalesquefilms.com/intimidad.html

Safman, R. M., & Sobal, J. (2004). Qualitative sample extensiveness in health education research. *Health Education & Behavior, 31,* 9–21.

Sagor, R. (2005). *Action research handbook: A four-step process for educators and school teams.* Thousand Oaks, CA: Corwin Press.

Said, E. W. (2007). *Music at the limits: Three decades of essays and articles on music.* New York: Columbia University Press.

Saldana, J. (2009). *The coding manual for qualitative researchers.* Thousand Oaks, CA: Sage.

Sampson, H. (2004). Navigating the waves: The usefulness of a pilot in qualitative research. *Qualitative Research, 4*(3), 383–402.

Sandelowski, M., & Barroso, J. (2003). Writing the proposal for a qualitative research methodology project. *Qualitative Health Research, 13,* 781–820.

Sanjek, R. (1990). On ethnographic validity. In R. Sanjek (Ed.), *Fieldnotes: The makings of anthropology* (pp. 385–418). Ithaca, NY: Cornell University Press.

Sariyant, T. P. (2002). *Knowing and understanding through auto/ethnography: Narrative on transformative learning experience of an international graduate student.* Unpublished doctoral dissertation, University of Massachusetts Amherst.

Saukko, P. (2003). *Doing research in cultural studies: An introduction to classical and new methodological approaches.* London: Sage.

Saukko, P. (2008). Methodologies for cultural studies: An integrative approach. In N. K. Denzin & Y. S. Lincoln (Eds.), *The landscapes of qualitative research* (3rd ed., pp. 457–475). Thousand Oaks, CA: Sage.

Saumure, K., & Given, L. M. (2008). Data saturation. In L. M. Given (Ed.), *The SAGE encyclopedia of qualitative research methods* (Vol. 1, pp. 195–196). Thousand Oaks, CA: Sage.

Schatzman, L., & Strauss, A. (1973). *Field research: Strategies for a natural sociology.* Englewood Cliffs, NJ: Prentice Hall.

Schensul, J. J. (2008). Methodology. In L. M. Given (Ed.), *The SAGE encyclopedia of qualitative research methods* (p. 519). Thousand Oaks, CA: Sage.

Scheurich, J. (1997). *Research methods in the postmodern.* London: Falmer Press.

Schram, T. H. (2006). *Conceptualizing and proposing qualitative research* (2nd ed.). Upper Saddle River, NJ: Pearson Prentice Hall.

Schwandt, T. A. (1996). Farewell to criteriology. *Qualitative Inquiry, 2,* 72.

Scott, J. W. (2003). The linguistic production of genderlessness in the superintendency. In M. D. Young & L. Skrla (Eds.), *Reconsidering feminist research in educational leadership* (pp. 81–102). Albany: State University of New York Press.

Seidman, I. E. (2006). *Interviewing as qualitative research: A guide for researchers in education and the social sciences* (3rd ed.). New York: Teachers College Press.

Seidman, S. (1996). *Queer theory/sociology.* Cambridge, MA: Blackwell.

Selener, D. (1997). *Participatory action research and social change.* Cornell, NY: Cornell Participatory Action Research Network.

Senge, P. (1990). *The fifth discipline: The art and practice of the learning organization.* New York: Doubleday.

Seymour, W. S. (2001). In the flesh or online? Exploring qualitative research methodologies. *Qualitative Research, 1*(2), 147–168.

Sfard, A., & Prusak, A. (2005). Telling identities: In search of an analytic tool for investigating learning as a culturally shaped activity. *Educational Researcher, 34*(4), 14–22.

Shadduck-Hernandez, J. (1997). *Affirmation, advocacy, and action: Refugee/immigrant student education and community building in higher education.* Research proposal to the Spencer Foundation, University of Massachusetts Amherst.

Shadduck Hernandez, J. (2005). *"Here I am now!" Community service-learning with immigrant and refugee undergraduate students and youth: The use of critical pedagogy, situated learning, and funds of knowledge.* University of Massachusetts Amherst. Unpublished doctoral dissertation.

Sharp, R., & Green, A. (1975). *Education and social control.* London: Routledge & Kegan Paul.

Shaw, I. (2003). Qualitative research and outcomes in health, social work and education. *Qualitative Research, 3,* 57–77.

Shaw, I., & Ruckdeschel, R. (2002). Qualitative social work: A room with a view. *Qualitative Social Work, 1,* 5–23.

Shostak, M. (1983). *Nisa: The life and words of a !Kung woman.* New York: Random House.

Silverman, D. (2000). Analyzing talk and text. In N. K. Denzin & Y. S. Lincoln (Eds.), *Handbook of qualitative research* (2nd ed., pp. 821–834). Thousand Oaks, CA: Sage.

Silverman, D. (2007). *A very short, fairly interesting and reasonably cheap book about qualitative research.* Thousand Oaks, CA: Sage.

Singal, N., & Jeffery, R. (2008). Transcribing and translating data. In *Qualitative research skills workshop: A facilitator's reference manual.* Cambridge, UK: RECOUP (Research Consortium on Educational Outcomes and Poverty). Retrieved February 27, 2009, from http://manual.recoup.educ.cam.ac.uk

Singer, M., Radinsky, J., & Goldman, S. (2008). The role of gesture in meaning construction. *Discourse Processes, 45*(4), 365–386.

Smagorinsky, P. (2007). Is "doing educational research" a matter of perspective? Two reviewers begin the dialogue. *Educational Researcher, 36*(4), 199–203.

Smith, C. S., & Faris, R. (2002). *Religion and the life attitudes and self-images of American adolescents.* Chapel Hill, NC: National Study of Youth and Religion.

Smith, D. E. (2005). *Institutional ethnography: A sociology for people.* Lanham, MD: AltaMira Press.

Smith, J. K. (1988, March). *Looking for the easy way out: The desire for methodological constraints in openly ideological research.* Paper presented at the annual meeting of the American Educational Research Association, New Orleans.

Smith, J. K., & Deemer, D. K. (2000). The problem of criteria in the age of relativism. In N. K. Denzin & Y. S. Lincoln (Eds.), *Handbook of qualitative research* (2nd ed., pp. 877–896). Thousand Oaks, CA: Sage.

Smith, M. (1999). Researching social workers' experiences of fear: Piloting a course. *Social Work Education, 18*(3), 347–354.

Soloway, I., & Walters, J. (1977). Workin' the corner: The ethics and legality of ethnographic fieldwork among active heroin addicts. In R. S. Weppner (Ed.), *Street ethnography* (pp. 159–178). Beverly Hills, CA: Sage.

Sparks, A. (1994). Self, silence, and invisibility as a beginning teacher: A life history of lesbian experience. *British Journal of Sociology of Education, 15,* 92–118.

Spradley, J. P., & Mann, B. J. (1975). *The cocktail waitress: Woman's work in a man's world.* New York: Wiley.

Spradley, J. S. (1979). *The ethnographic interview.* New York: Holt, Rinehart & Winston.

Spradley, J. S. (1980). *Participant observation.* New York: Holt, Rinehart & Winston.

Steedman, P. S. (1991). On the relations between seeing, interpreting, and knowing. In F. Steier (Ed.), *Research and reflexivity: Inquiries in social construction* (pp. 53-62). Newbury Park, CA: Sage.

Stein, A., & Plummer, K. (1996). "I can't even think straight": "Queer" theory and the missing sexual revolution in sociology. In S. Seidman (Ed.), *Queer theory/sociology* (pp. 129–144). Cambridge, MA: Blackwell.

Stephens, N. (2007). Collecting data from elites and ultra elites: Telephone and face-to-face interviews with macroeconomists. *Qualitative Research, 7*(2), 203–216.

Strauss, A., & Corbin, J. (Eds.). (1997). *Grounded theory in practice.* Thousand Oaks, CA: Sage.

Strauss, A. L. (1969). *Mirrors and masks.* Mill Valley, CA: Sociology Press.

Strauss, A. L., & Corbin, J. (1998). Basics of qualitative research: Techniques and procedures for developing grounded theory. Thousand Oaks, CA: Sage.

Stringer, E. T. (1996). *Action research: A handbook for practitioners.* Thousand Oaks, CA: Sage.

Stringer, E. T. (1999). *Action research: A handbook for practitioners* (2nd ed.). Thousand Oaks, CA: Sage.

Stringer, E. T. (2007). *Action research: A handbook for practitioners* (3rd ed.). Thousand Oaks, CA: Sage.

SurveyMonkey [Computer software]. Accessed March 5, 2009, from www.surveymonkey.com

Sutherland, E. H., & Conwell, C. (1983). *The professional thief.* Chicago: University of Chicago Press.

Skype [Computer software]. Accessed November 2, 2009, from www.skype.com

Szto, P., Furman, R., & Langer, C. (2005). Poetry and photography. *Qualitative Social Work, 4,* 135–156.

Taylor, S. J., & Bogdan, R. (1984). *Introduction to qualitative research methods: The search for meanings* (2nd ed.). New York: Wiley.

Tedlock, B. (2005). The observation of participation and the emergence of public ethnography. In N. K. Denzin & Y. S. Lincoln (Eds.), *The SAGE handbook of qualitative research* (3rd ed., pp. 467–481). Thousand Oaks, CA: Sage.

Temple, B., & Young, A. (2004). Qualitative research and translation dilemmas. *Qualitative Research, 4*(2), 161–178.

Tesch, R. (1990). *Qualitative research: Analysis types and software tools.* New York: Falmer Press.

Thomas, W. I. (1949). *Social structure and social theory.* New York: Free Press.

Thorne, B. (1983). Political activists as participant observer: Conflicts of commitment in a study of the draft resistance movement of the 1960s. In R. Emerson (Ed.), *Contemporary field research: A collection of readings* (pp. 216–234). Prospect Heights, IL: Waveland.

Tierney, W. G., & Lincoln, Y. S. (Eds.). (1997). *Representation and the text: Re-framing the narrative voice.* Albany: State University of New York Press.

Tilley, S. A. (2003). "Challenging" research practices: Turning a critical lens on the work of transcription. *Qualitative Inquiry, 9*(5), 750–773.

Titchen, A., & Bennie, A. (1993). Action research as a research strategy: Finding our way through a philosophical and methodological maze. *Journal of Advanced Nursing, 18,* 858–865.

Todres, L., & Galvin, K. T. (2008). Embodied interpretation: A novel way of evocatively re-presenting meanings in phenomenological research. *Qualitative Research, 8*(5), 568–583.

Toma, J. D. (2000). How getting close to your subjects makes qualitative data better. *Theory into Practice, 39*(3), 177–184.

Tong, R. (1989). *Feminist thought: A comprehensive introduction.* San Francisco: Westview.

Tsing, A. L. (1990). The vision of a woman shaman. In J. M. Nielsen (Ed.), *Feminist research methods* (pp. 147–173). San Francisco: Westview.

Tucker, B. J. (1996). *Teachers who make a difference: Voices of Mexican-American students.* Unpublished thesis proposal, Harvard University Graduate School of Education, Cambridge, MA.

Van Maanen, J. (1988). *Tales of the field: On writing ethnography.* Chicago: University of Chicago Press.

Villenas, S. (1996). Chicana ethnographer: Identity, marginalization, and co-optation in the field. *Harvard Educational Review, 66*(4), 711–731.

Viney, L. L., & Bousefield, L. (1991). Narrative analysis: A method of psychosocial research for AIDS-affected people. *Social Science and Medicine, 23,* 757–765.

VisualAnthropology.net [Web site]. Accessed March 3, 2009, at www.visualanthropology.net.

Walters, S. D. (2004). From here to *queer*: Radical feminism, postmodernism, and the lesbian menace (or why can't a woman be more like a fag?). In I. Morland & A. Willox (Eds.), *Readers in cultural criticism: Queer theory* (pp. 6–21). New York: Palgrave MacMillian.

Wang, C., & Burris, M. A. (1997). Photovoice: Concept, methodology, and use for participatory needs assessment. *Health Education & Behavior, 24*(3), 369–387.

Wang, C. C., & Pies, C. A. (2004). Family, maternal, and child health through photovoice. *Maternal and Child Health Journal, 8*(2), 95–102.

Warren, C. A. B. (2001). Gender and fieldwork relations. In R. M. Emerson (Ed.), *Contemporary field research: Perspectives and formulations* (2nd ed., pp. 203–223). Prospect Heights, IL: Waveland.

Wax, R. (1971). *Doing fieldwork: Warnings and advice.* Chicago: University of Chicago Press.

Weick, K. E. (1976). Educational organizations as loosely coupled systems. *Administrative Science Quarterly, 21,* 1–19.

Weis, L. (1990). *Working class without work: High school students in a de-industrializing economy.* New York: Routledge.

Weis, L., & Fine, M. (Eds.). (2000). *Construction sites: Excavating race, class, and gender among urban youth.* New York: Teachers College Press.

Weitzman, E. A. (2000). Software and qualitative research. In N. K. Denzin & Y. S. Lincoln (Eds.), *Handbook of qualitative research* (2nd ed., pp. 803–820). Thousand Oaks, CA: Sage.

Weitzman, E. A., & Miles, M. B. (1995). *Computer programs for qualitative data analysis.* Thousand Oaks, CA: Sage.

Welland, T., & Pugsley, L. (2002). *Ethical dilemmas in qualitative research.* Hants, UK: Ashgate.

Wengraf, T. (2001). *Qualitative research interviewing: Biographic narrative and semi-structured methods.* London: Sage.

Westby, C., Burda, A., & Mehta, Z. (n.d.). Asking the right questions in the right ways: Strategies for ethnographic interviewing. *The ASHA Leader Online.* Retrieved February 25, 2009, from www.asha.org/about/publications/leader-online/archives/2003/q2/f030429b.htm

Westley, W. A. (1967). The police: Law, custom, and morality. In P. I. Rose (Ed.), *The study of society* (pp. 766–779). New York: Random House.

Whyte, W. F. (1980). *The social life of small urban spaces.* Washington, DC: Conservation Foundation.

Whyte, W. F. (1984). *Learning from the field: A guide from experience.* Beverly Hills, CA: Sage.

Wilber, K. (1996). *Eye to eye: The quest for a new paradigm.* Berkeley, CA: Shambhala.

Williams, M. (2007). Avatar watching: Participant observation in graphical online environments. *Qualitative Researcher, 7*(1), 5–24.

Wilson, S. (1977). The use of ethnographic techniques in educational research. *Review of Educational Research, 47,* 245–265.

Winter, R. (1982). Dilemma analysis: A contribution to methodology for action research. *Cambridge Journal of Education, 12,* 161–174.

Wiseman, F. (Director). (1969). *High school* [Motion picture]. Boston: Zippora Films.

Wolcott, H. F. (1973). *The man in the principal's office: An ethnography.* Walnut Creek, CA: AltaMira Press.

Wolcott, H. F. (1994). *Transforming qualitative data: Description, analysis, and interpretation.* Thousand Oaks, CA: Sage.

Wolcott, H. F. (2001). *Writing up qualitative research.* Thousand Oaks, CA: Sage.

Wolcott, H. F. (2002). *Sneaky kid and its aftermath: Ethics and intimacy in fieldwork.* Walnut Creek, CA: AltaMira Press.

Wolcott, H. F. (2009). *Writing up qualitative research* (3rd ed.). Thousand Oaks, CA: Sage.

Wronka, J. (2008). *Human rights and social justice: Social action and service for the helping and health professions.* Thousand Oaks, CA: Sage.

Yablonsky, L. (1965). *The tunnel back: Synanon.* Baltimore: Penguin.

Yeh, C. J., & Inman, A. G. (2007). Qualitative data analysis and interpretation in counseling psychology: Strategies for best practices. *The Counseling Psychologist, 35,* 369–403.

Yihong, F. (2000). *Educating to liberate: Cross-boundary journeys of educators toward integration and innovation.* Unpublished doctoral dissertation proposal, University of Massachusetts Amherst.

Yin, R. K. (1984). *Case study research: Design and methods.* Beverly Hills, CA: Sage.

Yin, R. K. (2003). *Case study research: Design and methods* (3rd ed.). Thousand Oaks, CA: Sage.

Young, M. D., & Skrla, L. (2003). Research on women and administration: A response to Julie Laible's loving epistemology. In M. D. Young & L. Skrla (Eds.), *Reconsidering feminist research in educational leadership* (pp. 201–210). Albany: State University of New York Press.

Young, M. F. D. (Ed.). (1971). *Knowledge and control.* London: Collier-Macmillan.

Zelditch, M. (1962). Some methodological problems of field studies. *American Journal of Sociology, 67,* 566–576.

AUTHOR INDEX

SUBJECT INDEX